Ideology and Empire in Eighteenth-Century India

Robert Travers' analysis of British conquests in late eighteenth-century India shows how new ideas were formulated about the construction of empire. After the British East India Company conquered the vast province of Bengal, Britons confronted the apparent anomaly of a European trading company acting as an Indian ruler. Responding to a prolonged crisis of imperial legitimacy, British officials in Bengal tried to build their authority on the basis of an 'ancient constitution', supposedly discovered among the remnants of the declining Mughal Empire. In the search for an indigenous constitution, British political concepts were redeployed and redefined on the Indian frontier of empire, while stereotypes about 'oriental despotism' were challenged by the encounter with sophisticated Indian state forms. This highly original book uncovers a forgotten style of imperial state-building based on constitutional restoration, and in the process opens up new points of connection between British, imperial and South Asian history.

ROBERT TRAVERS is Assistant Professor in History at Cornell University. He has written articles in *Modern Asian Studies*, *Journal of Imperial and Commonwealth History* and *Past and Present*.

Cambridge Studies in Indian History and Society 14

Editorial board

Cambridge Studies in Indian History and Society publishes monographs on the history and anthropology of modern India. In addition to its primary scholarly focus, the series also includes work of an interdisciplinary nature which contributes to contemporary social and cultural debates about Indian history and society. In this way, the series furthers the general development of historical and anthropological knowledge to attract a wider readership than that concerned with India alone.

A list of titles which have been published in the series is featured at the end of the book

Ideology and Empire in Eighteenth-Century India

The British in Bengal

Robert Travers

Cornell University

CAMBRIDGE UNIVERSITY PRESS
The Edinburgh Building, Cambridge CB2 8RU, UK
Cambridge, New York, Melbourne, Madrid, Cape Town, Singapore, São Paulo

Published in the United States of America by Cambridge University Press,
New York

http://www.cambridge.org
Information on this title: www.cambridge.org/9780521861458

First published 2007

Printed in the United Kingdom at the University Press, Cambridge

A catalogue record for this book is available from the British Library

Library of Congress Cataloguing in Publication data
   Travers, Robert, 1972-
Ideology and empire in eighteenth century India : the British in Bengal, 1757-93 /
Robert Travers.
   p. cm. (Cambridge studies in Indian history and society; 14)
Includes bibliographical references and index.
ISBN 978-0-521-86145-8 hardback
1.   Bengal (India)–Politics and government–18th century.
2.   Legitimacy of governments–India–Bengal–History–18th century.
3.   Bengal (India)–Colonization–History–18th century. 4.   East India
Company–History–18th century. I.   Title. II. Series

DS485.B48T73 2007   954'.140296–dc22   2006100295

ISBN   978-0-521-86145-8   hardback

Contents

Preface and acknowledgements

This study originated in my fascination with the thought-worlds of British imperialists, and a sense that the ideological origins of British rule in India needed revisiting in the light of recent work on eighteenth-century British politics and political thought. As I was writing this book, an 'imperial turn' in the writing of British and European history has focused new attention on the role of empire in the political culture of eighteenth-century Britain, and in the intellectual culture of the enlightenment. My own study aims to contribute to these exciting revisions by providing an intellectual history of British politics and policy-making in Bengal, the 'bridgehead' to empire in eighteenth-century India.

This is not an intellectual history in the sense of being a history of intellectuals or of intellectual movements. Rather, following David Armitage's recent formulation, this is a study of how 'various conceptions of the British Empire arose in the competitive context of political argument'.[1] I am concerned with how policy-makers in Bengal sought to justify their political actions with reference to certain 'conventions, norms and modes of legitimation' operating in the wider sphere of British politics.[2] I argue that British conceptions of empire were also shaped by tense encounters with indigenous political culture. The twin dynamics of imperial legitimation and colonial governance led British officials to engage creatively with India's pre-colonial past, and especially with the history of the Mughal empire. British rulers attempted to legitimize their own power on the basis of an imagined form of constitutionality, supposedly discovered among the remnants of Mughal power in the province of Bengal.

The terms 'British' and 'Indian' as used in this book require some explanation. This study is mainly about elite British men who filled the

---

[1] David Armitage, *The Ideological Origins of the British Empire* (Cambridge, 2000), p. 5.
[2] John Brewer, *Party Ideology and Popular Politics at the Accession of George III* (Cambridge, 1976), p. 32.

high civilian ranks of the East India Company service in India, and elite politicians at home. It does not give a full account of the broad spectrum of those making up the 'British' communities in eighteenth-century India, which included Scots, Welsh, Irish and other 'Europeans', women as well as men, spanning from wealthy elites to poor soldiers. The East India Company was still often referred to as the 'English East India Company', though historians have suggested it was an important institution for forging a unified sense of 'Britishness'.[3] On the Indian side, even though some recent scholarship has argued that Indian nationalism had deep roots in early modern regional and imperial forms of patriotism, nevertheless, the term 'Indian' carries unavoidably anachronistic associations with the modern Indian nation state.[4] I use the term as a necessary shorthand, but it could be misleading if it was read to ascribe a homogenous 'national' identity to the diverse indigenous peoples brought under British rule.

This is a study of British political argument set in the context of political and social change. I have tried to describe and analyse changes at the level of political ideology rather than systematically discussing the extent to which particular ideological representations accurately reflected political events. There is relatively little in this work about the growth and uses of the British armies in India, about the establishment of British monopolies, or about bribe-taking and other scandals. This is partly because these subjects have been extensively studied before, but also because British attempts to justify their empire often skirted around its most problematic features.

This book is a poor form of tribute, but a tribute nonetheless, to the many wonderful teachers who led me to history and helped me to try it for myself. Mark Stephenson was the most demanding and inspiring history teacher any young person could wish for. Like all the best teachers, he strove through his own example to communicate the thrill of intellectual discovery. He would never have written a book about British India which paid so little attention to account books, cotton piece-goods and sailing ships, or to farmers and their crops. As an under-graduate, David Abulafia, Anna Abulafia, Christopher Brooke, Christine Carpenter and Mark Bailey were brilliant guides to medieval European history, as David Fieldhouse, Chris Bayly, Susan Bayly and Gordon Johnson were for imperial history and the history of colonial India.

---

[3] See H. V. Bowen, *The Business of Empire. The East India Company and Imperial Britain, 1756–1833* (Cambridge, 2006), p. 275; Linda Colley, *Britons. Forging the Nation 1707–1837* (1st edn. London, 1992, repr. 1994), pp. 127–9.

[4] C. A. Bayly, *Origins of Nationality in South Asia. Patriotism and Ethical Government in the Making of Modern India* (New Delhi, 1998).

David Smith gave me great encouragement at an important time. It was my enormous good fortune that Chris Bayly agreed to become my graduate supervisor. His unfailing personal kindness and intellectual generosity provide an inspiring example for a young historian. The breadth and depth of his historical imagination is something always to aspire to.

Peter Marshall offered generous assistance throughout the writing of this book. Many others gave valuable advice and support, among whom I would like particularly to thank: Muzaffar Alam, Seema Alavi, David Armitage, Bernard Bailyn, Ian Barrow, Sugata Bose, Huw Bowen, Kunal and Shubra Chakrabarti, Raj Chandavarkar, Linda Colley, Lizzie Collingham, Jeff Dolven, Natasha Eaton, Noah Feldman, Michael Fisher, Joseph Glenmullen, Jacob Hacker, Doug Haynes, Patrice Higonnet, Gene Irschick, Mary Lewis, Neil McKendrick, Tom and Barbara Metcalf, Steve Pincus, Maya Jasanoff, Mark Kishlansky, Susan Pedersen, Doug Peers, Katharine Prior, Emma Rothschild, Penny Sinanoglou, Mary Steadly, Judith Surkis, David Washbrook, Jon Wilson, Kathleen Wilson and Nur Yalman. I have been immensely lucky to benefit from the stimulating intellectual life of the history departments at Harvard and Cornell, and I thank all my colleagues and students warmly. Rachel Weil and Philip Stern took time out of busy schedules to provide astute comments on a late draft of this book, and for that I am immensely grateful. Thanks also to my excellent research assistants, Kambiz Behi and Amanda Hamilton. Needless to say, responsibility for any mistakes is entirely my own.

The Harvard Society of Fellows and the Milton Fund at Harvard University provided financial support for my research. At the Harvard Society of Fellows, Diana Morse is the presiding genius, and I have much to thank her for. Janet Hatch and her team in the Harvard history department, Patricia Craig and the other staff members at the Center for European Studies in Harvard, and Judy Burkhard and her crew in the Cornell history department have consistently put up with my administrative failings and provided unstinting support for my teaching and research. Grateful thanks go to many librarians and archivists, especially those at the Cambridge University Library and the British Library (especially the fantastic staff in the OIOC), in Calcutta at the State Archives of West Bengal, the National Library and the Victoria Memorial, and in America at the Harvard and the Cornell libraries.

Maureen McLane has been an immense source of moral, intellectual and comedic support throughout the writing of this book. Varsha Ghosh has cheerfully come to the rescue on numerous occasions. My parents, Pru and Chris, tactfully stopped asking many years ago when this book would be finished; for that and for many other reasons I thank them. My sister Olivia has been a constant source of strength and love, and she let me live in her house while I was conducting research in London. My children, Ravi and Lila, light up my life. And last, but most of all, I thank Durba Ghosh, my best friend and my best colleague, for countless and undreamt of blessings. I can confidently say that no one will be more relieved that I have finished this book than her!

Abbreviations and note on currency

Add. MSS	Additional Manuscripts
AHR	*American Historical Review*
BL	British Library, London
BLC	Bengal Law Consultations
BPC	Bengal Public Consultations
BRC	Bengal Revenue Consultations
BSC	Bengal Secret Consultations
COC	Committee of Circuit, 1772–3
CRO	County Record Office
Ct. of D.	Court of Directors
EHR	*English Historical Review*
FWIH	*Fort William – India House Correspondence*
HCSP	*House of Commons Sessional Papers of the Eighteenth Century*, Sheila Lambert (ed.), 145 vols. (Wilmington, Del., 1975)
HM	Home Miscellaneous
IESHR	*Indian Economic and Social History Review*
IOR	India Office Records
JBS	*Journal of British Studies*
JICH	*Journal of Imperial and Commonwealth History*
MAS	*Modern Asian Studies*
MP	Proceedings of Controlling Committee of Revenue at Murshidabad
MSS Eur.	European Manuscripts, Oriental and India Office Collections, British Library
NCHI	New Cambridge History of India
OHBE	*Oxford History of the British Empire*
OIOC	Oriental and India Office Collections
RCHC	*Reports from Committees of the House of Commons*

The Fifth Report   *The Fifth Report from the Select Committee of the House of Commons on the Affairs of the East India Company, 28 July, 1812,* W. K. Firminger (ed.), 3 vols. (London, 1917–18)

Note on currency

There were many denominations of coin circulating in eighteenth-century Bengal. Most often, figures for rupees refer to 'current rupees', a standard unit of account. P. J. Marshall, *East Indian Fortunes. The British in Bengal in the Eighteenth Century* (Oxford, 1976) estimated that one lakh of current rupees (Rs 100,000) was roughly equal to £11,000 before 1770, and £10,000 afterwards.

Glossary of Indian terms

Glossaries like this were often included in eighteenth-century British writings about India. They were part of an effort to translate Indian terms into fixed, normative meanings. It is part of the argument of this work that the meanings of these political and administrative categories were actually fluid and widely contested, and that they were being redefined in subtle or not-so-subtle ways by the British. Nonetheless, it may be helpful to provide here a very brief account of some important Indian terms that appear frequently in the chapters below.

This work follows the standard procedure of South Asian history of using the term 'land revenues' to refer to the land tax. Eighteenth-century British spellings of important terms will be given in brackets where appropriate. I have followed the form of transliteration of Indian words used in John McLane, *Land and Local Kingship in Eighteenth Century Bengal* (Cambridge, 1993).

adalats	name given to law courts established by the East India Company to administer justice to Indians
amil	(aumil) a revenue official appointed by the *nawab*'s government
band	a dam in a river
banyans	commercial agents of British officials
bigha	measurement of an area of land; roughly equivalent to one-third of an acre
dakaiti	a term for criminals, often used by the British to refer to a kind of highway robber, regarded as professional criminals
daroga	used by the British to refer to the chief officers or superintendents of the criminal courts (*faujdari adalats*) established by the East India Company in 1772

diwan	(dewan, duan) title of a Mughal officer of revenues and finance. The East India Company took the title of *diwan* of Bengal in 1765; the office of *diwan* was described by the contemporary historian Alexander Dow as 'receiver-general of the imperial revenues'. The British tended to define the responsibilities of the *diwani* branch of Mughal government as pertaining to revenues and the civil law. *Diwan* was also a title given to Indian revenue officials under the Company government
diwani adalat	(dewanny adaulut) name given to courts of civil law established by the East India Company in 1772
faujdar	(fougedar) literally a 'troop-commander'; applied to military officers of Mughal government with wide powers in local administration; defined by the British as officers of 'police'
faujdari adalat	name given to criminal courts established by the East India Company in 1772
firman/farman	a Mughal imperial order
ijara	a temporary lease of revenue-collecting rights over an area of land, usually translated by the British as a 'revenue farm'
ijaradar	person who holds an *ijara*, often termed 'revenue farmer'
jagir	an assignment of revenues often granted to Mughal officials as a kind of salary
jama	(jumma) the land-revenue assessment or demand, as dictinct from *hasil*, meaning the actual collections
kacheri	(cutcherry) a government office where records were kept and revenues received
khalsa	treasury or revenue department of the *nawab*'s government, moved by the East India Company from Murshidabad to Calcutta in 1772
lakh	one-hundred thousand, as in 1 lakh rupees = 100,000
mansabdar	a member of the Mughal nobility, holding an official rank and title
maulvi	a Muslim scholar, especially a legal scholar
mofussil	Persian term widely used in India, meaning hinterland or interior of the country

mufti	a type of Muslim law officer, often translated as expounder of legal opinions
naib	deputy, as in *naib subahdar*, deputy governor
nawab	(Nabob) a provincial governor of the Mughal empire; the title given to the eighteenth-century Mughal governors of Bengal
nawabi	the system of government under the *nawabs*
nizamat	branch of Mughal government attached to the office of *nazim*, another term for a Mughal provincial governor. According to the leading *nawabi* official, Muhammad Reza Khan, the *nazim* enjoyed extensive powers over all spheres of administration in concert with the *diwan*, but the *nizamat* was interpreted by the British to mean criminal justice or 'law and order' as distinguished from civil justice and revenues
nizamat adalat	another name for a criminal court under the British; used especially for the *sadr* (chief) criminal court
pandit	(pundit) a Brahmin scholar; usually used by the British to refer to a scholar of Hindu law
patta	(potta) a document describing the terms for revenue payments on a plot of land, used by the British to try to fix the revenue demand on peasants
puniya	a ceremony held at the court of the *nawabs* each year at the beginning of the revenue cycle, in which major revenue payers came to Murshidabad to negotiate revenue levels. Abolished by the Company in 1772
qanungo	keeper of revenue records; sometimes translated as 'registrar'
qazi	a Muslim judge, involved in various functions of local government
raiyat	(ryot) Mughal term for a peasant, and more broadly, for a subject of the empire; used by the British to refer to peasant cultivators
ray raiyan	(roy royan) the chief Indian officer in the *khalsa*
sanad	(sunnud) a written document or order conferring office or privileges
sepoy	Indian infantry soldier in the Company's armies
subah	a province under the Mughal empire
tahsildar	a government-appointed revenue collector

taluqdar	holder of a *taluq*, a form of land right ranking below a *zamindar*
zamindar	(zemindar, zemidar) literally meaning land (*zamin*) holder (*dar*), it was a Persian term applied by Mughal governments to a wide range of rural elites paying land revenues to the state. The exact nature of *zamindar* rights and duties was much disputed by the British, before *zamindars* were eventually defined as landowners
zamindari	the territory or jurisdiction of a *zamindar*

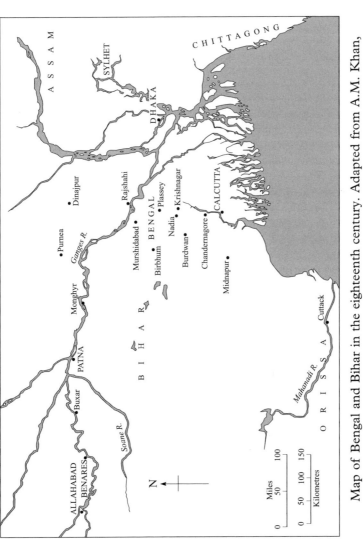

Map of Bengal and Bihar in the eighteenth century. Adapted from A.M. Khan, *The Transition in Bengal, 1756–75: a study of Muhammad Reza Khan*, Cambridge, 1969.

Introduction

> It is impossible, Mr Speaker, not to pause here for a moment, to reflect on the inconstancy of human greatness, and the stupendous revolutions that have happened in our age of wonders. Could it be believed when I entered into existence, or when you, a younger man, were born, that on this day, in this house, we should be employed in discussing the conduct of those British subjects who had disposed of the power and person of the Grand Mogul? This is no idle speculation. Awful lessons are taught by it, and by other events, of which it is not too late to profit.
>
> Edmund Burke, Speech on Fox's India Bill, 1783.[1]

Edmund Burke's pregnant pause invited the commons of Great Britain to gaze on the lonely, impoverished emperor of Hindustan, and to beware the fate of empires. Seven years after the publication of the first volume of Edward Gibbon's *Decline and Fall of the Roman Empire*, imperial history appeared to Burke as the record of 'awful lessons'. Britain's own imperial destiny hung in the balance. Her colonies in North America, after a long and bitter struggle, were breaking off to build a new model of republican liberty, much heralded by radicals in Britain itself. Meanwhile, a British trading company, the United Company of Merchants of England Trading to the East Indies (or East India Company for short), had conquered a 'vast mass' of territories, 'larger than any European dominion, Russia and Turkey excepted', 'composed of so many orders and classes of men . . . infinitely diversified by manners, by religion, by hereditary employments, through all their possible combinations'. 'The handling of India', Burke urged his compatriots, was a 'matter in a high degree critical and delicate. But oh! It has been handled rudely indeed'.[2]

When Edmund Burke 'entered into existence', as he so grandly put it, he did so as a British subject in England's oldest Atlantic colony, Ireland.

---

[1] Edmund Burke, *On Empire, Liberty and Reform. Speeches and Letters* (David Bromwich (ed.), Yale, 2000), pp. 298–9.

[2] Ibid., p. 296.

Born in 1729, Burke grew up with a conception of the British empire as a pan-Atlantic community of Britons that was 'Protestant, commercial, maritime and free'.[3] The imagined community of this empire, leaving out the vast numbers of slaves and indigenous peoples under its subjection, were white Protestants governed by the English common law and representative institutions. A sense of empire as a bulwark of British liberty against the threat of continental tyranny was worked out in trans-Atlantic dialogues during the early eighteenth century, and reached its patriotic apogee around the Seven Years War (1756–63).[4] Yet, in its moment of military triumph, the old empire began to unravel, as the pan-Atlantic community of the British shattered into warring tribes, and new conquests of alien peoples in distant lands began to divulge their 'awful lessons'.[5]

The East India Company's conquests in India had been swift and chaotic. Since it's founding in 1600, the Company had exercised its monopoly rights to trade with India through small forts and factories perched on the coasts. For much of this period, the Company was militarily weak, and dependent on the good will of Indian rulers, especially the Mughals, the central Asian dynasty that ruled over much of north India from the sixteenth to the eighteenth centuries.[6] Yet, in the middle decades of the eighteenth century, the balance of power in India decisively shifted. The Mughal empire, beset by factionalism, rebellion and new threats from beyond its frontiers, began to fragment. At the same time, European traders mobilized unprecedented naval and military resources in response to the globalizing dynamics of European warfare, but also in an effort to exert power and influence over Indian territories. As even Edmund Burke could not have guessed, these transformations in India signalled an epochal shift in world power, as militarizing European nation states cut into the great agrarian empires of Asia, establishing the foundations of modern colonial empires.[7]

[3] For this formulation, see David Armitage, *The Ideological Origins of the British Empire* (Cambridge, 2000), pp. 195–7.
[4] Ibid.; Kathleen Wilson, *The Sense of the People: Politics, Culture and Imperialism in England, 1715–1785* (Cambridge, 1995); Jack P. Greene, 'Empire and Identity from the Glorious Revolution to the American Revolution', *OHBE*, 2, pp. 208–31; Elijah Gould, *The Persistence of Empire: British Political Culture in the American Revolution* (Chapel Hill, NC, 2000).
[5] P. J. Marshall, *The Making and Unmaking of Empires. Britain, India and America, c. 1750–1783* (Oxford, 2005).
[6] For a good survey, see John Richards, *The Mughal Empire*, NCHI, 1.5 (Cambridge, 1993).
[7] C. A. Bayly, *Imperial Meridian: The British Empire and the World, 1780–1830* (London, 1989).

The British Company made its most startling conquests in the Mughal province of Bengal.[8] Bengal was a notable example of the regionalization of power which followed the death of the Mughal emperor Aurungzeb in 1707. Starting with Murshid Quli Khan (1700–27), Shia Muslim rulers styled as *nawabs* (provincial governors) succeeded in building a semi-independent regional state in Bengal.[9] From the 1740s, as the *nawabs* fought off incursions by Maratha invaders from western India, they ceased to pay any tribute to the hidebound emperors in Delhi. Within Bengal, meanwhile, the *nawabs* achieved significant fiscal innovations, and the assessed value of the Bengal revenues increased by 40 per cent between 1722 and 1756.[10]

The *nawabs* had some success raising tax revenues in an age of rural commercialization and expanding foreign trade.[11] Nevertheless, cut off from military reinforcements from the north, they were also intensely vulnerable to powerful interest groups within their realm. These included the powerful bankers who financed their regime, big land-holders (*zamindars*) and, most dangerous of all, European trading companies clustered on the coast, which could tap into global networks of trade and militarism. In 1756, an inexperienced young *nawab*, Siraj-ud-daula, provoked by the haughty and aggressive behaviour of British traders in their port settlement of Calcutta, swept into the city, and drove the British into a desperate retreat down the river Hughli. But this attempt to discipline unruly British traders fatally backfired. The East India Company had assembled a formidable naval and infantry force at its south Indian base in Madras. These forces, originally designed to combat the growing power of the

[8] The Bengal province or *subah* was a fluid geographical and political entity in the eighteenth century, for which term Bengal stands as a necessary shorthand. The eighteenth century *nawabs* of Bengal annexed the northerly *subah* of Bihar in the 1730s and (only nominally) the south-western *subah* of Orissa. The Company's acquisitions were thus described in formal British documents of the period as 'Bengal, Bihar and Orissa'. Orissa was wrestled away from the *nawabs* by Maratha invaders from the west in the 1740s, and not reconquered by the British until after 1803. P. J. Marshall, *Bengal: the British Bridgehead, Eastern India 1740–1828*, NCHI, 2.2 (Cambridge, 1987) pp. 48, 93. 'Bengal' should thus usually be read in this book to refer to Bengal and Bihar, which both came under the sway of the Company in this period.

[9] P. J. Marshall, *Bengal: the British Bridgehead Eastern India 1740–1828*, NCHI, 2.2 (Cambridge, 1987), pp. 48–69.

[10] John R. McLane, *Land and Local Kingship in Eighteenth Century Bengal* (Cambridge, 1993), p. 39.

[11] For the connections between agricultural expansion, commercialization and state-formation, see Richard M. Eaton, *The Rise of Islam on the Bengal Frontier, 1204–1760* (Berkeley, CA, 1993); Rajat Datta, *Society, Economy, and the Market: commercialization in rural Bengal 1760–1800* (New Delhi, 2000).

French, were hurriedly diverted to Bengal, where they were put to remarkable use.[12]

The commander of the Company's forces, Robert Clive, swiftly retook Calcutta. Within a year, Clive had struck deals with big financial and political interests within the Bengal government, and routed Siraj-ud-daula's army at the battle of Plassey (1757). Clive then installed a new *nawab* in the provincial capital of Murshidabad, and secured from this ruler a grant of new territories (and their tax revenues) around Calcutta.[13] Thereafter, the allure of more territorial revenues proved too enticing for the British to resist, and the regional state of Bengal swiftly collapsed under the weight of British demands. The Company cultivated a series of *nawabs* as allies until they were either set aside or they rebelled against the Company's voracious appetite for tribute. In 1765, Robert Clive, on his second stint as the Company's governor in Calcutta, engineered the appointment of the East India Company as *diwan* (roughly translated as treasurer or chief revenue collector) of Bengal, by the captive Mughal emperor, Shah Alam II. The Company used the grant of the *diwani* to extend their controlling power over the entire territorial administration of Bengal. By the early 1770s, the East India Company's 250 or so civilian servants in Bengal, backed up by a few hundred British army officers and over 20,000 Indian soldiers, had become the rulers of Bengal.[14]

In the same period, the East India Company was also seeking to extend its territories around Madras in south India and Bombay in the west, but its territorial gains in these regions were much slighter. In the south, Company traders preferred to prop up the relatively pliant *nawab* of Arcot, whose regime was in effect mortgaged to British creditors. Bombay at this stage lacked the resources to expand its territories to a significant extent.[15] The Mughal province of Bengal, therefore, became

---

[12] Brijen Kishore Gupta, *Sirajudaullah and the East India Company, 1756–7. Background to the Foundation of British Power in India* (Leiden, 1966).

[13] Some historians choose to emphasize how Company officials exploited an internal crisis within Bengal, while others argue that the internal crisis was deliberately engineered by the 'sub-imperialism' of the British. Compare, for example, Marshall, *Bengal: the British Bridgehead*, pp. 70–92, with Sushil Chaudhury, *The Prelude to Empire. Plassey Revolution of 1757* (New Delhi, 2000).

[14] The number of civilian 'covenanted' servants of the Company in Bengal rose from about 70 in the early 1750s to around 250 in the early 1770s, and this despite very high mortality during the wars of this period. By 1769 there were 3,000 British soldiers in Bengal, out of a total military force of more than 25,000. P. J. Marshall, *East Indian Fortunes: The British in Bengal in the Eighteenth Century* (Oxford, 1976), pp. 15–16, 218.

[15] P. J. Marshall, *The Making and Unmaking of Empires*, pp. 229–30.

the launching pad for further territorial expansion, and also the main laboratory for the development of new conceptions of empire.

Older ideas of an 'empire of liberty', connoting British settlers and the extension of English common law and representative assemblies, scarcely seemed to fit with the new conquests. These conquests were achieved by recruiting a large infantry force from among an indigenous population with sophisticated and varied cultural, religious and political traditions. They had been made, moreover, by a chartered trading company, which suddenly appeared to many in Britain as a new kind of *imperium in imperio*, a many-headed hydra threatening to disturb the turbulent frontiers of British constitutional politics. Meanwhile, the very idea of India in eighteenth-century Britain was veiled with pejorative and exotic connotations associated with 'Asiatic' peoples. It conjured up images of grand Islamic despots ruling tyrannically over timid pagans, florid and fanciful literature bred under a searing sun, and men corrupted by heat and the harem into terminal effeminates.[16]

Presenting the problems of Indian empire in these stark terms tends to efface the long history of the Company as both a military and territorial power in South Asia, and the elaborate systems of government and administration developed in the presidency towns of Calcutta, Madras and Bombay.[17] Nonetheless, the dramatic territorial conquests of the 1750s and 1760s brought India to new prominence in British imperial politics, and appeared to demand a serious rethinking of the very nature of empire.[18] Indeed, the Company's struggles to administer and police its new territories, its alarming financial instability, and the complex moral problems raised by the admixture of trade with

[16] For contemporary ideas of Asiatic or oriental despotism see, Nasser Hussain, *The Jurisprudence of Emergency. Colonialism and the Rule of Law* (Ann Arbor, MI, 2003), pp. 44–50; Susan Kingsley Kent, *Gender and Power in Britain, 1640–1990* (London, 1999), p. 97; John Brewer, *Party Ideology and Popular Politics at the Accession of George III* (Cambridge, 1976), p. 259. While modern scholars, following the work of Edward Said (*Orientalism*, 1978), have tended to use the term 'orientalism' to describe European studies of 'the east', the term Asiatic, as in 'Asiatic manners' or 'Asiatic despotism', was more commonly used than 'oriental' by eighteenth-century Britons. William Jones, in his first annual 'discourse' as President of the journal *Asiatick Researches* in 1784, argued that 'Asiatick' was the more classical and proper term to describe the region stretching from Japan to Turkey and North Africa, while 'Oriental' was merely 'relative' and 'indistinct'. *Asiatick Researches* 1 (Calcutta, 1788, repr. London, 1801), p. xii.

[17] This pre-history of British imperialism in India is only now getting the attention it deserves; see especially, Philip Stern, '"One body Corporate and Politick": the Growth of the East India Company-State in the Later Seventeenth Century' (unpublished Ph.D. thesis, Columbia University, 2004).

[18] H. V. Bowen, 'British Conceptions of Global Empire, 1756–63', *JICH*, 26 (1998), pp. 1–27.

government, and Europe with Asia, provoked an extended crisis of imperial nerve in Britain.[19] A massive famine, which overwhelmed many parts of Bengal in 1769–70, further magnified the sense of crisis. This coincided with major upheavals in the Atlantic world of empire, leading to the American rebellion and revolution. As the British government strove over several decades to control its over-mighty mercantile subjects in India, Burke and others unfurled their own florid rhetoric on the Nabobs, British traders turned Asiatic rulers, whom it was feared were establishing a 'tyranny that exists to the disgrace of this nation'.[20]

Historians in general have paid far more attention to Burke's high-minded rhetoric than to the self-representations of the Nabobs themselves, and in part because of this, the process of ideological rearmament that accompanied colonial state-formation in eighteenth-century India has remained obscure. This study focuses on British officials who devised policies for the government of Bengal in the late eighteenth century, mainly servants of the British East India Company. It shows how their conceptions of power in Bengal were intimately tied to languages of politics generated in Britain and the Atlantic world of empire, and how these notions were deployed alongside British arms in the construction of colonial authority.

This book describes a distinctive style of colonial state-building that has tended to lie buried under later notions of the British civilizing mission. In the nineteenth century, theorists of empire often justified British rule in India by reference to enlightenment ideas about stages of civilization. John Stuart Mill, for example, argued that there were 'conditions of society in which a vigorous despotism is in itself the best mode of government for training the people in what is specifically wanting to render them capable of a higher civilization'. It was incumbent on a 'more civilized people' to advance the condition of

[19] For a brilliantly original account of the crisis of legitimacy associated with 'Asiatic' conquests, P. J. Marshall, 'A Free though Conquering People': Britain and Asia in the Eighteenth Century. An inaugural lecture in the Rhodes Chair of Imperial History delivered at King's College, London (London, 1981).

[20] Burke, 'Speech on Fox's India Bill', in Burke, On Empire, Liberty and Reform, p. 370. For ideas about Nabobs, see Philip Lawson and Jim Phillips, 'Our Execrable Banditti: Perceptions of Nabobs in Mid-Eighteenth Century Briton', Albion, 16 (1984), pp. 225–41. 'Nabob' was a corrupted transliteration of the Persian word nawab, which literally means 'deputy', but was a title accorded to provincial governors within the Mughal empire. According to Holzman, one of the earliest uses of this word in England was Horace Walpole's reference in 1764 to 'Mogul Pitt and Nabob Bute', but Nabob came to refer in particular to returned Anglo-Indians. J. M. Holzman, The Nabobs in England. A Study of the Returned Anglo-Indian, 1760–1785 (New York, 1926), p. 8.

'a barbarous or semi-barbarous one'.[21] By the mid-nineteenth century it appeared to Mill that 'it was rapidly tending to become the universal condition of the more backward populations, to be held either in direct subjection by the more advanced, or to be under their complete political ascendancy'.[22]

Yet for Edmund Burke's generation, for whom the 'Grand Mogul' was until recently a vivid symbol of the enduring power of Asiatic empires, the naturalness of European colonial power could not be so much taken for granted. Nor were the ideas of 'advanced' and 'backward' peoples yet fixed into their nineteenth-century hierarchies.[23] India, after all, was still one of the world's biggest suppliers of manufactured textile goods, and Britain was only in the early stages of the gradual evolution of its own modern industrial economy. Indians were not, Burke argued, like the 'savages' found among the natives of the Americas, 'but a people for ages civilized and cultivated', with a 'nobility of great antiquity and renown; a multitude of cities, not exceeded in population and trade by those of the first class in Europe; merchants and bankers . . . millions of ingenious manufacturers and mechanicks; millions of the most diligent, and not the least intelligent, tillers of the earth.'[24]

Burke's rhetoric was distinctive and contentious in its day, but it reflected a wider fluidity in eighteenth-century conceptions of the world, before the hard edges of 'western modernity' had been sharpened and refined. Indeed, this work will argue that Burke's views of Britain's Asiatic empire can only be understood in the context of ideas developed within the service of the East India Company that he came to so mistrust. In eighteenth-century British debates about India, the rhetoric of barbarism and civilization was cut across by view of the world as a set of 'ancient constitutions', closely related to the particular 'genius' of different peoples.[25] This constitutional geography was strongly informed

---

[21] J. S. Mill, 'On the Government of Dependencies by a Free State', in *Considerations on Representative Government* (London, 1856), pp. 313–40. For a study which situates Mill in the wider history of liberal imperialism, see Uday Mehta, *Liberalism and Empire. A Study in Nineteenth Century British Liberal Thought* (Chicago, 1999).

[22] J. S. Mill, 'On the Government of Dependencies by a Free State', p. 323.

[23] For an excellent discussion of this theme, see Jennifer Pitts, *A Turn to Empire. The Rise of Imperial Liberalism in Britain and France* (Princeton, NJ, 2005), pp. 14–19.

[24] Burke, 'Speech of Fox's India Bill', in *On Empire, Liberty and Reform*, pp. 295–6. For a stimulating treatment of Burke's Indian thought, emphasizing the theme of 'threatened communities', see Mehta, *Liberalism and Empire*, pp. 153–90.

[25] The rhetoric of barbarism was not entirely absent; it was especially likely to be used against Muslims, and against hill tribes on the margins of agricultural and industrial society. For examples of the latter use, see Kate Teltscher, *India Inscribed. European and British Writing on India, 1600–1800* (Delhi, 1995), pp. 121–4.

by Montesquieu's idea of the spirit of the laws, but also by British understandings of their own constitution as an ancient inheritance refined by the wisdom of the ages. British strategies of colonial state-building in Bengal often involved excavating the constitutional history of India to find workable models for their own government.

The notion of the ancient constitution was a hallmark of early modern political thought in Britain. In its 'classic phase' in the early seventeenth century, the ancient constitution of England denoted a coherent world-view associated especially with English common-law scholars. This world-view asserted the continuity of the past and the present in English history, and the self-sufficiency of the common law as a system of law rooted in custom and reason.[26] The true nature of the ancient English constitution was widely contested between different political interests, and the idea of the connectedness of the present with the past became vulnerable in the eighteenth century to new forms of historicist critique. Nonetheless, the ancient constitution remained a prominent motif of British political debate in the second half of the eighteenth century.[27] Indeed, the quest for 'continuous, instructive and politically legitimating' pasts also defined political debate in other European monarchies in the early modern period.[28]

This book argues that the language of ancient constitutionalism was transplanted to Bengal, where the British tried to justify their rule by reference to an ancient Mughal constitution.[29] As in Britain itself, the ancient constitution was a political slogan that was variously and often loosely used. 'Ancient' often meant simply 'previous' – pertaining, for example, to the Mughal empire, which had first established itself in Bengal in the late sixteenth century. The term ancient constitution might imply an ongoing, present concern with deep historical roots; or, more commonly in India, it could refer to an old system of government that had become run down and needed to be restored. 'Ancient' might

---

[26] For the idea of the 'classic phase' of ancient constitutionalism, see Glenn Burgess, *The Politics of the Ancient Constitution. An Introduction to English Political Thought* (Philadelphia, 1992), p. 99. The classic modern account is J. G. A. Pocock, *The Ancient Constitution and the Feudal Law* (1st edn, 1957, repr. Cambridge, 1987); the Scots had their own versions of an ancient constitution based on the legendary Dalriadic kingdom. See Colin Kidd, *British Identities Before Nationalism. Ethnicity and Nationhood in the Atlantic World, 1600–1800* (Cambridge, 1999), pp. 123–45.
[27] Ibid., pp. 75–98; Brewer, *Party Ideology and Popular Politics*, pp. 257–64.
[28] Anthony Pagden, *Spanish Imperialism and the Political Imagination. Studies in European and Spanish-American Social and Political Theory, 1513–1830* (Yale, 1990), p. 91.
[29] Contemporaries wrote 'Mogul' to describe the dynasty descended from the central Asian warrior chief, Babur, in the late fifteenth century, but Mughal is the more usual transliteration today.

also denote great 'antiquity'. Indeed, an important feature of this concept was its tendency to push back into deep 'immemorial' time. Some Britons came to argue that the Mughals had in fact preserved elements of a more ancient constitution – comprising 'Hindu' forms of law and property – that predated the Islamic conquests of India.

The concept of an ancient Mughal constitution began as a device for justifying the transformation of a British trading company into a major territorial power, but it rapidly evolved into an ideological cornerstone of the Company's rule in Bengal. It was the frame through which early colonial politics were debated and disputed, by Company officials, by British critics of the Company like Edmund Burke, and also by Indian officials and land-holders trying to negotiate with or resist the growing power of the British. Finally, this book shows how the empire of constitutional restoration subsided before a new idea of British India in the late 1780s and 1790s, as the effects of Company rule corroded the older patterns of Mughal provincial administration, and the Company itself was tied more firmly to the decks of a globalizing British empire.

******

If to Burke the fall of the 'Grand Mogul' evoked something like astonishment and awe, to many Britons in the nineteenth century, it was a matter neither of surprise nor regret. When the imperial administrator and scholar, Sir Henry Elliot, produced his *Biographical Index to the Historians of Mohammedan India* (1849), an index of Arabic and Persian histories, he did so not 'on account of any intrinsic value in the histories themselves', for they had no claim 'to rank higher than annals', with their 'dry narration' leavened by speculations of 'the most puerile and contemptible kind'.[30] The index would serve, however, to warn the 'young Brutuses and Phocions' of India, if they should harbour 'romantic sentiments' about the 'Muhammadan period', that it was a 'dark period' of 'conspiracies, revolts, intrigues, murders and fratricides'.[31] Elliot's was an extreme view, and British writers continued to valorize some aspects of the Mughal empire – for example, the supposed enlightened tolerance of the Emperor Akbar or the glories of Mughal architecture. Nonetheless, few among the imperial race doubted

---

[30] 'Original Preface', 1849, reprinted in H. M. Elliot and J. Dowson (eds.), *History of India by its own Historians. The Muhammadan Period*, 8 vols. (Calcutta, 1867–77), vol. I, pp. xviii–xix.
[31] Ibid., xxiii, xix. For British historiography on the Mughals and other Indo-Islamic rulers, see Peter Hardy, *Historians of Medieval India. Studies in Indo-Muslim Historical Writing* (London, 1960), pp. 1–9, and J. S. Grewal, *Muslim Rule in India: the Assessment of British Historians* (Oxford, 1970).

that the rise of British power was a decisive break with the arbitrary despotism of the so-called 'Muslim period' of Indian history.

Yet the murky origins of their own empire remained a problem for British imperialists, as Burke's rhetoric against corrupt and rapacious Nabobs, greedy youths feasting on timid Asiatic prey, echoed down the decades. In the late nineteenth and early twentieth centuries, a growing band of British imperial historians, often employed by the imperial bureaucracy, put together a kind of reverse Whig theory of Indian history driven by the teleological pull of a benevolent colonial despotism. In this view, India had descended into a dark age after the Mughals imposed only a fragile and temporary order on its diverse peoples.[32] The depredations of the British Nabobs were merely one more symptom of the general anarchy and decay attendant on Mughal decline, and they were redeemed by the far-sighted state-building of imperial governors of Bengal like Robert Clive (1765–7), Warren Hastings (1772–85) and Lord Cornwallis (1786–93), and by the gradual assertion of parliamentary oversight.[33] The rise of British India in its nineteenth-century form was conceived as an entirely logical and rational development, as the British imperial state gradually imposed its genius for bureaucratic order on anarchic 'natives'.

In the twentieth century, as the British were forced to face 'the inconstancy of human greatness' themselves, imperial pomposity and its historical justifications were gradually deflated by first nationalist and later post-colonial critiques. Now the corrupt British Nabobs did not appear so much as brief aberrations from the imperial norm, but as infamous exemplars of the systemic plunder of India by an alien power.[34] More recently, stimulated by Edward Said's thesis that western knowledge of the orient was a type of 'discourse' through which imperial domination was established and sustained, scholars turned their attention to the epistemological violence perpetrated by colonialism.[35]

---

[32] A good example is W. K. Firminger's treatment of 'the broken down Mogul government', in 'Historical Introduction to the Bengal Portion of the Fifth Report', *The Fifth Report From the Select Committee of the House of Commons on the Affairs of the East India Company, 1812*, 3 vols. (Calcutta, 1918), vol. I, pp. xxii–li.

[33] The fullest narrative of this type was H. H. Dodwell (ed.), *The Cambridge History of India*, Vol. V, *British India, 1497–1858* (Cambridge, 1929). The teleology was made fully apparent in the title; late medieval India was not a nation-in-waiting but a colonial dependency-in-waiting. For a good discussion of Dodwell's work in the wider context of nineteenth-century imperial history, see Nicholas B. Dirks, *The Scandal of Empire. India and the Creation of Imperial Britain* (Cambridge, MA, 2006), pp. 326–7.

[34] See, for example, the classic liberal nationalist work of R. C. Dutt, *The Economic History of India Under Early British Rule* (London, 1901).

[35] Edward Said, *Orientalism* (New York, 1978).

Historians, anthropologists and literary critics examined British representations of India and related particular styles of representation to colonial technologies of rule.[36] The origins of empire provided particularly fertile ground for exploring the cultural tensions involved in the colonial encounter. Part of the goal of some of this work was to rescue indigenous systems of meaning from the condescension of imperial posterity. The Mughal empire and post-Mughal regional states, it has been argued, had their own complex forms of political rationality that were wilfully misinterpreted by British imperialists.[37]

Alongside this work on colonialism and its forms of knowledge, a different kind of reaction to the old imperial history has also flourished. New studies on the political sociology of eighteenth-century India have challenged the notion of a post-Mughal 'age of decline'. Studies of post-Mughal regional states revealed evidence of rapid commercialization, the emergence of commercial and landed entrepreneurs, and the growth of centralizing 'military–fiscal' regimes tapping into new forms of wealth to pay for growing armies.[38] The eighteenth century in India was still

[36] See, for notable examples of this work, Bernard S. Cohn, *An Anthropologist among the Historians and Other Essays* (Oxford, 1987) and *Colonialism and its Forms of Knowledge: The British in India* (Princeton, 1996); Nicholas B. Dirks, *The Hollow Crown: Ethnohistory of an Indian Kingdom* (Cambridge, 1987) and *Castes of Mind: Colonialism and the Making of Modern India* (Princeton, 2001); Sara Suleri, *The Rhetoric of English India* (Chicago, 1992); Teltscher, *India Inscribed*. For a set of essays surveying the fall-out of post-orientalist scholarship in South Asia, see Carol Breckenridge and Peter Van der Veer (eds.), *Orientalism and the Postcolonial Predicament: Perspectives on South Asia* (Philadelphia, 1993).

[37] Sudipta Sen, *Empire of Free Trade. The East India Company and the Making of the Colonial Marketplace* (Philadelphia, PA, 1998); Kumkum Chatterjee, *Merchants, Politics and Society in Early Modern India* (Leiden, 1996). For an important study of the clash of political cultures in early colonial Awadh, see Michael H. Fisher, *Clash of Cultures: Awadh, the British and the Mughals* (New Delhi, 1987). For contrasting notions of criminal justice in pre-colonial and colonial north India, see Radhika Singha, *A Despotism of Law. Crime and Justice in Early Colonial India* (New Delhi, 1998).

[38] C. A. Bayly, *Rulers, Townsmen and Bazaars. North Indian Society in the Age of British Expansion* (Cambridge, 1983); C. A. Bayly, *Indian Society and the Making of the British Empire*, NCHI, 2.1 (Cambridge, 1988); Richard B. Barnett, *North India Between the Empires: Awadh, Mughals and the British* (Berkeley, CA, 1980); D. A. Washbrook, 'Progress and Problems. South Asian Economic and Social History, c. 1750–1830', *MAS*, 22 (1988), pp. 57–91; Burton Stein, 'State Formation and Economy Reconsidered', *MAS*, 19 (1985), pp. 387–413; Muzaffar Alam, *The Crisis of Empire in Mughal North India: Awadh and the Punjab, 1707–48* (New Delhi, 1986). For a trenchant critique of some of these arguments, see M. Athar Ali, 'Recent Theories of Eighteenth Century India', *Indian Historical Review*, 13 (1986–7), pp. 102–10. Useful collections of essays on the eighteenth century in Indian history include Seema Alavi (ed.) *The Eighteenth Century in India* (New Delhi, 2002); P. J. Marshall (ed.), *The Eighteenth Century in Indian History, Evolution or Revolution* (New Delhi, 2003).

regarded as a period of crisis, from which Indian polities would emerge much weakened and increasingly subordinated to British imperial power. Yet there were, in one influential account, 'threads of continuity', especially in the endurance of 'intermediary groups' of officials, merchants and land-holders, stretching through the era of Mughal decline and British expansion.[39] Old visions of a powerful and cohesive British nation confronting a weakened and divided India were replaced by a picture of British traders forging strategic alliances with Indian capitalists.[40] Increasingly, the causes of British expansion were sought as much in indigenous processes of change like the 'commercialization of power' and the drift of 'intermediary groups' towards the East India Company, as in endogenous factors like the growth of British power or ambition.[41]

These two strands of recent historiography have often sat uneasily together. An emphasis on 'Indian agency' and social continuities has clashed with arguments about the cultural dislocations wrought by colonial discourse.[42] Yet both strands together have done much to uncover the complexity of early modern India from the narrowness and distortions of older imperialist accounts; and there is scope for intellectual cross-fertilization as well as conflict.[43] Moreover, a limiting factor which much of this scholarship shares in common is the tendency to frame colonial histories within the bounds of 'national' histories of India. This has meant that scholarship on trans-national institutions like the East India Company itself, and on the imperial dimensions of British

---

[39] Bayly, *Indian Society*, p. 5.

[40] For a subtle essay on this point, arguing that 'the East India Company state incorporated merchants', and gave them a 'political voice', see Prasannan Parthasarathi, 'Merchants and the Rise of Colonialism', in Burton Stein and Sanjay Subrahmanyam (eds.), *Institutions and Economic Change in South Asia* (Delhi, 1996), pp. 85–104.

[41] See, for example, Washbrook's often quoted statement that 'in a certain sense colonialism was a logical outcome of South Asia's own history of capitalistic development'. Washbrook, 'Progress and Problems', p. 76.

[42] For a particularly stern critique of some revisionist social histories, which accuses them of perpetuating colonial strategies for concealing the violence of conquest, see Dirks, *Castes of Mind*, pp. 303–15. This critique is extended in Dirks' more recent study, *The Scandal of Empire. India and the Creation of Imperial Britain* (Cambridge, MA, 2006).

[43] For a thoughtful essay on this theme, see Ian J. Barrow and Douglas E. Haynes, 'The Colonial Transition: South Asia, 1780–1840', *MAS*, 38 (2004), pp. 469–78; for an attempt, by a leading 'revisionist' to balance ' "continuity" manifested in aspects of revenue management and state structure with novelty and "change" evident in the central ideology of the Company's administration and its links with the international commercial economy', see C. A. Bayly, 'The British Military-Fiscal State on the Periphery', in Bayly, *The Origins of Nationality in South Asia* (New Delhi, 1998), pp. 238–75.

expansion, has lagged behind new work on Indian regional states, social structures and colonial knowledge.[44]

British and even 'imperial' histories, themselves often confined within conventional national limits, often went only a limited way towards connecting metropole and colony.[45] More recently, following an 'imperial turn' in British history writing, historians have begun to show how India became a crucial site for generating new British identities and ideas of the state.[46] P. J. Marshall has argued that the eighteenth-century conquests in India should be seen as an integral part of an interlinked crisis of empire in an era of globalizing warfare.[47] And Nicholas B. Dirks has suggested how Indian conquests fed into wider reconceptualizations of the relationship between state, economy and empire at home. Through the drama of the impeachment trial of Warren Hastings (1786–94), the British state re-imagined itself as the remedy

---

[44] The historiography of the British East India Company remains oddly fractured between studies of domestic faction fighting and parliamentary wrangles on the British side, and commercial and administrative histories on the Indian side. For the British side, see L. Sutherland, *The East India Company in Eighteenth-Century Politics* (Oxford, 1952); H. V. Bowen, *Revenue and Reform. The Indian Problem in British Politics, 1757–1773* (Cambridge, 1991); H. V. Bowen, *The Business of Empire. The East India Company and Imperial Britain, 1756–1783* (Cambridge, 2006); for studies of the Company's commerce, see K. N. Chaudhuri, *The Trading World of Asia and the English East India Company, 1660–1760* (London, 1978); Holden Furber, *John Company at Work, a Study of European Expansion in India in the Late Eighteenth Century* (Cambridge, MA, 1948); P. J. Marshall, *East Indian Fortunes: the British in Bengal in the Eighteenth Century* (Oxford, 1976); for administrative history, see B. B. Misra, *Central Administration of the East India Company, 1773–1834* (Manchester, 1959). For a stimulating recent collection of essays on the East India Company up to 1800, see H. V. Bowen, N. Rigby and M. Lincoln (eds.), *The Worlds of the East India Company* (Woodbridge, 2002).

[45] A notable exception was Vincent T. Harlow, *The Founding of the Second British Empire, 1763–1793*, 2 vols. (London, 1952–64), vol. II, pp. 7–224, which remains an immensely useful connected account of imperial politics in relation to India. The framing of Harlow's work, especially his sense of an imperial 'swing to the east' and a 'pursuit of markets in preference to dominion', now seems problematic. But he beautifully draws out the difficulty that Britons found in making pre-existing colonial models and precedents work in India, and Harlow is one of the few historians to explore (though briefly) the significance of the idea of an ancient constitution in Bengal politics, ibid., pp. 79–81.

[46] See, for examples, Sudipta Sen, *Distant Sovereignty: National Imperialism and the Origins of British India* (New York, 2002); C. A. Bayly, *Imperial Meridian*; P. J. Marshall, *A Free Though Conquering People. Eighteenth Century Britain and its Empire* (Ashgate, 2003); Kathleen Wilson, *A New Imperial History. Culture, Identity and Modernity in Britain and the Empire, 1660–1840* (Cambridge, 2004); Linda Colley, *Captives. Britain, Empire and the World, 1600–1850* (London, 2002); Maya Jasanoff, *Edge of Empire: Lives, Culture and Conquest in the East, 1750–1850* (New York, 2005).

[47] P. J. Marshall, *The Making and Unmaking of Empires. Britain, India, and America, c.1750–1783* (Oxford, 2005).

for the scandals of empire which Burke had brought to light, even as the blame for these scandals was rapidly displaced on to Indian society and culture.[48]

These works have further exposed the historiographical fault lines between approaches which emphasize the capacity of empire to build alliances with colonized elites based on shared in unequal benefits, and those which emphasize more the violent subordination of Indians and their interests in a colonial regime of conquest.[49] While these differences are important to acknowledge, the paradigms of 'negotiated empire' and the imperial rule of force can also be fruitfully held together as inseparable dimensions of colonial state-formation. This study emphasizes the way that empire was shaped by the encounter with the hierarchies, conventions and ideals of indigenous politics; but also how imperial power worked to set limits to this encounter, as much by translating indigenous voices into the new logic of the colonial archive, as by excluding those voices. It argues that British imperial ideology was formed at the intersection of exported European concepts and appropriated indigenous categories that were put to new uses by the colonial state.[50]

******

Histories of British India have sometimes sought to downplay the ideological motivations of empire, emphasizing the unplanned or ad hoc characteristics of expansion. This approach appeared to be especially applicable to India, because the East India Company's eighteenth-century conquests were deeply controversial in Britain, and because the Company itself, agonizing over the costs of empire, often argued that territorial aggrandizement had been thrust upon it through dire necessity. Yet the apparent hesitancy (or even reluctance) of British imperialists in eighteenth-century India was itself an element in the emerging ideological framework of British rule. As Charles Maier has recently argued, 'project managers of empire rarely have a vision of the whole. Nonetheless, empire does not emerge in a fit of absence of mind. Instead it represents a fit of what social scientists call path dependency, clinging to choices made early on whose reversal seems

---

[48] Dirks, *The Scandal of Empire.*
[49] Compare, for example, Marshall, *The Making and Unmaking of Empire*, pp. 270–2, with Dirks, *Scandal of Empire*, pp. 332–3.
[50] For other studies which have emphasized the way imperial knowledge grew out of interactions with indigenous sources and informers, see C.A. Bayly, *Empire and Information. Intelligence Gathering and Social Communication in India, 1780–1870* (Cambridge, 1996); Eugene Irschick, *Dialogue and History. Constructing South India, 1795–1895* (Berkeley, CA, 1994).

unthinkable'.[51] If, in imperial world-views, the absence of empire often appears literally unthinkable, this is in part because of the substantial material stakes in empire, and in part because of the elaborate conceptual webs through which empire is thought.

Previous attempts to write about the intellectual history of British Indian politics have often related British ideas about India to prevailing cultural 'attitudes', usually emanating out from Britain or Europe.[52] In this approach, the sympathetic view of Indian culture and politics sometimes taken by politicians like Warren Hastings and Edmund Burke was seen as symptomatic of a set of relatively latitudinarian attitudes associated with enlightenment philosophy, deistical Anglicanism and respect for customary forms of law. This approach has yielded important insights, though historical assumptions about prevailing attitudes in a given period tend to conceal how varied and inchoate 'British attitudes to India' or to Indians were at any one time. The problem is not just that attitudes were so varied, but also that political speech draws on available conceptual resources in ways that are strategic, contested and as much constitutive of broader 'attitudes' as simply reflective of them.

Another approach has seen the eighteenth century as a source of origins for nineteenth-century schools of Anglo-Indian thought, most notably that of the so-called 'orientalists'. This category, used in a pre-Saidian sense of denoting sympathy with and desire to rule through indigenous languages and cultural forms, gained currency in the battles over education reform in the 1820s and 1830s when 'anglicist' reformers sought to offer state sponsorship for English education in India. The battles between orientalists and anglicists were then read back into the eighteenth-century origins of British India, so that Warren Hastings (Governor of Bengal, 1772–85), who patronized scholarship on Indian laws, religion and history, was seen as an orientalist, whereas Lord Cornwallis (Governor-General of India, 1786–93), who championed English Whig forms of administration, was seen as anglicist.[53]

It is far from clear, however, that these distinctions are helpful in understanding the patterns of eighteenth-century politics. Indeed, this study will argue that Warren Hastings' attempt to found British

---

[51] Charles S. Maier, *Among Empires: American Ascendancy and its Predecessors* (Cambridge, MA, 2006), p. 21.

[52] G. D. Bearce, *British Attitudes to India 1784–1858* (Oxford, 1961); Clive Dewey, *Anglo-Indian Attitudes: the Mind of the Indian Civil Service* (London, 1993).

[53] The fullest exposition is David Kopf, *British Orientalism and the Bengal Renaissance; the Dynamics of Indian Modernization, 1773–1835* (Berkeley, CA, 1969). See also Eric Stokes, *The English Utilitarians and India* (Oxford, 1959), pp. 1–5.

authority on an ancient Indian constitution was as much an attempt to align the Company government with contemporary British idioms of political legitimation as an accommodation to Indian forms of rule. Anglicism, in the sense of using British notions of good government as a source for policy in Bengal, and orientalism, in the sense of justifying policy by reference to some notion of entrenched oriental custom, were not distinct schools of thought in the eighteenth century, but inter-connected rhetorical strategies which all political actors needed to deploy to justify their political actions.

Indeed, the importance of the concept of the ancient constitution was its capacity to appeal at once to British notions of political virtue, while simultaneously invoking some idea of Asiatic tradition. Modern historians have often noted in passing that eighteenth-century Britons frequently referred to an ancient constitution in India, but they have tended to treat this concept as an interesting side-light that is incidental to the main stream of imperial politics.[54] J. S. Grewal's brilliant essay on 'British historians of Muslim India' was the fullest exposition to date of this theme. Grewal noted both the critical importance of Mughal history to conceptions of the British empire in India, and the way that British officials tried to use Persian language sources to fill out an image of the Mughal constitution as a template for their own rule. He also saw that this attitude to the Mughal constitution had changed by the 1790s.[55] Yet Grewal's was a study of historiography rather than politics per se, so he was more concerned with how ideas of ancient constitutions promoted Persian scholarship than with their repercussions and uses in political argument.

Historians have failed to build on Grewal's insights, in part because the language of ancient constitutions threatens to disturb the strong historical association of European imperialism with modernity, and the concomitant sense of modernizing European ideologies confronting non-European 'tradition'. Ranajit Guha, for example, in his classic intellectual history of early British rule in Bengal, noted that 'in England, in particular, it almost became a matter of convention for a writer on East India affairs to preface his remarks about the English government in Bengal by a dissertation on the "ancient constitution" of the country'. Yet Guha understood this practice as a form of superficial

---

[54] For examples, see Marshall, *Bengal: the British Bridgehead*, p. 53, and Bayly, *Empire and Information*, pp. 48–53. Recently, Dirks has drawn the line between Burke's espousal of ancient constitutionalism in relation to both Britain and India. Dirks, *Scandal of Empire*, pp. 192–201.
[55] Grewal, *Muslim Rule in India*, pp. 23–7.

'myth-making', which was much less important than modernizing theories of economic development.[56] Guha argued that the British 'rule of property' in Bengal was an application of physiocratic political economy, a Western 'bourgeois' form that was 'bent backwards to adjust itself to a semi-feudal society'.[57] Thus, the modernizing imperative of colonialism was destined to fail, and semi-feudal Indian landholders failed to evolve into capitalist farmers. Within the framework of this Marxist meta-narrative, language about the ancient Mughal constitution appeared an odd contradiction at best, and disingenuous at worst, an attempt to confer a sense of 'spurious continuity' on the rupture of colonial conquest.[58]

Yet, however spurious the invented genealogies of British rule now appear, the historicist and constitutionalist aspects of early colonial thought deserve careful study as a critical aspect of colonial state-building. For all the richness and sophistication of his analysis, Guha's conception of the relationship between feudalism, capitalism and Western modernity led him to downplay aspects of eighteenth-century British opinion which came to understand private property in land, not just as a theoretical construct of enlightenment thought, but as an important element in the constitutional history of India itself. For example, Philip Francis, Supreme Councillor in Bengal (1774–80) and a central figure in Guha's study, certainly deployed the language of physiocracy in his plans for the regeneration of the agrarian society of Bengal; but he also framed his plan for securing landed property as a return to the wise and benevolent policies of the Mughal emperors.[59] For Francis and many of his contemporaries, potentialities of 'commercial society' existed within Asiatic constitutions, and were not the imported prerogative of European colonizers.[60]

Taking the language of historical constitutionalism seriously as a critical rather than ornamental aspect of imperial ideology reminds us that 'modern' European empires had their roots in 'early modern'

---

[56] Ranajit Guha, *Rule of Property for Bengal. An Essay on the Idea of Permanent Settlement* (Paris, 1963), pp. 25, 101, 103–4.

[57] Guha, *A Rule of Property:* 'Preface to the Second Edition', p. 6.

[58] Ranajit Guha, *Dominance Without Hegemony. History and Power in Colonial India* (Cambridge, MA, 1997), p. 2. See also Guha's argument that early colonial officials turned to writing of Indian history because they were locked out of contemporary indigenous information systems by their own linguistic and cultural ignorance and the resistance of Indian officials. Ibid., pp. 161–3.

[59] This argument is further developed in chapter 4.

[60] This point is emphasized in Jon E. Wilson, 'Governing Property, Making Law: Land, Local Society & Colonial Discourse in Agrarian Bengal, 1785–1830' (unpublished DPhil. thesis, Oxford University, 2000), introduction.

conceptions of politics in which provenance, lineage and custom remained crucial markers of legitimacy.[61] Moreover, eighteenth-century ideas about ancient constitutions tend to complicate the binary distinction between 'similarity' and 'difference' in relation to British Indian thought. Thomas Metcalf has argued that there was an 'enduring tension between two ideals' in British ideas about India, 'one of similarity and the other of difference'.[62] Yet, while this dichotomy may work well in analysing later nineteenth-century debates, it is less relevant for the eighteenth century. Similarity and difference in early modern political thought were often treated as interconnected rather than contradictory categories. Colin Kidd has argued that scholarly elites in Britain, imbued with biblical notions of monogenesis, 'did not think in essentialist terms of ethnic *difference*, but historically in terms of processes of *differentiation* from a common stock'.[63] Similarly, Sankar Muthu has argued that a powerful strand in enlightenment philosophy understood the 'wide plurality of individual and collective ways of life and the dignity of a universal shared humanity as fundamentally intertwined ethical and political commitments'.[64]

Muthu was writing of enlightenment critics of empire. Yet in order to legitimize their rule over alien peoples, eighteenth-century empire-builders were also concerned to reconcile entrenched notions of cultural and historically produced difference with universal political ideals. One way of doing this was to imagine an empire of ancient constitutions, fitted for the particular genius of different peoples, yet at the same time according with universal or natural law. In this way, respecting constitutional difference, as Edmund Burke argued, did not necessarily mean settling for a 'geographical morality'.[65] The English common law, imagined as the repository of both local custom *and* universal or 'natural' reason working together through the wisdom of the ages, was a jurisprudential key to this pattern of thought.[66] Indeed, the

---

[61] For a discussion of eighteenth-century notions of British identity emphasizing these themes, see Kidd, *British Identities Before Nationalism*, pp. 287–91.

[62] Thomas R. Metcalf, *Ideologies of the Raj*, NCHI, 3.4 (Cambridge, 1995), p. x. Though he organized his excellent survey in these terms, Metcalf recognized that British ideas about Indians were 'shot through with contradiction', and also that the British sometimes deployed ideas of similarity and difference simultaneously.

[63] Kidd, *British Identities Before Nationalism*, p. 290.

[64] Sankar Muthu, *Enlightenment Against Empire* (Princeton, 2003), p. 10.

[65] For recent discussions of what Jennifer Pitts calls Burke's 'peculiar universalism', see Pitts, *Turn to Empire*, pp. 77–85, and Dirks, *Scandal of Empire*, pp. 201–2.

[66] For eighteenth-century understandings of the common law, see David Lieberman, *The Province of Legislation Determined: Legal Theory in Eighteenth Century Britain* (Cambridge, 1987), pp. 35–46.

redeployment of the idea of the ancient constitution in India led to a significant revision of entrenched stereotypes about Asiatic despotism, even if this revision proved highly unstable and ultimately short-lived in the official discourse of British India.

******

The concept of the ancient Mughal constitution had a dual life in imperial politics: as a way of legitimizing empire in an idiom familiar to British elites; and as a way for policy-makers in Bengal of organizing new information about their recent conquests. Yet given conventional stereotypes about 'Asiatic despotism' and the moral corruption of Muslim societies, and also the vicious delegitimization of Indian rulers which accompanied wars of conquest, the colonial project of ancient constitutionalism was no easy task.[67] Nonetheless, it was a necessary task within the conventions of British political and legal theory. A British judge serving in Calcutta noted in 1777 that:

According to the known law of England, with respect to conquered or ceded countries, if they have already Laws and Courts of their own, the King may indeed alter and change their Institutions, or give them, absolutely or in Part, the Law of England, but till he does actually change them, the ancient Laws, including Courts and the Practice of those Courts, remain, unless contrary to the Laws of God.[68]

This was the narrow legal statement of a wider political presumption that the rights of conquest were constrained by pre-existing constitutions, especially where the conquering power was not the British Crown, but a subordinate trading company. The argument could be made, and occasionally was made, that the despotic regions of India had no proper courts or laws, and that British laws should therefore be extended in full. Yet this was hardly an attractive argument for Company servants trying to protect their territorial prerogatives from the British state; nor was it easy to reconcile with the growing weight of evidence that Indian governments were composed of elaborate legal and constitutional arrangements.

Indeed, the British preoccupation with the Mughal constitution in part reflected the remarkable endurance of the Mughal empire as a 'cultural system' even after the decline in the power of the

---

[67] For invocations of Asiatic despotism and Muslim barbarism to justify conquest, see Robert Travers, 'Ideology and British Expansion in Bengal, 1757–72', *JICH*, 33 (2005), pp. 7–27.

[68] Justice Robert Chambers' decision in the case of Kamal-ul-din, Hilary Term, BL Add. MSS 38,400, fo. 71.

emperors.[69] Within the composite culture of 'Mughal imperial society', the Mughal empire endured as an elaborate system of political ideals and routines, a bureaucratic lexicon, and an ethic of state service.[70] Over the seventeenth and eighteenth centuries, Mughal service groups gradually developed a 'growing sense of corporate identity, of uniform standards of conduct and good administration, and of strong loyalty to the empire'.[71] This political culture was tied together by Persian, the language of Mughal government, and by norms of gentlemanly conduct that cut across internal religious and social distinctions.[72]

The British quest for a usable ancient constitution in Bengal intersected with a determined rearguard action from within the old Mughal and post-Mughal elites of Bengal, which aimed to defend indigenous systems of governance and meaning from outside assaults.[73] As Kumkum Chatterjee has argued in a path-breaking study, diverse figures from within the old administration, from high-ranking *mansabdars* (nobles) to lesser scribal technicians, constructed an idealized image of a 'classicized Mughal past' as a foil for the perceived disorders of the present.[74] They were involved in the 'recasting of a political tradition', as Mughal virtue was separated out from the persons of the emperors and located in a set of administrative routines upheld by loyal service groups.[75] As Chatterjee also recognized, much of this literature of complaint was actually commissioned by British officials trying to access the Persianate culture of Bengal high politics to generate new information about conquered territories.

The responses of indigenous political elites to the British conquests included migration out of Bengal, armed rebellion and attempts to

---

[69] Eaton, *Rise of Islam on the Bengal Frontier*, pp. 311–12; Bayly, *Indian Society*, pp. 14–18.
[70] For the concept of Mughal 'imperial society', see David Ludden, *India and South Asia. A Short History* (Oxford, 2002), pp. 84–91. M. Alam, *The Crisis of Empire in Mughal North India: Awadh and the Punjab, 1707–48* (Delhi, 1986).
[71] J. F. Richards, 'Norms of Comportment Among Imperial Mughal Officers', in Barbara Daly Metcalf (ed.), *Moral Conduct and Authority: the Place of Adab in South Asian Islam* (Berkeley, CA, 1984), p. 256.
[72] Muzaffar Alam, *The Languages of Political Islam: India, 1200–1800* (Chicago, 2004); Muzaffar Alam and Seema Alavi (trans., ed.), *A European Experience of the Mughal Orient* (New Delhi, 2001), pp. 14–18, 60.
[73] Khan, *Transition in Bengal*, esp. pp. 15–16, 264–96. Marshall, *Making and Unmaking of Empires*, pp. 266–70; Bayly, *Origins of Indian Nationality*, pp. 57–9, 63–4. Rajat K. Ray, *The Felt Community. Commonality and Mentality before the Emergence of Indian Nationalism* (Oxford, 2003), pp. 213–334.
[74] Kumkum Chatterjee, 'History as Self-Representation: The Recasting of a Political Tradition in Bengal and Bihar', *MAS*, 32 (1998), pp. 913–48; see also F.L. Lehmann, 'The Eighteenth Century Transition in India: Responses of Some Bihar Intellectuals' (unpublished Ph.D. thesis, Univ. of Wisconsin, Madison, 1967).
[75] Chatterjee, 'History as Self-Representation', pp. 936–8.

withhold vital information about local resources or populations.[76] Many, however, tried to strike a balance between defending their honour and status and supplicating the new British rulers. Meanwhile, the East India Company hoped to exploit ongoing traditions of state service in order to extract an imperial tribute from Bengal. This set the scene for a series of tense engagements and confrontations, as British officials tried both to appropriate indigenous technologies of rule, but also to reframe them within their own distinctive notions of an ancient constitution.

These encounters made their mark on the colonial archive, in the form of petitions, treatises and letters, and in 'questions to the natives', a peculiar bureaucratic practice designed to elicit specific answers about administrative problems from indigenous informers regarded as author-itative by the Company government. Translated from indigenous lan-guages, and forming part of the colonial state's record of itself, these documents cannot be read as authentic representations of 'indigenous opinion'.[77] Yet, if these documentary traces of colonial encounter can take us only a limited way into the thought-worlds of pre-colonial polities, they can provide valuable insights into how British officials appropriated, displaced and distorted indigenous knowledge as they built the colonial state.[78]

The British attempt to discover an ancient Mughal constitution did suggest some interesting points of overlap or intersection between colonial and pre-colonial systems of political knowledge. These occurred at both a philosophical and a more pragmatic level. For example, a feature of political discourse shared between British and Mughal elites

---

[76] Rajat K. Ray, 'Colonial Penetration and the Initial Resistance: the Mughal Ruling Class, the East India Company and the Struggle for Bengal, 1756–1800', *IHR*, 12 (1985–6), pp. 1–106. Marshall, *Making and Unmaking of Empires*, pp. 263–6.

[77] Although this study mainly relies on the colonial archive and British private papers, indigenous language sources, especially Persian manuscripts, do exist from this period, which could be used to explore the nature of colonial encounter from indigenous perspectives. Before now, these sources have been mainly used to cast light retrospectively back on issues of Mughal governance. See, for example, B. R. Grover, 'Nature of Land Rights in Mughal India', *IESHR*, 1 (1963), pp. 2–15, and N. A. Siddiqi, *Land Revenue Administration under the Mughals* (Delhi, 1989).

[78] For a useful approach to colonial knowledge production, which aims to steer between on the one hand the '"Todorov model" of semiotic incompatibility' which asserts the radical incommensurability of different cultures, and on the other hand the 'counter-position which argues that everything was translatable' in a dialogic encounter between colonizer and colonized, see Sanjay Subrahmanyam, 'Frank Submissions: the Company and the Mughals between Sir Thomas Roe and Sir William Norris', in Bowen et al. (eds.), *The Worlds of the East India Company*, pp. 93–4. See also Stuart B. Schwartz (ed.), *Implicit Understandings. Observing, Reporting, and Reflecting on the Encounters between Europeans and Other Peoples in the Early Modern Era* (Cambridge, 1994), introduction, pp. 2–3.

was the notion of climatic influence on forms of rule, and the need for rulers to study and to recognize particular local customs.[79] In a different vein, British efforts to squeeze more tribute out of the Bengal tax system picked up on earlier attempts by the *nawabs* to achieve more detailed surveys of agrarian resources. Meanwhile, British critiques of the Company's mercantile sovereignty found echoes in indigenous concerns over the effects of rampant commercialization on habits of political virtue.[80] Contrary to stereotypes of Asiatic despotism, the British also discovered sophisticated notions of customary right, and of the mutual obligations of rulers and ruled, expressed within indigenous political discourse. Indigenous appeals to ancient custom served to reinforce British notions of an ancient constitution.

Such moments of intellectual cross-fertilization should not obscure the deep sense of cultural antipathy which existed on both sides of the emerging colonial divide. Persianate elites frequently commented on the strangeness of the 'hat-wearing' invaders, and their peculiar social customs and bodily habits.[81] They reacted with scorn and disgust to British bullying tactics, and to dramatic cuts in different forms of political, religious and cultural patronage. Instrumental struggles over status and resources intersected with profound intellectual and moral concerns, which often coalesced around issues of good counsel. While some Britons were willing to credit the Mughal constitution with settled laws and even property rights, few were willing to recognize any settled forms of community representation or consultative rulership in the despotic monarchies of India. Indian writers, however, frequently bemoaned the way that British rulers distanced themselves from the people, abandoned old practices of holding 'public audiences', and excluded the old nobility from the corridors of power.[82]

As they worked to subordinate Indian officials, British rulers also redeployed indigenous categories within their own ideas of the state. One crucial feature of these ideas was a relatively hard conception of singular sovereign power. The ancient Mughal constitution became a vehicle for imagining a uniform and comprehensive model of

---

[79] See, for example, Eaton, *Rise of Islam on the Bengal Frontier*, pp. 168–9.
[80] For a broad discussion of similar connections, see C. A. Bayly, *Birth of the Modern World, 1780–1914* (Oxford, 1994), pp. 288–9.
[81] See, for example, the speech attributed to Narayan Singh, a *nawabi* official, reported in a Persian history, the Muzaffar-Namah, written in 1772. 'What honour is left to us, when a few traders, who have not yet learnt to wash their bottoms (*hamoz bakun-shustan kho-gar nashuda*) reply to the ruler's orders by expelling his envoy?' Jadunath Sarkar (ed., tr.), *Bengal Nawabs* (1st edn, 1952, repr. Calcutta, 1985), p. 63.
[82] See the discussion in Dirks, *Scandal of Empire*, pp. 291–4.

sovereignty, in which public authority was rigorously distinguished from private right. This hard view of sovereignty arose both from the unprecedented fiscal and military resources of the Company state compared to pre-colonial rulers, but also from the strong emphasis on unitary sovereignty which was a feature of eighteenth-century British politics.[83] This contrasted sharply with the fluid pattern of shared sovereignty which characterized the Mughal empire and other pre-colonial states in South Asia.[84] As other historians have recently noted, British views of sovereignty tended to delegitimize forms of dispute resolution and legal authority that were not directly attached to the central state, as well as to redefine numerous little kingdoms with Bengal as private landed estates.[85]

Yet British ideas about the state were not themselves uniform, but rather highly contested; and these contests were played out through contrasting versions of the ancient Mughal constitution. Disputes arose in part from problems of translating and interpreting diverse indigenous representations of Mughal tradition. The crises of conquest and famine in Bengal also fuelled intense factionalism and party disputes among the British, as the East India Company and the British state competed for the spoils of empire. In particular, Philip Francis and Edmund Burke elaborated a distinctively Whig view of the ancient Mughal constitution as part of their critique of the mercantile tyranny of the Company. They imagined the Mughal empire as a form of limited monarchy, a rule of law and a rule of property, which carefully preserved the ancient rights of the original 'Hindu' inhabitants of Bengal. British debates about Bengal thus tended to echo old disputes about the ancient constitution in England, especially around the issue of the royal prerogative and its limits. An absolutist theory of the Mughal prerogative, which became especially associated with Warren Hastings, was opposed by a view of the ancient constitution in India as a source of

[83] John Brewer, *The Sinews of Power, War, Money, and the English State, 1688–1783* (London, 1989), pp. 22–3.

[84] For different treatments of this theme, see Bernard S. Cohn, 'Political Systems in Eighteenth-Century India', *Journal of American Oriental Society*, 82 (1962), pp. 312–20; Bayly, *Birth of the Modern World*, p. 75; Andre Wink, *Land and Sovereignty in India: Agrarian Society and Politics under the Eighteenth Century Maratha Swarajya* (Cambridge, 1986); Dirk H. A. Kolff, 'End of the Ancien Regime: Colonial War in India, 1798–1818', in J. A. de Moor and H. L. Wesseling (eds.), *Imperialism and War* (Leiden, 1989), pp. 22–49. For a longer perspective, which highlights notions of monolithic sovereignty as a major legacy of colonialism in the region, see Sugata Bose and Ayesha Jalal, *Modern South Asia: History, Culture, and Political Economy* (New York, 1997), especially pp. 239–40.

[85] Singha, *Despotism of Law*; McLane, *Land and Local Kingship*.

rights that were prior to and independent of the Mughal conquests. As in Britain, opponents of absolutism in Bengal tended to cast the landed nobility as the virtuous bulwark of the state.

Disputes over the ancient constitution in Bengal should thus be seen as part of a wider crisis of imperial sovereignty in the 1760s and 1770s, as centralizing, militarizing and tax-raising regimes across the British empire provoked a rash of new opposition movements.[86] The Seven Years War was a tipping point in many different imperial theatres, as the attempt to meet military costs and to strengthen executive powers encountered new forms of resistance.[87] Wilkeite Radicals in Britain, the Rockingham Whig opposition in parliament, Grattan's patriots in Ireland, and the patriotic rebels of North America differed much in philosophy and aims, but they shared a sense of crucial constitutional rights at threat from grasping and spendthrift executives.[88] What made Bengal distinctive was that, here, the rhetoric of constitutional patriotism and ancient rights was being deployed by agents of the imperial state against the East India Company, rather than by opponents of the Crown.

This helps to explain why Bengal played such a prominent role in the reconstruction of imperial authority after the loss of America in 1783. If, as many British historians have argued, Whig fears of absolutist pretensions at the court of George III were more imagined than real, the idea that the East India Company represented a new brand of absolute power had much more substance.[89] Prodded by Burke's diatribes,

---

[86] John Brewer developed the notion of the 'fiscal-military state' in eighteenth-century Britain, arguing that the growth of the central state was driven by the needs of military finance, in his *Sinews of Power*. South Asian historians have argued that 'military-fiscalism' was also a noted feature of Indian regional states; see, for example, B. Stein, 'State Formation and Economy Reconsidered' in *MAS*, 19 (1985), pp. 387–413. Bayly has connected the dots between military-fiscalism and imperialism most comprehensively in his essay 'The First Age of Global Expansion', *JICH*, 28 (1998), pp. 29–47.

[87] J. G. A. Pocock, 'Political Thought in the English Speaking Atlantic, 1760–90: I, The Imperial Crisis', in J. G. A. Pocock (ed.), *The Varieties of British Political Thought* (Cambridge, 1993), pp. 246–82. For another good synthetic treatment of the 'fiscal-military state and its discontents', see Philip Harling, *The Modern British State. An Historical Introduction* (Polity Press, Cambridge, 2001), pp. 49–55.

[88] For English oppositionist politics, see Brewer, *Party Ideology and Popular Politics*, and Frank O'Gorman, *The Rise of Party in England. The Rockingham Whigs, 1760–82* (London, 1975); for patriotism in Ireland, see R. F. Foster, *Modern Ireland, 1600–1972* (London, 1988), pp. 241–58; for ideologies of American patriotism, see Bernard Bailyn, *The Ideological Origins of the American Revolution* (Cambridge, MA, 1967), and Jack. P. Greene, *Peripheries and Center. Constitutional Development in the Extended Polities of the British Empire and the United States, 1607–1788* (Athens, GA, 1986).

[89] For historical debates around George III and the politicians, see Brewer, *Party Ideology and Popular Politics*, pp. 26–31.

William Pitt the Younger's India Act of 1784, subordinating the Company government to ministerial control, was part of a broader effort by the British state selectively to appropriate the rhetoric of patriotic opposition by cracking down on potential sources of corruption within the realm.[90]

Yet the state's triumph over the Company in 1784, heralding a more unified form of national imperialism in India, was followed by the gradual erosion of the idea of the ancient Mughal constitution as a basis for British rule in Bengal. The confusing and rancorous disputes of the trial of Warren Hastings suggested that the ancient Mughal constitution remained a fluid and unstable slogan rather than a coherent foundation for British imperial policy. The trial worked to expose inherent problems in the idea of the ancient Mughal constitution. For example, the premise of a uniform Mughal constitution struggled against the varied regional configurations of Mughal rule, and its change through time. The meanings of Indian administrative terms were not fixed, as the British often tried to read them, but fluid and contested political categories. British Persian scholarship remained young and little-developed, so that British interpretations of the Mughal constitution were founded on scattered and very limited sources. Moreover, the idea of ancient Mughal constitution continued to coexist uncomfortably with entrenched notions of Asiatic tyranny and Muslim depravity associated with theories of oriental despotism.

Ultimately, the idea of an ancient Mughal constitution was more useful as a critique of the Company's mercantile government than as a basis of British rule in the long term. In domestic British politics, government propagandists often tried to distance themselves from the notion of an idealized ancient English constitution, arguing instead that modern liberty was a more recent consequence of the development of commercial society.[91] Similarly, in British India, officials gradually moved towards a progressive narrative of colonial enlightenment, posing a stark break between arbitrary Asiatic despotism and a British rule of law and property. While the Company was now subordinated to the British state, the governor-general and his council in Calcutta were also newly empowered as a legislative body. Lord Cornwallis' code of administrative regulations for Bengal, promulgated in 1793, made the old language of ancient constitutions increasingly redundant. The 'bureaucratic-military despotism' of the colonial state eventually

[90] Philip Harling, *The Waning of the Old Corruption. The Politics of Economical Reform in Britain, 1779–1846* (Cambridge, 1996), pp. 42–55.
[91] Brewer, *Party Ideology and Popular Politics*, pp. 259–61.

preferred to make its own rules, than to hold itself hostage to some putative indigenous constitution.[92]

Yet the idea of the ancient Mughal constitution had framed crucial decisions about the nature of sovereignty, legality and property in India. And even while the British moved to distance themselves from the idea of an ancient Mughal constitution, it left a powerful imprint on their ideas of India, and especially their sense of Indian history. Colin Kidd has noted the tendency of English constitutionalism in the eighteenth century to become 'more decidedly ethnocentric and exclusively Saxonist'. The origins of the ancient constitution were increasingly located among the Saxons, imagined as the 'nation's ethnic core', by contrast with the conquering Normans, who were thought to have disrupted, while they never entirely vanquished, the spirit of Gothic freedoms.[93] Similarly, in India, the language of ancient constitutionalism gradually took on an ethnographic logic, attaching in particular to the broad religious categories of Hindu and Muslim. Even Britons sympathetic to the Mughals, tended to argue that the Mughal conquest of Bengal, like the Norman conquest of Britain, had overlaid an ancient system of customary right – represented by Hindu law and property. The rhetoric of ancient constitutionalism, therefore, rendered the Mughals intensely vulnerable to the taint of the 'Norman Yoke'.

Indeed, the way that the language of ancient constitutions worked to entrench the idea of Muslims as 'foreign' invaders, and the Hindus as the ancient 'inhabitants of India' may have been one of its most important legacies in the longer term. There was a great irony in this outcome, related to the familiar dynamic of the unintended consequences of colonialism. British enthusiasts for the ancient Mughal constitution frequently appealed to the tolerant traditions of Mughal state-craft, looking in particular to the Emperor Akbar (1556–1605) as a kind of deistical ruler, highly appealing to latitudinarian Anglicans. Yet, at the same time, British notions of Muslims as conquerors, and Hindus as conquered subjects, tended to read stark differences into the far more complex and composite reality of Mughal political culture. Modern scholarship has shown how the Mughal empire fostered a diverse imperial elite, in which notions of honour, loyalty and political

[92] R. Singha, *A Despotism of Law*. David Washbrook has recently characterized British India in the early nineteenth century as a 'rule by law', in which 'while the state may make law for its subjects, it posits itself as above that law and unaccountable to it', see D. Washbrook, 'The Two Faces of Colonialism: India, 1818–1860', in *OHBE*, 3, p. 407.
[93] Kidd, *British Identities Before Nationalism*, pp. 83, 91.

ethics cut across religious distinctions.[94] In Bengal, not only were
'Hindus' fully incorporated into the ruling elite, but also a large
proportion of the peasantry, especially in East Bengal, were Muslim.[95]
Moreover, the very categories of Muslim and Hindu, considered as
generalized, bounded identities, were far less prevalent in pre-modern
South Asia than they would later become.[96]

The breakdown of the ancient Mughal constitution into Muslim
rulers and Hindu subjects did not simply arise from the pre-history of
English ancient constitutionalism and the shadow of the Norman Yoke.
It also related to the material dynamics of colonial state-formation in
Bengal. Bengal was a frontier province of the Mughal empire, where
Mughal and *nawabi* rule had always depended on striking alliances with
local land-controllers – frequently given the broad designation of
zamindars. British rule quite quickly siphoned profits and patronage
away from the old *nawabi* capitals of Murshidabad, Dhaka and Patna,
and from the broad class of officials who depended on grants, pensions
and salaries from the *nawab*'s government. Yet the British recognized
early on that *zamindars* would be necessary intermediaries linking the
Company's military–fiscal regime with the commercialized agrarian
society of Bengal.[97] Nearly all of the bigger *zamindars*, especially in West
Bengal, were non-Muslim, while they sometimes legitimized their
authority through the symbols and rituals of Hindu kingship, and by
appealing to notions of ancient custom. This gave some plausibility to
the notion that the Mughal state was a military superstructure over a
more ancient constitution of Hindu property. In fact, however, as some
Britons recognized, most of these large *zamindari* estates had actually
grown up under the patronage of the later Mughals and the *nawabs*.

The British 'award' of private property to the *zamindars* in 1793 was
both a recognition of the resilience of *zamindars'* authority in the
countryside, and also an attempt to recast *zamindari* rights as a
benevolent gift of the enlightened colonial power. At the same time, the
discoveries of William Jones about the connections between Sanskrit

[94] For an important recent study of Mughal political thought which emphasizes these themes, see Muzaffar Alam, *The Languages of Political Islam: India, 1200–1800* (Chicago, 2004); see also Barbara D. Metcalf, 'Too Little, Too Much: Reflections on Muslims in the History of India', *Journal of Asian Studies*, 54 (1995), pp. 951–67.
[95] For the British ignorance about the extent of Islamic influence in Bengal, see P. J. Marshall and Glyn Williams, *The Great Map of Mankind. British Perceptions of the World in the Age of Enlightenment* (London, 1982), pp. 16–17.
[96] David Gilmartin and Bruce B. Lawrence, *Beyond Turk and Hindu. Rethinking Religious Identities in Islamicate South Asia* (Gainseville, FL, 2000).
[97] McLane, *Land and Local Kingship*; Anand Yang, *The Limited Raj: Agrarian Relations in Colonial India, Saran District, 1793–1920* (Berkeley, CA, 1989).

and classical European languages offered a new point of historical connection between rulers and ruled in colonial India.[98] The classical civilization of the ancient Hindus, apparently rescued from Muslim bigotry by tolerant Britons, was used to prop up a new conception of colonial enlightenment. Just as in Europe, an emerging 'enlightenment narrative' understood modern commercial society as a reawakening of civilization from the long darkness of 'barbarism and religion', so in India the colonial government imagined itself as rescuing the once great classical civilization of the Hindus from a long night of Islamic medievalism.[99]

The failings, and the eventual abandonment, of more nuanced and sympathetic views of Mughal government, at least in official rhetoric, should not efface the creative possibilities opened up by British encounters with the traditions of Mughal rule in eighteenth-century Bengal. Nonetheless, this study tends to qualify a recent strand of British imperial historiography which has painted a beguiling picture of a pre-racialist eighteenth-century empire as it intersected with the cosmopolitan ethos of the Mughals.[100] The British adoption of the language of ancient constitutionalism was certainly related to the distinctive power dynamics of the eighteenth century, in which the British could not yet imagine for themselves all-India paramountcy. It also fitted with a strand of enlightenment thought which sought to revise conventional stereotypes of Asiatic peoples. At the same time, however, languages of cross-cultural reconciliation always coexisted with fierce denunciations of the inherent corruption of Asiatic peoples. And the search for points of connection with Indian tradition was cut across by the need to draw clear distinctions between colonizer and colonized.

In the capitals of surviving post-Mughal states, British residents sometimes adopted the courtly dress and styles of Mughal elites.[101] Yet the language of ancient constitutions had relatively little effect on the broader cultural idioms of the emerging British capital in Calcutta – on public ceremonial, on architecture or on social life. It is true that Nabobs were often ridiculed for their luxurious tastes, their long trains of

[98] Thomas Trautman, *Aryans and British India* (California, 1997), and Tony Ballantyne, *Orientalism and Race. Aryanism in the British Empire* (New York, 2002).
[99] For the European 'enlightenment narrative', see J. G. A. Pocock, *Barbarism and Religion*, 2. *Narratives of Civil Government* (Cambridge, 1999), pp. 2–4.
[100] For a fine exposition of this view, see William Dalrymple, *White Mughals: Love and Betrayal in Eighteenth-Century India* (London, 2002).
[101] For examples from eighteenth century Lucknow, see Jasanoff, *Edge of Empire*, pp. 45–88.

servants, and their habits of hookah-smoking.[102] Yet, as P. J. Marshall has argued, British social life in Calcutta even in the eighteenth century was marked by racial exclusivity and the attempted reconstruction of European urban life.[103] Inter-racial sexual relations were common, but also officially discouraged, and maintaining a proper European comportment among Company servants was regarded as crucial to the integrity of the empire.[104] Meanwhile, Calcutta was built up as a city of neo-classical, rather than neo-Mughal, palaces.

British appropriations of the Mughal imperial past never came close to evolving into a distinctive form of colonial patriotism, comparable, for example, to the emergence of creolized identities in early modern Spanish America.[105] The small East India Company settlements were too small and too closely tied into wider imperial networks to imagine a patriotic identity distinct from the metropole. In this context, the eventual displacement of ancient constitutionalism by the modernizing narratives of colonial enlightenment reflected the emergence of a new kind of imperial style. The British in India were destined to remain a society of temporary exiles rather than settlers, and a class of rulers rigidly separated from those they ruled. Despite their frequent attempts to cast the Mughals as 'foreign' rulers, the British were destined to remain the most stubbornly foreign of all India's imperial powers.

In the longer history of imperial political thought, British imaginings of the ancient Mughal constitution were part of the process in which a self-styled empire of liberty became acclimatized to a modern military despotism. For eighteenth-century Britons of Edmund Burke's genera-tion and stamp, despotism was the ultimate political slur, which evoked not only the fear of an ambitious absolutism in France, but also the historical memory of the royal house of Stuart.[106] To enjoy the fruits of its Asiatic empire, Britons had to adjust their most cherished

---

[102] For a good account of the 'Indianization' of the European body, and also the 'limits of Indianization', see E. M. Collingham, *Imperial Bodies. The Physical Experience of the Raj, 1800–1947* (Cambridge, 2001), pp. 13–49.

[103] P. J. Marshall, 'The White Town of Calcutta Under the Rule of the East India Company', *MAS*, 34 (2000a), pp. 307–31; P. J. Marshall, 'British Society and the East India Company', *MAS*, 31 (1997), pp. 89–108.

[104] Durba Ghosh, *Sex and Family in Colonial India: The Making of Empire* (Cambridge, 2006).

[105] For efforts of Hispanic settlers to associate themselves with Aztec and Inca pasts, see Pagden, *Spanish Imperialism and the Political Imagination*, pp. 91–132; for a comparison of creolized colonial identities in Spanish America and Ireland, see Kidd, *British Identities Before Nationalism*, pp. 179–81.

[106] R. Koebner, 'Despot and Despotism: Vicissitudes of a Political Term', *Journal of the Warburg and Courtauld Institutes*, xiv, 3–4, 1951, pp. 275–302. For a recent discussion of the ways that colonial conquests evoked fears about despotism within Britain itself, see Hussain, *The Jurisprudence of Emergency*, p. 24.

assumptions about themselves. Rehabilitating the idea of Asiatic despotism, and representing the Mughal empire as a rule of law and property, was one way to proceed; yet this quickly proved too confining and confusing. Instead, the British embraced what they hoped would be a new kind of colonial despotism, a despotism of law underpinned by racial segregation and the rule of force, that would increasingly be justified by Europe's supposed higher rank on the ladder of civilization.

******

The following chapters have a broadly chronological organization. Chapter 1 situates the Company government of Bengal within the wider networks of British politics and political argument. Chapter 2 explores the initial encounters between British officials and the complex power structures existing within the regional state of Bengal and considers these in the context of the famine of 1769–70. Chapter 3 examines the attempt by Warren Hastings (Governor of Bengal, 1772–85) to justify his reforms of the Bengal state by reference to 'the legal forms of Mogul government', and chapter 4 shows how Hastings' rivals, notably Philip Francis, constructed a different version of Mughal history to brand Hastings' rule as an unconstitutional tyranny. Chapter 5 examines the critical debates about the Supreme Court of Judicature in Calcutta, and about the proper limits of English law in India. Finally, chapter 6 explores the gradual eclipse of the ancient Mughal constitution as a theme in British imperial politics, despite memorable evocations of the Mughal past in the rhetoric of Edmund Burke.

1 *Imperium in imperio*: the East India Company, the British empire and the revolutions in Bengal, 1757–1772

The 'age of revolutions' arrived early in India, nowhere more so than in Bengal. Contemporary Britons frequently used the term 'revolutions' in describing the East India Company's rise to military and political pre-eminence in eastern India, and Indo-Persian sources used a similar term, *inqilab*.[1] Academic histories of this period of revolutions have been mainly structured around explanations of British 'expansion' or imperialism. They have tended to focus on key moments of war and conquest in the 1750s and 1760s as the Company subjugated the faltering regime of the Bengal *nawabs*. In analysing these events, historians have weighed the role of different causal factors: the expansion of European commerce and Anglo-French wars in south India; Mughal decline and instability within Indian regional states; the corrosive effects of British 'private trade' on Indian polities; or the inexorable momentum of militarization. By contrast, this chapter seeks to understand the shifting institutional and ideological settings in which contemporary Britons themselves interpreted the various revolutions in Bengal. The aim here, and in chapter 2, is to probe the links between processes of conquest and colonial state-formation, and to show how narratives of conquest fed into ideologies of rule.

Two points in particular are emphasized in this analysis. First, while historians have generally privileged material incentives for the Company's territorial expansion, especially expanded access to the markets of Bengal, and new revenues from territorial revenues, it is important to see how these material interests were embedded in particular institutional and ideological contexts. A second, related point, is that the 'sub-imperialism' of British officials in Bengal, responding

---

[1] An early use of the term 'revolution' was William Watts' pamphlet, *Memoirs of the Revolution in Bengal* (London, 1760, repr. Calcutta, 1988). For a discussion of the use of the term *inqilab*, derived from the root verb *qalb* (to invert) in Persian sources, see F. L. Lehman, 'The Eighteenth Century Transition in India', p. 18, and Rajat K. Ray, 'Indian Society and the Establishment of British Supremacy, 1765–1818', *OHBE*, 2, p. 508.

to fast-moving events at six months sailing distance from Britain, never floated entirely free from networks of anglophone politics far beyond India. Even if there was no coherent 'imperial programme' directed from London, policy-makers in far-flung outposts like Calcutta were profoundly influenced by currents of political debate in the wider British empire. Empire building in India was always a kind of performance for home authorities, designed to garner support, military, financial and moral, for Company servants abroad. A British governor of the Company's factories in Bengal was becoming not just a 'man on the spot' but a 'man in the spot-light' of national scrutiny. The Company's emerging territorial empire was forged not just out of the military competition with Indian regional states, but also in a series of negotiations between British authorities in India and Britain.

To explore the ideological and performative dimensions of the Company's territorial expansion after 1757, this chapter is divided into three sections. The first section examines the institutional linkages that tied together the different limbs of the Company's operations, and which bound the Company into the broader fabric of empire. The second section takes a broad overview of some of the key terms of political debate in the eighteenth-century British empire, and how the Company's changing situation in India was variously understood within these terms. The final section looks in greater detail at attempts by East India Company servants to interpret their fast-changing role in Bengal in their own writings, especially in pamphlets published in Britain in the era of expansion.

The connected worlds of the East India Company

By 1756, Calcutta was the East India Company's most important trading post in India. Founded in the 1690s on the site of a few coastal villages by a maverick Company servant, Job Charnock, it soon became a 'presidency' town, with a governor and council, and an extensive fort complex, Fort William.[2] In the early eighteenth century, Calcutta became the major source of British textile exports, and after the 1720s shipments from Bengal generally made up at least half the value of the Company's exports from India.[3] Approximately 30 ships,

---

[2] J. P. Losty, *Calcutta, City of Palaces. A Survey of the City in the Days of the East India Company, 1690–1858* (London, 1990), pp. 16–19.
[3] P. J. Marshall, 'The British in Asia: Trade to Dominion, 1700–1765', *OHBE*, 2, p. 490.

called 'East Indiamen', sailed every year to the Company's India stations, bringing back cargoes valued at around £2 million per annum by the 1750s.[4]

Calcutta in the early eighteenth century sat on the unstable periphery of two major early modern empires: the slowly collapsing land-based empire of the Mughals, and the expanding sea-borne empire of the British. The Company's governor and council sought powers and privileges from Mughal emperors as well as British kings and parliaments, and the government of Calcutta reflected these hybrid sources of authority. In 1698 the Company purchased from the Mughal emperor the rights to collect rents from the villages that made up the growing settlement of Calcutta. Thereafter, one member of the Company's ruling council held the official title of *zamindar*, collecting rents and administering justice to the Indian population. In 1717, the Company purchased *zamindari* rights to 38 more villages from the Mughal emperor Farukhsiyar, as well as obtaining a *farman* (imperial order), granting that the Company's trade should pass free of duties in Bengal.[5] The scope of the Company's legitimate trading rights became a major source of contention with provincial governors in Bengal (*nawabs*), as the latter emerged as semi-autonomous regional rulers under a declining Mughal sovereignty.

Meanwhile, the governor and council in Calcutta also derived powers to regulate trade and administer justice from a series of British royal charters which established the Company's monopoly of the British import/export trade with Asia, and enabled it to govern its settlements abroad according to English law. 'Charters of justice' issued in 1661, 1726 and 1753 authorized the Company to found civil and criminal courts of English law in its Indian settlements, and established a line of appeal to the English Privy Council.[6] Company agents were also subject to detailed instructions sent out regularly to India by the Company's directors in Leadenhall Street in London. Meanwhile, the 24 directors were answerable to, and elected by, the 'court of proprietors' or 'general court', made up of over 2000 East India stock-holders.[7] A highly developed system of bureaucratic record keeping and accounting held together the far-flung operations

---

[4] P. J. Marshall, *Problems of Empire: Britain and India, 1757–1813* (London, 1968), pp. 81–2.

[5] S. Bhattacharya, *The East India Company and the Economy of Bengal, 1704–1740* (London, 1954), pp. 28–9.

[6] M. P. Jain, *Outlines of Indian Legal History* (3rd edn, Bombay, 1972), pp. 7, 35–47.

[7] Marshall, *Problems of Empire*, p. 65.

of the Company, and helped to ensure steady profits for investors, with dividends running at 7 or 8 per cent between 1722 and 1755.[8]

The lines of authority which framed the government of Calcutta in the early eighteenth century were shattered by the 'revolutions' of 1756–7. For some time, Company authorities in Bengal had tried to convert ambiguous privileges garnered from increasingly powerless Mughal emperors into claims of 'extra-territoriality' or complete immunity from the authority of provincial governors. Their pretensions led to frequent quarrels with the *nawabs* of Bengal over trading dues and other issues.[9] In earlier times the Company had been forced to compromise with Mughal officials for lack of a large military force. In 1756, however, after *Nawab* Siraj-ud-daula invaded Calcutta, Company servants diverted naval reinforcements from their wars against the French in south India, and also began to recruit sepoy infantrymen in Bengal. This military strength meant that the Company broke through all previous limits on its regional power.

In treaties with weakened *nawabs* after the battle of Plassey in 1757, the Company helped itself to the local rights it had long craved, including expanded territorial revenues, and duty free trade in the interior of Bengal.[10] This inaugurated the period often known in Indian history as the 'post-Plassey plunder' or 'the shaking of the pagoda tree', as Company servants used their new found military power to fill their boots with extravagant gifts extorted from Indian rulers, and most of all with profits drawn from the expansion of British 'private trade' in the internal commerce of Bengal.

The dramatic assertion of power in Bengal, if it rapidly undermined the authority of the *nawabs*, also threw the Company's own hierarchies into a period of relative disorder. As revolution followed revolution, some British observers worried that the private commercial ambition of Company traders had hijacked the Company. Directors had long been uneasy about the extent of British participation in the local 'country trades'; since the seventeenth century they had allowed their 'covenanted' servants to supplement small nominal salaries by participating on their own accounts in local and inter-regional Asian trades not covered by the Company's monopoly of the trade between Europe

[8] Ibid., p. 27; K. N. Chaudhuri, *The Trading World of Asia and the English East India Company, 1660–1760* (Cambridge, 1978), pp. 29–39.
[9] C. A. Bayly, 'The British Military-fiscal State and Indigenous Resistance', pp. 246–7; Sen, *Empire of Free Trade*, pp. 60–88.
[10] P. J. Marshall, *East Indian Fortunes. The British in Bengal in the Eighteenth Century* (Oxford, 1976), pp. 112–13.

and Asia.[11] After Plassey, British profiteering burst all its former bounds, and the directors' letters remonstrated with Company servants for taking extravagant bribes or gifts, excessive expenditure, luxurious living, and seizing and monopolizing valuable local trades in products like salt, beetel nut and tobacco. Robert Clive, when he returned to Bengal as governor in 1765, felt that the excessive profiteering of relatively junior Company servants had undermined standards of morality in Calcutta, and threatened to subvert the traditional hierarchy of the Company based on seniority. His diagnosis that 'luxury in every shape' had so corrupted Calcutta that 'all distinction ceased' was picked up eagerly by the directors, who complained of 'the universal depravity of manners' in the settlement, tending towards a 'dissolution of all government'.[12]

There is no question that military expansion and accompanying political upheavals put new power into the hands of Company agents in India, and that this power was used to promote 'private interests' as well as the aggrandizement of the Company. Directors often felt themselves to be losing control of the situation, or blamed their servants for the unwelcome costs and dangers of warfare. Yet the expansion of the Company's territorial ambitions was not wholly the work of opportunistic 'men on the spot'. Directors in London, like officials in Calcutta, quickly appreciated the desirability of collecting local revenues from taxation, and of establishing military superiority over Indian rulers. By 1761, directors were urging the 'judicious management and improvement of our new acquired lands'.[13] In 1765, they reappointed Robert Clive as governor in Bengal, with extraordinary powers, knowing that he wished to expand the Company's armies, and that he would insist on close military and political controls over the *nawab* of Bengal.[14] When Clive assumed the Mughal office of *diwan* (roughly translated as state treasurer) of Bengal on behalf of the Company in 1765, he delegated the actual administration of much of Bengal to Indian deputy governors in the old capitals of Murshidabad and Patna. But by 1769, the directors themselves were pushing for increased involvement of Company servants in the collection of land taxes in the so-called *diwani* territories.[15]

---

[11] Marshall, *East Indian Fortunes*, p. 19.

[12] Clive to Ct. of D., 30 September 1765, with reply, 17 May 1766, cited in John Malcolm, *Life of Robert, Lord Clive*, 3 vols. (London, 1836), vol. II, pp. 335–7.

[13] See, for example, letter of Ct. of D. to President and Council at Fort William, 13 March 1761, *FWIH*, 3, p. 83.

[14] Malcolm, *Life of Robert, Lord Clive*, vol. II, pp. 302–16.

[15] Ct. of D. to Ft. William, 28 August 1771, *FWIH*, 6, p. 123.

The Company's lines of command and control frayed in this period, but they did not entirely break down. For the governor and his council in Bengal, outright rejection of the Company's directives from London was only sustainable in cases where circumstances had totally superseded the directors' orders. Openly defying these orders risked invoking heavy sanctions, including possible dismissal from the Company. The relationship between directors and local governors was thus usually one of tense negotiation and eventual compromise rather than outright opposition. The Company's system of discipline had long rested on a combination of abstract notions of honour and loyalty with hard facts of coercion. The first line of defence was the covenants which defined the civil or 'covenanted service', in which officials promised under oath to give faithful service on penalty of fines, and offered securities for these fines. In the 1760s, directors moved to strengthen these covenants, adding new prohibitions on inland trade and taking presents from Indians.[16] Though these covenants were frequently broken, this was not always with impunity. If local officials were found to have disobeyed orders or broken their covenants, the directors might dismiss them from the Company's service and withdraw their licence to reside in the Indian settlements.[17]

Within the Company's settlements, the powers of governors were also strengthened to meet the perceived crisis of authority. Between 1765 and 1767, Robert Clive was allowed to operate independently of the council at Fort William through a smaller 'select committee' of hand-picked supporters.[18] Governors also exercised powers to suspend refractory officials from the Company service and even to deport them from Bengal. Robert Clive acted sternly to put down a mutiny of Company army officers in 1765, and in September 1766 Governor Verelst forcibly deported a notorious 'private trader', William Bolts.[19] British traders often complained that the Company governors in India enjoyed 'despotic' powers, and these extraordinary powers themselves quickly became an object of scrutiny in Britain. Indeed, the long tradition of limiting the powers of governors through the influence of

---

[16] Marshall, *East Indian Fortunes*, pp. 9, 139.

[17] For example, five members of the council at Calcutta were dismissed from service after harshly criticizing the directors in 1759. See Malcolm, *Life of Robert, Lord Clive*, vol. II, p. 133.

[18] B. B. Misra, *The Central Administration of the East India Company (1773–1854)* (Manchester, 1959), pp. 66–7.

[19] H. H. Dodwell, 'Bengal, 1760–1772', in Dodwell (ed.), *Cambridge History of India, Vol. V, British India, 1497–1858* (Cambridge, 1929), pp. 178–9; N. Chatterji, *Verelst's Rule in India* (Allahabad, 1939), pp. 169–70.

their councils soon reasserted itself, while governors could also be pursued at home in the English courts either by the directors or political rivals.[20] Governor Verelst was tirelessly pursued in this way by William Bolts, while Robert Clive eventually was subject to investigation by a committee of the House of Commons.[21]

The political, legal and bureaucratic complexity surrounding the Company's operations, meant that Company servants in India were not as autonomous as contemporary polemics against corrupt British Nabobs suggested. Both the directors and parliament moved quite quickly to exert greater controls over the Indian settlements, and Marshall's research showed that by the early 1770s a tightening framework of regulations, in conjunction with a general trade depression, blocked some of the avenues of private profiteering available in the aftermath of Plassey.[22] A broader consideration, of course, was that Company servants in Bengal depended on the home authorities not only for their appointments and licences to trade in Bengal, but also for necessary reinforcements in manpower, weapons and money to secure their vulnerable settlements. Between 1762 and 1772 the Company spent over £1.6 million (over twice the annual investment in Bengal textiles) on building a new fort complex in Calcutta.[23] This was a potent sign both of the new ambition and impressive resources of the Company in Bengal, and also the continuing sense of vulnerability even in the Company's regional headquarters.

A number of structural changes in Company politics also expanded the web of connections between the Company's headquarters in Leadenhall Street and the Indian factories in the post-Plassey period, blurring the lines between the 'centre' and 'periphery' of the Company's empire. After 1757, the Company's directorate remained largely made up of city gentlemen, drawn from a close-knit oligarchy of banking, cloth and shipping interests. At the same time, however, returning Company servants, known as East Indians, began to play a bigger role in the Company's domestic governance, reinvesting their windfall profits in commercial and political influence.[24] The so called 'Bombay faction'

---

[20] Harlow, *The Founding of the Second British Empire*, pp. 23, 30–1.

[21] For Bolts' career, see W. G. J. Kuiters, *The British in Bengal, 1756–73. A Society in Transition Seen through the Biography of Rebel, William Bolts, 1739–1808* (Paris, 2002). For Clive, see Bowen, *Revenue and Reform*, p. 167.

[22] Marshall, *East Indian Fortunes*, p. 243.

[23] *RCHC*, 4, p. 459.

[24] Bowen, *Business of Empire*, pp. 128–9. See also J. Gordon-Parker, 'The Directors of the East India Company, 1754–1790' (unpublished Ph.D. thesis, University of Edinburgh, 1977).

which formed around the returned Company servant Laurence Sulivan, exploited the sudden instability in Company affairs provoked by the 'revolutions' in Bengal to take control of the Company in 1758.[25]

Sulivan's novel tactics of presenting a rival 'list' of directors to the court of proprietors, and unsettling the established channels of commercial oligarchy, had far reaching repercussions. Sulivan's coup presaged a new era of instability in Company politics marked by heavily contested directorial elections. Robert Clive, the hero of Plassey, emerged after 1763 as Sulivan's major rival for control of the direction. Clive and other Company servants felt increasing need to enter the politics of Leadenhall Street to protect their own far-flung interests; Clive's party, for example, was heavily invested in protecting its leader's right to a valuable *jagir* (an assignment on the Bengal revenues, worth over £20,000 per year) gifted by the *nawab* of Bengal.[26] These factional conflicts were also fuelled by disputes over policy in Bengal, as the Company became controversially engaged in further rounds of wars and conquests. Finally, Company politics were energized by disputes about 'private trade' in Bengal. As governor from 1765–7, Clive's attempt to restrict what he saw as the destabilizing and corrupting scope of British private trade brought him into conflict with a group of wealthy servants. The Sulivan party made an opportunistic alliance with these anti-Clive forces and regained control of the Company from the Clivites in 1768.[27]

Factional conflicts have rightly been viewed as a source of the disorders in Company affairs, marked by changeable personnel and policies, financial instability and a wavering stock price. But these factions also forged powerful networks of allegiance spanning from London to the Indian factories. Among the major weapons available to the competing party leaders in London was patronage. Writer-ships in the Company's civil service, positions in the Company armies, or just licences to trade were valuable prizes in the gift of directors, especially the Chairman and Deputy Chairman. In the 1760s, both the value and the number of jobs in the Company service in Bengal rose quickly, as the profits of war and conquest became evident.[28] At the same time, the

---

[25] Sulivan, an Irishman, was a Company servant in Bombay from 1740–52, who invested his fortune in a country estate (Ponsborne Manor in Hertfordshire) and politics; he became a director of the Company in 1755 and an MP in 1762. Sutherland, *The East India Company in Eighteenth Century Politics*, pp. 59–65, 71–3.

[26] Bruce Lenman and Philip Lawson, 'Robert Clive, the "Black Jagir" and British Politics', *Historical Journal*, 26 (1983), 801–29.

[27] Sutherland, *The East India Company in Eighteenth Century Politics*, pp. 139–40, 187–90.

[28] Marshall, *East Indian Fortunes*, pp. 14–15.

speed with which Company servants made their fortunes in the 1760s, expulsions for disciplinary reasons, and frequent regime changes in London, meant that some Company servants travelled much more frequently back and forth between Britain and India, becoming fully trans-national operators.[29]

New conquests also pushed Company directors and servants into the wider orbit of British and imperial politics during the turbulent early years of George III. The accession of George III in 1760 began a decade of short-lived, unstable ministries as the Whig party that previously dominated parliament fragmented into competing factions. The great corporations of the City of London were also drawn into these political contests. Influence in the East India Company's direction had many attractions for British ministers, just as directors needed to curry favour with the government of the day. The Company was an important cog in the machinery of state finance and patronage, one of the wealthiest corporations of the City of London, and a major underwriter, through loans to the government and revenues from taxes on trade, of the national debt.[30] About 23 per cent of MPs held stock in the East India Company in the 1760s, and many used their stock to participate in the contested politics of East India House.[31]

Meanwhile, Company directors and returned Company servants entered parliament in part to protect their commercial interests. Money and great estates exercised great influence over narrow parliamentary electorates, especially in so-called 'rotten boroughs', and returning Company servants often saw parliamentary seats as a sound investment. Clive, for example, used his massive personal fortune not only to become an Irish peer and great landowner in Surrey and Shropshire, but also to command a small troop of seven MPs elected under his patronage.[32] These votes were very useful for him in leveraging

---

[29] For example, Robert Clive first went to Madras in 1743, returning to Britain between 1753 and 1755 after famous victories against the French; after defeating Siraj-ud-daula he returned to Britain in 1760, became Baron Clive of Plassey, and went back to Bengal from 1765–7. He returned to Britain again between 1767 and his death in 1774. Another crucial figure in Bengal politics, Warren Hastings, served in Bengal between 1750 and 1764, before returning to Britain. In 1769 he took another appointment in Madras and then in 1772 was appointed governor of Bengal.

[30] Marshall, *Problems of Empire*, p. 29.

[31] Bowen, *Revenue and Reform*, p. 31.

[32] For an entertaining recent account of Robert Clive's career as a collector of titles, members of parliament, great houses and estates, and expensive art (notably portraits of himself), see Maya Jasanoff, *Edge of Empire. Lives, Culture and Conquest in the East, 1750–1850* (New York, 2005), pp. 32–9.

influence with ministers, and defending himself publicly against charges of corruption and oppression in Bengal.

Clive's notoriety was a sign that the Company's dramatic military and territorial expansion in Asia was becoming an inescapable issue of national political interest. The government spent approximately £8 million on naval and military reinforcements for the East India Company during the Seven Years War (1756–63), as India came to be seen as a vital theatre in the global war with the French.[33] Ministers were soon demanding some return on this investment. From 1767, the British government claimed an annual tribute of £400,000 from the Company's territorial revenues, hoping that this windfall would help Britain to weather the financial and political strains arising from debts accumulated in the recent wars with France.[34]

At the same time, the system of competitive elections for directorships discouraged directors from resisting organized pressure for higher dividends. The dividend rose from 8 per cent to an unsustainable 12½ per cent in March 1771.[35] In order to meet these costs, directors tried to expand the Company's commercial investment in Indian goods, but without adequately assessing whether markets in Europe and the Atlantic could absorb this new volume of Indian cotton or Chinese teas. In the short term, at least, they would not, and little mountains of unsold goods piled up in the Company's warehouses.[36] Meanwhile, projections of new territorial revenues in India fell short of expectations, or were swallowed up by expanding military costs. In 1772 a European-wide crisis of credit brought the Company's severe financial problems to light in London. The Bank of England was unwilling to underwrite the Company's losses, and the directors turned to the government for a loan, submitting to a new raft of parliamentary inquiries.[37]

Thus, the East India Company developed in the 1760s into a highly complex network of interconnected interest groups, straddling several different political systems, and vulnerable to shocks and stimuli from many different directions. It existed as a long chain of committees cut across by chains of faction, which themselves reached out beyond the formal structures of the Company into British and Indian politics.

---

[33] Marshall, *The Making and Unmaking of Empires*, pp. 128–9.
[34] Bowen, *Revenue and Reform*, p. 64.
[35] Ibid., pp. 125–6, 184.
[36] H. V. Bowen, 'Tea, Tribute and the East India Company, c. 1750–1775', in S. Taylor, R. Connors and C. Jones (eds.), *Hanoverian Britain and Empire. Essays in Memory of Philip Lawson* (Woodbridge, 1998), pp. 158–76.
[37] Bowen, *Revenue and Reform*, pp. 126–7.

The Company was both strongly hierarchical and authoritarian, but also relatively open, even democratic, in its system of elections to the direction; for example, unlike in parliamentary elections, no one was excluded from voting in Company elections on the basis of nationality, religion or gender.[38] Above all, the Company existed, like the British state itself, as a set of voluble competitors for power, generating reams of argument and counter-argument, opinion and analysis, that would frame its evolution into a powerful limb of empire.

British power in India emerged as a system of 'negotiated empire', a phrase recently used to describe the empires of the early modern Atlantic world.[39] This system of negotiation also incorporated some powerful Indian figures. Indian politicians quickly recognized the importance of the Company's trans-oceanic political networks, and tried on occasion to break into them.[40] The *nawab* of the southern state of Arcot forged direct lines of communication with Britain, maintaining clients among British MPs.[41] Other Indian politicians and merchants exploited their connections with Company servants, and their role as financiers of British trade, to build up their interests in Britain. For example, a leading Indian official in Bengal, Maharaja Nandakumar, kept up a correspondence with directors in London, and fed them information that was damaging to his rivals.[42] Others used the English courts to press claims against Company servants.[43]

Even in the embryonic phase of colonialism, however, the power of British officials in Bengal depended crucially on their ability to limit the terms on which Indian voices and interests were admitted to the wider politics of negotiated empire. To many Indian politicians, the twists and turns of Company politics must have appeared as a peculiar puppet show in which the strings and puppeteers remained hidden and mysterious. According to the Governor of Bengal, Warren Hastings, the *nawab* of the north Indian state of Awadh complained to him of

---

[38] Marshall, *Problems of Empire*, p. 25.
[39] C. Daniels and M. V. Kennedy, *Negotiated Empires. Centers and Peripheries in the Americas, 1500–1820* (Routledge, 2002). This idea of 'negotiated empire' is also extended to India by Marshall, *Making and Unmaking of Empires.*
[40] Michael H. Fisher, *Counterflows to Colonialism: Indian Travellers and Settlers in Britain, 1600–1857* (Delhi, 2004), pp. 50–102.
[41] Sutherland, *East India Company in Eighteenth Century Politics*, pp. 323–4, 380. J. D. Gurney, 'The Debts of the *nawab* of Arcot, 1763–1776' (unpublished DPhil., Oxford University, 1968).
[42] A. M. Khan, *The Transition in Bengal: A Study of Seiyid Muhammad Reza Khan* (London, 1969), pp. 300–1.
[43] P. J. Marshall, 'Nobkissen versus Hastings', *Bulletin of the School of Oriental and African Studies*, 27 (1964), pp. 382–96.

'the perpetual hazard to which he was exposed of losing the English friendship by the continual changes of their chiefs', and by shifting factions on the Company's council.[44] Of course, the shifting politics of home often undercut British officials as well. Ultimately, however, the oceanic politics of empire was the life-blood of the colonial power. The Company's international operations enabled Company servants to draw on men, money and firepower from sources more varied than those of other Indian rulers. And the vast linguistic and cultural gulf that separated Bengal from London meant that Company servants were usually better able than Indian politicians to navigate the shifting sands of imperial politics. Company servants were certainly vulnerable as they were drawn into the unstable orbit of imperial politics, but Indians were doubly so.

The helplessness that many Indians felt in the face of the new oceanic politics is poignantly captured in the person of Mir Jafar, Robert Clive's nominee as *nawab* of Bengal. Mir Jafar tried to establish a strong personal alliance with Clive, whom he addressed in the Mughal style with the titles: *Zubdat ul Mulk* (Select of the Kingdom), *Muin-ud-daulah* (the Eminent in the State) and *Sabut Jang* (Firm in War). Yet early in 1760 Clive left Bengal for Britain, and Mir Jafar wrote to Clive that 'a separation from him is most afflicting to me'.[45] Indeed, within a few months of Clive's departure, Mir Jafar was summarily deposed by the new governor Henry Vansittart. A translator in the Company armies, Mr Lushington, wrote to Clive on 3 December 1760, describing the scene in Murshidabad as Mir Jafar was confronted by hostile British soldiers. Lushington recorded that the broken *nawab* made a dramatic speech, declaring 'The English placed me on the musnud;[46] you may depose me if you please. You have thought proper to break your engagements. I would not mine'. He added, 'I will desire you will either send me to Sabut Jung (Lord Clive), for he will do me justice, or let me go to Mecca'.[47] It is typical that our only record of this speech is in an English translation, reconstructed ('as well as I can remember') by a Company servant. Lord Clive, of course, was across the waters in England and could no longer protect Mir Jafar. The sources of power in

---

[44] Letter of Warren Hastings to Ct. of D., Ft. William, 11 November 1773, printed in G. R. Gleig, *Memoirs of the Life of the Right Honourable Warren Hastings*, 2 vols. (London, 1841), vol. I, p. 369.

[45] Cited in Khan, *The Transition in Bengal*, p. 11. For a list of Mughal titles awarded to leading Company servants, see ibid., pp. xii–xiii.

[46] A throne marking the *nawab*'s status.

[47] Lushington to Clive, 3 December 1760, cited in Malcolm, *Life of Robert, Lord Clive*, vol. II, p. 268.

Bengal, as Mir Jafar recognized, were increasingly being taken out of Indian hands.

The terms of negotiation

What, then, were the key terms that shaped the emerging 'negotiated empire' of the British in India? The tone and substance of British debates about India reflected the varied terrains of the East India Company's operations. The Company service itself had generated a set of vocabularies for describing itself and its relationship to India over the 150 years of its existence since 1600; this conceptual inheritance, especially notions of Indian despotism, depravity and corruption, were remarkably resilient as they were passed down the close-knit commercial societies of the Indian settlements. The expansion of the Company into Indian politics brought Company servants into contact with a range of Indian 'informers' and texts that would, in a form that was highly mediated by British translations and interpretations, shape the course of British Indian thought.

Meanwhile, after 1757, and especially after 1765, Company servants were forced to address a set of wider concerns generated from within the British and Atlantic politics. Increasingly Company servants had to explain their Indian predicament not just to other 'East Indians' or the Company directors and proprietors, but to a wider political nation, represented in parliament. The Company's state-building in Bengal was thus entangled with concepts of the state generated within the broad spectrum of British political thought. Three terms in particular, crucial concepts in eighteenth-century British politics, would have wide resonance in debates over the Company government in Bengal. These key terms were sovereignty, constitutions and political economy, and they can be viewed as thematic headings representing overlapping clusters of political ideas that were deployed in innovative ways in debates over India.

In the 1760s and 1770s the issue of sovereignty, the locus of ultimate political power within the realm, gained a new prominence in Britain, not only as a debating point of high political theory but also as a subject of everyday polemic.[48] A variety of circumstances brought the issue of sovereignty forward. A new king, George III, keen to assert himself over a fractious parliament, raised the spectre (at least in the imagination of

---

[48] For a recent treatment of this theme in relation to empire, see E. Rothschild, 'Global Commerce and the Question of Sovereignty in the Eighteenth Century Provinces', *Modern Intellectual History*, 1 (2004), pp. 3–25.

opposition groups) of a new Toryism, a royal absolutism that Britons hoped had been buried once and for all by the Glorious Revolution of 1688 and the banishment of the Stuart dynasty. A growing standing army and inflated national debt, legacies of the Seven Years War of 1756–63, raised fears about the corruption of parliament by tax-hungry ministers. And above all, a new empire, another legacy of global warfare, raised troubling questions about the status of new conquests, the costs of defending expanded territories, about command and control over distant provinces, and ultimately about the integrity of the growing empire under the sovereignty of the king-in-parliament.[49]

Debates about India, and especially about the Company's growing power in Bengal, took their place in this wider set of debates about empire and sovereignty in the 1760s. India, in this period, was in some sense only the poor cousin of the British empire in the Atlantic. The value of Atlantic trade still dwarfed that of Asian trade, and North America and the West Indies were far more familiar than Bengal and Madras to British political society.[50] Yet bald comparisons of trade figures cannot properly describe the importance of India in British politics. For one thing, the high value of East Indian capital on the London markets, and the real fear that this stock of capital was coming to the verge of ruin, forced India to the top Parliamentary agenda by 1772–3, raising fears of another financial crash on the scale of the South Sea bubble. For another, the astonishing appearance of a chartered trading company, for so long operating from small coastal factories in Asia, and now transformed into a territorial colossus to rival even its parent state, raised thorny questions not only about the relative rights to Indian revenues, but also the desirability for Britain of an empire of conquest in Asia.

The Company's Indian 'factories', Bombay, Madras and Calcutta, had long been regarded as existing under the sovereignty of the king-in-parliament expressed in royal charters.[51] But the Company's Indian trade also brought the British into the realms of Indian sovereignty, especially during the 'revolutions' of the 1750s and 1760s. Until 1765 it appeared that the old structures of Indian sovereignty, running from the Mughal emperor through the provincial *nawab*, were still in place. From 1765, however, as the Company formalized its claims to Indian territorial revenues as *diwan* of Bengal, it increasingly appeared that, in the words of one prominent critic of the Company, 'the Company are

---

[49] For a general view, see Pocock, 'The Imperial Crisis'.
[50] Bowen, *Revenue and Reform*, p. 17.   [51] Ibid., pp. 53–4.

become sovereigns of extensive, rich and populous kingdoms', 'the Merchant-sovereign and the Sovereign-merchant'.[52]

The idea of a divided sovereignty, and of a body like the Company springing up from within the realm as an *imperium in imperio*, was profoundly disturbing to many among Britain's political elite. While Britons both at home and overseas had learned to think of their own constitutional forms as the bulwark of liberty, valorizing the checks and balances inherent in the relationship between the Crown and the two houses of parliament, they also frequently argued that liberty and property depended on a strong and undivided sovereign power to act as the ultimate guarantor of legal government. William Blackstone, the foremost legal theorist of his day, argued that security and good order necessitated an 'absolute despotic power, which must in all govern-ments reside somewhere', and which in England resided in the 'sovereign and uncontrollable' power of parliament.[53] A strong unitary sovereignty was important in avoiding the perils of disunity or even civil war, especially in an era of global competition with the French.[54] Many British politicians came to believe that the integrity of the realm depended on maintaining the unity of king-in-parliament in the face of American protests against a more assertive parliamentary sovereignty.[55]

This strand of British thinking about the exclusive prerogatives of a central sovereign power had an important impact on debates about India. As we shall see, a version of it informed the East India Company's critique of post-Mughal Indian states. Many British observers thought that the endless division and proliferation of small sovereignties, unre-strained by the failing imperial power of the Mughals, had led to endemic anarchy. But the East India Company itself, as it became an Asian potentate, was liable to a similar critique in Britain, by those who feared that its overmighty servants were tearing the precious fabric of British imperial sovereignty. British ministers undertook major inquiries into the Company's affairs in Bengal in 1766–7, 1772–3, 1781 and 1783–4, on each occasion claiming for parliament a sovereign's right to

---

[52] William Bolts, *Considerations on Indian Affairs; Particularly Respecting the Present State of Bengal Dependencies*, 3 vols. (London, 1772–5), pp. vi–vii. See also T. Pownall, *The Right, Interest, and Duty of Government, As Concerned in the Affairs of the East Indies* (1st edn, 1773, repr. London, 1781), p. 3; 'the Merchant is become the Sovereign'.

[53] Cited in David Lieberman, *The Province of Legislation Determined. Legal Theory in Eighteenth-century Britain* (Cambridge, 1989), pp. 50–3.

[54] P. J. Marshall, 'Empire and Authority in the Late Eighteenth Century', *Journal of Imperial and Commonwealth History*, 15 (1987b), pp. 105–22.

[55] Pocock, 'The Imperial Crisis', p. 275.

regulate (and to tax) their subjects overseas.[56] By 1784 an enduring set of institutional controls over the Company government, centred on a ministerial 'Board of Control' for India, was established. Yet the Company had maintained a significant degree of autonomy within this framework, and the issue of formal British sovereignty over the Indian territories was not legally defined until the early nineteenth century.[57]

There were several important obstacles to the formal assertion of British sovereignty in India. Pre-eminent among them was the Company's vigorous defence of its property overseas as an inviolable component of rights granted by parliament through the Company's charters of incorporation. A legal opinion from 1757 suggested a distinction between territories conquered by British arms, which would be subject to both the dominion and dominium (sovereignty and property) of the Crown, and territories leased or granted from Indian rulers which would remain the property of the Company.[58] Thus, by claiming to hold much of Bengal as *diwan* by grant from the Mughal emperor, the Company sought to define its territorial revenues as its own property. In 1766–7 and again in 1772–3 the Company rallied significant support around the issue of chartered rights, while the Rockingham Whigs (including Edmund Burke) opposed ministerial interventions in Company affairs as presaging a broader attack on property rights.[59] Another dimension of this argument suggested that if ambitious ministers managed to take control of the vast pool of wealth and patronage represented by the Company, they could by-pass or manipulate the legislature and establish a new tyranny. This view helped to defeat Charles Fox's ambitious 1783 bill which would have replaced the court of directors with commissioners nominated by the Crown's ministers.[60]

---

[56] Bowen, *Revenue and Reform*, pp. 170–1, notes that the House of Commons on 10 May 1773 passed a resolution *vis-à-vis* Indian affairs stating that 'all acquisitions made under the influence of a military force, or by treaty with foreign princes, do of right belong to the state'. Yet, as Bowen also showed, this was merely an expression of parliamentary opinion rather than a resolution of the ambiguous legal position.

[57] For an interesting, if dated, account, see H. H. Dodwell, 'The Development of Sovereignty in British India', in Dodwell (ed.), *Cambridge History of India*, vol. V, pp. 589–608.

[58] The so-called Pratt/Yorke opinion, delivered by the Solicitor and Attorney Generals in 1757, is discussed in Bowen, *Revenue and Reform*, pp. 53–5, and Dodwell, 'The Development of Sovereignty', p. 593.

[59] H. V. Bowen, 'A Question of Sovereignty? The Bengal Land Revenue Issue, 1765–7', *JICH*, 16 (1988), pp. 155–76.

[60] Marshall, *Problems of Empire*, p. 41.

A further factor, complicating the issue of sovereignty, was the issue of other European powers, and the standing of the Company's territories in international law. Company servants often emphasized that maintaining the paraphernalia of Indian sovereignty in Bengal protected them from potential liabilities with regard to other European traders; in 1769, for example, Governor Harry Verelst (writing four years after the assumption of the *diwani*) worried that 'an open avowal of sovereignty' in Bengal would have the effect of 'awakening the jealousy of foreign nations'.[61] If Bengal was declared British territory, it could be attacked by the French or the Dutch on the outbreak of war elsewhere in the empire. Similarly, if the Company was seen to exercise sovereign powers in Bengal, then complaints by other European powers in India might be directed to the Privy Council or other channels of diplomatic influence within Britain, making further trouble for the Company. Thus, the Company was careful to act against other trading companies in Bengal through the established channels of the *nawab's* administration, long after the *nawabs* were denuded of any real autonomy. Moreover, in international treaties between Britain and other European powers, Britain stopped short of declaring its sovereignty over the Company's extensive territories before 1814.[62]

A further and related set of uncertainties surrounded the issue of the constitutionality of the Company government in Bengal. In conventional wisdom, the power of the sovereign, if it was not to become arbitrary – threatening the liberty and property of its subjects – was expressed and contained within a constitution, a set of 'fundamental laws' that both described and circumscribed the operations of the sovereignty. The English constitution was often described as an 'ancient constitution', a series of political and legal procedures evolved and perfected through long experience and refinement. At the core of this 'ancient constitution' lay the 'common law' and parliamentary representation, perceived as the twin bedrocks of English liberty and property. For many eighteenth-century Whigs, a key aspect of the idea of an ancient constitution was the notion of sources of right rooted in ancient custom, independent of the will of sovereign kings. Government propagandists disputed with radical opponents whether or not the eighteenth-century British state represented the triumphant vindication, or a terrible backsliding, from the glories of the ancient constitution.[63]

---

[61] H. Verelst, *A View of the Rise and Progress and Present State of the English Government in Bengal* (London, 1772), Appendix, p. 123.

[62] Dodwell, 'The Development of Sovereignty', pp. 595–7.

[63] Brewer, *Party Ideology and Popular Politics*, pp. 260–1.

As Colin Kidd has detailed, the concept of the ancient constitution was highly malleable and much contested. Ancient Britons, Saxons and even the conquering Normans (especially in some royalist versions) were all credited in different degrees with establishing the principles of the ancient constitution. In the eighteenth century, a modernist Whig account of British history grew up to challenge the idea of an ancient constitution. The modernist Whigs, notably David Hume and Josiah Tucker, drew on Harrington and others to argue that British liberty was rooted in the more recent evolution of commercial society and in the consolidation of modern forms of property.[64]

Notwithstanding this critique, however, the ancient constitution remained a central element in the rhetoric of the age. Blackstone, for example, understood modern liberty as 'a gradual restoration of that ancient constitution, whereof our Saxon forefathers had been unjustly deprived, partly by the policy, and partly by the force, of the Normans'.[65] Edmund Burke, too, relied on the sense of the constitution as a precious, ancestral inheritance in his response to the radicalism of the French Revolution, praising the 'powerful prepossession towards antiquity, with which the minds of all our lawyers and legislators, and all the people whom they wish to influence, have always been filled'.[66]

British constitutionalism had an internationalist as well as a nationalist dimension in the eighteenth century, related in particular to the widespread influence of Montesquieu's treatise on comparative politics, *The Spirit of the Laws* (1748).[67] In this work, Montesquieu offered a typology of different 'constitutions' shaped by climatic and historical conditions and organized around various animating principles. For example, the organizing principle of a republic was virtue, and of a despotism, fear. Montesquieu greatly admired the British constitution, which he saw as a blend of monarchy, aristocracy and republican forms, capable of withstanding the corrupting tendencies of each form, and uniquely fitted for liberty. British elites, in turn, greatly admired Montesquieu.[68]

---

[64] Kidd, *British Identities Before Nationalism*, pp. 93–4.

[65] Blackstone, *Commentaries on the Laws of England*, vol. IV, pp. 401–2, 413, cited in Kidd, *British Identities Before Nationalism*, p. 97.

[66] Edmund Burke, *Reflections on the Revolution in France* (1st edn, 1790, repr. J. G. A. Pocock (ed.), Indianapolis, 1987), p. 28. See also, Pocock, 'Burke and the Ancient Constitution', in *Politics, Language, Time. Essays on Political Thought and History* (New York, 1973), pp. 202–32.

[67] Montesquieu, *The Spirit of the Laws* (tr., ed.), Anne M. Cohler, Basia Carolyn Miller, Harold Samuel Stone (Cambridge, 1989).

[68] F. T. H. Fletcher, *Montesquieu and English Politics* (London, 1939).

Montesquieu's text suggested a hierarchy of constitutional forms. Despotism (particularly associated with hot climates and Asiatic peoples) was clearly a pejorative term, describing a system of cruelty and servitude, in which base impulses of fear and aggression substituted for honour and virtue. Despotism, in this view, was 'endlessly corrupted because it is corrupt by nature'. Yet, Montesquieu's thought was also tinged by relativism. Despotism had its own rationale, and might maintain itself 'when circumstances, which arise from the climate, the religion, and the situation of the genius of the people, force it to follow some order and to suffer some rule'.[69]

As Britain acquired an Asiatic empire, it appeared that the poles of liberty and despotism, and temperate and torrid zones, were suddenly being ratcheted together. Before the Seven Years' War, it was possible to understand the constitution of the British empire as an extension of the domestic constitution into settler colonies. After 1763, however, Britons were confronted with a vastly expanded territorial empire, bigger land armies, and large populations of non-white, non-British inhabitants – who were not in general slaves (as in plantation economies of the Atlantic empire) but subjects.[70] Two conquest territories in particular, Canada (with its large population of French Catholics) and Bengal, posed novel problems for theorists of the imperial constitution. Contention arose not only from the alien populations but also from the fact of conquest. The conventions of the law of conquest granted the British king power to abrogate pre-existing laws in conquered territories and to replace them with the laws of England.[71] Coke's famous opinion in Calvin's Case suggested that Christian laws would continue in force until the king moved to abrogate them, but 'infidel' laws automatically lapsed.[72] On the other hand, there was a tradition of legal diversity under the Crown (the Scottish, for example, retained their own distinctive laws), which many cherished as a mark of the 'Romanic' toleration of the British for alien customs.

---

[69] Montesquieu, *Spirit of the Laws*, p. 119.

[70] This is not to say that forms of domestic and even plantation slavery were entirely absent from the 'Asiatic empire'; indeed, as Chatterjee has detailed, they were quite widespread. Indrani Chatterjee, *Gender, Slavery and the Law in Colonial India* (Oxford, 1999). Moreover, the Mughal empire was sometimes construed by British observers as a system of despotism that reduced its subjects to the condition of slaves.

[71] For a discussion of the law of conquest, see Nasser Hussain, *The Jurisprudence of Emergency*, pp. 23–5.

[72] Marshall, 'Britain and the World in the Eighteenth Century: IV. The Turning Outwards of Britain', *TRHS, 6th Series*, 11 (2001), p. 6.

The confusion of home authorities presented with new conquests was reflected in the complete reversal of British policy in Quebec, from the initial declaration of conquest in 1763, which implied that French law would be abolished and replaced by English laws and forms of rule, to the decision in 1774 to allow French civil law to be administered in Quebec under a governor and council operating without an elected assembly.[73] Just as the Quebec Act raised a storm of criticism from protestants who feared Catholic pollution of the stream of English liberties, so the Company's conquests in Bengal seemed to presage a new form of more authoritarian empire, as well as the much heralded onset of 'eastern luxury'.[74]

In Bengal, the issue of constitutionality was complicated by the long tradition of thinking of 'Asiatic' government as despotic, founded on arbitrary whim rather than settled law, and absolute power rather than liberty. Yet English law, it was widely assumed, could not be easily introduced into what was perceived as the dramatically different social environment of India. Thus, after the conquest of Bengal, Britons began searching for sources of legality within the constitutional history of India. The main strands of British thinking about constitutionality, the 'ancient constitutionalism' of the English, and the comparative constitutionalism of Montesquieu, came into an uncomfortable yet creative relationship. Montesquieu's great work presented a conundrum; despotism was both a corrupt form of government but also an organic product of 'Asiatic' climates. British politicians and thinkers tried to solve this conundrum in many different ways, from embracing despotism as a cultural necessity, to using British supervision or even English legal remedy to mitigate the worst excesses of Asiatic corruption, and to asserting that Asiatic despotism in India was not as destructive as Montesquieu and others had claimed. The sophisticated administrative forms of the Mughal empire, as well as growing knowledge of the rich traditions of Muslim and Hindu law, could be used to argue that Bengal had its own kind of ancient constitution by which the Company could be guided.

Many Britons, as we shall see, distinguished between the legitimate sovereignty of the Mughal emperors and the chaotic 'usurpations' of provincial governors (*nawabs*) or large landholders (*zamindars*) which they assumed had followed from the corruption of the empire in the eighteenth century. Indeed, this narrative of Mughal corruption fitted

[73] Peter Marshall, 'British North America, 1760–1815', *OHBE*, 2, pp. 375–8.
[74] Marshall, *Making and Unmaking of Empires*, pp. 333–4.

well with Montesquieu's idea that despotism, founded solely on fear rather than any other species of loyalty, 'is destroyed by internal vice if accidental causes do not prevent its principle from becoming corrupt'.[75] Thus, one way of legitimizing the Company's government in Bengal was to imagine that it was restoring some version of an ancient constitution that had degenerated during the decline of the Mughal empire.

The final key term of British political thought, after sovereignty and constitutions, through which Britons analysed the revolutions in Bengal, was political economy. As in legal and historical thought, writings on political economy tended to invoke a strong view of the role of the central sovereign power. As Keith Tribe argued, eighteenth-century political economy often did not conceive of the 'economy' as a domain distinct from 'polity', governed by its own laws of supply and demand. 'Economy' was often used to refer to practices of frugality, moderation and good management in the head of a household, or by analogy to a household, in the state. 'What oeconomy is in a family, political oeconomy is in a state', so wrote James Steuart, in his *Inquiry into the Principals of Political Oeconomy* of 1768.[76] Steuart conceived of the polity as a system of circulation of money and goods. The role of the sovereign was to order the affairs of the nation so as to quicken the flow of wealth through the veins of the body politic.

As in theory, so in practice, the eighteenth-century British empire was marked by the strong arm of the sovereign in regulating production and commerce. The 'navigation acts' of the seventeenth century provided an enduring framework of regulations for overseas trade, marked by preferential tariffs and specific embargos, designed to centre the profits of trade in Britain, and to promote the strength of the British nation (and especially the British merchant and naval fleet) versus its continental competitors.[77] Within this imperial framework of protected trades, the East India Company's military victories in the 1750s and 1760s could be interpreted as a major triumph for the nation, as they checked the growth of French commercial power in a lucrative branch of world trade. The Company's monopoly of trade east of Suez, its grants

---

[75] Montesquieu, *Spirit of the Laws*, p. 119.

[76] James Steuart, *An Inquiry into the Principles of Political Oeconomy* (1st edn, 1768, repr., A. S. Skinner (ed.), 2 vols., Edinburgh 1966), pp. 16–17, cited in Keith Tribe, *Land, Labour and Economic Discourse* (London, 1978), p. 84.

[77] P. K. O'Brien, 'Inseparable Connections: Trade, Economy, Fiscal State, and the Expansion of Empire, 1688–1815', in *OHBE*, 2, pp. 53–77. For the assumptions that lay behind 'economic nationalism' in the eighteenth century, see also Keith Wrightson, *Earthly Necessities. Economic Lives in Early Modern Britain, 1470–1750* (Yale, 2000), pp. 250–1.

from the king-in-parliament of powers of government for its trading stations, and the support of the British navy for Asian trade, were fulfilling their imagined role in enabling British merchants to beat off foreign competition.

As the Company's publicists often stressed, the 'amazing revolution' in Bengal after 1757, which provided the Company with a new income from territorial revenues, solved some of the perceived flaws of the Indian trade within the imperial system. No longer would the Company need to export bullion to pay for its 'investment' in Indian textiles; rather, it would pay for its cotton from local revenue surpluses of silver rupees.[78] Nor would the new Indian territories require a drain of manpower from Britain (unlike the American colonies); silver rupees would pay for Indian troops (sepoys) to police the Company's domains. Proponents of the Company's military expansion in the 1760s tended to see landed settlements as necessary adjuncts of an essentially maritime empire, creating self-financing settlements with extra provision against future danger.

From early on in the process of the Company's conquest of Bengal, however, dissenting voices both within and without the Company questioned the effects of Asiatic empire on the Company's trade, British national well-being and the welfare of Bengal itself. As wars led swiftly to more wars, and the military costs of the Company ballooned, a leading Company official, J. Z. Holwell testified before a parliamentary committee that 'a Commercial and Military Company cannot long subsist at the same time for the Expansion and Inconvenience on the one side must over-balance the advantages on the other'.[79] Others in Britain, associating Asia with the corrupting effects of 'luxury' on national manners, were worried at the potential new influx of wealth into the kingdom, and what such wealth might do to the delicate balance of the constitution. In Samuel Foote's play, *The Nabob*, first produced in June 1772 at the Haymarket Theatre, the country gentleman and MP, Sir Thomas Oldham, complained to Sir Matthew Mite, a returned Nabob, that 'your riches (which perhaps too only are ideal) by introducing a general spirit of dissipation, have extinguished labour and industry, the slow, but sure source of national wealth'.[80]

---

[78] Watts, *Memoirs of the Revolution in Bengal*, pp. 63–4.
[79] Evidence of J. Z. Holwell, before a Committee of the House of Commons on the State of the East India Company, 30 March 1767, BL, Add. MSS, 18,469, fo. 12v.
[80] By talking of the Company's 'ideal' riches, Oldham was invoking the ghost of the South Sea Company. Samuel Foote, *The Nabob. A Comedy in Three Acts* (Dublin, 1778), p. 52.

Within Bengal, theories of Asiatic despotism worked often to justify encroachments on the powers of Indian states or Indian officials. As we shall see in chapter 2, few Company officials believed that the *nawabs* were effective stewards of the Bengal lands, and many argued that British officials were bound to be more effective administrators than degenerate Asiatics. These views appeared to be backed up by the writings of European travellers, especially François Bernier, who worked as a physician at the Mughal court in the mid-seventeenth century. Bernier taught that the Mughal emperor was the sole owner of the lands in his domain, that there was no private property in India, and warned that the imperial territories were being impoverished as a result.[81] Throughout the period of expansion, versions of the thesis of Asiatic despotism and native depravity gave meaning and justification to the Company's territorial ambitions.

In the short term, however, the Company's territorial expansion appeared to profit neither Company shareholders in London, nor the British government, nor the people of Bengal. In the context of a major famine in Bengal (1769–70) and the near bankruptcy of the Company at home, the Company's new incarnation attracted multiple criticisms from theorists of political economy.[82] Its problems centred on the notion of the sovereign as the patriarchal guardian of the public good, ordering the flow of wealth in the kingdom to maintain the public welfare and maintain the social balance. It was unclear whether a commercial Company could be safely entrusted with this charge of sovereignty, or whether the private interests of its shareholders were compatible with the 'public' interests of either Britain or Bengal.

In a mercantilist world of protected markets and monopoly, it was argued that the Company's interest in maximizing its profits from the Indian trades would inevitably force other Indian merchants out of Bengal. Meanwhile, the Company's new ability to pay for goods both in India and in China using rupees garnered from the Bengal revenues resulted in what many thought of as an 'unrequited' drain of wealth from Bengal. James Steuart addressed the problem of currency drain by noting that the usual rules of 'balance of trade', that 'exportations enrich

---

[81] P. J. Marshall and G. Williams, *The Great Map of Mankind. British Perceptions of the World in the Age of Enlightenment* (London, 1982), pp. 18–19, and Kate Teltscher, *India Inscribed. European and British Writing on India (1600–1800)* (New Delhi, 1995), pp. 28–34.

[82] For the sense, among contemporary political economists, of the 'global scandal' of mercantile sovereignty, see Rothschild, 'Global Commerce and the Question of Sovereignty', p. 17.

a country, and that importations impoverish it' no longer pertained in Bengal, where the country received no outside remuneration for the Company's exports.[83] Steuart believed this problem might be mitigated if the Company promoted free trade in products over and above its own investment, 'to increase the demand of strangers'.[84] But he had few illusions that the Company's demands on Bengal needed to be strictly delimited, and 'it is vain to think of a remedy without sacrificing the interest of Great Britain, and of the Company itself to that of Bengal'.[85]

Adam Smith went still further, arguing that the narrow interests of a merchant company in securing cheap and exclusive access to Bengal's manufactures was diametrically opposed to the wider interest of a proper sovereign power, and that the Company was 'altogether unfit to govern its territorial possessions'.[86] Such arguments against the Company's monopoly often aimed to replace the mercantile sovereignty of the Company with the purified sovereignty of the king-in-parliament; but while ministers fitfully asserted their supervisory powers over the Company's Indian regimes, too much wealth and power was staked in the Company for its critics to have their way.

On the other hand, debates about political economy profoundly influenced policy-makers within the Company, as they sought to render their mercantile sovereignty respectable within the theoretical conventions of the day. Particularly important in this regard were new doctrines of agricultural improvement. The disastrous Bengal famine of 1769–70, following closely on the heels of the Company's conquests, cast a long shadow over Company politics. European agricultural theorists and Company servants themselves began to develop schemes for the regeneration of Bengal, centring on private property rights, moderate taxation and free commerce in agricultural products. While criticisms of the Company's own monopoly were resisted and deflected, theories of agrarian development were incorporated into the workings of the Company government, combining English Whig notions of private landed property as the foundation of political security, with the

[83] James Steuart, *The Principles of Money Applied to the Present State of the Coin of Bengal* (London, 1772), p. 81. See also the useful discussion of this text in W. J. Barber, *British Economic Thought and India, 1600–1858. A Study in the History of Development Economics* (Oxford, 1975), pp. 73–85.
[84] Steuart, *The Principles of Money Applied to the Present State of the Coin of Bengal,* pp. 82–3.
[85] Ibid., p. 64.
[86] Adam Smith, *The Wealth of Nations, Books IV–V* (ed.), A. S. Skinner (Penguin, London, 1999b), pp. 221–2, 343.

prescriptions of the French physiocrats for agricultural investment and improvement.[87]

What needs to be stressed, however, is that doctrines of political economy were only one element in a wider fabric of debate about imperial sovereignty and constitutionality that engulfed the East India Company from the mid-1760s. This is why notions of 'improvement', expressed through arguments about money or land, were encased within a conception of legitimate sovereignty structured by organic and historically formed constitutions. In a Montesquieuan world, in which political forms were related to the 'genius' of different peoples, the exercise of 'improvement' was of necessity mediated by the texture and shape of pre-existing forms of sovereignty. Thus, Indian forms of government did not appear simply as a foil for the saving grace of British virtue, or only as a flawed 'other' that might illuminate the virtues of the 'self'. Early colonial state-building was marked by the quest for a stable form of sovereignty which both ensured the security of British military and commercial interests, and which could be represented as compatible with the historical forms of rule in Bengal. Colonial state-building in Bengal was conceived as the reconstruction of a wounded sovereignty, both at home and abroad, that was also, of necessity, a process of historical reconstruction.

This happy revolution?

The growing body of pamphlets and treatises on Indian affairs, and in particular on Bengal, printed in London between 1757 and 1772, show in greater detail the dynamic reconceptualization of the East India Company, and of its place in the wider frame of Indian history, which accompanied the process of territorial expansion. Many pamphlets were written by Company servants who had returned to London, and wished to justify and explain their Indian careers, or to promote a particular line of policy. Often, these works contained so-called authentic documents culled from official records of the Company as a means of disseminating a preferred interpretation of events. Taken together, they charted a course from euphoria to anxiety and disillusionment as the hoped for profits of military expansion evaporated after 1768. But they also developed new ways of thinking about Indian politics and history. Early pamphlets justified the Company's conquests by highlighting the

---

[87] The classic treatment is Ranajit Guha, *A Rule of Property for Bengal* (Paris, 1963). See also Richard Drayton: *Nature's Government. Science, Imperial Britain & the 'Improvement' of the World* (London: Yale, 2000), pp. 117–18

corruption and instability of Asiatic despotism. Increasingly, however, as British conquests were perceived to have destabilized British national finances and brought misery to the inhabitants of Bengal, some writers enunciated a more positive account of former Indian governments, especially the Mughal empire, which began to serve as a foil for a new era of Company oppression.

British pamphlets on Bengal in this period revealed the tense coexistence of contrasting views about Indian history and politics. On the one hand, the experience of small but armed groups of European traders coexisting uneasily with powerful Indian rulers enabled stereotypes of the tyrannical cruelty of Asiatic governments to flourish. These stereotypes often connected the idea of Asiatic despotism with Islam and its alleged corrupting effects. On the other hand, Company servants had for many decades appealed to the sovereign power of Mughal emperors as a means of legitimizing their trade. Most importantly, the basis of the Company's claim to duty-free trade in Bengal was the *farman* granted by the Emperor Farrukhsiyar in 1717. These claims to legal rights under the Mughal empire had spawned a different way of talking about the Mughals. In this view, the Mughal empire was a kind of legal sovereignty – with its own form of viable constitution, which had apparently been eroded by the 'usurpations' of the Bengal *nawabs*.

The earliest defenders of the revolution of 1757, mainly acolytes of the chief revolutionary Robert Clive, framed the Company's defeat of *Nawab* Siraj-ud-daula, as part of a longer narrative of the breakdown of Mughal imperial authority. William Watts, for example, who published his *Memoirs of the Revolution in Bengal* in 1760, argued that the Company had been forced to defend itself from the rapacious greed of successive Bengal *nawabs* in order to protect trading rights derived from the Mughal *farman*. Watts' *Memoirs* gave a stereotypical account of Asiatic despotism. The Hindus were kept in 'abject slavery' by the race of Moors. 'The whole country belongs' to the emperor, 'his subjects having no other laws but the dictates of his will'. When emperors were fatally weakened by luxurious pursuits, 'a kind of anarchy' overtook India marked by endless 'civil wars'. There was 'hardly any such thing as legal authority subsisting in any part of the empire'. On the other hand, the British rights to duty-free trade and to hold land around their factories were 'as solid and firm . . . as the constitution could give', having been obtained 'when the Mughal Empire was in its most flourishing condition'.[88] Siraj, who attacked those rights, was an illegitimate ruler, and the East

---

[88] Watts, *Memoirs of the Revolution in Bengal*, pp. 3–4, 6.

India Company, in deposing him, had merely been defending their just rights enshrined in the Mughal *farman*. The best that Watts could say in defence of Siraj-ud-daula was that 'he had a view of sovereignty from his infancy'; bred up in the corrupting habits of the seraglio and among the Mughals who were 'addicted to luxury, fierce, oppressive and for the most part very rapacious', Siraj was a natural product of his race.[89] After the 'amazing Revolution' and 'happy changes' of 1757, Watts claimed, Robert Clive was received into the *nawab*'s capital in Murshidabad 'with the utmost expression of joy and the loudest acclamations of the people'.[90]

There was an obvious tension in Watts' account between his disparagement of the lawless and degenerate Mughal despotism, and his claim that the Company's trading rights derived from a putative imperial 'constitution'. Similarly, the idea that the 'amazing Revolution' of 1757 was simply aimed to protect British trade by 'restoring the old form of rule', would not have reassured the attentive reader, taught to think of this old form of government as unstable and corrupt.[91] Luke Scrafton's text, *Reflections on the Government of Indostan*, first published in 1761, was more aware of these dilemmas. Scrafton, another Clivite, deployed the idiom of neo-classical narrative, posing as a statesman reflecting from retirement on the virtues and vices of great historical figures.[92] Like Watts, Scrafton emphasized the cruel and salacious character of Siraj-ud-daula, making use, for example, of J. Z. Holwell's account of the supposed massacre of 128 Britons and Indians in the Black Hole dungeon of the old Fort William in 1756.[93] The eventual nemesis of Siraj-ud-daula was recounted by Scrafton with a sense of providential relish. Robert Clive's military successes, by contrast, were seen as emblematic of his natural genius.[94] Both figures, Siraj and Clive, were conceived of as natural products of the 'genius' of their respective peoples.

A particular vitriol often attached to Muslims in these accounts. 'I am sensible', Scrafton wrote, 'that I have everywhere given the Moors a

---

[89] Ibid., pp. 58, 2.   [90] Ibid., p. 57.   [91] Ibid., p. 59.

[92] For the neo-classical tradition of history writing, see J. G. A. Pocock, *Barbarism and Religion*. Vol. II. *Narratives of Civil Government* (Cambridge, 1999), pp. 8–9.

[93] Luke Scrafton, *Reflections on the Government of Indostan. With a Short Sketch of the History of Bengal, from the Years 1739 to 1756, and an Account of the English Affairs to 1758* (2nd edn, London, 1763), pp. 58–9. For the original narrative of the Black Hole, see J. Z. Holwell, *A Genuine Narrative of the Deplorable Deaths of the English Gentlemen, and Others, who were suffocated in the Black Hole in Fort-William, at Calcutta* (London, 1758). Historians now agree that Holwell's account must have substantially exaggerated the numbers of dead.

[94] Scrafton, *Reflections on the Government of Indostan*, p. 100.

detestable character; and I am sorry to say it is so universally true, that I never knew above two or three exceptions'.[95] But Scrafton also addressed the contradiction between the widespread notion that Indian Muslims were a people without virtue, and the long duration and great extent of Mughal power through two centuries. In what would be an influential formulation, Scrafton characterized the Mughal government in its prime as a kind of limited despotism, built on a partial conquest of the gentle and industrious (if also weak and divided) race of the Hindus. Scrafton was 'amazed to see that all the writers have asserted that there are no laws in this country; that the land is not hereditary; and the emperor is the universal heir'. He agreed that there were 'no written institutes', 'no acts of Parliament' and 'no power to control the emperor'; nonetheless 'they proceed in their courts by established precedents'. When the Mughals conquered India, they 'made no innovations, so that the old Gentoo laws still prevailed', including the laws of succession. Only when central control broke down, after the invasions of Nadir Shah of Persia in the 1740s, did the regional *nawabs* undermine the old established forms of Hindu property and inheritance through their unremitting plunder.[96]

Scrafton's elaboration of the 'constitution' of the Mughal empire was designed in part to defend his patron, Robert Clive's right to his valuable *jagir*, or personal revenue assignment.[97] When Clive's enemies on the court of directors challenged his legal right to the *jagir* in the English courts, the 'constitution of Indostan' became a term of English law and politics.[98] Other contemporary writers also began their narratives, like Scrafton, with a disquisition on the historical forms of Indian government. Robert Orme, for example, prefaced the first volume of his massive history of British military transactions in India in 1764, with 'a Dissertation on the Establishments made by Mahomedan Conquerors in Indostan'.[99] Orme, a long-time servant of the Company, sought to highlight the military genius of the British as exemplified in their honourable and victorious deeds in India. His history was a confident appeal to imperial patriotism, rooted in the notion that the disciplined ranks of British-trained infantry would always vanquish the disordered rabble of native infantry.[100] But he shared Scrafton's view of the layered

[95] Ibid., p. 23.   [96] Ibid., pp. 26–7.
[97] Ibid., p. 125. Scrafton describes the *jagir* as 'not unlike the lands formerly held in England, by Knight's service'.
[98] Malcolm, *Life of Robert, Lord Clive*, vol. II, pp. 216–21.
[99] Robert Orme, *History of the Military Transactions of the British Nation in Indostan*, 3 vols. (London, 1763, repr. Madras, 1861), vol. I, p. 1.
[100] Ibid., p. 293.

pattern of Mughal government, arguing that 'ancient India' was divided into many 'distinct sovereignties', and that Muslim conquerors had left 'many Indian princes in possession of their respective sovereignties'.[101] Interestingly, in the light of future controversies over land rights in Bengal, Orme argued that the Mughal imperial claim to own all landed property was more designed to check the power of local chiefs than to engross all wealth or oppress the people. 'Such slavery', wrote Orme, 'would leave the monarch little grandeur'.[102]

The sense of the Mughal empire as a kind of limited despotism would play an influential role in Company politics in the decades to come, as Company officials tried to justify their own authority by Mughal precedent. In the short term, however, narratives of rapacious despotism were put to work by Company officials in opposition to the rapid succession of *nawabs* who followed Siraj-ud-daula. The cluster of ideas that surrounded the notion of Asiatic despotism, including fraud and forgery, venal and cruel officials, hoarding and engrossing of wealth, could relatively easily be deployed to justify attacks on Indian rulers. Robert Clive himself regarded Muslims in general as 'villains enough to undertake anything which might benefit themselves at another's expense'.[103] As early as 1759, Clive, in a famous letter to William Pitt, was arguing that further instability in Bengal would eventually give the Company the chance to take over the whole sovereignty for itself.[104]

By this stage, most Company servants believed that the Company's survival in Bengal required a strong military presence. But the aims and consequences of the Company's assertive stance were still contested. Further 'revolutions' in Bengal, as the Company deposed one *nawab* (Mir Jafar) in 1760, then went to war with another (Mir Qasim) in 1763–4, sparked further disputes and controversy both in Bengal and Britain. The factional disputes over Mir Qasim's war, as they were played out in pamphlet literature in London, also turned on contrasting interpretations of the 'Mughal Constitution'. The critical issue was the true nature of the Mughal *farman* granted to the Company in 1717. This *farman* was the basis for *dastaks*, or trade passes, distributed to Company servants to allow their goods to pass duty free along the rivers and roadways of Bengal. The question of whether this *farman* applied just to the official export trade of the Company, or to the private trade of

---

[101] Ibid., pp. 24–5.   [102] Ibid., p. 27.
[103] Malcolm, *Life of Robert, Lord Clive*, vol. I, pp. 381–2.
[104] Clive to William Pitt the Elder, Calcutta, 7 January 1759, repr. in ibid., vol. II, pp. 120–6.

Company officials as well, was long a matter of contention between the *nawabs* and the British. The expanded use of *dastaks* by British private traders was a major cause of Mir Qasim's turning against the Company.[105]

The debate over *dastaks* demonstrated again the tension between the idea of a Mughal 'constitution' as a system of ordered sovereignty, and the notion of rapacious, lawless despotism. On one side, Governor Henry Vansittart strongly defended the *nawab*'s right to tax British private trade as an indispensable element of Mughal sovereignty. Vansittart argued on a priori grounds that the Emperor Farrukhsiyar would not have acted with such prejudice against his own 'natural subjects', both merchants and producers, by giving foreign traders an unfair advantage in the internal commerce of his domains. The emperor's aim must have been to promote foreign exports, not to allow foreigners to swarm through internal markets. Nor would Farrukhsiyar have renounced the sovereign's natural right to tax trade in return for his protection. Vansittart here conceived of the Mughal empire as a system of rational political economy, guided by the imperial patriarch into the paths of fair trade and justice.[106]

Vansittart's enemies, by contrast, bothered little about the motives or otherwise of the emperor, basing their arguments on the evidence of precedent. They argued that British traders and the Indian agents were accustomed to using the *dastak* in private trade, an established right that should not now be abolished.[107] Further, they emphasized their horror at the thought of being subjected to the wild and unrestrained authority of *nawabi* officials, painting a classic image of lawless despotism, replete with kangaroo courts and venal, arbitrary judges. John Cartier, for example, who would become governor of Bengal between 1770 and 1772, argued that 'the nature of the government in every part of Indostan, being in all respects oppressive and venal', it would be impossible for British traders to submit to the judicial authority of the *nawabs*.[108] This visceral reluctance to submit to Indian authority helped to sway the vast majority of the council to reject Vansittart's policy of appeasement of Mir Qasim.

By 1772, it was the Company's own government which appeared to many in Britain as 'oppressive and venal'. Faltering finances, factional

---

[105] Sen, *Empire of Free Trade*, pp. 85–6.
[106] Extract of Consultations on the Bengal Council, 1 March 1763, Henry Vansittart, *Narrative of the Transactions in Bengal* (London, 1766, repr. Calcutta 1976), p. 98.
[107] See, for example, the opinions of Watts, Marriott and Hay, ibid., pp. 289–301.
[108] Ibid., p. 309.

splits, and reports of war and famine in India had undermined the credibility of the Company and its directors. In this context, critics of the Company began to invoke the Mughal constitution nostalgically, as a foil for the Company's misgovernment. One of the best known of these critics was William Bolts, a Dutchman by birth, who was expelled from Calcutta for illegal trading. Returning to Britain, Bolts sought legal remedies against his persecutors in the Company.[109] In his tract *Considerations on Indian Affairs*, published in the early months of 1772, Bolts took his case to the court of public opinion, cleverly exploiting the growing furor about the Company's finances. Anticipating parliamentary intervention in Indian affairs, Bolts addressed himself to the King of Great Britain, suggesting that he should assume his rightful role as sovereign of Bengal, thus extending his beneficent rule over his 'subjects in Asia', both European and Indian.[110]

Bolts argued that the Company's claim to have obtained the *diwani* by treaty with independent princes was a sham, and that they 'are become sovereigns of extensive, rich and populous Kingdoms, with a standing army of above sixty thousand men at their command'.[111] The *nawab* of Bengal and the emperor himself were merely 'nominal nabobs', 'puppets' of the Company's whim, and all the so-called grants of territory since the *farman* of the Emperor Farruksiyar of 1717 were 'not legally valid, according to the Constitution of the Mogul Empire, but possessions acquired and held either by violence or usurpation'. This was because 'no such laws or empire exist'.[112] The Mughal empire as a legal entity was entirely broken down and had been replaced by various categories of usurper. The Company in fact had conquered Bengal and was now an *imperium in imperio*. Moreover, because of the unnatural confusion of commerce and government in one body, the Company had become 'an absolute government of monopolists', which was impoverishing Bengal, and working against long-term British interests in the region.[113] It was time for the British government to acknowledge that 'the Sovereign of Great Britain is now an Asiatic Potentate' and to 'separate the Merchant from the Sovereign'.[114]

Bolts also founded his argument on history, contrasting the commercial policies of the Company unfavourably with those of the Mughals. As we shall see in chapter 2, even most Company servants thought that the Bengal economy was in decline in this period, as they

---

[109] For a recent account of Bolts' career, see Kuiters, *The British in Bengal*.
[110] William Bolts, *Considerations on Indian Affairs; Particularly Respecting the Present State of Bengal and its Dependencies*, 3 vols. (London, 1772–5), vol. I, pp. v–vi.
[111] Ibid., p. vi.   [112] Ibid., p. 49.   [113] Ibid., p. vii.   [114] Ibid., pp. 221–2.

experienced currency shortages and high prices in the 1760s, and especially as they considered the progress and impact of the 1769–70 famine. Bolts blamed this decline squarely on the Company, especially what he regarded as its disastrous attempt to increase its investment, using its new revenues and military might to enforce a virtual monopoly of Bengal's textile trade. Bolts contrasted this with the wisdom of the Mughal government, which appeared as a model of fair trade principles in its steady encouragement of merchants and artisans. 'Such', Bolts concluded, 'was the wise and benignant internal policy, and such were the humane and just laws of the Mogul government'.[115]

A similarly benign view of Mughal rule was also taken by Alexander Dow in his highly influential *History of Hindostan*.[116] Dow was a writer of greater literary pretensions than William Bolts, hobnobbing with the aristocrats of British high culture like David Hume and Joshua Reynolds.[117] Dow was also a former officer in the Company armies who had been sacked after the mutiny against Lord Clive's military reforms of 1765–6. Like Bolts, Dow was strongly opposed to Clive and his friends, and some of his third volume was devoted to a bitter attack on Clive and his policies. Also like Bolts, Dow dedicated his volume to the British King, George III. The third volume of his history, published in 1772, was explicitly designed to encourage parliament to make sweeping reforms of the Bengal government, treating Bengal as a British sovereign territory conquered by British arms. 'The British nation', Dow insisted, 'have become the conquerors of Bengal'.[118]

While Dow's version of Mughal government, like Bolts', was a foil for the supposed depredations of the Company, Dow founded his opinions on a far more detailed understanding of the Indian history drawn from translations of Persian chronicles. A large part of Dow's history consisted of a loose translation of the *Tarikh-i Firishtah*, a seventeenth-century history of Muslim rulers in India written by a servant of the sultans of Bijapur. Dow began the third volume of his history with a 'Dissertation on the Origin and Nature of Despotism in Hindostan', which began by reciting Montesquieuan verities about the links between hot climates and despotic constitutions, adding a discussion,

[115] Ibid., pp. 13–14.
[116] Dow, *A History of Hindostan, from the Death of Akbar, to the Complete Settlement of the Empire under Aurugzebe*, 3 vols. (London, 1768–72).
[117] For good summaries of Dow's career and writings, see J. S. Grewal, *Muslim Rule in India: the Assessments of British Historians* (Oxford, 1970), pp. 6–22, and Guha, *A Rule of Property for Bengal*, pp. 21–42.
[118] Dow, *History of Hindostan*, vol. III, p. cxvi.

probably taken from Boulanger, of the despotic tenets of Islam.[119] But Dow argued that 'the despotic form of government is not, however, so terrible in its nature, as men born in free countries are apt to imagine'.[120] Indeed despotism appeared 'in its most engaging form, under the Imperial house of Timur. The uncommon abilities of most of the princes, with the mild and humane character of all, rendered Hindostan the most flourishing empire in all the world during two complete centuries'. Not only the wisdom of benevolent emperors, but also the mildness inherent in the Hindu religion was seen to mitigate the worst aspects of despotism in Mughal India. While the emperors were bound by no civil regulation, 'there is one great law, the ideas of mankind with regard to right and wrong, by which he is bound'. Moreover, the emperors created their 'humane despotism' by respecting the large bodies of Muslim and Hindu laws, by guarding their subjects' welfare and by encouraging trade and commerce.[121]

In his 'Enquiry into the STATE of BENGAL', which followed the treatise on despotism, Dow painted a picture of a highly centralized, rule-bound Mughal government. Drawing on evidence of official documents of appointment, Dow argued that ever since Akbar's conquest in the late sixteenth century, Bengal was governed 'by established rules and regulations' which fixed the land rents at established rates, and prescribed a series of checks on local officials.[122] While Dow followed Bernier and others in thinking that all property originally belonged to the state, he did allow for the development of some hereditary private property out of government grants of assignments on land revenues like *jagirs*, and limited amounts of transferable private property in towns.[123] Furthermore, in Dow's view the Mughal had allowed the ancient Hindu rajas of Bengal to retain most of their local powers.[124] Muslim jurists, *qazis*, were attached to each district administering Islamic law, and the separation of military and civil government, represented by the distinct offices of *nawab* and *diwan*, was formerly strictly adhered to.[125]

Dow thought that the elaborate controls of the Mughal constitution broke down in the course of the eighteenth century after the 'mildness' of the emperors 'degenerated into indolence'. 'Usurpers' in the provinces threw off the established regulations and only a 'mock form

---

[119] Dow, *History of Hindostan*, vol. III, pp. vii–xxii. For Dow's use of Montesquieu and Boulanger, see Guha, *A Rule of Property for Bengal*, pp. 26–9.
[120] Dow, *History of Hindostan*, vol. III, p. xxii.
[121] Ibid., pp. xxii, xxiii, xxv.   [122] Ibid., p. xlii.   [123] Ibid., pp. xxvii, l.
[124] Ibid., pp. xliii–xliv.   [125] Ibid., pp. liii–lviii.

of empire' now remained. In Dow's view, however, the real decline of Bengal from its former prosperity dated from the rise of the English Company, which added stringent monopolies to higher taxation, and began to drain Bengal of its specie. The Company had employed corrupt Indian officials, who had leased rights of tax collection to temporary farmers, and were reducing the population to penury and starvation.[126]

Like William Bolts' treatise, Dow's text reflected the sense of disillusionment with the East India Company after the initial euphoria of conquest; but his attempt to describe the official forms of Mughal rule from Persian sources represented an advance on Bolts' reliance on old European travel accounts. Dow should be placed beside Voltaire as one of the principal figures in a wider European reassessment of Asian polities and of the idea of despotism itself; in the works of some enlightenment philosophers, stereotypes of Aristotelian tyranny and slavery were being replaced by more nuanced portraits of eastern empires marked by laws, ancient learning and economic prosperity.[127] In Dow's view, the Mughal empire at its height was a system of regulated despotism, marked by a respect for official conventions, for Muslim laws and for the ancient usages of the indigenous Hindus. In this view, the old constitution of Bengal was an amalgam of different forms of rule. Muslims had engrafted their own institutions on to 'regulations which Brahma transmitted, with his followers, from remote antiquity'.[128]

Yet Dow's celebratory view of the Mughals did not lead him to advocate the reconstruction of the old constitution. Rather, he argued that the king-in-parliament should recognize the duties and opportunities afforded by the conquest of Bengal, and that the British should 'extend some part of their own fundamental jurisprudence to secure their conquests'.[129] Dow's ideas for the regeneration of Bengal drew, as Guha showed, on mercantilist and bullionist economic theory which emphasized the importance of a favourable balance of trade and a ready money supply for commercial prosperity.[130] Internal monopolies on trade should be abolished, paper currency should be introduced, and landed property should be put on a sound basis by a general sale of lands – as a stimulant to industry and investment.[131] Dow's remedies for the improvement of Bengal were drastic and far-reaching, and even

---

[126] Ibid., pp. lxv–lxvi, lxx–cv.
[127] For this trend, see J. G. A. Pocock's discussion of Voltaire in *Barbarism and Religion*, vol. II, pp. 102–12.
[128] Dow, *History of Hindostan*, vol. III, pp. cxv–cxvi.
[129] Ibid.   [130] Guha, *A Rule of Property for Bengal*, pp. 33–42.
[131] Dow, *History of Hindostan*, vol. III, pp. cxvii–cxxxiii.

included arguing that 'the laws of England, in so far as they do not oppose prejudices and usages which cannot be relinquished by the natives, should prevail'. This was because the inhabitants of Bengal were 'divided into two religious sects, the Mahommedan and Hindoo', and 'one party will not now submit to the laws of the other'.[132]

Bolts' and especially Dow's texts were important in publicizing relatively sympathetic views of the Mughal empire, and in harnessing these historical claims to a sharp attack on the Company government in Bengal. Yet their radical prescriptions for the extension of royal protection to Bengal were unlikely to appeal to cautious ministers more interested in stabilizing the finances of the Company than in overhauling its Indian administration. Moreover, Dow's view that a foreign system of law could easily be extended into India was not widely shared. Nonetheless, Bolts' and Dow's idea of a once glorious form of centralized Mughal sovereignty would become one of the organizing principles of British political thought in Bengal in the 1770s. Resuscitating the sinews of the old Mughal constitution appeared to offer a solution to the Company's present troubles which would fit with the British penchant for ancient constitutions.

Meanwhile, British views of Indian history continued to be shot through with contradictions. Even the fashionable idea of an era of stability and prosperity under the Mughals could not eradicate the stain of despotism. Responding to Bolts and Dow, for example, the former governor of Bengal, Harry Verelst, wrote his *View of the Rise, Progress and Present State of the English Government in Bengal*, questioning whether these rosy views of Mughal government could be substantiated. Verelst was sceptical of these revisionist views of Mughal history which were 'apt to charm the imagination and mislead the judgement of men'. 'In truth', he argued, 'the condition of a people under despotic power must perpetually vary with the virtues or vices' of the governors. Verelst's treatise contained an extended defence of the Company government of Bengal in the 1760s, which emphasized the political considerations that weighed with Clive and Verelst 'in preserving the Moorish government' in 1765. But Verelst's scepticism about the Mughal empire did not mean that he wished to replace Asiatic forms of rule with imported English institutions. Indeed, whereas Bolts and Dow had argued in different ways for the extension of British jurisprudence to Bengal, Verelst emphasized the contrasting 'spirit of the laws' in Britain and India, and the very different principles of law and government in the

---

[132] Ibid., p. cxliii.

two countries. 'As well might we transplant the full-grown oak to the banks of the Ganges', he declared, 'as dream that any part of a code, matured by patient labours of successive judges and legislators in this island, can possible coalesce with the customs of Bengal'.[133] Thus, Montesquieuan notions of legal geography could be deployed to fend off attempts to extend British law to Bengal. But the question of what kind of Asiatic government the Company would become remained highly contentious and uncertain.

[133] H. Verelst, *View of the Rise, Progress and Present State of the English Government in Bengal* (London, 1772), pp. 64, 67–72, 132.

2 Colonial encounters and the crisis in Bengal, 1765–1772

Mir Qasim (1760–3) was the last *nawab* of Bengal to aspire to any real measure of independence from the Company's control. In 1763–4, the Company's army comprehensively defeated the combined forces of Mir Qasim, Shuja-ud-daula (*nawab* of the northern province of Awadh and *vizier* of the Mughal empire) and the impoverished Mughal emperor himself, Shah Alam II. From this point on, the Company was clearly the dominant military power in eastern India, even if Company officials still feared Maratha invasions from the west and the possibility of French attacks from the sea.

The *nawab* of Awadh was forced to pay a hefty tribute to the Company, and his military capacities were deliberately circumscribed. The captured emperor was settled under the protection of the Company's forces in Allahabad, and by a treaty of 1765 he appointed the Company as *diwan* of Bengal, an office described by Alexander Dow as the 'receiver-general of the Imperial revenues in the province'.[1] Mir Jafar, and after him his sons, held the office of *nazim* or imperial governor of Bengal, but they were in effect pensioners of the Company. Robert Clive, the governor of Bengal from 1765–7 who engineered the grant of the *diwani*, wrote to the directors that we must 'become the Nabob ourselves in fact, if not in name'.[2]

The years after the grant of the *diwani* were crucial in the political education of the East India Company service in Bengal. Between 1765 and 1772 the Company began to reimagine itself as a vehicle not just of British national trade, but of the political reconstruction of a Mughal province. While the Company's rapid takeover of the territorial administration was driven by the lure of corporate and personal gain from taxes and trade, it also developed a powerful ideological momentum fuelled by stereotypes of native depravity, Muslim faithlessness and Asiatic despotism. The critique of the *nawabs* of Bengal as despotic

[1] Dow, *History of Hindostan*, vol. III, p. xlvi.
[2] G. W. Forrest, *Life of Lord Clive*, 2 vols. (London, 1918), vol. II, pp. 256–7.

plunderers, deployed so aggressively by Company propagandists in the recent wars, was now extended more generally to apply to other Indian officials and power-holders. As Company servants invaded key institutions of central and local government, they often portrayed the *nawabi* as corrupt to the core, a system of organized fraud and plunder, in terms familiar from Montesquieu's critique of despotic forms of rule.

At the same time, the Company's aspirations to govern and draw tribute from vast and unfamiliar territories also led its servants into new forms of engagement with the same indigenous institutions which they often professed to disdain. The Company's army was already powerful, comprising (in 1770) about 3,000 European and 28,000 Indian soldiers.[3] But this large standing army, divided into three brigades, was designed mainly to defend major cities and territorial frontiers from invading armies. Soldiers, especially the so-called *pargana* sepoys, could be a valuable resource in enforcing the Company's will within Bengal – for example, against recalcitrant landholders or frontier peoples.[4] Nonetheless, the limits of centrally organized coercive power were quickly reached in the day-to-day business of governing diverse territories. To maintain order and to keep its revenues flowing, the Company needed to co-opt and manipulate the hierarchies and routines of power established under the Mughals and the *nawabs*. Thus, this chapter explores how the Company's ideological critique of the Indian state was refracted through the complex negotiations which underpinned the emerging colonial order.

Contemporary Britons tended to think of the eighteenth-century state in Bengal as a corruption of a more settled and ordered form of centralized Mughal governance. Recent scholarship has tended rather to emphasize both how Bengal was always a frontier region within the Mughal empire marked by distinctive forms of rule, but also how the eighteenth-century *nawabs* extended and adapted Mughal institutions in creating a semi-independent regional state.[5] Starting with Murshid Quli Khan (1716–27), *nawabs* began to combine in their own person the two major provincial offices of *nazim* and *diwan*, and eventually established a provincial state in which power centred on the regional capital of Murshidabad rather than Delhi. Even though the *nawabs* stopped sending regular tribute to Delhi in the 1740s, they continued to identify

[3] Michael H. Fisher, *The First Indian Author in English. Dean Mahomed (1759–1851) in India, Ireland and England* (New Delhi, 1996), pp. 35–9.
[4] Seema Alavi, 'The Company Army and Rural Society: the Invalid Thanah, 1780–1830', *MAS*, 27 (1993), pp. 147–78.
[5] Richard M. Eaton, *The Rise of Islam on the Bengal Frontier*; P. Calkins, 'The Formation of a Regionally Oriented Ruling Group in Bengal, 1700–1740', *JAS*, 29 (1970), pp. 799–806.

strongly with the traditions of Mughal rule.[6] After 1765, as the British sought to investigate and reform the central institutions of government in Murshidabad, most importantly the *khalsa* (revenue department), *nawabi* officials vigorously defended their administrative practices by reference to Mughal imperial customs.[7]

The Company's expanding ambition also drew its servants out into the districts of Bengal, to the towns, markets and villages that dotted the countryside. The Company's often clumsy and ill-informed interventions in systems of local government sparked a new set of material and conceptual contests. Company servants ran up against a very diverse constellation of local power-holders that characterized the layered pattern of Mughal and late Mughal governance. Some of these groups – for example, *amils* (revenue collectors), *faujdars* (military governors) or *qazis* (Muslim law officers) appeared to be clearly tied to the *nawab*'s government as officials of state. Others, however, seemed to occupy a more ambiguous intermediary position between state and society. Especially important was a broad category of rural elites known as *zamindars* (literally, landholders), who held complex bundles of rights to collect agricultural and commercial taxes over areas ranging from one or a few villages to huge territories amounting to little kingdoms. They formed a privileged group among the different layers of co-sharers in the produce of the land in Mughal India.[8] *Zamindars* in eighteenth-century Bengal derived their incomes from their right to a share of the taxes collected from the *raiyats* (peasants) and markets, and from profits derived from certain personal lands, which they often held tax free, employing peasants as share-croppers.[9]

Zamindars and other categories of rural elite like *taluqdars*[10] rapidly came to occupy a critical place in British debates about the government

---

[6] Marshall, *Bengal: the British Bridgehead*, pp. 49–52.

[7] The classic study is Khan, *The Transition in Bengal*, and I draw on this work often in this chapter. Whereas Khan's study of the crucial figure of Muhammad Reza Khan was framed as the last gasp of a dying Mughal tradition, my concern is to show how Reza Khan's 'rearguard action' on behalf of the Mughal order intersected with British notions about upholding the 'ancient constitution'.

[8] For good surveys of different forms of land right under the Mughals, see B. R. Grover, 'Nature of Land Rights in Mughal India', *IESHR*, 1 (1963), pp. 1–22; Irfan Habib, *The Agrarian System of Mughal India* (2nd edn, Oxford, 1999), ch. 5. Interestingly the nearest Habib comes to a general definition is the statement that *zamindari* was a 'right which belonged to a rural class other than, and standing above, the peasantry'; ibid., p. 174.

[9] Datta, *Society, Economy and the Market*, pp. 155–61.

[10] *Taluqdar*: a form of right in the land, typically ranking below *zamindar*, paying rent either directly to the government or to a *zamindar*. For a detailed discussion, see ibid., p. 138.

of Bengal, in part because of their entrenched role as intermediaries between central government and peasant producers, and in part because of the difficulties that Britons experienced in classifying them.[11] On the one hand, *zamindars* appeared like quasi-officials, holding *sanads* or certificates of appointment from the Mughals or the *nawabs* enjoining them to collect and pay taxes and to keep order in their domains. Some large *zamindars* were also incorporated into the Mughal nobility as *mansabdars* with official rank and attached salaries.[12] On the other hand, *zamindari* tenures also had features of landed property rights; they were usually hereditary, and they were often bought, sold and mortgaged. Further confusing the issue, both for British rulers and later historians, the term *zamindari* was attached to varied forms of right with diverse origins; *nawabi* officials commonly distinguished, for example, between *zamindari* rights originating in clearance of wastelands, or purchase, or official appointment.[13]

Zamindari rights had also changed through time. In the early eighteenth century, *Nawab* Murshid Quli Khan substantially raised the government demand on Bengal by making new measurements of agricultural lands, coercing or dispossessing *zamindars*, or employing temporary revenue farmers who offered fixed payments for the right to farm certain taxes.[14] Gradually, certain *zamindars* had been allowed to expand their domains by force and purchase, creating huge lordships. By the 1760s, 60 per cent of the land tax demand was paid by 15 of these large *zamindars*. A few of these large *zamindars* descended from long-standing local lordships, but most were relatively recent creations in the late seventeenth and eighteenth centuries by families associated with military or administrative service to the Mughals and the *nawabs*.[15] The raja of Burdwan, one of the largest *zamindars*, employed nearly 30,000 servants in the 1760s, ranging from high ranking scribes to lowly pykes (armed guards).[16] Below these large lordships stood a complex hierarchy of smaller gentry and small-holding peasants with diverse forms of title to occupy a plot or to share in the produce of the soil.

---

[11] For good discussions of the nature of *zamindari* tenure in Bengal, and British confusion around this institution, see Marshall, *Bengal: the British Bridgehead*, pp. 53–8; McLane, *Land and Local Kingship*, pp. 8–15; Ratnalekha Ray, *Change in Bengal Agrarian Society, c. 1760–1850* (New Delhi, 1979).

[12] Mclane, *Land and Local Kingship*, p. 10.

[13] Datta, *Society, Economy and the Market*, p. 136.

[14] McLane, *Land and Local Kingship*, p. 35.

[15] Ray, *Change in Bengal Agrarian Society*, pp. 24–36.

[16] McLane, *Land and Local Kingship*, p. 187.

Historians have often emphasized how the layered system of proprietary interests appeared to clash with British ideas of exclusive individual ownership of plots of land. A more immediate problem for British observers was in reconciling the density and complexity of claims on the land in Bengal with received European stereotypes about Asiatic despotism. If secure rights to hold property were the defining mark of a free-born Briton, then the absence of such rights was supposed to be the defining mark of despotism. Alexander Dow's writings on the Mughal empire reflected the emerging tension between received theory and actual experience on this question. Dow followed Bernier in arguing that in the Mughal empire 'no real property exists'. Indeed this commonplace notion justified his plan for a general sale 'to dispose of all the lands in Bengal and Behar, in perpetuity, at an annual sum'.[17] Yet, earlier in his treatise, Dow argued that political expediency led earlier Muslim conquerors to allow 'many of the Rajas, or indigenous Indian princes . . . to retain a great part of their ancient possessions'. Thus, in Bengal 'many districts of greater extent than any county in Britain, are still possessed by the aboriginal Rajas'. Dow seems to have considered these rajas as leaseholders, dependent on the empire, rather than freeholders, and he defined *zamindars* as 'farmers of the Imperial rents'. *Zamindari* rights, he argued (perhaps thinking of the Company's own claim to the *zamindari* of Calcutta), typically originated in bribes to the 'venal' imperial court, but sometimes evolved into hereditary lordships.[18]

One way the British dealt with the claims of *zamindars* and others (for example, holders of rent-free lands) to rights to the agrarian surplus was to treat them as 'usurpations' resulting from the absence of close imperial supervision during the decline of the Mughal empire. One of the greatest ironies of early British rule, given the vaunted British respect for 'liberty and property', was the cavalier attitude of some Company servants to Indian forms of tenure. For example, in the 24 Parganas, one of the first territories ceded by the *nawabs* to the Company in 1757, *zamindars* were summarily dispossessed of their domains and the lands leased out by public auction to new revenue farmers.[19] This kind of dispossession was justified both by the supposed absence of landed property in India, but also by the widespread sense that *zamindars* collected substantially more from the peasantry than they ever admitted to government, and were cheating the state out of its rightful revenues.

[17] Dow, *History of Hindostan*, vol. III, p. cxix.   [18] Ibid., pp. xliv, l, xlv.
[19] W. K. Firminger, 'Historical Introduction to the Bengal Portion of the Fifth Report', in *The Fifth Report*, pp. c–ciii.

One Company servant, giving evidence to Parliament in 1767, suggested that the 'real produce' of the Bengal lands was three or four times as much as the government collected, a discrepancy arising from 'unwarrantable frauds'. Thus, the revenues could be hugely augmented if *zamindars* were set aside, and lands let at public auction to find their 'real value'.[20] Others in the Company, while suspicious of the *zamindars*, viewed the idea of such a drastic intervention as impolitic and impractical.[21]

The question of the nature of land rights in Bengal, and the scope for reform of existing systems, would become a major source of disagreement among Company officials. Adding to the chaotic atmosphere of early Company rule, the catastrophic famine of 1769–70 presented scenes of astonishing deprivation and suffering. After the wars and political revolutions of the previous decade, Bengal was plunged into a massive economic crisis following a weak monsoon rain in 1768 and an unprecedented failure of the monsoon in 1769.[22] The all-important winter harvest of rice fell off dramatically, especially in western and northern districts. The natural disaster of drought became a human tragedy through the operations of socially constructed markets. Prices for staple goods spiked, pushing many of the most vulnerable in Bengal society into a major subsistence crisis. In early 1770, more than 500 people were said to be dying of starvation and disease every day in the town of Murshidabad.[23] Recent studies have tended to question contemporary estimates that a third of the Bengal population died in the famine, noting that an extensive contraction of the acreage under cultivation seems to have been confined to the worst hit northern districts. Nevertheless, the human devastation was immense.

Historians have generally agreed that the response of the Company authorities to the famine was slow and terribly inadequate. Officials tried to place embargoes on grain being exported from certain badly affected districts.[24] But their main priorities were to feed the army and maintain the tax revenues. Few remissions of revenue were allowed to relieve the burden of taxation, and little state provision was made either for

---

[20] Evidence of J. Z. Holwell, 30 March 1767, in 'Evidence taken before the Committee [of the House of Commons] on the state of the East India Company', BL Add. MSS 18,469, fos. 13–19.

[21] See, for example, the testimony of Henry Vansittart and Warren Hastings, ibid., fos. 3, 22–3.

[22] Sugata Bose, *Peasant Labour and Colonial Capital: Rural Bengal since 1770*, NCHI, 3.2 (Cambridge, 1993), pp. 17–19; McLane, *Land and Local Kingship*, pp. 194–207; Datta, *Society, Economy and the Market*, pp. 238–84.

[23] Datta, *Society, Economy and the Market*, p. 252.

[24] W. W. Hunter, *Annals of Rural Bengal* (Calcutta, 1868), pp. 43–5.

immediate food purchases for the indigent, or for advancing seeds or credit to vulnerable peasants to enable recovery from the famine.[25] For all the patent inadequacy of the Company's response, however, the famine had important repercussions in British ideas about the government of Bengal. Coming in the context of the Company's attempts to squeeze more money out of the Bengal tax system, the famine raised troubling questions about the long-term health of the Bengal economy, and its capacity to service the Company's voracious demands for tribute.

The rest of this chapter explores political disputes that arose in Bengal during this period of acute political and economic instability. First, it describes the conflicts between the Company's councils in Calcutta and the surviving remnants of the *nawab*'s government in Murshidabad, showing how the Company's critique of the Indian state provoked a vigorous defence of the ongoing traditions of Mughal rule. Second, it shows how Company servants were becoming embroiled in disputes in the districts, as they ran up against entrenched notions of customary right. Meanwhile, at different levels of power in Bengal, the reformist ambitions of Company servants were starkly challenged by the onset of famine and depopulation.

Contesting power in Murshidabad

From 1760, the Company was drawing sizeable revenues from the so-called 'ceded districts', granted by Mir Qasim as one of the conditions of his appointment as *nawab*. After the assumption of the *diwani* in 1765, the territorial revenues of Bengal were widely regarded as the keystone of the Company's finances. On assuming the *diwani* revenues, Clive projected 'a clear gain to the Company of 122 lakhs of Sicca Rupees, or £1,650,900 sterling, which will defray all the expence of the investment', as well as supplying the Company's other stations in India and China, leaving 'a considerable balance in your treasury besides'.[26] At the same time, Clive sought to decorate the Company's new found wealth and power in the paraphernalia of Mughal legitimacy. He offered the impoverished Mughal emperor an annual tribute of Rs 26 lakhs, over a quarter of a million pounds, for the grant of the *diwani*.[27]

---

[25] Datta, *Society, Economy and the Market*, pp. 256–60.

[26] Clive to Ct. of D., 30 September, 1765, *FWIH*, 4, pp. 337–8.

[27] Khan, *Transition in Bengal*, p. 101, n. 4. By 1772, the arrears of payment to the emperor stood at £60,406; ibid., p. 288. The Company withdrew its financial and military assistance to the emperor after he made alliance with the Marathas in 1771 in an attempt to retake his capital in Delhi. *Calendar of Persian Correspondence*, 11 vols. (Calcutta, 1919), vol. III, introduction, pp. xxviii–xxix.

Meanwhile, Mughal *sanads* of appointment were obtained on behalf of high-ranking Indian officials, chosen by the Company to act as deputy governors in the old provincial capitals of Murshidabad in Bengal and Patna in Bihar. The Indian 'prime ministers' were charged with the day-to-day administration, acting under the supervision of British 'residents'. These deputies were granted large allowances of over 53 lakhs of rupees, approximately £500,000, to cover the expenses of government, an indication that Company officials were unwilling or unable at this stage to dispense with the central institutions of the *nawab*'s government.[28] A contemporary Indian historian wrote that the British 'in those beginnings of their dominion were more careful and inclined to conciliate the hearts of the natives'.[29]

The Company was especially careful to deploy indigenous officials in its dealings with other European traders. A French trader, complaining in 1768 about curtailment of French trading privileges, noted that 'the English know well that it would be indecent to make their name appear in these vexatious affairs. They act in the name of the nawab; the latter is but a paid servant of theirs constrained to act conformable to their wishes.'[30] Meanwhile, the directors continued to invoke Mughal precedent in fighting the extension of the 'private trade' of their own servants in 'Salt, Beetle Nut or Tobacco, or in any other Articles produced or consumed in the Country.' They argued that the Mughal *farman* of 1717 confined duty-free privileges 'within the Ancient Limits of our [that is the Company's] Export and Import Trade', and that the further intrusion of British private trade through special privilege was a violation of 'the natural right of the Natives of the Country'.[31]

Indeed the directors' continuing suspicion of the profiteering of their own servants was a major reason why they approved of Clive's scheme to preserve 'the ancient forms of government' in Bengal. The Company had been administering the three 'ceded' territories of Burdwan, Midnapur and Chittagong since 1760, but the alleged corrupt dealings of Company servants in these areas had convinced the directors 'how unfit an Englishman is to conduct the collection of the revenues and to follow the subtle native through all his arts to conceal the real value of his country'. Therefore, the *diwani* 'was not the office we wish to

---

[28] Khan, *Transition in Bengal*, p. 101.
[29] Ghulam Husain Khan Tabatabai, *Seir Mutaqherin*, 3 vols., trans. Nota Manus (Calcutta, 1789, repr. 1906) vol. III, p. 27.
[30] This letter is cited in Chatterji, *Verelst's Rule in India*, p. 137.
[31] Ct. of D. to Fort William, 20 November 1767, *FWIH*, 5, p. 56.

exercise ourselves', but by delegation to Indian deputy governors.[32] If this was not exactly a rousing vote of confidence in the capacities of the 'subtle native', it represented the widespread feeling that the Company's small service of foreign traders was ill-fitted for the difficult task of territorial administration.

The Company's need to make Bengal pay, and its continuing reliance on Indian intermediaries, gave some degree of leverage to the Indian deputies. Muhammad Reza Khan, formally styled as *Naib Subahdar*, or deputy for the young *nawab* (a minor), was the chief administrator in Murshidabad. Born around 1717, the son of a Persian physician from Shiraz, at the age of 10 he migrated to India with his father. Eventually, Reza Khan's father took service in the court of *Nawab* Alivardi Khan in Bengal, and Reza Khan himself married into the ruling family.[33] By 1765, he had extensive experience in high-ranking government posts. Another experienced official, Maharaja Shitab Rai, was appointed deputy governor for the region of Bihar. These two began reassembling the damaged authority of the central government.

They were careful to cultivate good relations with their British patrons, holding lavish dinners and entertainments which drew elite Britons into the courtly world of late Mughal governance; they also fulfilled traditional charitable obligations to the poor and religious mendicants, as well as to poets and musicians.[34] Reza Khan assisted leading Company servants in establishing a monopoly in imports of raw cotton from western India, and Shitab Rai acted as a valuable source of intelligence about other Indian powers in north India.[35] Meanwhile, the Indian ministers continued the courtly rituals of incorporation, granting *khilats* (robes of honour) to visiting *zamindars* and receiving *nazrs* (donations) in return. Behind these rituals lay tense negotiations between central and local power-holders over the extraction of revenue. Under the later *nawabs*, especially Mir Qasim (1760–3), the tax demand had been raised very dramatically in an attempt to mobilize

---

[32] Ct. of D. to Fort William, 17 May 1766, *FWIH*, 4, p. 184.

[33] Khan, *The Transition in Bengal*, pp. 17–19.

[34] For a nice evocation of the ceremonial dimensions of governance in Patna in this period, see Chatterjee, *Merchants, Politics and Society*, esp. pp. 207–11. See also the contemporary memoir of Dean Mahomed, the servant of an Irish soldier serving in the Company armies. 'The Raja Sataproy', he wrote – referring to Raja Shitab Rai in about the year 1770 – 'had a very magnificent palace in the centre of the city of Patna, where he was accustomed to entertain many of the most distinguished European Gentlemen, with brilliant balls and costly suppers'. Fisher, *The First Indian Author in English*, p. 17.

[35] *FWIH*, 5, introduction, pp. 23–4; *Calendar of Persian Correspondence*, vol. III, pp. xxv, 6.

resources for war with the British. Reza Khan reduced the revenue demand somewhat from the inflated and uncollectable assessments of Mir Qasim's time, but continued Mir Qasim's attempt to tighten government control, especially in former frontier provinces of north Bengal and Bihar. These regions had yielded relatively little revenue under the earlier *nawabs*.[36]

Clive had hoped that this system of 'double government' would finally stabilize the Company's position in Bengal after an era of expensive wars and conflict. Yet the attempt to establish a system of indirect rule quickly floundered. Harry Verelst, governor of Bengal from 1767–9, later blamed the 'too eager desire of parliament, and the proprietors of India stock, to derive immoderate advantage from the acquisitions of the Company' for undermining both the Company's position and the wider economy of Bengal.[37] As the Company's costs rapidly ate into new revenues, pressure mounted on the Indian deputy governors to meet the growing demand for tribute. At the same time, Muhammad Reza Khan's patrons in the Company lost their former influence, and Clive's rivals eventually gained control of the directorate. Sharp cuts began to be made in the expenses ear-marked for the *nizamat* in Murshidabad. Disappointing tax collections from the unsettled northern districts offered excuses to the British resident in Murshidabad, Francis Sykes, to begin his own inquiries into the revenues, and at the same time to extend his own private commercial interests in the districts.[38]

In this period of the Company's fiscal crisis, the Indian deputy governors were also intensely vulnerable to the pervasive critique of 'Asiatic manners'. Company servants directly administered the so-called 'ceded districts' of southern Bengal, and trumpeted their ability to uncover the deceits of Indian intermediaries. Harry Verelst served as supervisor in the ceded districts between 1765 and 1767, self-consciously aiming to root out the profiteering of Company servants and their Indian agents in the land revenues. In the 24 Parganas, he instituted detailed surveys and land measurements, which purported to discover a large proportion of rent-free land secretly alienated from the rent rolls by the *zamindars*.[39] In Burdwan district, one of the largest *zamindaris* of Bengal, Verelst continued to maintain the *zamindar* as the official head of the district, but worked to reduce administrative costs

---

[36] Khan, *Transition in Bengal*, pp. 129–30.
[37] Verelst, *View of the Rise, Progress and Present State*, p. 84.
[38] Khan, *Transition in Bengal*, pp. 159–61.
[39] J. Grant, 'An Historical and Comparative Analysis of the Finances of Bengal' (1786), *The Fifth Report*, p. 425.

by down-sizing the *zamindar*'s military and civilian administration, and reforming the system of revenue farming. He abandoned the practice of selling lands at 'public outcry', which he thought had encouraged a set of 'desperate adventurers' to bid for revenue rights. Instead Verelst granted farms to 'men of substance', forbidding the *zamindar*'s own officials to hold revenue farms. The farms were granted for a three-year term to encourage farmers to invest in the improvement of their domains, and the revenue demand was set to rise each year.[40]

The directors were impressed by Verelst's figures, which showed a substantial increase in revenues received in each of the ceded districts after 1765; Verelst's own accounts suggested that the Burdwan revenues rose from Rs 3,567,854 in 1765–6 to Rs 4,288,171 in 1766–7.[41] These successes contrasted with the large arrears of revenue building up in the *diwani* territories administered by the Indian deputies. Company servants in the ceded districts enjoyed many advantages not shared by Muhammad Reza Khan and Shitab Rai, not least their ability to persuade the wealthy *banyans* or commercial agents of the Company in Calcutta to invest in revenue farms. Yet the directors tended to blame shortfalls in the *diwani* revenues on the depravity of 'Asiatic' manners, referring to 'modes of Oppression which have been in use so long as the Moorish Government has Subsisted'. Happily, these were apparently now mitigated in the ceded districts by 'the Constant and Minute direction of our Covenanted Servants'.[42] The system of revenue farming for a term of years, pioneered by Verelst in Burdwan, now appeared to offer a workable model of administration which would cut through the deceits of Indian officials and *zamindars*.

The portentous decision to send British officials into the *diwani* districts was taken almost simultaneously in Calcutta and in Britain. In June 1769, soon after hearing the disastrous news from Madras about a new war with Hyder Ali of Mysore, with the Company's stock price plummeting in London markets, the directors wrote to Bengal ordering a full investigation of local government in the *diwani* districts.[43] This would be conducted by two 'controlling councils' of British officials, one at Murshidabad in Bengal proper and one in Patna in Bihar.

---

[40] Verelst, *View of the Rise, Progress and Present State*, pp. 70–2; McLane, *Land and Local Kingship*, pp. 189–91.

[41] Verelst, *View of the Rise, Progress and Present State*, pp. 72; Ct. of D. to Ft. William, 30 June 1769, *FWIH*, 5, p. 211.

[42] Ct. of D. to Ft. William, 30 June 1769, *FWIH*, 5, p. 212.

[43] Company stocks had dipped sharply after 26 May, and the order was sent on 30 June 1769. Sutherland, *The East India Company in Eighteenth Century Politics*, pp. 191–2.

These councils would supervise other Company servants working in the districts. The directors emphasized their wish to reduce the charges of collection in the *diwani* lands by cutting off the 'large Salaries now paid to idle Dependents appointed to useless Offices by the Country Government'.[44] Even before this letter reached Bengal, Governor Verelst and the council in Calcutta had come to their own decision to send Company servants as 'supervisors' into the *diwani* districts.[45]

Governor Verelst drew up a series of instructions for these supervisors, approved by the select committee in Calcutta on 16 August 1769.[46] This is a fascinating document, which fleshed out the Company's critique of corruption at different levels of the *nawab*'s government. *Zamindars* now emerged as a crucial category of analysis and an object for reform. The 'instructions' defined a *zamindar* as the 'head-collector' of a district, though they acknowledged that *zamindars* often held their powers over local revenue collection on a hereditary basis. Verelst also recognized a limited proprietary right of the *zamindars* over their specified home territories or personal land (*nankar* lands).[47] The main thrust of the 'instructions' was a concern for the rights of the *raiyats* or peasant agriculturalists apparently oppressed by the arbitrary demands of greedy landlords and revenue collectors. Supervisors were encouraged 'to convince the Ryot that you will stand between him and the hand of oppression . . . that after supplying the legal due of government, he may be secure in the enjoyment of the remainder'.[48] The 'instructions' painted a Montesquieuan vision of despotic government as a system of plunder. In order to evade the rapacious demands of the *nawabs*, *zamindars* had learnt to collude with corrupt officials to defraud the government, alienating lands from the rent rolls by charity and other grants, giving in false accounts of the amount of land in cultivation, setting arbitrary taxes on local markets, and by fining peasants on a variety of pretexts. Great attention was given to how the supervisors could penetrate collusive networks of local officials, and obtain authentic knowledge of the real value of the lands in their

---

[44] Ct. of D. to Ft. William, 30 June 1769, *FWIH*, 5, p. 214.
[45] A. M. Khan has detailed the factional disputes around the decision to appoint British supervisors. He described how Governor Verelst, who had previously tried to uphold the authority and independence of the Indian deputy governor in Murshidabad, Muhammad Reza Khan, was bounced into instituting the plan for the supervisors by other members of the council. Khan, *The Transition in Bengal*, pp. 195–7. Yet, though Governor Verelst was initially reluctant to intervene more strongly in the *diwani* lands, he appears to have shared the consensus view that the Bengal government was deeply corrupted.
[46] The 'Instructions' are reprinted in Verelst, *A View of the Rise, Progress and Present State*, Appendix, pp. 227–38.
[47] Ibid., pp. 230–3.   [48] Ibid., p. 228.

districts. They were to prepare a new *hastobud*, or rent roll, comparing the existing records of central government with detailed investigations made in the actual villages. Where officials had destroyed local records to confuse the government, the supervisors were to seek out old men, knowledgeable and uncorrupt, to break through the veil of deceit that supposedly characterized the old regime. If *zamindars* resisted the supervisor's investigations, they were to be threatened with dispossession.[49]

On the face of it, these were remarkably radical proposals for penetrating the intermediary groups standing between the Company as *diwan* and the peasant producers of Bengal, and building the Company's power on a more direct relationship with the peasant producers. The 'instructions' were somewhat undercut, however, by their limited conception of the actual powers of the supervisors in the districts. They suggested more of a scheme of research as a basis for future reforms. For example, the supervisors were asked to compose a history of the district, outlining 'the form of the ancient constitution of the province, compared with the present'.[50] This reflected the widespread view that a more settled administration had existed before the 'age of revolutions'. The supervisors were advised to trace local histories only as far back as the *nawab* Shuja-ud-din Khan (1727–39), 'as, at that aera of good order and good government, no alterations had taken place in the ancient divisions of the country'.[51] At other points, however, the 'instructions' depicted corruption and abuse as innate properties of Asiatic governments. Commenting on law courts in Bengal, Verelst was unsure 'whether the original customs or the degenerate manners of the Mussulmen has most contributed to confound the principles of right and wrong in the province', but 'certain it is that almost every decision of theirs is a corrupt bargain with the highest bidder'.[52]

The 'instructions' to the supervisors represented an enduring strand of British opinion about the government of the *nawabs* as a system of barely regulated plunder. What is remarkable about the document is the new-found confidence that British officials, apparently now more knowledgeable in Indian languages, could themselves come to an exact knowledge of the Bengal lands. In fact, there was a huge gap between the heated rhetoric of this document and the still fragile appearance of the Company's actual power. The 12 Company servants chosen as supervisors for the different districts covered immense tracts of land, and they relied heavily on the assistance of Indian agents and officials. Moreover, the rhetoric of the instructions concealed real disagreements

[49] Ibid., pp. 230–1.   [50] Ibid., p. 227.   [51] Ibid., p. 229.   [52] Ibid.

about whether or not the young men of the Company service were fit instruments for such reforms. The future governor of Bengal, Warren Hastings, wrote from Madras praising the content of the instructions, but wondering (with more than a touch of irony) whether 'the Service [would] furnish Lockes, Humes and Montesquieus in Number sufficient for each Department'.[53]

There were, after all, other explanations for the Company's fiscal problems and the poor performance of the *diwani* territories that focused less on the deceits of Indian officials and more on the intermingling of the Company's commercial and political roles. Harry Verelst, the author of the 'instructions', frequently remonstrated with the directors about the shortage of currency in Bengal, which he blamed on the sudden stoppage of bullion imports after the acquisition of the *diwani*, and also the directors' insistence on exporting rupees from Bengal to pay for its investment in China.[54] Verelst argued that the Company's demand on Bengal was gradually strangling the life out of Bengal's commercial economy.[55] The directors, on the other hand, were unwilling to countenance what they called the 'speculative apprehensions' of its servants in Bengal about a scarcity of silver.[56]

Meanwhile, as the Company flexed its political muscle in Bengal, it provoked new forms of resistance from within the indigenous state system, in the context of a developing agrarian crisis of massive proportions. Muhammad Reza Khan vigorously defended his weakening position, finding an ally in Richard Becher, the Company's resident at Murshidabad. Becher apparently felt his own power compromised by the new assertiveness of the Calcutta council. Becher and Reza Khan managed to stall the full implementation of the supervisor scheme during the early months of 1770; only four supervisors were initially sent out to the districts.[57] Early reports of famine mortality reinforced Reza Khan and Becher's claim that harsh revenue demands were partly to blame for the miseries of the people. Many observers, both British and Indian, tended to blame grain merchants, including British officials and their agents, for forcing up the price of grain to unprecedentedly high levels; yet Reza Khan's request for a general ban on British trade in rice was refused by the Calcutta council.[58]

[53] Hastings to G. Vansittart, Ft. Saint George, 23 December 1769, BL Add. MSS 29,125, fo. 22r.
[54] Verelst to Ct. of D., 5 April 1769, *FWIH*, 5, pp. 546–53.
[55] See also Verelst's review of the currency problem, in Verelst, *A View of the Rise, Progress and Present State*, pp. 84–104.
[56] Ct. of D. to Ft. William, 11 November 1768, *FWIH*, 5, p. 144.
[57] Khan, *Transition in Bengal*, p. 209.   [58] Ibid., p. 222.

Meanwhile, Becher and Reza Khan staged a more dramatic resistance to the supervisor scheme in April 1770. In a fascinating episode, redolent with the tensions and compromises of colonial expansion, they claimed that the *zamindars* of Bengal were refusing to contract for the revenues at the annual ceremony of the *puniyah*, if the British supervisors were granted a controlling power over the local administration.[59] In the districts, meanwhile, some *zamindars* refused to acknowledge the official demands of supervisors, claiming that they were answerable only to Muhammad Reza Khan. Reza Khan wrote in a letter to the new governor John Cartier, 'When I speak to the zamindars and farmers about the terms of the *band-o-bast*, they straightway reply "we have no power and footing in the districts".'[60] In a later letter Reza Khan added more diplomatically that though the new plan of supervisorships was 'truly wise and judicious . . . yet as the natives of this country look no further than the present, they failed to appreciate these advantages and with one voice raised objections'.[61] Further grist to the mill was the apparent refusal of Indian bankers to advance monies to the *zamindars*, because the position of the latter under the new order only inspired a lack of confidence.[62] On the back of these arguments that the collections would be irreparably damaged, Becher and Reza Khan forced the Calcutta select committee to issue an order in June 1770 abolishing the controlling power of the supervisors over local officials and landlords.[63]

As A. M. Khan astutely noted in his detailed study of the period, *nawabi* officials and *zamindars* increasingly looked to Reza Khan as their last protector against the depradations of the Company.[64] The example of the 24 Parganas and the Company's ceded districts suggested that tax increases and dispossession of *zamindars* was the likely outcome of direct British administration. Yet the mood in Calcutta was turning violently against Reza Khan, boosted by impatient letters from the directors. Hence, the Company's ruling council overruled the select committee, and the supervisors were again granted powers over local government.[65] Indian *amils* (revenue officials) were withdrawn from most of Bengal and

---

[59] The *puniyah* was an annual assembly of *zamindars* held in the *nawab*'s capital in Murshidabad, where *zamindars* settled their accounts with the government. McLane, *Land and Local Kingship*, pp. 48–52.

[60] Reza Khan to President and Council at Calcutta, 2 June 1770, *Calendar of Persian Correspondence*, vol. III, p. 71.

[61] Reza Khan to President and Council at Calcutta, 12 July 1770, ibid., p. 88.

[62] Khan, *Transition in Bengal*, p. 242.

[63] Ibid. On the recommendation of Reza Khan, only four supervisors were allowed to maintain their controlling power.

[64] Ibid., p. 128.   [65] Ibid., p. 251.

replaced by supervisors. Richard Becher, the resident at Murshidabad, was replaced by a new four-man controlling council, who had full powers to manage the *diwani* territories. Reza Khan had been reduced to a shadow of his former power, advising the controlling council and adding his own seal to their orders.

During this period when Muhammad Reza Khan's powers were being heavily constricted, he made some of his most influential political statements and manoeuvres. In the context of famine, Reza Khan exploited the Company's need to maintain the 'exteriors of power' and the aura of Mughal legitimacy, articulating a complex defence of Mughal imperial institutions. For example, he managed to keep small pockets of his administration intact. *Amils* were allowed to remain in the districts of Hughli and Dacca where they policed the activities of rival European traders.[66] When the British wanted to tighten their super-vision of French and Dutch traders in 1770, Reza Khan described how it was 'the ancient custom in Hindustan that whenever some important business is taken in hand, three officers, namely the darogah, the writer of occurences, and the writer of reports' were appointed to manage it; these all corresponded separately with the ruler to act as checks upon each other; furthermore, *harkarahs* (spies) wrote secret diaries and transmitted them to the ruling magistrate. In this case Reza Khan's view of the 'ancient custom of Hindostan' was approved by the governor in setting up a new checkpoint for searching European ships going up the river Hughli.[67]

Reza Khan's emphasis on the Mughal empire as a subtle system of checks and balances in which local officials were carefully monitored by central authorities offered a direct contradiction to British accounts of the tyranny of *amils*, *zamindars* and other Indian agencies. In September 1769 Reza Khan reacted angrily to the broad-brush criticism of 'idle hordes' of Indian officials in the directors' latest dispatch from England, and their call to reform the revenue collections of the *diwani* lands by farming districts for a term of years. Reza Khan claimed it would be 'impossible to farm them out at once', and he insisted that *amils* were not, as the British painted them, desperate plunderers appointed only on a temporary basis for a year, but 'men of capacity, principle and religion', chosen for their proven experience in the revenue branch. The Mughal government, he argued, was always sensitive to the appeals of *raiyats*, and its law courts in the districts were not venal and corrupt

---

[66] Khan, *Transition in Bengal*, p. 259.
[67] Reza Khan to President and Council at Fort William, 3 March 1770, *Calendar of Persian Correspondence*, vol. III, pp. 25–6.

as the British tended to think. Rather, he said, fines were never used as a replacement for proper punishments; if they were, he suggested, the Mughal government could not have thrived. Watchful imperial officials would have rooted out such abuses.[68]

Later, as the British extended their researches into local government, and attempted to cut back administrative expenses, Reza Khan gave detailed accounts of the histories of various official positions of the Mughal empire.[69] Reza Khan seems to have had a sharp sense of the continuing constraints operating on Company officials even in their hour of reformist enthusiasm. As Verelst had worried in his last minute as governor in 1769, the Company had reached the 'supreme line' beyond which lay the clear appropriation of sovereignty in Bengal, and it remained unclear whether the directors would be willing to take this final step. What was perhaps Reza Khan's most influential rearguard action played on this uncertainty, by reminding the British that the young *nawab* Mubarak-ud-daula remained the duly appointed *nazim* (or provincial governor) of Bengal. In defending the rights of the *nizamat*, Reza Khan resurrected a set of distinctions which had been rendered effectively redundant earlier in the century as the Bengal *nawabs* had united the office of *nazim* and *diwan* in their own person. In a representation to the Company council in Murshidabad, Reza Khan detailed the extensive duties of the *nizamat*, which included the appointments of jurists (*naibs* and *qazis*), the rooting out of robbers, the management of the *nawab*'s household, and even giving approval to various actions of the *diwan*, and asked that they should be carried out independently under his own seal.[70]

As British supervisors clashed with local law officers in the districts, the Calcutta council issued orders that the *diwani* lands were 'still subject to the Moorish jurisdiction and usages'.[71] Unwilling to assume formal sovereign power over Bengal, the Company had little choice but to proffer continued allegiance to existing legal regimes. After 1770 the British tended to parse the distinction between *diwani* and *nizamat* as that between civil and criminal law, though in Reza Khan's formulation the *nizamat* was more broadly conceived as an agent of imperial authority, overlapping with and complementary to the *diwani*. Here again, Reza Khan offered an image of delicate checks and balances

---

[68] Reza Khan's note enclosed with Becher's letter, BSC, 25 September 1769, OIOC, IOR, P/A/9.
[69] Khan, *Transition in Bengal*, pp. 277–9.
[70] MP, 3 December 1770, cited in Khan, *Transition in Bengal*, p. 266.
[71] MP, 4 February 1771, cited in ibid., p. 269.

within an idealized Mughal order. Even though the Company squeezed the rights of the *nizamat* both in terms of function and geography, the notion of the criminal law as a distinct sphere of government administered by Muslim jurists under the authority of the *nawab* would provide a significant niche for Muhammad Reza Khan and his dependents in the coming decades.

Reza Khan's defence of Mughal custom between 1769 and 1772 invoked a subtle set of relationships between the continuing sovereignty of the Mughal emperors, the precepts of Islam, and the historically formed rights and responsibilities of the rulers and the ruled in Bengal. Nostalgia for the old imperial ways only grew in the midst of the famine, which hit Murshidabad and surrounding districts especially hard. Reza Khan wrote of the vast numbers of the dead, and of fires sweeping through the tinder dry houses and granaries.[72] Disease was at least as big a killer as starvation itself, and not even the vice-regal house of the *nawabs* was spared; *nawab* Saif-ud-daula and several other members of his family were carried off by smallpox.[73]

Richard Becher, writing to the Calcutta council in 1771, caught the sense of panic among Bengal's elites, as well as pinpointing the radical agenda of some British reformers, when he addressed his colleagues on the implications of recent directoral orders and the instructions to the supervisors. 'The directors seem to think', he noted, 'that there need be few intermediate people between the Ryot or Tenant and the Treasury'. Meanwhile, in Bengal, *zamindars* and *amils* were apprehensive that 'they shall be deprived of all advantages they derive from holding lands'. He urged caution, and (like Reza Khan) he argued that new plans for farming out the lands on three-year terms should only be introduced slowly, 'by degrees'. Economic improvements would only follow from a 'Freedom of Trade', which was maintained 'even under a despotic government', but lessened under the English.[74] In Becher's view the decline of Bengal's agricultural economy followed not from native corruption, but from unwarranted attempts by the Company to increase the tax demand 'beyond what the general Welfare of the Country would bear'.[75] He referred to the policy of the former nawabs, who 'tho' arbitrary and despotick to the highest Degree left the Zemindars to live in a state of power, parade and independence' which allowed

---

[72] Muhammad Reza Khan's letter, May 15 1770, *Calendar of Persian Correspondence*, vol. III, p. 64.
[73] Ghulam Husain Khan, *Seir Mutaqherin*, pp. 25–6.
[74] Becher's Minute, MP, 23 November 1770, OIOC, IOR G/27/1, pp. 336–9.
[75] Becher's Minute, MP, 3 December 1770, OIOC, IOR G/27/1, p. 424.

'the Zemindars to get rich and the soubahs knew they could when necessary on extraordinary Occasions draw their Resources from them'; now the *zamindars* were in a 'much inferior situation'.[76]

Becher's voice was drowned out by harsher rhetoric from others on the new Murshidabad controlling council. Lawrell and Graham, for example, responding to Becher's observations, could now point to directoral orders which seemed to share their diagnosis of native corruption and peculation. They noted that the directors, while wishing not to overturn the old 'Constitution', had 'plainly expressed their Ideas of the great Improvement that may be effected in the Duannee Collections'. They invoked the example of the Company's farming system in Burdwan. It was in the Company's interests, they argued, to promote 'farmers and other useful subjects', and even *zamindars* should be allowed their 'ancient profits and emoluments'. However, they assumed that the *zamindars* currently enjoyed profits beyond these 'ancient' rights. They invoked the notion of Asiatic despotism to argue that the *zamindars*, 'familiarized to almost continual Breaches of public Engagements, arbitrary Seizures of their Property', would gradually be conciliated by the 'proved Experience of the Lenity, Mildness, and Justice of our Authority'.[77] By 1771, the radicals seemed to have the upper hand in Murshidabad and Calcutta and they were eager to try their hand at remoulding the Bengal government, and slashing the emoluments of the supposed despotic and corrupt indigenous officialdom.

Power in the districts

The aggressive sentiments of the directors or Verelst's instructions to the supervisors, suggesting a sweep out of corrupt administrators and tax lords, could only be a threatening opening bid in a longer negotiation over the shape of the colonial state in Bengal. What the British called the 'farming' system, which meant leasing revenue rights for a fixed price for several years, appeared to offer a way of simplifying the tax system, and even of circumventing the power of the *zamindars*. Except in unsettled frontier regions, *zamindars* and other rural elites did not possess sufficient concentrations of military power to resist the Company's claims entirely. But they could draw on substantial political resources, both material and ideological, to blunt the Company's

---

[76] Ibid., pp. 425–6.
[77] Lawrell and Graham's Minute, MP, 26 November 1770, G/27/1, pp. 375–8.

reformist ambitions. The authority of *zamindars* rested in part on their ability to mobilize material resources of people, produce and money in the localities. But it also rested on complex structures of legitimation, combining appeals to Mughal documents of appointment (*sanads*), with other markers of distinction such as caste status, or prestige derived from religious and educational patronage. Especially in the large Hindu *zamindaris* of west Bengal, *zamindars* patronized Brahmin learning and piety, appealing to established norms of Hindu kingship.[78]

The rest of this chapter follows a young Company servant out into the districts of Bengal, to explore the emerging dynamics of colonial power in the countryside. The private papers of George Vansittart, a junior but well-connected East India Company official, offer an unusually vivid portrait of the dynamics of colonial state-formation in the very early period of British rule. Vansittart was employed as a revenue collector in one of the ceded districts (Midnapur) between 1766 and 1769, and then worked as one of the twelve supervisors in the north Bengal district of Dinajpur in 1770; his private journals and notebooks, as well as letter books survive from this period.[79] Vansittart's papers afford only a partial view of systems of local government, and they need to be treated with some care. His representations of local society were filtered through his own strategies of self-representation and self-justification. Nonetheless, sources of this kind are immensely valuable for understanding the way that British ideologies of rule were being shaped by interactions 'on the ground' with indigenous power-holders. In particular, Vansittart's writings reflected his struggle to reconcile the Company's voracious demand for new revenues with claims of local people that their traditional rights be respected and upheld.

George Vansittart was the younger brother of Henry Vansittart, governor of Bengal from 1760–4. George's high-powered connections helped him to rise quickly through the Company's ranks. He was appointed 'writer' on the Bengal establishment in 1761 and he worked as 'Assistant under the President' (his brother) until 1764, at which point he progressed to being a Persian translator during Clive's second governorship (1765–7).[80] In 1766 George Vansittart received his first appointment in the interior of Bengal as the Company's 'resident' in Midnapur. His position nicely illustrated the dovetailing of commercial

---

[78] McLane, *Land and Local Kingship*, pp. 13–15; David L. Curley, 'MahaRaja Krisnacandra, Hinduism, and Kingship in the Contact Zone of Bengal', in Richard B. Barnett (ed.), *Rethinking Early Modern India* (New Delhi, 2002), pp. 85–118.

[79] 'Vansittart Collection: Papers of George Vansittart (1745–1825), East India Company Servant, Bengal', OIOC, MSS Eur. F331.

[80] 'Bengal Civil Servants', 1760–83, OIOC, IOR, Financial Department, L/F/10/2.

and political functions within the Company by this date. His duties included managing the commercial investment in the region, in cotton and silk products, as well as collecting the territorial revenues and keeping the peace. Meanwhile Vansittart was also carrying on extensive private concerns in the inland trade of Bengal, operating (like many others in this period) in a series of partnerships with other Company servants.

For all the novelty of his situation, Vansittart's conception of his official position in Bengal sometimes drew on Mughal analogies. For example, he described himself to a French trader in the region as the 'Fougedar' of the 'Midnapore Cutcherry'.[81] A *faujdar* was the title typically given to military governors of large districts under the Mughals. As we have seen, it was common for Company men to invoke the authority of the Mughal empire when they were dealing with other Europeans. Meanwhile, Vansittart's friend, the future governor of Bengal Warren Hastings, described Vansittart as Lord Lieutenant of Midnapur, suggesting an analogy with English lords of the shires or colonial governors in Ireland.[82] In these early stages of colonial state-formation, Company officials were operating in an eclectic semantic context, drawing selectively on many different languages of power to interpret their novel situation.

Midnapur, along with Burdwan and Chittagong, was one of three districts in the south of Bengal ceded by *nawab* Mir Qasim in 1760 to satisfy the Company's demands for revenue. It was a major rice-growing region in south-western Bengal, and also stood on the dangerous frontier with Maratha-dominated territories to the west. In Vansittart's time, Company sepoys patrolled the western borders, making raids against recalcitrant chieftains.[83] Vansittart frequently reported his fears of impeding Maratha attacks from the west; but he also tried to increase revenues collected from so-called 'jungle Rajas', and hoped that Company rule would make frontier peoples 'more civilized' as they applied 'themselves more to the business of cultivation'.[84]

The flat lands in the east of the division, well-watered plains dominated by rice cultivation, were the main focus of the Company's revenue-raising interests. These areas encompassed especially complex forms of agrarian relations. Unlike other areas of Bengal where large

---

[81] Vansittart to Dr Blossom, Midnapur, 12 April 1769, OIOC, MSS Eur. F331/1, fo. 142.
[82] Hastings to Vansittart, Ft St George, 11 September 1769, BL Add. MSS 29,125, fo. 3 r–v.
[83] L. S. S. O'Malley, *Bengal District Gazetteers. Midnapur* (Calcutta, 1911), pp. 34–5.
[84] OIOC, MSS Eur. F331/1, pp. 2, 138, 141–2.

zamindari little kingdoms had expanded across huge areas in the eighteenth century, the agricultural tracts of Midnapur were character-ized by a succession of relatively small and scattered *zamindaris* and *taluqdaris*.[85] Vansittart's notebooks recorded how the local power of *zamindars* and *taluqdars* was cut across by networks of officials appointed by the *nawabs* to collect the revenues. Some *zamindars* who were regarded as particularly loyal or trustworthy dealt directly with the government *kachari*, but others had to contend with *tahsildars* (a type of collector) and other government officials stationed in their domains.[86] Many *zamindaris* were also subdivided into lands directly adminis-tered by *zamindars*, and lands that were leased to revenue farmers or *ijaradars*. The complex interlacing of revenue officials and landholders accorded with Muhammad Reza Khan's account of Mughal administration written for the British in 1775; he wrote that *zamindars* were duly honoured while they paid their taxes, but if they failed, 'Amils were sent', not to dispossess, but to scrutinize and regulate local collections.[87]

Vansittart's journal from 1767, compiled as he travelled around his province with an entourage of Indian sepoys and subordinate officials, is testament to the inquisitiveness and reach of the fledgling colonial power. He recorded topographical details, the position of *zamindar* forts, and population figures for different villages. Much of this information was clearly designed for taxation purposes; for example, he listed data about crop prices and yields, about the amount of land under culti-vation, waste land and rent-free land.[88] He also took a lively interest in the taxation history of different areas, noting that some increases occurred under *Nawab* Alivardi Khan to pay for the defence of the region against Maratha incursions; others were imposed by Vansittart's predecessors as residents in the region. In fact, as in the other ceded districts, the Company had tried various schemes in previous years to increase the value of the Midnapur revenues. According to Governor Verelst's figures, the land tax collections increased quite sharply from Rs 732,055 in 1765–6 to Rs 1,005,882 in 1766–7, and in the next few years they tended to hover around 9 lakhs.[89]

---

[85] The biggest *zamindar* in Midnapur, the raja of Kasijora, paid about Rs 200,000 in revenues per annum, compared with bigger *zamindaris* such as Dinajpur which paid about Rs 2,000,000.

[86] 'Journal of a Circuit of the Midnapore and Jallesore Provinces', OIOC, MSS Eur. F331/35, fos. 3v, 8r, 10r, 33r.

[87] Reza Khan's note, February 1775, Francis papers, OIOC, MSS Eur. E 28, fo. 345v.

[88] OIOC, MSS Eur. F331/35, fos. 1–2, 8, 12.

[89] Firminger, 'Historical Introduction', *The Fifth Report*, p. cxxxi.

Company residents in Midnapur had also resisted more dramatic schemes for tax reform suggested by authorities in Calcutta. The first resident, John Johnstone, claimed to have generated increases by discovering frauds in *zamindar* accounts. But a plan formulated by the Calcutta council in 1764 (in the heat of the wars with Mir Qasim and Awadh) to annul the collection rights of the *zamindars*, allowing them only a fixed income, and collecting the revenues directly from peasant cultivators, was firmly rejected by the resident Hugh Watts as 'very prejudicial to the country'. The Company, he explained, would be forced to maintain some 3000 families out of the revenues, and 'so many would be deprived of lands which they have either held for generations or have bought of the zemindars'. A later resident, Thomas Graham, objected to a Calcutta plan to let lands on more advantageous terms, because he felt that it was based on a misunderstanding of 'the constitution of the province', the whole being possessed of 'hereditary zemindars', 'who derive their rights from original sunnuds granted to their ancestors'. At the same time, Graham searched out wastelands on which peasants might be encouraged to extend cultivation, and also inquired into the titles of rent-free lands.[90]

Thus, Company officials sometimes invoked local claims to hereditary rights in an attempt to limit the revenue demands on the locality. These incidences reflected the active resistance of local elites, as well as the concern of Company servants to limit their own liabilities as tax collectors. George Vansittart represented his own administration in Midnapur as a series of negotiations between the Company and local rights-holders. One common issue was the question of control of water channels in the wetlands of Midnapur. The river systems of lower Bengal were notoriously fickle and shifting, and in the monsoon season from June to September rivers and streams were liable to break their banks and flood. Rice crops demanded a degree of flooding, but too much water could completely submerge the paddy and destroy it.[91] Meanwhile, local cultivators and landholders strove to manipulate the shifting river channels to the best advantage of their plot of land. Villagers also used their concerns over the water supply as a bargaining tool in negotiations with the central state over revenues.

For example, people in Amarsi *pargana* complained to Vansittart in 1767 that inundations were preventing them from realizing the

---

[90] Ibid., pp. cxxv–cxxvii.
[91] Bose, *Peasant Labour and Colonial Capital*, pp. 9–14; Datta, *Society, Economy and the Market*, pp. 38–54.

stipulated land revenue.[92] Inhabitants of Amarsi blamed the floods on the effects of a *band* (dam) built by the Marathas in what they said was previously a 'publick water course'.[93] The Maratha *band* was blocking the drainage of water away from Amarsi. Vansittart therefore took 'an obligation from the Maratha officers of Petanpore to break down the Band' and to repair another one. This done, the Amarsi *zamindars* signed a written agreement to cultivate more land, and to pay more revenue in the ensuing season.[94]

This incident suggests how Vansittart was able to insert himself into local disputes over resources. Colonial state-building, as a top down process of demand and extraction, was also entangled with longer histories of state-formation, a more dispersed process in which local interests tried to appropriate the authority of the central state for local purposes. Even as he increased the tax demand, George Vansittart recognized a certain obligation in the government to protect the customary rights of taxpayers, even if his role in this case amounted only to an official order that might or might not be enforced. We do know that in January 1769, Amarsi flooded again, and this time Vansittart advanced Rs 1,500 to the *zamindars* on top of the usual allowance granted by the government for repair of *bands*.[95]

Another type of engagement with local society arose from the Company's attempts to increase its commercial profits in Bengal. As resident of Midnapur, Vansittart was under pressure to expand the acreage under mulberry, as part of the Company's drive to expand its commercial investment in Indian silk.[96] In March 1768, he wrote to Richard Becher (then the Company's 'collector-general'), informing him that he had granted 100 *bighas* of waste ground in Midnapur *pargana* as a *taluq*, with the *taluqdar* engaging to cultivate half the area with mulberry for raw silk, and to leave the other half to the disposal of the *raiyats*. The *taluqdar* would pay a rent to the *zamindar*, which would gradually increase over four years up to 100 sicca rupees. This was 'rather less than a Common Renter would pay', but the lenient rates were granted as an inducement to the *taluqdar* to make the

---

[92] OIOC, MSS Eur. F331/35, fos. 30–1. The place Vansittart calls 'Omercey' is almost certainly present-day Amarsi, a south-eastern division of Midnapur. 'Pergunna' or *pargana* is an administrative term for a group of villages forming a revenue unit.

[93] Ibid. Pockets of Maratha-controlled territory remained in Midnapur into the early nineteenth century.

[94] Ibid., fo. 30v.

[95] Vansittart to James Alexander, Midnapur, 12 January 1769, W. K. Firminger (ed.), *Bengal District Records, Midnapur* (Calcutta, 1914–26), p. 131.

[96] N. K. Sinha, *The Economic History of Bengal, from Plassey to the Permanent Settlement*, 3 vols. (Calcutta, 1956), vol. I, p. 18.

necessary investment of labour and capital to introduce the cultivation of mulberry.[97]

Vansittart recognized that this scheme might antagonize *zamindars*, by carving new *taluqs* out of their domains, but he hoped it would act as a warning to *zamindars* to cultivate more wastelands. He wrote that the *zamindars'* 'unwillingness to be deprived of any part of their hereditary estates will induce them to exert their utmost endeavours that their lands may not remain uncultivated and be liable to be taken from them'. A few weeks later, Vansittart wrote to Becher again, representing the objections of the *zamindars* of Midnapur to his scheme for creating mulberry *taluqs*. Vansittart again expressed the hope that the *zamindars* themselves would agree to cultivate mulberry to preserve the integrity of their *zamindaris*. In the meantime Vansittart encouraged Becher to accept 'at least conditionally' the proposals of those 'Calcutta people' who were 'desirous of Taalucs'.[98] One of these 'Calcutta people' was none other than Gokhalchandra Ghosal, one of the most successful Calcutta entrepreneurs of the period, who used his extensive contacts with Company agents to expand his portfolio in commercial contracts and land revenue farms.[99]

Vansittart's mulberry scheme shows not only the Company's desire to use its new-found territorial power to pursue its commercial goals, but also how Company officials were forced to reckon with competing claims of rural elites. On 19 April 1768, Vansittart reported that the *zamindars* themselves had agreed to cultivate 400 *bighas* of mulberry. Some *zamindars* still refused to cultivate more mulberry, and in these *zamindaris* Vansittart was at first willing to create some new *taluqs* for Calcutta investors, if the investors also imported sufficient labour to work the lands.[100] Yet by 19 July, Vansittart had decided he was unwilling 'to deprive the Zemindars of any part of their patrimonial estates so long as they themselves seem disposed to improve them as much as is in their power'. Instead of creating *taluqs* for the likes of Gokhal Ghosal to purchase, Vansittart proposed granting *ijaras* (revenue farms) for 10 or 12 or more years. The system of sub-letting land as *ijaras* was already widespread within the *zamindaris* of Midnapur. Rather than acquiring permanent rights to a plot of land or *taluq* independently of a *zamindar*, investors would thus acquire the

---

[97] Vansittart to Becher, Midnapur, 22 March 1768, OIOC, MSS Eur. F331/1, pp. 57−8.
[98] Vansittart to Becher, Midnapur, 1 April 1768, ibid., pp. 59−60.
[99] Vansittart to Becher, Midnapur, 19 July 1768, ibid., pp. 93−4. For more information on the varied interests of Gokhal Ghosal see McLane, *Land and Local Kingship*, pp. 191, 217−20.
[100] Vansittart to Becher, Midnapur, 19 April 1768, MSS Eur. F331/1, p. 65.

temporary right to profit from cash-cropping in an *ijara*, which would remain part of the original *zamindari*. By following this course, Vansittart argued that he could both satisfy Gokhal Ghosal's desire for a profitable investment and also 'the Zemindar's hereditary rights'.[101]

Gokhal Ghosal apparently decided that the *ijaras* were not a sufficiently attractive investment, and Vansittart was left trying to decide whether to revert to *taluqs* or to abandon the mulberry scheme altogether.[102] Yet Vansittart's attempt to reconcile the Company's aggressive pursuit of profit with *zamindari* claims to 'hereditary rights' is a nice demonstration of the conceptual struggles inherent in colonial state-formation. By the late 1760s British understandings of Indian society were not only being shaped by theorists and pamphleteers in Calcutta and London, but also by day-to-day negotiations in the districts of Bengal. In this case, it appears that a notion of hereditary right over particular lands was vigorously asserted by *zamindars* themselves in the face of pressures from the Company and its commercial friends. Vansittart's acknowledgement of 'patrimonial' rights, however belated and provisional, suggested that conventional stereotypes about absence of 'real property' under Asiatic despotism were being modified in the engagement with elites in the Bengal countryside.

Vansittart's experience in the 'ceded' district of Midnapur made him particularly well qualified to profit from the expansion of the Company's direct administration into the *diwani* territories of Bengal after 1769. Thus, in 1770, Vansittart received a new appointment as the supervisor at Dinajpur, a rural district in north-central Bengal, lying between the two great river courses of the Ganges and Brahmaputra. Like eastern Midnapur, Dinajpur was a major rice-producing area, intersected by numerous small and large water courses. His jurisdiction was a diverse one: the northern areas could sustain two rice crops in a year; by contrast, southern Dinajpur was marked by less fertile clay soil.[103] Vansittart arrived in Dinajpur in the spring of 1770, and he left sometime between 14 October and December of the same year to take up an appointment on the new Company council in Patna in Bihar.[104]

Vansittart's situation in Dinajpur differed markedly from his stay in Midnapur, for a number of reasons. In Midnapur, Vansittart followed

[101] Vansittart to Becher, Midnapur, 19 July 1768, ibid., pp. 93–4.
[102] Vansittart to Becher, Midnapur, 8 August 1768, ibid., pp. 105–6.
[103] J. C. Sengupta, *West Bengal District Gazetteers: West Dinajpur* (Calcutta, 1965).
[104] The earliest date given in his private papers for his residence at Dinajpur is 30 April 1770, and the last letter from Dinajpur is dated 14 October 1770, MSS Eur, fo. 331/1/ pp. 120, 126. He had taken up his new post in the Company's council at Patna by 11 December 1770. OIOC, MSS Eur. *Vansittart* F331/3, p. 1.

a procession of other British officials who had already begun to make systems of local government intelligible to the Company. By contrast, in Dinajpur he replaced Indian *amils* appointed by Muhammad Reza Khan, the beleaguered deputy governor in the old capital of Murshidabad. Moreover, Vansittart travelled to Dinajpur at a moment of agrarian crisis as the famine engulfed rural populations, especially in northern and western Bengal, and as the Company sought to mitigate its own financial woes with new interventions in local government. Understandably, Indian officials and landholders were keen to take shelter from this onslaught, and to make life difficult for the new British investigators; meanwhile, their efforts to conceal local resources would be interpreted as further evidence of Indian corruption.

The famine of 1769–70 is now thought to have been worst of all in the northern and western districts of Bengal such as Dinajpur. Vansittart worried that government regulations exacerbated the problem of hunger. In July 1770, he complained to Richard Becher, advising him against the policy of imposing embargoes on rice exportation from one district to another. He considered that such embargoes were stopping rice moving out from places like Rangpur, where rice could still be procured at 15–20 seers per rupee, compared with only 6 seers per rupee in Dinajpur.[105] The talk of local embargoes suggests how the famine diverted the supervisors' attention away from their original 'instructions'. At the same time, declining harvests would put even greater pressure on the supervisors to meet the revenue demands of their superiors.

Dinajpur also presented Vansittart with a very different model of local government from that of Midnapur. In Midnapur, Vansittart dealt with a complex topography of many different *zamindars* and *taluqdars* and he was sometimes able to insert his authority into the fault lines between competing local interests. In Dinajpur, however, he was asked to regulate one of the great local kingdoms that had grown up in early eighteenth-century Bengal under the stewardship of the *nawabs*. Eighteenth-century Dinajpur was entirely encompassed by one large *zamindari*, the Dinajpur raj, which covered over 4,000 square miles by the 1760s.[106] The seventeenth-century founder of the Dinajpur raj worked in the *qanungo* (record keeping) department of the Mughal government, and used this official position as a stepping stone to the status of local *zamindar*. The Dinajpur rajas were not Bengali by origin,

[105] Vansittart to R. Becher, Dinajpur, 6 August 1770, OIOC, MSS Eur. F331/2, pp. 111–13.
[106] McLane, *Land and Local Kingship*, p. 144.

but north-Indian Kayasths, a group often associated with scribal and administrative skills. The major growth of the Dinajpur raj came under the great rajas Prannath (1682) and Ramnath (1733–60), who expanded their domains by grant from the *nawabs*, by purchase, and sometimes by force. By 1728, Dinajpur was one of the four largest *zamindaris* in Bengal. On Vansittart's arrival in 1770, the state's revenue assessment of the Dinajpur raj was about Rs 1,900,000 or not much under a tenth of the total revenue assessment for Bengal in this period.[107] Over the coming decades, British officials often treated such large landholders with considerable suspicion, perceiving them as threatening blocks of power that could prevent the Company from exercising proper controls over local government.

When Vansittart arrived in Dinajpur he found the raj in a state of considerable disrepair. *Nawab* Mir Qasim (1760–3), and then the Company's Indian deputy governors, had substantially raised the revenue assessment of Dinajpur and sent central government agents into the *zamindari* to extract bigger collections. This revenue assault from the centre coincided with a succession crisis in Dinajpur after the death of raja Ramnath in 1760. The authority of Ramnath's first son, Baidhanath, was undermined by the competition of his half-brother Kantunath; in 1770, Vansittart described the brothers as sworn rivals.[108] Moreover, the raja had fallen badly into debt in attempting to meet the heavy revenue demands.[109]

Echoing the reformist agenda of the 'instructions' to the supervisors, George Vansittart was unimpressed with the administrative agencies of both the *zamindar* and the *nawab*'s *amils*. One of his first letters from Dinajpur describes the systems of revenue collection in the region as 'extremely oppressive', characterized by arbitrary exactions by the various types of revenue officials, whose peculations and oppressions in the districts went undetected.[110] Acting in the spirit of his 'instructions', he immediately moved to cut back administrative costs and personnel at all levels of the *zamindari*. For example, his own supervisor's establishment at Dinajpur was set at Rs 1,000 per month, whereas the former *amil*'s establishment cost over Rs 3,000 per month. Similarly, the allowances of the *zamindar*'s own central office (*kachari*) in the town of Dinajpur were cut back from Rs 2,000 per month to Rs 1,694.

---

[107] Vansittart to R. Becher and Council at Murshidabad, 14 October 1770, OIOC, MSS Eur. F331/2, p. 131.
[108] Vansittart to Becher, no date, OIOC, MSS Eur. F331/2, p. 119.
[109] Vansittart to Becher, 14 October 1770, ibid., p. 129.
[110] G. Vansittart to R. Becher, Dinajpur, 6 July 1770, ibid., p. 96.

Meanwhile, the annual pay awarded to *zamindari* servants in the *parganas* of Dinajpur was reduced from Rs 4,749 to Rs 3,001. Rent-free lands used to support *zamindari* servants were also sharply cut back.[111] Such restrictions on the established system of *zamindari* patronage must have been felt particularly keenly, to say the very least, in an era of high food prices and famine.

Apart from their obvious fiscal motives, Vansittart's reforms were also couched in a rhetoric of state power which posited the exclusive rights of the sovereign to regulate the public realm of revenue collection and judicial administration. In other words, Vansittart's cost cutting was also an attack on the capacity of the Dinajpur raja to act independently of central government, dispensing patronage and administering justice in his local kingdom. Vansittart tried to stop the practice of *zamindari* officials levying fines on cultivators, or making the traditional claim of *chauth* or a quarter of the value of goods disputed in litigation in the *zamindar*'s courts.[112] He also stipulated that all administrative orders issued under the *zamindar*'s seal concerning revenue matters 'or any other publick business' should be copied into 'the Dufter [record office] of the Hakim's Dewan' as well as 'the Dufter of the zemindarry'.[113] By constructing more detailed Company records in parallel with the *zamindar*'s own records, Vansittart was trying to tie the *zamindari* little kingdom more firmly into the emergent Company state.

Perhaps the most potent symbol of the Company's ambition to suffocate the Dinajpur Raj, in its search for a 'regular' system of 'public authority', was Vansittart's heavy-handed intervention in the household finances of the raja. In October 1770 Vansittart wrote that he had restricted the raja's personal income to a 'fixed allowance'. This was fixed at Rs 100,000 per annum, although it was thought that the raja would also gain some Rs 30,000 from his own personal estates (*khamar* lands) and from some revenue farms that he held in his own hands. The Company was trying to impose specific limits on the profits of local kingship, but leave enough, as Vansittart hoped, for the raja to support his family, repair buildings ('which are all falling to ruin') and preserve at least a 'small share of grandeur he may be judged intitled to whilst the public Business is conducted in his name and apparently under his direction'. The allowance was to be conditional on the good

---

[111] G. Vansittart to R. Becher, 14 October, 1770, ibid., pp. 126–8.

[112] G. Vansittart to Becher, Dinajpur, 6 July 1770, p. 97.

[113] 'Abstract of Regulations Established by Mr Vansittart at Denagepore 30 April–30 September, 1770', OIOC, MSS Eur. F331/2, p. 122.

behaviour of the raja, and his continued cooperation with the supervisor 'for the Publick good'.[114]

Much of Vansittart's energy went in settling of the *jama* (revenue assessment) for Dinajpur in 1770. His professed goal was to establish fixity in tax collections, and to avoid both the extra exactions made by local officials for their own profits and the shortfalls in the government collections which characterized the previous administration. Vansittart termed these balances as 'embezzlements', and he blamed the collusive practices of local revenue officials. 'Embezzlements' for the previous year stood at Rs 169,662 (nearly a tenth of the assessment), which he considered 'dissipated among upwards of fifty Tahsildars [*zamindari* collectors] and their underlings'.[115] The Dinajpur raj was divided into *khas* lands, in which collections from the cultivators were administered directly by *zamindari* officials, and *ijara* lands which were leased to revenue farmers. Vansittart's expedient for improving the collections was to increase the number of *ijaras* or revenue farms, and to issue signed agreements with the farmers (*pattas*), which would stipulate the precise amount to be paid to the government. Such fixed revenue farms, issued for a term of years, were the 'only means for putting a final stop to the abuses which the officers of this pergunna are guilty of'.[116] However, under great pressure from above to maintain the revenue at high levels, Vansittart set the assessment at Rs 1,900,000, exactly the same as the previous year, despite the ill effects of the famine.[117]

Vansittart's aggressive regulation of the Dinajpur raj closely followed the 'instructions' provided by his superiors in Calcutta. His fixed, three-year revenue farms, for example, were an imitation of the farming system pioneered by Governor Verelst in Burdwan. But two revealing passages of Vansittart's letters suggest that his attempts to set in train long-term reforms of local government in Dinajpur met with very limited success. One of his flagship proposals, the limitation of fines exacted by *zamindari* officials on the *raiyats*, was strenuously resisted by the raja and his officials. According to Vansittart, the raja's servants 'allowed that the regulations would contribute much to the security of the Ryots' but 'protested so strongly against such an encouragement (as they called it) being given to fornication and adultery' that

---

[114] G. Vansittart to Becher, 14 October 1770, ibid., pp. 129–30.
[115] Vansittart to R. Becher, 14 October 1770, ibid., p. 130.
[116] Ibid., p.132.
[117] Ibid., p. 131. For the 'form of *patta*' issued by Vansittart to farmer holders of *ijaras*, see 'Abstract of Regulations', pp. 123–4.

Vansittart resisted his planned abolition of all fines and referred the matter to higher authorities.[118]

A few months after he left Dinajpur, Vansittart explained to his successor how his attempt to introduce a new system of fixed-revenue farms was also thwarted by local custom and the resistance of *zamindari* officials. In fact, a system of farming (*ijara*) was already well established in Dinajpur, but these *ijaras* were very different from the fixed leases envisaged by Vansittart's regulations. Vansittart explained that the established custom was for *ijaradars* to retain their holdings automatically each year, unless they gave their resignation in writing to the *kachari*. But rather than having their revenue payments fixed in a *patta*, they only entered into negotiations with officers of the *zamindari kachari* over the amount of their payments at the close of each Bengal financial year. In these negotiations the demand on the *ijaradar* would be adjusted according to the nature of the harvest; new *abwabs* (increases) might be added, or old ones removed. Vansittart had hoped in his time at Dinajpur to reconstitute this farming system around the practice of issuing fixed *pattas* for a term of years. But in the end he had given up on this idea because 'creditable people were not to be found' to take up the farms, and the raja and officers were also 'totally averse to such a plan'. The old system was long established and it was 'not possible to set it aside in the course of a few months and under the disadvantage of a drought'.[119]

Thus, the Company's desire for a fixed income was temporarily thwarted by older patterns of more flexible negotiations over revenue payments. As it turned out, Raja Baidhanath also demanded a reduction in his revenue payments in 1771. Vansittart told his successor that such demands for reduced taxes would continue while the central government had no good 'mofussil hustabood' or revenue survey.[120] In other words, in Dinajpur, the comparative ignorance of the central government about the true extent of local resources meant that officials had no effective means of testing the *zamindar*'s claims for revenue reductions. Vansittart's reference to the inability of the government to penetrate the *zamindar*'s local information systems highlighted the continuing dependence of the early Company raj on local power-holders, and the enduring (if now increasingly risky) capacity of a large *zamindar* like Baidhanath to bargain for better terms.

---

[118] Ibid., pp. 133–4.
[119] G. Vansittart to J. Graham, Patna, 14 February and 13 March 1771, OIOC, MSS Eur. F331/3, pp. 173–4, 186.
[120] Vansittart to J. Graham, 14 February 1770, ibid., pp. 173–4.

Conclusions: crisis and nostalgia

In the late 1760s and early 1770s, Company servants in Bengal were struggling to transform ideologies of conquest into languages of rule. Crude stereotypes of Asiatic depravity and corruption served both to justify the Company's rapid takeover of territories and also offered the hope that Bengal and its revenues could be dramatically improved under European management. Perhaps no document better illustrates this momentary self-confidence than a letter of Gerard Ducarel, a 24-year-old Company servant, recently appointed as supervisor of Purnea district in northern Bengal:

Certainly it is that we have it in our Power to perform the noblest task that can be allotted to men of honor and humanity, that of changing the condition of a people from a state of Oppression to Happiness, and the Country from desolation to Prosperity, and that the scheme will in general have this effect is undoubted, by the advantages English gentlemen have over Natives of this Country in education, principles and disposition.[121]

Ducarel was writing this even as famine began to decimate his district, which suggests how the agrarian crisis could also reinforce simple notions of Asiatic corruption. Yet the famine also appeared as a terrible warning about increasing the burden of taxation on rural society. Within a few months of the above letter, Ducarel was concluding that Purnea was much more flourishing under the Mughals than in the period of the Company's *diwani*, a situation he blamed in part on improvident tax demands.[122]

This kind of nostalgic looking back to the imagined stability and prosperity of earlier eras was increasingly common during and after the catastrophe of famine. According to his modern biographer, Muhammad Reza Khan idealized the administration of *Nawab* Alivardi Khan from the 1740s and 1750s.[123] George Vansittart recorded that the rule of Raja Ramnath in Dinajpur (1733–60) was 'still celebrated in the province and his memory greatly revered'. Even among the British, Bengal's troubles provoked a harking back, as in the works of Dow and Bolts, to an imagined golden age of the Mughal empire.

Meanwhile, Company servants at the cutting edge of territorial administration in Bengal, many of them armed with conventional

---

[121] Ducarel Papers, G. G. Ducarel to his mother, 15 December 1769, D2091, fo. 11, Gloucestershire Country Record Office.

[122] Ducarel to Controlling Council at Murshidabad, 3 December 1770, in W. K. Firminger (ed.), *Proceedings of the Controlling Council of Revenue at Murshidabad*, 12 vols. (Calcutta, 1919–24), vol. II, pp. 68–70.

[123] Khan, *Transition in Bengal*, p. 13.

theories of Asiatic despotism as corrupt, corrupting and oppressive, were suddenly confronting powerful streams of indigenous politics concerned with the rights of subjects and the responsibilities of rulers. The dissonance between the theory and the actual experience of Asiatic politics would provoke a major rethinking of the nature of the Mughal empire in the years to come. Meanwhile, as Company servants strove to give some coherence and stability to their chaotic territorial government, they sought to appropriate the continuing aura of Mughal legitimacy and to reconcile their own power with the deep traditions of Indian rulership.

3   Warren Hastings and 'the legal forms of Mogul government', 1772–1774

Warren Hastings (governor of Bengal from 1772 and governor-general of the British territories in India from 1774 to 1785) stands not least among those 'imperial icons' that dominated old pro-consular histories, and his dramatic career has launched a large shelf-full of biographies.[1] Hastings' particular genius, in some old versions, was for seeing beyond the vacillations and hesitations of his colleagues, and masterfully grasping Britain's historic destiny as an imperial power.[2] For others, following the famous attacks on his character by Edmund Burke and Lord Macaulay, Hastings' career stood as a horrifying example of the dangers of imperial hubris and brutality. Another durable and more sympathetic tradition has cast Hastings as an enlightened cosmopolitan and 'orientalist' in the non-pejorative, pre-Saidian sense of that word – a notable patron of Indian arts and scholarship.

This chapter tries to understand Hastings' governorship against the swirling backdrop of Company politics in the 1760s and early 1770s. It argues that Warren Hastings' attempts to reform the Bengal government in the early 1770s did indeed constitute a critical moment in the refashioning of the English East India Company as a branch of empire. This was not, however, because Hastings had visions, as if through a crystal ball, of the later history of British India. Hastings' reforms were part of a wider pattern of crisis management, as the East India Company confronted the aftermath of the Bengal famine and growing financial and political problems in Britain. These reforms drew on the widespread British sense that the Indian provincial government of Bengal was now broken down, but also the idea that a workable constitutional tradition existed within the erstwhile Mughal empire. Hastings' governorship was an uneasy mix of economizing administrative accountancy, attempts to

---

[1] P. J. Marshall, 'The Making of an Imperial Icon: the Case of Warren Hastings', *JICH*, 27 (1999), pp. 1–16.
[2] See, for example, P. E. Roberts, 'The Early Reforms of Hastings in Bengal', Dodwell (ed.), *Cambridge History of India*, vol. V, pp. 205–14, and M. E. Monckton Jones, *Warren Hastings in Bengal, 1772–4* (Oxford, 1918).

extend the coercive powers of the central state, and grand gestures designed to legitimize the Company government as steward of an ancient constitution. But Hastings would be undermined, like others before him, by the disabling legacies of conquest and famine, by factional and party conflicts, as well as by the ideological contradictions thrown up by the effort to cast a European trading company as a virtuous Asiatic ruler.

Governor Hastings in context

When Warren Hastings was appointed governor of Bengal in 1771, he had spent the past two years as the second in the Company's council in Madras. A long-time Company servant, who had served in Bengal from 1750 to 1764, Hastings was a close ally of Robert Clive's major rival for control of the directorate in London, Laurence Sulivan.[3] Widely admired for his administrative expertise, Hastings arrived in Bengal in February 1772 and spent the next months analysing the recent stream of directorial orders, as well as the voluminous records of the Company's expanding bureaucracy in the region.

Robert Clive's system of 'double government' was now on its very last legs, and Muhammad Reza Khan was an increasingly isolated and compromised figure. The directors' letters to Fort William had become steadily more hostile to Reza Khan, accusing him of revenue fraud, of contributing to the impact of the famine by monopolistic practices, and charging his official agents with widespread corruption.[4] The directors also attacked their own servants for disobeying restrictions on their private trade, in particular in the 'staple' goods of salt, tobacco and betel-nut. They railed against deficiencies in the revenues, and the unnecessary expenses they felt were undermining the Company's finances. 'How greatly must we be alarmed', they wrote to their Bengal council in August 1771, 'at seeing the Dewanny Collections scarce answering any other purpose than Defraying the Civil and Military Charges of our Presidency of Bengal'. In the same letter, the directors announced their wish 'stand-forth as Duan [sic, Diwan], and by the Agency of the Company's servants to take upon ourselves the entire Care and Management of the Revenues', to remove Muhammad Reza Khan from his duties, and to 'adopt such Regulations and pursue such Measures as shall at once ensure to us every possible Advantage'.[5]

---

[3] Sutherland, *The East India Company in Eighteenth Century Politics*, pp. 190–2, 205.
[4] Monckton-Jones, *Warren Hastings in Bengal*, pp. 126–39.
[5] Ct. of D. to President and Council at Fort William, 28 August 1771, *FWIH*, 6, pp. 122–3, 128.

This order was the starting point for major political reforms instituted by Warren Hastings and his council from the spring of 1772 to late 1774. In response to brewing crises at different levels of its operations, the Company was now moving to extend its direct control over all the *diwani* territories. The Company's fast-growing establishments in Bengal were barely paying for themselves, let alone supporting the Company's other trading stations and its swelling obligations to investors and the government in Britain. By 1772 the Company's bonded debt in Calcutta stood at over 10 million rupees.[6] Warren Hastings needed both to enhance revenue flows and trim the Company's expenses, yet this fiscal squeeze would run up against the bitter aftershocks of the recent famine, with falling grain prices and a sudden contraction in the supply of agricultural labour. Increasingly, Hastings would take advantage of sources of profit beyond the frontiers of Bengal, in tribute extracted in exchange for military protection from allied rulers in Awadh and Benares.[7] But this in turn would leave him exposed to charges of disobeying directorial orders to restrain from offensive military operations in north India. There was also evidence that war and famine were translating into growing problems of political order within Bengal. Senior Company servants thought that rent collections had been 'violently kept up to its former standard' after the famine.[8] In the early 1770s the Company's forces frequently clashed with armed groups of religious mendicants, *faqirs* and *sannyasis*, especially on the northern frontiers of Bengal.[9]

Related to financial difficulties, and to problems of governance in Bengal, the Company was also facing a crisis of confidence in Britain. The orders to 'stand forth' in Bengal were part of a wider slew of measures proposed by the directors in 1771 and 1772 to restore the good reputation of the Company and protect it from parliamentary regulation.[10] Company servants like Warren Hastings were well aware that the 'Temper of the Times' had turned against them in Britain.[11] By at least October of 1772, Hastings was hearing from friends in England that some form of parliamentary regulation of the Company

[6] For Hastings' own account of the fiscal crisis of the early 1770s, see his letter to a Company director, Richard Becher, 19 September 1776. BL Add. MSS 29,128, fo. 10r.
[7] R. B. Barnett, *North India Between the Empires: Awadh, the Mughals and the British, 1720–1801* (Berkeley, CA, 1980), pp. 90–5.
[8] Revenue Board to Ct. of D., 3 November 1772, *FWIH*, 6, p. 419.
[9] A. K. Dasgupta, *The Fakir and Sannyasi Uprisings* (Calcutta, 1992).
[10] Sutherland, *The East India Company in Eighteenth Century Politics*, pp. 217–18.
[11] For Hastings' use of this phrase, see his letter to another (unnamed) Company servant, Madras, 2 October 1771, BL Add. MSS 29,125, fo. 82r.

was likely.[12] By then, he was also receiving information about the latest treatises on Indian affairs authored by William Bolts and Alexander Dow, including a copy of the latest volume of Dow's *History of Hindustan*, which was sent to India 'reeking from the press'.[13] Hastings was roused to indignation by what he considered 'medlies replete (though not in equal degree) with abominable untruths, base aspersions and absurdities'.[14] He admitted that Dow's work had an 'Elegant Stile', and even that 'some things which he asserts are true', but thought that in general Dow's text was 'grossly deficient in the knowledge of the Revenue, Forms of Office and Justice, and in many other points respecting Bengal'.[15]

In the context of such attacks on the Company and its servants, Hastings' reforms in Bengal after 1772 were an exercise in political legitimation as much as financial rationalization. But the six-month, or sometimes longer, time lag for the communication of news between Calcutta and London created uncertainty on all sides. Even as he drew up new schemes for the administration of Bengal, Hastings knew that 'some great Change in the Constitution of the British Establishments in India' would likely soon arrive from home.[16] Hastings also knew that his reforms in Bengal would likely be subject to parliamentary scrutiny and revision. He was, however, thoroughly suspicious of parliamentary intervention, thinking it 'a contradiction of the common notions of equity and policy that the English gentlemen of Cumberland and Argyleshire should regulate the polity of a nation which they know only by the lakh which it has sent to Great Britain, and by the reduction which it has occasioned in the land tax'.[17]

While Hastings defended the superior right of experienced Company servants like himself to direct the Bengal government, he agreed with Bolts and Dow at least to the extent of sharing their highly jaundiced view of the current state of Bengal, and of the Company's establishments there. 'The new Government of the Company', he wrote to a colleague on the Bengal council in July 1772, 'consists of a confused Heap of indigested materials, as wild as the chaos itself. The Powers of Government are undefined; the collection of the Revenue, the Provision of the

---

[12] Letters of Ralph Leycester to Hastings, 12 March 1772 (recd 11 October 1772) and 4 April 1772, BL Add. MSS 29,133, fos. 72–3, 93.

[13] John Macpherson to Hastings, Madras, 12 October 1772, BL Add. MSS 29,133 fo. 262r,v.

[14] Hastings to Robert Palk, 11 November 1772, Add. MSS 29,127, fo. 49r.

[15] Hastings to L. Sulivan, 11 November 1772, Add. MSS 29,127, fo. 44v.

[16] Hastings' 'Diary of Transactions and Occurrences in a Voyage to Benaris, in 1773', BL Add. MSS 29,234, fo. 157r.

[17] Hastings to J. Dupré, 6 January 1773, BL Add. MSS 29,127, fo. 64v.

Investment, the Administration of Justice (if it exists at all), the Care of the Police, are all huddled together, being exercised by the Same Hands'.[18] A year later he wrote that while the extent and resources of Bengal were 'equal to those of most states in Europe', its difficulties were 'greater than those of any, because it wants both an established form and powers of government, deriving its actual support from the unremitted labour and personal exertion of individuals in power instead of the vital influence which flows through the channels of a regular constitution, and imperceptibly animates every part of it'.[19] The sense of trying to mould a 'confused heap of materials' into a 'regular constitution', infusing new life into the moribund polity of Bengal, was a recurrent theme of Hastings' busy schematizing in the months and years ahead.

While Hastings' own sense of the urgency of reform, and the directors' order to 'stand forth' as *diwan*, both pointed to a more aggressive assertion of Company sovereignty, Hastings also inherited his predecessors' sense of the delicacy of the Company's position as a merchant body straying into unfamiliar Asiatic territories. The Company's own 'constitution' derived from 'ancient charters which were framed for the jurisdiction of your trading settlements', and was incompetent 'for the government of a great Kingdom'.[20] Hastings' early letters from Bengal were preoccupied with the difficulty of effectively controlling the district supervisors, whom he regarded as ill-suited for their large responsibilities. In a letter to the chairman of the directors, which uncannily anticipated the rhetoric of Hastings' future nemesis, Edmund Burke, he feared that 'the Country by these revolutions [was] in Danger of being thrown to the Mercy of raw inexperienced Boys' and to 'tremble at the Consequences'.[21]

A document called 'Regulations Proposed for the Government of Bengal', with annotations in Warren Hastings' own hand, probably dating from early 1772, reflected Hastings' desire both to overhaul the territorial administration and at the same time to rein in the Company service.[22] On the one hand, these regulations declared that

[18] Hastings to R. Barwell, Kasimbazar, 22 July 1772, BL Add. MSS 29,125, fo. 113r,v.
[19] Hastings to Ct. of D., Ft William, 11 November 1773, printed in G. R. Gleig, *Memoirs of Warren Hastings*, 3 vols. (London, 1841), vol. I, p. 368.
[20] Ibid.
[21] Hastings to George Colebrooke, Ft William, 20 April 1772, Add. MSS 29,127, fo. 34v.
[22] Two copies of these 'Regulations' survive, one in OIOC, MSS Eur. Orme/41, and the other (a better copy) in BL Add. MSS 29,203, fos. 1–16. For a printed version, and a discussion of the date of production, see Monckton-Jones, *Warren Hastings in Bengal*, p. 152.

the Company should openly assert its powers as the 'civil magistrate' of Bengal, managing the territorial government from 'the General Cucherree [*kachari*], which should be in Calcutta, and under the immediate Direction of the President and Council'.[23] On the other hand, suspicious of the oppressions committed by junior Company servants, Hastings wanted to restrict all Europeans to Calcutta, except junior servants working from the up-country 'factories'.[24] Europeans should not themselves be employed in the administration of the districts, Hastings argued, because Company servants were sufficiently employed by other business, and they should not be allowed beyond the juridical reach of the English law court in Calcutta. 'There is besides', he wrote, 'a fierceness in the European manners, especially among the lower sort', he argued, 'which is incompatible with the gentle temper of the Bengalee'.[25] The functions of government in the *mofussil* would thus continue in the hands of Indian officials, because 'by the principles of justice the inhabitants of every country are entitled to a share of its emoluments'.[26]

Thus, Hastings' 'proposed regulations' envisaged that the Company would continue to govern Bengal at a certain distance, as the steward of a reformed Indian administration. According to these proposals, 'the Mahomatan and Gentoo inhabitants shall be subject only to their own laws'; in Calcutta, native inhabitants were necessarily subject to English courts regarding their transactions with Europeans, but not in their dealings with each other.[27] Hastings' proposals were animated by a Montesquieuan sense of legal geography, in which different 'esprits des lois' attached to different peoples. There would be occasions, however, when the demands of natural justice overrode allegiance to indigenous practice. Hence, echoing a previous order from the directors, he considered it would be impossible to allow an English council to act like a Mughal prince in enforcing the resumption of the estates of office holders on their deaths. Instead the English should encourage the evolution of 'the natural rights of inheritance'.[28] Hastings parsed this uneasy partnership of constitutional variation and natural law with this ringing declaration:

In a word let this be the ruling principle in our Government of the People whose Ease and Welfare we are bound both by Justice and Policy to preserve; to make

---

[23] BL Add. MSS 29,203, fo. 4v.
[24] Hastings' views of this were shaped by the troubles of his friend Henry Vansittart in the early 1760s, whose governorship was marred by disunity among councillors widely dispersed across Bengal and acting at cross purposes.
[25] Ibid. [26] Ibid., fo. 5r. [27] Ibid., fo. 5v. [28] Ibid., fos. 10r–11v.

their laws sit as light on them as possible, and to share with them the Privileges of our own Constitution, where they are capable of partaking of them consistently with their other Rights and the Welfare of the State.[29]

These proposed regulations anticipated key themes of his governorship, not least his sense that the Company government could best function by employing Indian officials and Indian laws, while occasionally infusing English constitutional principles. Hastings was unusual among the Company servants of the 1770s in that he had personal experience of the relative order of *Nawab* Alivardi Khan's rule, before the implosion of the regional state of Bengal. Indeed in the early 1760s Hastings was one of the last defenders of the independence of the *nawabs*, and he tended to reject generalized characterizations of *nawabi* officials as degenerate.[30] Hastings shared in the notion that Mughal and *nawabi* rule was a species of despotism, very different from the free constitutions of the British state and empire; but he seems to have regarded this kind of Asiatic despotism as a viable, if occasionally 'barbaric', form of sovereignty.

Like William Bolts and Alexander Dow, Hastings thought that the Mughal empire at its height possessed a highly centralized and regulated system of government. Thus, when he began to investigate systems of land revenue in Bengal, he asked a colleague to outline the rights and duties of various participants 'according to the legal forms of Mogul government'.[31] Sending an early draft of revenue plans to the chairman of the Company, Hastings stated his goal 'not to introduce fresh Innovations, but to restore the Government of the Country to its first principles'. 'Many other correspondent Regulations will be necessary, but not one perhaps which the original constitution of the Mogul Government hath not before established or adopted, & thereby rendered familiar to the People'.[32]

While Hastings talked grandly of 'the original constitution of the Mogul Government', this did not mean that he had a very clear view of what this was. Generations of imperial historians, portraying Hastings as a masterful founder of empire, tended to underestimate the vagueness and uncertainty with which he and his colleagues confronted the daunting tasks of Indian governance. 'In many cases', he wrote in

---

[29] Ibid.

[30] See, for example, Hastings' minute of 1 March 1763, printed in Henry Vansittart, *Narrative of the Transactions in Bengal*, pp. 302–4.

[31] Hastings to Thomas Motte, Madras, 27 September 1769, BL Add. MSS 29,125, fo. 10r,v.

[32] Hastings to G. Colebrooke, 26 March 1772, BL Add. MSS 29,127, fo. 13r,v.

July 1772 to another Company servant, 'we must work as an arithmetician does with his *Rule of False*. We must adopt a plan upon conjecture, try, execute, add, & deduct from it, till it is brought into a perfect shape'. Yet this approach was liable to 'many inconveniences', not least that 'the Losses, Troubles and Embarrassments attending the first Experiment, & unavoidably incident as you justly observe to all Innovations will be charged to the account of the first projectors'.[33] Meanwhile, Hastings constantly bemoaned the limits of his powers as governor. He was, he complained, 'no more than a Mere Member of the Board', with a casting vote in the Company's council of 14 senior servants.[34]

In this context, the idea of the 'Mogul constitution' was less a coherent programme of governance than a way of attaching the upstart sovereignty of the Company to some idea of stability and longevity. It was a hopeful intimation that some ordered system existed among the apparently confusing byways of Indian politics. All the time, however, shadowing this idea of an organic, pre-existing constitution, was the lingering sense of Asiatic barbarism and venality, and the perceived need to expunge the most repugnant elements of Indian custom. Moreover, Hastings' relationship with the idea of despotism remained highly ambiguous. Theories of Asiatic despotism were not just a foil for British virtue, they also offered alluring justifications for a masterful colonial executive.

A revolution in sovereignty

When the Company's ship, the *Lapwing*, arrived in Bengal on 23 April 1772, it carried not just the public orders to 'stand forth' as *diwan*, but also secret orders, read only by the governor, for the immediate arrest and trial of the Indian 'prime ministers', Muhammad Reza Khan and Maharaja Shitab Rai, on charges of fraud in revenue collections and hoarding during the famine.[35] Hastings set about breaking down the residual power of the *nawab*'s household in Murshidabad, removing the central agencies of territorial government, most importantly the *khalsa* (revenue office), to Calcutta. By November 1772 he was writing that his reforms together amounted to 'an entire revolution in the State and Government of this Country without Bloodshed'.[36] 'Calcutta', he

---

[33] Hastings to R. Barwell, Kasimbazar, 22 July 1772, BL Add. MSS 29,125, fo. 113r.
[34] Hastings to L. Sulivan, 11 November 1772, ibid., fo. 43v.
[35] A. M. Khan, *The Transition in Bengal: A Study of Seyid Muhammad Reza Khan* (London, 1969), p. 294.
[36] Hastings to John Purling, 11 November 1772, BL Add. MSS 29,127, fo. 48r.

declaimed, 'is now the Capital of Bengal, and every Office and trust of the Province issues from it'.[37] It was time, he told Laurence Sulivan, 'to establish the Line of the Company's Power, & habituate the People, and the Nabob to their Sovereignty'.[38]

Yet the 'revolution' of 1772 was somewhat more equivocal than this new rhetorical assertion of the Company's sovereignty might have suggested. Hastings' assault on Reza Khan and the *nawabi* was, as he put it, a 'matter of much delicacy'.[39] Hastings knew that Reza Khan had 'established an interest' with other senior servants, who would not be pleased by his arrest.[40] Reza Khan was held under house arrest in Calcutta, but Hastings did not begin proceedings in his 'trial' on charges of corruption for many months. Blaming this delay on the weight of business and the difficulty of procuring evidence, Hastings suggested that it did not much trouble Reza Khan himself, who 'buoyed himself up with the Hopes of a Restoration to his Former Authority by the Interest of his Friends & a change in the Direction, & his Letters and the Letters of his Dewan to the City declared these Expectations'.[41]

In June 1772, Hastings set out for Murshidabad to preside over the reorganization of the major offices of the *nawab*'s household. On the advice of the directors, he planned to use one of Muhammad Reza Khan's great rivals in Bengal politics, Maharaja Nandakumar, former chief minister of *Nawab* Mir Jafar, to help eradicate Reza Khan's influence. Thus, he appointed Nandakumar's son, Gurudas, as the new *diwan* of the *nawab*'s household. Meanwhile, Munni Begum, the widow of Mir Jafar and an inveterate enemy of Reza Khan, was appointed guardian of the young *nawab*. Hastings thought Munni Begum a particularly suitable choice because, as a widow whose children had all died, she could not herself aspire to become *nawab* as a male relative might.[42] Meanwhile, Hastings halved the expenses granted to the *nizamat* from Rs 32 lakh to 16 lakh. In an apparently forensic operation he drew up lists of officers and pensioners retained under the patronage of Reza Khan, and either reduced or abolished their pensions.[43]

[37] Hastings to J. Dupré, 11 November 1772, ibid., fo. 63v.
[38] Hastings to L. Sulivan, Kasimbazar, 7 September 1772, ibid., fo. 38v.
[39] Hastings to J. Dupré, 8 October 1772, BL Add. MSS 29,125, fo. 155r,v.
[40] Hastings to Secret Committee of Ct. of D., Kasimbazar, 1 September 1772, BL Add. MSS 29,125, fo. 137r.
[41] Ibid.   [42] Ibid., fos. 140–1.
[43] 'State of the Nizamut Accounts shewing the Expense of Nabob Mobareck ul Dowlah's household under the different Heads together with an Establishment formed agreeable to the late Reductions of his stipend', 23 January 1773, OIOC, IOR, BPC, P/154/38.

Hastings' attack on the surviving patronage structures of the *nawabi*, coming after a decade of war and famine, provoked outrage among the nobility and service gentry in the old capitals of Murshidabad and Patna. A Mughal scholar/administrator from Patna wrote how the parsimony of the Company was exacerbated by the corruption of those appointed to manage the *nawab*'s affairs, so that the Murshidabad pensioners 'in these hard times have not a single resource under the canopy of the Hindostany heaven', and were 'reduced to such miseries, as God relieve mankind from'.[44] Another Mughal official, Karim Ali, had held a monthly pension from the *nawabs* since the reign of Alivardi Khan; a protégé of Muhammad Reza Khan, he composed a Persian history in 1772, the *Muzaffarnama*, which savagely attacked the Company's regime and Hastings in particular. When Hastings visited Murshidabad, Karim Ali wrote, 'all the employees of Bengala from top to bottom were dismissed from their services and around fifty persons were appointed afresh'. The English were 'the most distinguished in wisdom, warfare and strength of power among the hat-wearing nations', yet they have shown that after all 'they are business men' by persecuting Reza Khan over a few lakhs of rupees. Calcutta, meanwhile, was a pestilential town where even birds flying over were prone to die, and the 'elite of the town are wont to destroy the Muslims'.[45]

Warren Hastings took an unsentimental view of the real locus of power in Bengal, 'the Dewanee', he declared, 'being ours by right, and the military and political affairs by Prescription'.[46] Despite all his efforts, however, he was not able entirely to seal off and neutralize the influence of the old *nawabi* elite. The inquiries against Muhammad Reza Khan and Shitab Rai proceeded slowly, and by 1774 both had been acquitted. Hastings distrusted the chief informer against Reza Khan, Maharaja Nandakumar, regarding him as an 'inconsiderate villain'.[47] Moreover, the governor soon realized, in part because of panicked letters from England, that detailed inquiries into the accounts of the *nawabs* would uncover illicit payments to senior Company servants.[48]

[44] Ghulam Hussain Khan, *Seir Mutaqherin*, vol. III, p. 46.
[45] Shayesta Khan (ed., tr.), *Bihar and Bengal in the Eighteenth Century. A Critical Edition and Translation of Muzaffarnama, a Contemporary History* (Patna, 1992a), pp. 42–3, 45.
[46] Hastings to Wm. Aldersey, Kasimbazar, 24 June 1772, BL Add. MSS 29,125, fo. 102.
[47] Hastings to Wm. Aldersey, Kasimbazar, 11 July 1772, ibid., fo. 219v. Hastings told Dupré (governor in Madras), in his letter of 8 October 1772, that Nandakumar 'stands convicted of treasons against the Company while he was a Servant of Meer Jaffier, and I helped to convict him'. BL Add. MSS 29,125, fo. 156r.
[48] Hastings to S. Middleton, 10 February 1774, BL Add. MSS 29,125, fo. 267v.

Justifying his own profits, the former resident at Murshidabad Francis Sykes wrote, 'it was this, whether it would go into a black man's pocket, or my own'.[49] Hastings came to believe that Reza Khan was innocent of the charges of trading in grain during the famine, and that even if he had committed revenue frauds, these would be impossible to discover.

The difficulties Hastings faced in gathering details about Reza Khan's administration suggested widespread resistance within the old capital to the Company's inquiries. Meanwhile, inside knowledge about the private profiteering of Company servants remained a potential source of leverage for Indian politicians. Despite Warren Hastings' reforms, the *nawab* was still in theory the *nazim* or Mughal governor in Bengal, and the Company continued to deploy this constitutional fiction in dealings with other European traders. Furthermore, the Company's attempts to justify its own policies by reference to the Mughal constitution sustained a demand for elite informers from the old order. Thus, in the early 1770s, both Muhammad Reza Khan and his rival Nandakumar moved to Calcutta, and they would continue to play an important role in Company politics in the years to come.

Standing forth

Touring Nadia district in western Bengal in June 1772, Warren Hastings wrote to a colleague that 'it is an exhausted country, and has been much oppressed'.[50] In fulfilling the directors orders to 'stand forth' as *diwan*, Hastings needed to find ways to stabilize the Company's revenues and cut its costs, while at the same time acknowledging the calamity of the recent famine and developing policies for the regeneration of Bengal. In making policy, Hastings was often, as he himself recognized, a 'compiler of other men's opinions', drawing on ideas of reform that were already commonplace in the Company service.[51] What was new, however, was the attempt to implement a systematic overhaul of the Bengal government by recentring power in the Company's capital in Calcutta.

Several of Hastings' early measures aimed to address the perceived downturn in the trade of Bengal, and the related problem of currency shortage. Bowing to pressure from Company servants, the directors by

[49] F. Sykes to Hastings, no date, BL Add. MSS 29,133, fos. 347–54.
[50] Hastings to Wm. Aldersey, Krishnanagar, 24 June 1772, BL Add. MSS 29,125, fo. 88v.
[51] Hastings to G. Colebrooke, Ft William, 26 March 1772, BL Add. MSS 29,127, fo. 14r.

1773 had stopped sending bullion out of Bengal to pay for the China tea trade.[52] In 1772, Hastings used the currency problem as the excuse for ending the annual *diwani* tribute to the Mughal emperor.[53] Like former governors, he persisted in trying to control the issue and value of silver coinage, establishing coins from the year 1773 as the base value for all future *sicca* rupees, centralizing the production of *siccas* in the Calcutta mint, and abolishing the old custom of annual depreciations on circulating coin.[54] Hastings' plan to open up inland commerce by reducing taxation on trade was also supposed to encourage inflows of specie from other parts of India. A proclamation of 1773 abolished the numerous *zamindari* tolls; in theory, only the Company's customs houses situated in five major cities were supposed to levy taxes on internal trade.[55] The *dastak* system of trade passes was also abolished, in a bid to end the special privileges enjoyed by Company servants and their agents in the inland trade. At the same time, however, Hastings established the lucrative trades in salt and opium as monopolies for the Company. The profits of monopoly and customs dues remained an important supplement of the Company's territorial income well into the nineteenth century.[56]

The centre-piece of Hastings' reforms was his plan for the reorganization of the land revenues. Hastings' policy of farming out rights to collect taxes on five-year contracts was both a rationalization of the Company's previous experiments in Indian land tax and a piece of crisis management after the famine, designed to provide a vital infusion of cash into the Company's treasury. As we have seen, different versions of revenue farming had become widely popular among Company officials in the 1760s as a means of achieving 'fixity' in the revenues. Yet Hastings needed to square the practice of revenue farming with growing recognition of the hereditary rights and entrenched local influence of Bengal's *zamindars*.

In 1767, giving evidence before the British parliament, Hastings expressed concern that a general scheme for leasing the Bengal lands to

---

[52] P. J. Marshall, *East Indian Fortunes. The British in Bengal in the Eighteenth Century* (Oxford, 1976), p. 98.

[53] Monckton Jones, *Warren Hastings in Bengal*, pp. 168–9.

[54] W. W. Hunter, *Annals of Rural Bengal* (Calcutta, 1868), p. 311, and S. Chakrabarti, 'Intransigent Shroffs and the English East India Company's Currency Reforms, 1757–1800', *Indian Economic and Social History Review*, 34 (1997), 81.

[55] R. Datta, *Society, Economy and the Market*, pp. 203–5. For a broader treatment of the Company's attempts to decouple local lordship from market controls in Bengal, see Sen, *Empire of Free Trade*.

[56] Marshall, *East Indian Fortunes*, pp. 143, 147; Marshall, *Bengal: the British Bridgehead*, pp. 110–12.

farmers by public auction would be a 'a very pernicious custom for you must dispossess the Zemindars who have a prior right and the Farmers would distress the People'.[57] His 'proposed regulations' of 1772 similarly acknowledged 'the natural and just rights of the Zemindar already in possession', but also noted that 'the great Zemindars have been ever dangerous checks upon Government', and that 'in all invasions and rebellions they have always born a considerable part'. His draft regulations suggested that the Company should adopt the Mughal practice of appointing *sezawuls* (temporary officials) to police *zamindars*, and dividing the largest *zamindaris* up into smaller *taluqs*.[58]

In May 1772, Governor Hastings assumed the chairmanship of a four-man 'committee of circuit' (COC) appointed from among senior Company servants to make a new tax settlement for the Bengal lands.[59] The council in Calcutta had already accepted the recommendation of the directors for 'letting of lands on long leases'.[60] But the eventual plan for a general farming system aimed to achieve a balance, at least on paper, between 'the just claim Government has upon their lands for a revenue adequate to their real value, or of the zemindars and talookdars in support of their rights and privileges, grounded upon the possession of regular grants, a long series of family succession, and fair purchase'.[61] In justifying the plan to the directors, the Bengal council described the bad state of the provinces owing to the recent famine, criticizing the lack of 'regular process' in the revenue administration since 1765. 'Every zemindaree and every taaluk was left to its own peculiar customs', but these were 'not inviolably adhered to' and 'every change added to the confusion which involved the whole'. According to the council, these problems had roots in the despotic nature of the *nawab*'s government. 'The Nazims exacted what they could from the zemindars, and great farmers of the revenue, whom they left at liberty to plunder all below them'.[62] In this now familiar account of Montesquieuan despotism, rapacity was the mother of mendacity, as *zamindars* and peasants strove to conceal their true wealth from tyrannical rulers.

In the new scheme, rights of revenue collection would be awarded for five years to revenue farmers who tendered written bids for the farms. Former *zamindars* and *taluqdars*, those in other words who held *sanads*

---

[57] Hastings' evidence, 31 March 1767, BL Add. MSS 18,469, fo. 22v.
[58] Monckton-Jones, *Warren Hastings in Bengal*, pp. 157, 159.
[59] Firminger, 'Historical Introduction', *The Fifth Report*, pp. ccxiii–ccxiv.
[60] Hastings to G. Colebrooke, Ft William, 26 March 1772, BL Add. MSS 29,127, fo. 14r.
[61] Public letter to Ct. of D., 3 November 1772, *FWIH*, 6, p. 423.
[62] Ibid., pp. 419–20.

for certain lands from the *nawabs*, would be given preference wherever possible because of their established local authority and 'perpetual interest' in their lands. The plan thus recognized the expressed wish of the directors not to 'alter the constitution, nor deprive the zemindars etc., of their ancient priviledges and immunities'. At the same time, the farming system would work as a shot against the bows of *zamindars*, by establishing 'the government's right' to appoint new revenue farmers, and tending to put *zamindars* on 'good behaviour'.[63] If *zamindars* were outbid by competitors, even though they would lose their powers over the collections, they would still be awarded an annual share in the revenues, usually between 10 and 20 per cent, considered as their hereditary right.[64]

A professed goal of the plan was to stabilize both the government revenues and the demands on the peasantry. Instead of annual negotiations over the revenue rates in Murshidabad, the revenue demand would be established for the five-year duration of the farms in written agreements, signed by the farmer. The farmers were also supposed to grant *pattas*, or lease agreements, to their *raiyats* to prevent peculation or oppression lower down the scale. At the same time, certain taxes on the peasantry, deemed oppressive, were abolished.[65] It was hoped that farmers and peasants would now be encouraged by the fixed demands to invest in the improvement of their domains. Meanwhile, the bidding system would help the government to assess the 'real value of the lands' (a much repeated mantra among Company officials).[66] Hastings hoped that competition for the farms would gradually reveal their true value, and that the accountants appointed by government to supervise the revenue farmers would provide invaluable information for the government at the end of five years.

Beneath ambitious declarations about 'security of property' lurked some hard-nosed political and financial calculations.[67] The Calcutta council argued that long-term farms provided a method 'the most simple, and therefore the best adapted to a government like that of the

---

[63] Ibid., p. 424.
[64] 'In addition', McLane writes, 'most *zamindars* were granted small farms of small- or medium-sized estates so that their revenue-collecting rights were not totally discontinued', see McLane, *Land and Local Kingship*, p. 213.
[65] Public letter to Ct. of D., 3 November 1772, *FWIH*, 6, p. 422.
[66] Hastings to Secret Committee of Ct. of D., 1 September 1772, BL Add. MSS 29,125, fo. 136v.
[67] 'The Security of private property is the greatest Encouragement to Industry, on which the wealth of every State depends'. President and Council to Ct. of D., 3 November 1772, *FWIH*, 6, p. 421.

Company which cannot enter into the detail and Minutiae of the collections'.[68] Further, the central revenue offices would now be moved to Calcutta, encouraging a 'great increase of inhabitants, and of wealth' in the Company's settlement.[69] As it turned out, the COC retained former *zamindars* or *taluqdars* as farmers in about half the lands covered by their survey.[70] In other places, revenue farms were often granted to *banyans*, the commercial agents of British officials. Warren Hastings' own *banyan*, Krishna Kanta Nandy, took sizeable farms in 1772.[71] Despite formal prohibitions, there is no doubt that Company servants also profited handsomely from the farming system, either through bribes from prospective farmers or by holding farms secretly themselves.[72] The farming system was thoroughly characteristic of this early phase of colonial government in Bengal, combining the simultaneous extension of public authority and private profiteering.

Like the supervisors before them, the COC cut back many of the customary charges on government revenue.[73] On paper, at least, the COC enforced significant cuts in the numbers and allowances of local government officers, from accountants, to armed enforcers, to religious attendants such as Brahmins. The rationale for the cuts was that the new revenue farmers and not the Company were supposed to bear the costs of collections. Company officials also thought that some of these charges were artificially inflated by *amils* or *zamindars* to conceal local resources from the Company.[74] Thus, the Company continued to invade the coercive and patronage power of landholders, despite growing evidence that such measures were causing hardship among the lower ranks of territorial officials.[75] Hastings later came to believe that these economies in the provision for local service groups may have contributed to local disorder and violence.[76] Meanwhile, the total revenue demand for

---

[68] Calcutta Committee of Revenue, BRC 14 May 1772, OIOC, IOR P/67/54, p. 247.
[69] President and Council to Ct. of D., 3 November 1772, *FWIH*, 6, p. 427.
[70] Firminger, 'Historical Introduction', *The Fifth Report*, p. ccxix.
[71] S. C. Nandy, *Life and Times of Cantoo Baboo, the Banian of Warren Hastings* (Calcutta, 1978a), pp. 46–50.
[72] McLane, *Land and Local Kingship*, pp. 217, 219, 222.
[73] President and Council to Ct. of D., 3 November 1772, *FWIH*, 6, p. 423.
[74] See, for example, BRC, 8 January 1773, OIOC, IOR P/49/38, p. 511.
[75] The Company Council at Patna wrote to the President and Council at Ft. William, on 17 December 1772, noting the bad effects of cutbacks in collection charges. 'Many of the dismissed servants not finding employment here, retire in quest of it to neighbouring countries.' The diminution of 'ryots' (peasant cultivators) was therefore smaller than that of other classes, so that grain was produced 'for which there does not remain an adequate number of consumers'. BRC, 29 January 1773, ibid., p. 683.
[76] Governor-general's minute, BRC, 19 April 1774, in Monckton-Jones, *Warren Hastings in Bengal*, pp. 208–9.

Bengal continued at the very high levels of previous years, despite the recent famine and depopulation;[77] the demand was also supposed to rise in increments during the five years of the farms.

Governor Hastings had hoped to limit the powers of Company servants in the districts as well as the 'usurpations' of Indian landholders. Initially, he wanted to recall the supervisors, 'nor suffer a Christian to remain in the Country beyond the bounds of the factories'.[78] In the event, he shied away from a measure which would have adversely affected 'so many Sons, Cousins, or élèves of Directors, and Intimates of Members of this Council'.[79] Instead, in the new plan, supervisors were renamed 'collectors', supervising the revenue farms in conjunction with Indian *diwans*. A year later, however, the directors (on Hastings' urging) ordered the withdrawal of the British collectors from the districts, aiming both to cut administrative costs and to prevent Company servants from monopolizing inland commerce.[80] Now the collectors were replaced by six provincial councils stationed in major towns, each made up of five Company servants advised by provincial *diwans*; beneath these councils, Indian deputies were supposed to conduct revenue and judicial affairs in the hinterlands. Hastings viewed the provincial councils as a temporary expedient, and hoped that when the Company's authority became better entrenched, Company servants could be finally withdrawn to Calcutta.[81]

The ancient constitution of law

Despite the rhetoric of benevolent interest in the welfare of the peasantry, the revenue farms suggested that the Company was in effect renting out its territorial powers to the highest bidder (often its own commercial partners) in each locality. Hastings and the COC sought to counteract this perception, and to bolster their rhetoric of 'security of property', in a new plan for the administration of justice. Hastings viewed the judicial plan as an essential corollary to the revenue farms. It was supposed to establish a competent network of law courts which would assist in the liquidation of debts at interest, deal with disputes between *raiyats* and farmers or between farmers and government officers, and to decide on questions of inheritance.[82]

---

[77] Datta, *Society, Economy and the Market*, p. 334.
[78] Hastings to G. Colebrooke, Ft William, 26 March 1772, BL Add. MSS 29,127, fo. 14r.
[79] Hastings to J. Dupré, Ft William, 6 January 1773, ibid., fos. 62v–63r.
[80] Misra, *Central Administration of the East India Company*, p. 119.
[81] Hastings to L. Sulivan, 10 March 1774, BL Add. MSS 29,127, fo. 119.
[82] Hastings to J. Graham, 23 July 1772, BL Add. MSS 29,125, fo. 116v.

But the institution of new law courts raised profound problems of authority and legality. On the one hand, most Company servants thought that indigenous law courts under the supposedly despotic rule of the Mughals and *nawabs* were thoroughly degenerate. In 1773, a committee of the House of Commons, after consulting widely among returned Company servants, concluded that the administration of justice even during 'the vigour of the Mogul Government' was in 'a great measure discretionary' and 'liable to great Abuse and Oppression'.[83] On the other hand, the introduction of a 'foreign' system of law was widely regarded as impractical; and it was far from clear that the Company government, whether considered as *diwan* of the Mughal empire, or as delegates of a chartered Company, had sufficient constitutional authority to remodel local judicatures.

Hastings and the COC confronted these difficulties by implying that their judicial plan aimed to restore and improve existing courts, rather than overturn them. They claimed that they 'confined themselves with scrupulous Exactness to the constitutional Terms of Judicature already established in this Province', only deviating from 'the known Forms' in order to 'recur to the original Principles' or because of 'some radical Defect in the Constitution of the Courts in being'.[84] Yet their review of the existing law courts in the *nawabi* capital of Murshidabad repeated conventional stereotypes about venal and arbitrary practices. The courts attached to the various offices of government were apparently 'never known to adhere to their prescribed bounds', but exercised conflicting and overlapping jurisdictions. The committee found that the *qazi*'s court for administering Islamic law was 'formed on wiser Maxims, and even on more enlarged Ideas of Justice, and civil Liberty, than are common to the despotic Notions of Indian Governments'. If the presiding judges disagreed over a decision, the case was referred to a 'general assembly' of legal experts, but the COC decided that, in practice, this assembly rarely met. A major problem with all these courts, according to the COC, was that they exercised no effective jurisdiction beyond the bounds of Murshidabad. Thus, they thought that the remainder of Bengal was prey to a variety of dubious claimants to judicial authority, including *zamindars* and *qazis*, who had converted justice into 'Sources of private Emolument'.[85]

---

[83] '7th Report of the Secret Committee of the House of Commons, *RCHC* 4, pp. 324–5.
[84] COC to Council at Ft. William, 15 August 1772, ibid., p. 346.
[85] Ibid., p. 347.

The apparent lack of *nawabi* officers of justice in the districts was likely in part a result of the recent encroachments of the Company, which led Muhammad Reza Khan to recall many of his officers from the countryside.[86] But the COC's critique also reflected a particular 'state-centric' view of justice. Recent studies of pre-colonial Indian legal systems have described a system of 'distributive justice', in which powers of judicial determination were delegated and shared along a complex hierarchy of regional and local lordships. Much of what the British described as 'criminal law', for example, rather than constituting a distinct sphere of the state bureaucracy, was bound up with a system of military retainership. Meanwhile, the judicial apparatus of the *nawabi* coexisted with a range of other tribunals, from village *panchayats* or assemblies, to *dalapatis* enforcing regulations of caste, to the *rajbaris* or kingly courts of the Bengal *zamindars*.[87] Meanwhile, networks of Brahmin *pandits*, often patronized by *zamindars*, studied, taught and proclaimed Sanskritic legal traditions.[88]

The diversity and dispersal of forms of judicial authority in Bengal now appeared troubling to the Company. The judicial plan of 1772 invoked an idea of singular sovereign power to delegitimize forms of judicial and coercive power beyond the direct purview of the central state. For example, it described the judicial powers of *zamindars* as beyond the 'Laws of the Land' of the Mughal empire.[89] The irony of this approach was apparently lost on Company servants, who for many decades had been exercising such 'usurped' powers by administering justice in their own *zamindari* of Calcutta.

Hastings claimed that the judicial plan of 1772 made only two 'material changes' 'to the Ancient Constitution of the country', by establishing a clearer distinction between civil and criminal law, and moving the central law courts to Calcutta.[90] To replace the several overlapping jurisdictions the COC found in Murshidabad (which they interpreted as three for property disputes and one for criminal law), the judicial plan created two chief courts for Bengal — a *diwani sadr adalat*

[86] Khan, *Transition in Bengal*, p. 267.
[87] Radhika Singha, *A Despotism of Law: Crime and Justice in Early Colonial India* (Delhi, 1998); see also Singha, 'Civil Authority and Due Process: Colonial Criminal Justice in the Banaras Zamindari, 1781–95', in Anderson and Guha (ed.), *Changing Concepts of Rights and Justice in South Asia* (Delhi, 2000), pp. 30–81.
[88] S. Sinha, *Pandits in a Changing Environment* (Calcutta, 1993).
[89] COC to Council at Ft William, 15 August 1772, *RCHC*, 4, p. 347. The Company did, however, allow *zamindars* and farmers to hear and determine very small disputes, concerning property under Rs 10.
[90] Hastings to J. Dupré, Ft William, 6 January 1773, BL Add. MSS 29,127, fo. 64r.

(chief civil court) and a *nizamat sadr adalat* (chief criminal court). These would both sit in Calcutta, acting as courts of appeal for lower civil and criminal courts sitting in the districts in Bengal. Each district would have two courts, a *mofussil diwani adalat* 'for the Cognizance of Civil Causes' and a *faujdari adalat* 'for the Trial of all Crimes and Misdemeanours'.[91] The civil courts would be presided over by the Company officials, senior council members in the chief *adalat* and collectors in the districts. (After the withdrawal of collectors in 1773, the five provincial councils presided over *diwani* courts, and Indian deputies held courts in the districts.) In the criminal courts, which in theory remained as part of the *nizamat* branch of government under the *nawabs*, Muslim law officers (*qazis* and *muftis*) would preside, but even these criminal courts came under the supervisory control of Governor Hastings.

The judicial plan picked up on earlier efforts by the Company to crackdown on apparently unregulated local officials. As before, the Company's strong conception of prerogatives of sovereignty coincided with its fiscal parsimony. The practice of taking *chauth*, or a percentage of the value of monies recovered in some civil suits, much derided by Company officials, was prohibited, together with the exaction of fees by law officers.[92] Instead, Indian officers of the courts were to be supported by salaries, the highest of which were set at Rs 100 per month, compared to several thousand rupees in official earnings for some Company servants. Yet despite the rhetorical aspiration for a more 'equal' administration of justice, it remained unclear in practice how the Company's scattered courts would achieve this. Collection of revenues remained the Company's first priority, and the new courts were expressly discouraged from intervening in revenue farms, especially during the crucial harvest months. The protection of peasant rights through *pattas* or revenue contracts, theoretically enforceable in the courts, remained a dead letter.[93]

After the rhetorical assertion of the exclusive rights of sovereignty, the most important and subsequently famous goal of the 1772 judicial plan was the preservation of indigenous laws. Clause XXIII of the new regulations stipulated that 'in all suits regarding Inheritance, Marriage, Caste and all other religious Usages or Institutions, the Laws of the Koran with respect to Mahometans, and those of the Shaster with respect to Gentoos shall be invariably adhered to'. 'Moulavies or Brahmins attending on the court' would expound the law in

[91] 'Plan for the Administration of Justice', *RCHC*, 4, p. 348.
[92] Ibid., p. 349.   [93] McLane, *Land and Local Kingship*, pp. 210–11.

these cases.[94] This provision has been viewed as the foundation of the modern development of Hindu and Muslim 'personal laws' in colonial India, and much attention has been given to explaining its intellectual origins. Bernard S. Cohn argued that the clause reflected Hastings' fundamentally 'theocratic' view of Indian society.[95] J. D. M. Derrett suggested that the specification of certain reserved topics as subject to 'religious' law may have echoed the role of 'ecclesiastical courts' in English legal practice.[96] Historians have broadly agreed, however, that subsequent British patronage of Sanskrit and Arabic legal treatises tended eventually to privilege certain classical or scriptural versions of Hindu and Muslim law over more diverse forms of royal and customary law existing in pre-colonial India.

That indigenous laws were related to different faith traditions appeared obvious to Company officials. Since 1753, after jurisdictional disputes between the Mayor's Court and the *zamindar*'s court in Calcutta, the categories of 'Hindu' and 'Muslim' had defined those inhabitants of the Company's settlement who were exempted in most cases from the jurisdiction of the English Mayor's Court.[97] Legal regimes in Calcutta and the other 'presidency towns' were supposed to protect the right of indigenous peoples to their own law. Warren Hastings also seems to have had the sense, perhaps derived from observing the workings of the law in the Calcutta courts, that 'Hindu' law (at least in Bengal) was a relatively uniform institution. In a revealing letter written from Madras, before he was appointed governor of Bengal, Hastings wrote that 'if I mistake not the Shaster is their [the 'Gentoos'] Law for all their Casts and the Professors of it competent Judges to decide in all cases'.[98]

There was, however, a more immediate context for Clause XXIII in the 1772 judicial plan. It seems very likely that this provision related back to a recent exchange, in the spring of 1772, between the Calcutta council and Muhammad Reza Khan, the *naib diwan*, over the correct administration of law according to Mughal custom. One source of contention was the attempt by the Company to encourage the use of arbitration to settle civil suits. In March 1772, Reza Khan insisted that some kinds of cases were not amendable to arbitration, but rather

---

[94] 'Plan for the Administration of Justice', *RCHC*, 4, p. 350.
[95] Cohn, *Colonialism and its Forms of Knowledge*, p. 65.
[96] J. D. M. Derrett, *Religion, Law and the State in India* (New York, 1968), pp. 233–4.
[97] M. P. Jain, *Outlines of Indian Legal History*, p. 60.
[98] Hastings to Major Grant, Ft St George, 19 October 1770, BL Add. MSS 29,125, fos. 57v–58r. He was comparing this relative unity of the Hindus in Bengal with the schismatic tendencies of the 'left' and 'right' caste groups of Madras.

fell 'under the Cognizance of the Magistrate' to be 'enquired into by People acquainted with the Laws of religion and the Precepts of the Commentators'.[99] The Bengal council apparently agreed with Reza Khan on this point, and in May 1772, Reza Khan affirmed that it was 'proper and adviseable' that matters concerning 'Inheritance, Marriages and other Disputes, which can be determined by the Express Dictates of Mahomedan Religion, should be decided by a Magistrate, the Religious officers and men of Learning'.[100] This exchange was referred to in 1773 by the committee of the House of Commons investigating judicial administration in Bengal, which suggests that committee members understood it to be part of the relevant background to the judicial plan.[101] It is significant, too, that regulation XXIII of the judicial plan, referring to the reserved cases in which Muslim and Hindu law would be applied, immediately followed a regulation encouraging the appointment for arbitrators to resolve commercial disputes. This genealogy also fitted with the Company's concern to justify its measures by reference to the 'ancient Mughal constitution'.

Clause XXIII appears, therefore, to be connected to Muhammad Reza Khan's notion that certain categories of civil cases were not amenable to arbitration but should fall under the purview of proper religio-legal authorities. Yet the Company's attempt to extend the logic of Reza Khan's ideas to the Hindu law drew sharp criticisms from the *naib diwan*. In 1771, the directors issued orders that all legal officials, including *qazis* and Brahmin *pandits*, should be issued with *sanads* of appointment and officially registered, and also be prevented from imposing 'arbitrary fines' on litigants.[102] In response, Reza Khan argued that the official appointment of Brahmins as law officers would be 'an innovation in Mohammedan laws and religion', that Muslims had the power to decide all disputes in the empire and that disputes among Hindus were often decided 'agreeable to the Mahommedan Laws'. Even such cases 'as relate to the Customs of their Cast, their Rules of Society and the like after being referred to the arbitration of Bramins and People of their own Cast are ultimately decided by Mussulmen'.[103]

Responding to these assertions, Warren Hastings and his council tried to reassure Reza Khan that 'all cases of inheritance, marriage or other

[99] 'Representation from the Naib Duan', MP, 26 March 1772, OIOC, IOR G/27/6.
[100] 'Naib Duan's Representation', MP, 4 May 1772, OIOC, IOR G/27/7.
[101] '7th Report of the Secret Committee of the House of Commons', RCHC, 4, pp. 328–9.
[102] See the account of this exchange in Khan, *Transition in Bengal*, pp. 270–2.
[103] 'Representation from the Naib Duan', MP, 26 March 1772, OIOC, IOR G/27/6.

matters for which Mahomedan law has made a provision', would be decided by established magistrates, who would also decide such cases for Hindus, 'assisted by Bramins', 'the invariable practice of all Mohamedan Governments in India'.[104] Muhammad Reza Khan, however, was not satisfied with the Company's clarification. His angry reaction posited a very different interpretation of the workings of law in the Mughal empire. Reza Khan strongly denied the Company's argument that Muslim magistrates were commonly assisted by Brahmins 'throughout the whole Indian empire'. On the contrary, he claimed that 'none of the former Emperors down to the present ever appointed a Brahmin to assist a Magistrate'; such a practice would be 'repugnant to the Rules of the Faith'.[105] In Reza Khan's view of Mughal justice, the emperors tolerated non-Muslim customs, but they could not allow these to impinge on the law of the 'true faith'. 'The Magistrate does not compel them to come and complain. But when their Disputes cannot be settled by their Brahmins & the Heads of their Casts, they complain to the Magistrates from whose decrees they cannot deviate.' Once they appealed to a Muslim magistrate, 'was the magistrate to disregard the Rules and Usages of his Jurisdiction and conform in his Decree with the Determinations of a Brahmin, the Foundation of the System of Justice, which has for a long Series of Time been binding on the whole Body of the People whether Mussulmen or Jentoos, must undergo a subversion'. But if Hindus decided matters among themselves, however, 'it is not the Business of the Magistrate' to interfere.[106]

Reza Khan's abhorrence of British judicial 'innovation' was part of his wider rearguard action against the Company's progressive encroachments on the powers of the *nawabs* and their servants. It is unclear what distortions were introduced by British translators of his views, or indeed how much this prescriptive view of Mughal justice corresponded to actual practice. What appeared to be at stake for Reza Khan was the integrity of imperial authority, as expressed through 'Mussulmen magistrates' throughout the empire. There was a strong link, in this view, between the emperor's authority and the 'Rules of the Faith'. There are reasons to be very wary of taking this to mean that Mughal governments routinely imposed the tenets of Islamic law on non-Muslims. Not only

---

[104] President and Council's letter of 13 April 1772, cited in Khan, *Transition in Bengal*, p. 271.

[105] 'In a country under the dominion of a Mussulman Emperor it is improper that any order should be issued inconsistent with the rules of his faith, that any innovations should be introduced in the administration of justice'. 'Naib Duan's Representation', Murshidabad Factory Records, 4 May 1772, OIOC IOR, G/27/7.

[106] Ibid.

did Reza Khan allow for dispute resolution within Hindu communities distinct from the state's law, but there is also substantial evidence that Muslim magistrates in Mughal Bengal were careful not to disturb Hindu law and custom in cases pertaining to Hindus.[107] Moreover, 'the rules and usages of his [the magistrate's] jurisdiction' were unspecified, and likely referred to a flexible system of imperial jurisprudence rather than a rigid code of specifically 'Islamic' law.[108]

Reza Khan went on to give a more developed account of the reason for maintaining the authority of Muslim magistrates even in cases pertaining to Hindus. The first issue was the necessity of maintaining the authority of the emperor, which was tied to the 'Rules of the Faith'. Second, the imperial magistrates possessed far greater 'exactness and accuracy' than the Brahmins. Third, if Brahmins were appointed to assist magistrates, this would be a source of 'continual contentions' within the government. Fourth, what Reza Khan called the 'Sect of the Gentoos' had a number of 'different tribes' listed as 'Bengallees, Hindoostanees, Khetrees, Kashmerees, Guzerattees & ca.', whereas the local Brahmins were mainly Bengalis. 'Each separate Tribe has its own distinct Customs and Laws'. Reza Khan thus anticipated later critiques of the British notion of a unified Hindu law, noting the great variations of customary law within different 'Hindu' groups.[109]

From Reza Khan's perspective, the system that modern historians have described as a layered or dispersed sovereignty in pre-colonial Indian states, allowing for forms of judicial authority below the level of Mughal magistrates, worked to insulate Islamic rulers from the polluting effects of an alien law. The British, on the other hand, with their stern view of singular sovereignty, were setting themselves up as arbiters between Muslim and Hindu, and eventually, as arbiters of what both the Muslim and Hindu law would entail. The realignment and restructuring of the state was as dramatic and disastrous as could be from Reza Khan's perspective, and as uncontroversial and necessary as could be in the eyes of Warren Hastings.

This exchange, perhaps more than any other, showed how colonial state-building even in its early stages involved much more than the transfer of power from one government to another; rather, it went with

---

[107] Eaton, *Rise of Islam on the Bengal Frontier*, pp. 179–83.

[108] A recent study of Mughal government in the port of Surat showed the centrality of Muslim *sharia* law to the rituals of Mughal sovereignty, but also how *sharia* was in practice a fluid and contested domain of jurisprudence rather than a rigid 'code' of law. See Farhat Hasan, *State and Locality in Mughal India. Power Relations in Western India, c. 1572–1730* (Cambridge, 2004), pp. 71, 128.

[109] 'Naib Duan's Representations', MP, 4 May 1772, OIOC, IOR G/27/7.

a profound disjuncture in political ethics. Britons like Warren Hastings imagined themselves as tolerant, enlightened rulers; in his view, the wisest of Muslim conquerors had protected and nurtured indigenous Hindu laws, and he was doing the same. Yet Hastings' understanding of religious and legal tolerance was predicated on the exclusive domain of legal sovereignty and on the notion of distinct categories of religio-legal subject-hood under a single sovereign state. Reza Khan's vision of a unified body of the people under imperial sovereignty suggested a different model of a multicultural polity, with Muslim magistrates and imperial law standing at the supreme final point of dispute resolution, but allowing for the self-regulation of different communities.

Muhammad Reza Khan was arrested soon after this exchange, while Hastings and the Company rejected his scruples about appointing Brahmin *pandits* as public officials. Moreover, despite Reza Khan's objections to the employment of Brahmins, Warren Hastings continued to justify his judicial plan by reference to the ancient Mughal constitution. Towards the end of 1772, he became increasingly concerned that parliamentary intervention would supersede his own regulations. In October he wrote to a colleague that 'a new judicature, and a new code of Laws are framing at home, on Principles diametrically opposite to ours, which is little more than a Renewal of the Laws and Forms established of old in the Country'.[110] He regarded his own measures as 'simple, and adapted to the Customs and understandings of the People', but he feared that parliament would try to 'subject the Natives of Bengal to the Laws of England'.[111]

As it turned out, Hastings' fears dramatically overestimated the interest of British ministers in creating a new form of government in Bengal. Yet even as late as March 1774, Hastings was concerned enough about the prospects of a 'new judicature' to write what became a very famous letter to the Lord Chief Justice, Lord Mansfield. This letter showed how the effort to legitimize the Company government by reference to an ancient Mughal constitution could work to modify cruder stereotypes about Asiatic despotism. Hastings criticized the view of many British writers that Indians were 'governed by no other principle of justice than arbitrary wills, or uninstructed judgements'. The 'Hindoos' or 'original inhabitants of Hindostan', he wrote, possessed written laws 'which have continued unchanged, from the remotest antiquity'. Brahmin 'professors of these laws, who are spread over the whole empire of Hindostan', 'suffered no diminution from the

---

[110] Hastings to J. Dupré, Ft William, 8 October 1772, BL Add. MSS 29,125, fo. 157r.
[111] Hastings to L. Sulivan, 11 November 1772, BL Add. MSS 29,127, fo. 46r.

introduction of Mohammedan government'; rather, Muslim rulers had left 'the people to remain in quiet possession' of their ancient laws. In the Company's administration, 'no essential change was made to the ancient constitution of the province'. Interestingly, in an apparent reference to Muhammad Reza Khan's opinions, Hastings stated that *pandits* did not by 'the practice of this country' act as judges in law courts, but only as 'expounders of the Hindoo law', giving opinions to recognized magistrates. Meanwhile, the Muslim law, which Hastings regarded as the 'guide at least of one fourth of the natives', was 'as comprehensive, and as well defined, as that of most states in Europe'.[112]

Hastings also sent Mansfield part of a new 'code of Gentoo laws' commissioned from a 'synod' of 10 of 'the most learned pundits' who had been invited from 'different parts of the province' to Calcutta.[113] This code was then translated from Sanskrit (which no Briton could read at this stage) into Persian, and from Persian into English by the Company servant Nathaniel Halhed.[114] Halhed's translation, which was published in England in 1776, was both a propaganda exercise designed to represent Hastings and the Company as benevolent stewards of ancient laws, and a guide for British officials presiding over the Company's courts. While the compilation became a point of reference for Company officials, it was not regarded as authoritative by many *pandits*, and was viewed even by many Britons as an inadequate guide to Hindu law.[115] At this early stage of colonial state-building, the embodied authority of *pandits* or *maulavis* as interpreters of Hindu and Muslim laws was more important to the working of the Company's courts than translated codes. Meanwhile, Hastings also patronized British translations of Muslim law books, for example, the Emperor Aurungzeb's legal digest, the *Fatawa-i Alamgiri*, and the *Hidaya* (a major text of the Hanafite school of Islamic law prevalent in Mughal India).[116] Initially, Hastings was not able to locate a good manuscript copy of the *Fatawa-i Alamgiri* (an indication, perhaps, that Aurungzeb's code was not

---

[112] Hastings to Lord Mansfield, Ft William, 21 March 1774, Gleig, *Memoirs of Warren Hastings*, vol. I, p. 404.
[113] Ibid.
[114] Nathaniel Brassey Halhed, *Code of Gentoo Laws; or Ordinations of the Pundits* (London, 1776). For Halhed's career, see Rosane Rocher, *Orientalism, Poetry and the Millennium. The Checkered Life of Nathaniel Brassey Halhed, 1751–1830* (Delhi, 1983).
[115] Derrett, *Religion, Law and the State*, pp. 240–2.
[116] Singha, *A Despotism of Law*, pp. 13–16. For Hastings' patronage of legal scholarship, see also P.J. Marshall, 'Warren Hastings as Scholar and Patron' in Anne Whiteman, J.S. Bromley and P.G.M. Dickson (eds.), *Statesmen, Scholars, and Merchants. Essays In Eighteenth Century History Presented to Dame Lucy Sutherland* (Oxford, 1973), pp. 246–8.

necessarily in widespread use in Bengal before the Company took it up).[117]

Hastings' attempt to produce authoritative codes or digests of legal opinions fitted with his broader project of asserting the exclusive rights of the sovereign state to administer public justice. A tendency to homogenize Indian 'tradition' was thus inherent in his sense of a comprehensive and undivided sovereignty. Hastings and Halhed also tended to emphasize the universal authority of Brahmin *pandits* among the Hindus, noting how they were worshipped 'almost to the point of idolatry' by superstitious 'Gentoos'.[118] In turn, Hastings thought that the *pandits* were so attached to the ancient Sanskrit texts of the 'Shaster' that they could not be prevailed upon to revise certain passages 'to render them fit for the public eye'.[119] Interestingly, Hastings seems to have viewed the 'Shaster' not as a set of fixed rules, but rather as containing 'the Principles upon which many of their Laws were formed'.[120] Similarly, Halhed thought that Brahminical laws derived authority not just from ancient texts but also because they represented the customary forms of law actually in use in Bengal.[121] It may well be, therefore, that Hastings and Halhed understood the 'Hindu' law as an expression of both scripture and custom, or of ancient principles applied through the reason of the *pandits*. This model of law suggested an analogy with the English common law, as ancient custom proved in the reasoning of the courts; yet, in its 'Asiatic' form, customary law was seen to be overdetermined by religious superstition.[122]

The Company's patronage of Brahmin *pandits* and Hindu laws eventually had important effects on British perceptions of their government in Bengal. By the 1780s and 1790s, as British Sanskritists like William Jones came to be seen as significant outriders of the European enlightenment, the idea of the emancipation of the Hindus from 'bigoted' Muslims would gain in prominence. In the 1770s, however, when

---

[117] Hastings to S. Middleton, 22 July 1774, BL Add. MSS 29,125, fo. 336v.
[118] Halhed, *Code of Gentoo Laws*, p. x.   [119] Hastings' preface, ibid., p. iv.   [120] Ibid.
[121] See Halhed, *Code of Gentoo Laws*, p. xi, where Halhed argued that 'long usage' had persuaded the Hindus of the equity of their laws.
[122] Jon E. Wilson has argued that this common-law mentality informed the 'digests' of Hindu law made in the 1780s and 1790s by William Jones; the law was viewed as 'the custom of the country' not just as unchanging scriptural prescription. See Wilson, 'Governing Property, Making Law, Land, Local Society and Agrarian Discourse in Colonial Bengal' (unpublished Ph.D. thesis, Oxford, 2000), pp. 184–94. In this context, Hastings' comment to Mansfield that Hindu laws had continued 'unchanged, from the remotest antiquity', may have implied continuity rather than stasis; in this sense, English common law was also regarded as 'unchanged' since time immemorial.

British understandings of their rule were still tied to the 'legal forms of Mogul government', this narrative had more limited play. Even so, we can see the seeds of this view in Nathaniel Halhed's poem from around 1773, 'The Bramin and the Ganges'. In this poem, the river goddess urges a melancholy Brahmin, suffering under Muslim tyranny, to embrace the rule of his enlightened and tolerant new masters, the British.[123] A short 'preliminary discourse' to Halhed's *Code*, supposedly written by the Brahmins themselves, also expressed gratitude to the Company for patronizing Hindu laws and contrasted this with the intolerance of Muslim rulers. Here, Muhammad Reza Khan's account of the supremacy of Muslim magistrates is echoed with a very different valence; 'the Laws of Mahomed were the Standard of Judgement for the Hindoos. Hence Terror and Confusion found a Way to all the People, and Justice was not impartially administered'.[124] Interestingly, the Sanskrit original of this preface, if it ever existed, no longer survives.[125] While it is important not to impose anachronistic ideas of unified and antagonistic 'communal' identities on this period, it is likely that critiques of Mughal rule, which drew on Hindu religious symbols and images, did exist in Bengal.[126] Over time, the new British rulers forged a narrative of colonial justification which posited Hindus as ancient inhabitants of India, long suffering under the yoke of Muslim 'invaders'. When the language of Mughal constitutionalism eventually broke down, this alternative narrative would increasingly take its place.

Questions to the natives and the custom of the country

Because the 1772 judicial plan has often been regarded as the originary moment of Anglo-Indian law, historians have tended to overestimate its clarity and coherence, and to underestimate how many aspects of judicial administration remained uncertain and ill-defined after 1772. As we have seen, the judicial plan was supposed to represent a reversion to the ancient constitution, which meant that outstanding issues arising

---

[123] Rosane Rocher, 'Alien and Empathetic: The Indian Poems of N. B. Halhed', in B. B. King and M. N. Pearson (eds.), *The Age of Partnership* (Honolulu, 1979), pp. 215–35.
[124] Halhed, *Code of Gentoo Laws*, p. 4.
[125] This is according to a personal communication with Dr Rosane Rocher, who made an extensive study of the genesis of Halhed's code.
[126] There are hints of this in Bengali *mangalkabyas*, long narrative poems often produced in the *zamindari* courts; McLane writes that 'Bharatchandra's Annadamangal, completed in 1752–3, suggested that the Maratha invasions had been a Hindu crusade to punish the Yavannas (Muslims) for damaging temples at Bhubaneshwar in Orissa in Alivardi's reign'. McLane, *Land and Local Kingship*, p. 174.

from the operation of the courts would raise further questions about earlier Mughal and *nawabi* custom. The boundaries between 'religious' law and the constitutional or administrative laws of the Mughal empire remained to be worked out in detail. Indeed, one crucial test case from 1773 raised exactly the question of the relationship between 'religious' law and constitutional practice. In resolving the case, the Company council deployed a particular investigative methodology, by placing written questions about the 'custom of the country' before selected Indian informers. This way of proceeding by 'questions to the natives' was designed both to decide a particular dispute and to perform the constitutionality of the Company government.

In a sign of Hastings' concern to recentre power in the Company's headquarters in Calcutta, the judicial plan of 1772 reserved all disputes over the succession of *zamindars* and *taluqdars* for the ultimate decision of the governor and council sitting as a 'revenue board'. In January 1773, the council was asked to decide over contradictory claims to the *zamindaris* of Mysadel and Tamluk, in the division of Hughli. These were potentially very valuable rights because Mysadel and Tamluk were major centres of salt production.[127] The dispute arose from a petition of Ramchurn Roy, a long-term ally of the Company, who had served as *banyan* to leading Company servants and military officers.[128] During his residence at Allahabad with General Richard Smith, Ramchurn had managed to procure *sanads* from the Mughal emperor himself for the *zamindaris* of Mysadel and Tamluk.[129] In January 1773, he asked the Company to confirm him in these possessions, which he had not yet taken up, noting his former loyal service to the Company. He also claimed that the present incumbents were two elderly widows who had never been confirmed by the Company's *sanad*, and who, because they were women, had no right to the inheritance according to the 'established Regulations of the Country, that Women shou'd not be the Acting Officers of the Government, excepting in cases where they are Guardians to Lawful heirs during their Minority'. If granted possession, Ramchurn promised to maintain the widows with an allowance deposited in the Company's treasury.[130]

Ramchurn's petition, founded on loyal service, Mughal authority and the claims of patriarchy, was referred by the revenue board to the 'superintendent of the *khalsa*', the Company servant charged with

---

[127] N. K. Sinha (ed.), *Selections from District Records. Midnapur Salt Papers. Hijli and Tamluk, 1781–1807* (Calcutta, 1984).
[128] 'Petition of Ramchurn Roy', BRC, 12 January 1773, OIOC, IOR P/49/38, pp. 562–8.
[129] Ibid., p. 564.   [130] Ibid., p. 565.

overseeing the central revenue and accounting offices, which had recently been moved to Calcutta. The superintendent discovered a complex web of local claimants based on kinship and inheritance. In Mysadel, the current holder was Rani Janooky, the widow of the last male *zamindar*. In Tamluk, Kisna Pareea held the 9 *anna* division of the *zamindari* as the widow of the last male *zamindar*, but neither she nor her husband had ever had possession of the smaller 7 *anna* branch. Meanwhile, Annund Narrain, the last heir in a younger branch of the family, who had apparently been adopted by Kisna Pareea, claimed the smaller division.[131] Interestingly, the superintendent found that both *zamindaris* had been disputed between rival claimants in the past few years. The Company had previously inquired into the rights of Rani Janooky after complaints that she was not truly the widow of the previous *zamindar*.[132] These disputes suggest both how the political revolutions of recent years had contributed to an unsettled environment for land rights, and also that female landholders may have been especially vulnerable to attacks on their rights.

Faced with the conflicting claims of Ramchurn's petition, and the local heirs and heiresses, the revenue board resolved to put a series of questions to different types of Indian officials and authorities.[133] These questions and answers were then recorded in the proceedings of the board and were used to extract general principles and precedents for future cases. The questions revolved around two main issues. First, whether the source of *zamindari* right lay in legal inheritance according to 'lineal descent' independent of government fiat, or whether legal succession to *zamindaris* required an act of government to establish the right. Second, the questions probed the rights of females and minor branches to inherit *zamindar* property, and asked at what point vacated estates reverted to government.[134]

Initially, the questions were put to the leading Indian officials of the *khalsa*, the *rai raiyan* (the head officer) and *qanungos* (a kind of imperial registrar), who were accustomed to investigating disputes over land rights, and whose responsibilities included issuing and registering *sanads* to *zamindars* and *taluqdars*. The council asked them to answer the questions 'according to the usage of the Country Government of Bengal'.[135]

---

[131] The 'pedigrees' of each family were eventually attached to the resolutions of the Board of Revenue Consultations, BRC, 11 June 1773, OIOC IOR P/49/40, pp. 2097–100.

[132] Superintendent's minute, BRC, 9 February 1773, OIOC IOR P/49/38, p. 795.

[133] BRC, 6 April 1773. These consultations, and those of 1 June, also pertaining to the same inquiry, are reproduced in 'Extracts from the Consultations of the Committee of Revenue Relative to the Administration of Justice', BL Add. MSS 29,079, fos. 4r–9v.

[134] Ibid., fo. 4v.   [135] Ibid., fo. 4v.

As befitted officers of the state treasury, the answers of the *rai raiyan* and *qanungos* took a relatively expansive view of royal authority. They posited the ultimate right of 'the king' to dispose of the lands of Bengal as he wished, even though principles of justice would generally lead him to uphold the claims of just inheritors. 'After the Death of a Zemindar the Zemindarry devolves to his son, although the Country belongs to the King, and he may indeed give it to whom he pleases, yet it is neither conformable to justice nor to the Custom of the Country that he give it to any other, in case the deceased Zemindar has left a son.' It was usual for sons to seek a *sanad* from the ruler recognizing his succession. Wives and daughters could also inherit (though it was 'not normal' for them to take possession themselves). Brothers and brother's sons could inherit if they were appointed as heirs by the previous *zamindar*. The *khalsa* officers also listed the different occasions on which the government might dispossess *zamindars*, including if someone had wrongly obtained a *sanad* by intrigue, or if a *zamindar* defaulted on revenue or otherwise 'offended against his Majesty'. In these cases, or if there were no heirs, the king could dispose of the lands to 'whomsoever he pleases'.[136]

Parts of these answers might seem to have favoured Ramchurn's petition in their expansive conception of the king's prerogative; at the same time, they suggested that lineal inheritance was regarded both as the usual course and the most just. The much briefer answers of the four *pandits*, who were asked to decide by reference 'to the Laws of the Gentoos', clearly reinforced the claims of the 'natural' heirs. Their answers listed the rightful heirs in order of precedence 'according to the Shaster': first son, then wife, grandson and daughter. Younger brothers and their descendants could also succeed, and while there were proper heirs, the property could not revert to government. The *pandits* professed incompetence to decide on the role of the king in the process of inheritance. 'Whether or not the King's Sunnud is necessary to put him in possession is not written in the Shaster'.[137]

The council apparently decided that they needed further clarification about the proper procedure to be followed in the case, because in June, they met to consider the answers of Muhammad Reza Khan and Shitab Rai. Conveniently enough, the former *naib diwans* were currently under house arrest in Calcutta being investigated for fraud and corruption; apparently, however, they were still valued as authentic witnesses to the ancient constitution. Muhammad Reza Khan based his answers

---

[136] Ibid., fos. 5v–6r.   [137] Ibid., fo. 6v.

on 'the Law of the Coran', detailing the rights of descendants according to the 'famous Magistrates and doctors' of Islamic law.[138] 'The Laws of the Coran' here seemed to indicate more than simply scriptural law, but to encompass the customs of Mughal imperial government more generally. The clear tendency, again, of his answers was to uphold the claims of inheritance independent of government. The king's right was limited only to the 'established revenue'. If there was no other heir, then a daughter could succeed to the whole; otherwise she was entitled to a specific share 'as Decreed in the Holy Scriptures'. Minor branches could also inherit down to a grandson's grandson, even if they had not been in possession for many generations. The inheritor might procure a *sanad* from the king 'for the sake of establishing his Credit, and to get his name enrolled on the Records' but this did not affect the basic right of inheritance either way. Only if the *zamindar* died without connections would the property revert to the king. If a *zamindar* defaulted on the revenue, the king might appoint another relative or some other person to manage the local collections, but even in this case the *zamindari* right could not be transferred by the government, and the established perquisites should continue to be paid to the rightful owner.[139]

Muhammad Reza Khan also noted that 'Zemindars are of a different kind'; some ancient estates predated the Muslim conquests, some were granted by emperors to encourage the spread of cultivation, some were purchased and some were granted as free gifts. In all these, the *zamindar* was 'Sole property and Master', and the king had no other claim on him than rent collection. If the renter fell behind in revenue payments, the ruler might send a *sezawul* to manage the collections, but he could not dispossess the *zamindar* of the share of the rental income that was his due inheritance. According to Reza Khan, there were other kinds of 'sunnudy' *zamindars*, who had been appointed by the king to vacant lands; a *zamindar* of this kind was 'a type of public officer', and the king could dispose of his lands as he wished.[140] Finally, Shitab Rai gave his opinions on *zamindari* inheritance 'according to the Custom of the Subah of Bahar [Bihar]'. Like Reza Khan, he claimed that on the death of a *zamindar*, a son or other heir would normally succeed independently of the will of the ruler, but would also usually apply for a *sanad* from the ruler to confirm the inheritance. Shitab Rai agreed with Reza Khan on the major principle that 'The revenue belongs to the King, but the Land to the zemindar.'[141]

---

[138] Ibid., fos. 6v–8r.   [139] Ibid., fo. 7r–v.   [140] Ibid., fo. 8r–v.   [141] Ibid., fo. 9v.

These translated answers pose many problems of interpretation, not least because they were procured from Indian officials who were either in the pay of the Company or (in the case of the *naib diwans*) under coercive confinement. Yet, taken together, these answers appeared as a clear rebuke to the European tradition, following Bernier, of assuming that the Mughal emperor was the sole landowner in Hindustan and that (as Alexander Dow argued) no real property existed in India. Even if we consider *zamindari* rights as a form of co-share coexisting with other layers of proprietary interests, rather than exclusive ownership of the soil, the claim to transferable rights of property appeared well established through varied sources of administrative and customary law.

In the immediate case under discussion, these answers suggested to the Company's revenue council that *zamindaris* were at least ordinarily hereditable independent of a *sanad*, and they rejected the petition of the old banyan Ramchurn Roy, noting him as a worthy case for future indulgence. However, while they confirmed the two widows in possession, they also limited their rights of adoption. At their deaths, it was decreed that their possessions should pass not to adopted sons but to the heirs of the younger branches, or in the female line. Even though the issue of adoption had formed no part of the questions put to the indigenous experts, no adoption would henceforth be recognized without express permission of the government.[142] This was a significant move that showed both the Company's urge to centralize and standardize conceptions of right, and how within the approximate framework of local law and custom the Company could try to manoeuvre for its own advantage. In eighteenth-century Bengal, adoption was a common way for families, and especially women, to protect their inheritances both from competitors and from the greedy eyes of the government (to whom an estate might revert if there were no heirs). By seeking to limit inheritance to 'legitimate' ties of kinship, the Company would seek to impose new controls over the management of family estates.[143] Company authorities continued to be highly suspicious of female *zamindars*, whom they often regarded as aberrations within what they imagined to be a pervasive system of secluded and dependent womanhood.[144]

[142] BRC, 11 June 1773, OIOC, IOR, P/49/40, p. 2098.
[143] For similar evidence relating to the management of property held by the ruling family (*nizamat*) in Murshidabad, which over time restricted the property rights of women and slaves in particular, see Chatterjee, *Gender, Slavery and Law in Colonial India*, pp. 131–2.
[144] McLane, *Land and Local Kingship*, pp. 224–5.

The apparently sound legal foundations of *zamindar* rights in the answers of Indian experts did not by themselves dislodge deeply engrained British stereotypes about the nature of Asiatic despotism. Even though Warren Hastings thought that Dow's plan for a general sale of land would be an 'infamous oppression' that would 'distress the Zemindars of their hereditary possession', he still felt able to claim in 1774 that landed property 'by the Constitution is solely vested in the Government'.[145] In a later document, prepared in the context of his impeachment trial, Hastings tried to reconcile an idea of *zamindar* property as usually hereditary, with an absolutist view of the imperial prerogative 'to alienate or assume a zemindarry'.[146] Hastings invoked the 1773 answers of the *rai raiyan* and *qanungos* to argue for an extra-legal power of dispossession 'conformable to the fundamental principle of Despotism' that 'the Check must be in his [the supreme magistrate's] own Breast'.[147] He also made a marginal note in his copy of the answers of Muhammad Reza Khan in 1773. Beside Reza Khan's assertion that it was not 'in the King's power' to dispose of land as he pleased, Hastings wrote that 'This must be an error in Translation, as the sense evidently shows that it can only mean legal power.'[148] Nonetheless, Muhammad Reza Khan's stern view of the limits of royal right would eventually provide crucial ammunition for Hastings' rivals as they tried to portray the 1772 revenue farms as a tyrannical usurpation of ancient rights of property.[149]

The reinvention of Mughal government: courts, criminals and the police

It was one thing for Warren Hastings to generate paper plans for the administration of justice in the districts, but quite another to mobilize sufficient local resources to enact his plans. Most historians have assumed that the implementation of the judicial plan remained very

---

[145] Hastings to L. Sulivan, 11 November 1772, and 10 March 1774, BL Add. MSS 29,127, fos. 45v, 124v.

[146] See 'A Definition of the Nature of the Office of a Zamindar: sent for the use of Mr Pitt, a day or two before the 13th June, 1786, on which day he used it and voted for the Benares article (in Warren Hastings' hand-writing)', BL Add. MSS 29,202, fos. 32–7.

[147] Ibid., pp. 32r–v.   [148] BL Add. MSS 29,079, fo. 6v.

[149] Philip Francis included the 1773 'answers of the natives' as an appendix to his famous 'Plan for the Settlement of the Revenues' of 1776. Philip Francis, *Original Minutes of the Governor General in Council . . . January, 1776* (London, 1985), p. 73. Francis' views are discussed further in chapter 4.

sketchy in the 1770s.[150] Hastings remained deeply suspicious of Company servants stationed in the districts. He preferred to appoint Indian officials and feared that the provincial councils, like the collectors before them, would become unregulated tyrannies.[151] He worried that Company servants and their agents were reducing cotton weavers to a 'state of absolute, irredeemable vassalage' by forcing them to produce for the Company, and that the *adalats* (law courts) were 'made a means of supporting' such monopolies.[152] In some places, *adalats* were simply not established at all. When George Bogle took over as Collector of Rangpur in 1780, for example, he found that there was no regular *diwani adalat* in the region, but there was a great demand for one because 'the Causes [were] multiplied to a heap that makes me tremble'.[153]

In the sphere of criminal law, Hastings came closest to his ideal, as outlined in the earlier 'proposed regulations', of employing only 'native magistrates' under the watchful attention of the governor himself. The Company considered that criminal law (which was assumed to be the Muslim criminal law under the Mughal constitution) was properly under the authority of the *nizamat* rather than the *diwani*, and remained in formal terms a prerogative of the *nawab* and his servants. Hastings admitted that his inclusion of criminal law in the judicial plan of 1772 was 'almost an act of injustice', but argued that prosecution of crime was so closely connected to the revenues, and the Muslim courts 'so abominably venal', that the Company was justified in intervening.[154] 'To obviate the reproach of Irregularity', the Muslim officers of the superior criminal court (*nizamat adalat*) received *sanads* of appointment from the *nawab*.[155] Over the coming years, the Company continued to shelter behind the constitutional mask of the *nizamat*, while invoking their own conceptions of the Muslim criminal law to extend the coercive arm of the colonial state.

For Hastings this constitutional fiction offered the chance to exert his personal authority over criminal jurisprudence independent of the bureaucratic apparatus of the Company. But his attempt to reorder the *nizamat* involved him in tense negotiations with Muslim law officers.

---

[150] See, for example, McLane, *Land and local Kingship*, pp. 221–2, and Misra, *The Central Administration of the East India Company*, pp. 233–5.
[151] Hastings to L. Sulivan, 10 March 1774, BL Add. MSS 29,127, fos. 122v–123r.
[152] Hastings to Richard Barwell, Ft William, 10 June 1774, BL Add. MSS 29,125, fo. 317r.
[153] Bogle to David Anderson, Rangpur, 12 February 1780, BL Add. MSS 45,421, fo. 94v.
[154] Hastings to J. Dupré, Ft William, 8 October 1772, BL Add. MSS, 29,125, fos. 156v–157r.
[155] Hastings to J. Dupré, Ft William, 6 January 1773, BL Add. MSS 29,127, fo. 64v.

Hastings' *modus operandi* was to appoint an old servant of the *nawabs*, Sadr-ul-Haq Khan, as the *daroga* (superintendent) of the chief criminal court, and to monitor the proceedings of the new court in Calcutta.[156] Apparently, the officers of the court were from the start ambivalent about their appointments. Hastings wrote that 'it was not without much difficulty and great delay that I could prevail on the Officers of the Nizamut Adalat to open their new court'. Then, because its 'first Proceedings were likely to become a precedent for all future Cases', Hastings spent time 'revising' them in the presence of the *daroga*. Decrees which he found 'hurtful to the peace and good order of society' were 'recommended to the court for reconsideration'. Yet the law officers frequently resisted these recommendations, sticking to their own interpretations of the law. At this point, Hastings forwarded the disputed judgements to the *nawab* in Murshidabad for his final decision.[157] The elaborate formality of these proceedings, at least in Hastings' own account of them, suggested how important the performance of constitutionality had become to the Company government.

One of Hastings' major goals was to crack down on what he regarded as the pervasive problem of 'dacoity' (*dakaiti*), which he defined as a particular genre of highway robbery committed 'by a Race of Outlaws who live from Father to Son in a state of warfare against Society'. Hastings thought that the leaders of these hereditary marauders were often under 'the almost avowed Protection both of the Zemindar of the Country and the first Officers of the Country', which strongly suggests that the category of *dakaiti* comprehended diverse forms of resistance to the Company government.[158] Regulation XXXV of the Judicial Plan decreed not only that *dakaiti* should be punishable by death, but also that the families of convicted *dakaits* should be sold into slavery.[159] In justifying these harsh measures, which the COC admitted were repugnant to the 'maxims of the English constitution', Hastings and his

---

[156] For an account of Sadr-ul-Haq Khan's career, see Khan, *Transition in Bengal*, pp. 229–30. Sadr-ul-Haq was described as being old and infirm in 1778 by the contemporary historian Ghulam Husain Khan Tabatabai. He 'had become one of the Governor's acquaintances, as early as the latter's first appearance in Bengal; and at his second coming he had proved himself an assiduous worshipper at the altar of his power'. Thus, Hastings' patronage was an award for 'personal attachment'. Ghulam Husain Khan, *Seir Mutaqherin*, vol. III, p. 91.

[157] Hastings to Council at Ft William, Murshidabad, 10 July 1773, BL Add. MSS 29,127, fo. 13v.

[158] Hastings to Council at Ft William, Murshidabad, 3 August 1773, Add. MSS 29,079, fos. 14v–15r.

[159] 'Plan for the Administration of Justice', *RCHC*, 4, p. 354.

colleagues argued that the 'no Conclusion can be drawn from the English Law, that can properly be applied to the Manners and State of this Country'. They further suggested that household slavery in India was fundamentally different to plantation slavery in the Americas, and that Indian slaves were treated as 'Children' by their masters, often attaining 'a much happier State by their Slavery'.[160]

While local manners and customs were invoked to justify exemplary punishments, the Indian law officers were in fact highly reluctant to act as agents of the Company's coercive goals. They repeatedly refused to apply the death penalty on those Hastings regarded as *dakaits*, unless the robbery was also attended with murder, resting their opinions on 'the express law of the Koran'. Hastings complained about the 'lenient principals' of Muslim law, and its 'abhorrence of bloodshed'.[161] He was further frustrated by other aspects of the decision making of the law officers, for example, their view (justified by the 'opinion of the Haneefa') that 'killing is not Murder unless it is performed by an Instrument formed for distructions'. Hastings preferred to judge murder according to the conventional English measure of intention to kill, and he claimed that many Hanafite scholars and other 'learned men' among Muslims also agreed. Yet he was unable 'to persuade our Judges of the Nizamut to adopt this Principal'.[162]

When Hastings visited the *nawab*'s court in Murshidabad in the summer of 1773, he found that the *nawab* had not yet affixed his warrant to any of the decrees of the superior criminal court, 'not chusing to confirm such of the decrees as I had objected to without consulting me upon the subject', but at the same time 'being advised not to deviate from the Law to which the first decrees were conformable'. Hastings ordered him to 'follow the advice which was given him', and immediately sign the decree, which he did, presumably rejecting Hastings' interpolated death sentences. At this point, Hastings sought further authority from the Calcutta council to interpose his preferred sentences independently of the *nawab*. His justification was partly the superior responsibility of the 'Sovereign power' of the Company, but partly also what he perceived as the established practice of Muslim rulers 'to interpose and by his mandate to correct the Imperfection' in the Muslim law.[163]

[160] Extract from Proceedings of Committee of Circuit at Krishnanagar, 28 June 1772, in G. W. Forrest (ed.), *Historical Documents of British India*, 2 vols. (repr. New Delhi, 1985), p. 19.
[161] Hastings to Council at Ft William, 10 July 1773, BL Add. MSS 29,079, fo. 15.
[162] Hastings to S. Middleton, Ft William, 24 May 1773, ibid., fo. 19r–v.
[163] Hastings to Council at Ft William, 10 July 1773, ibid., fos. 13–14, 15.

The council agreed that 'in this Country it has not only been the custom but seems to be a maxim interwoven into the Constitution that every case of Importance where the precise Letter of the Law would not reach the root of the Evil should be submitted to the Justice of the Hakim or Ruler of the Country by an Express reference added to the Sentence'.[164] Hastings and the council may have been invoking the Islamic doctrine of *siyasa*, which granted the ruler an independent right to decide on cases not covered by existing provisions of *sharia* law.[165] Yet this embracing of the alleged masterly prerogative of Asiatic sovereigns was highly ironic, given the Company's rhetorical use of Asiatic despotism to justify its conquests, and also given the determination of the Muslim lawyers to apply the rules of settled law.

Hastings quickly tired of his conflicts with Muslim law officers in Murshidabad over the appropriate sentences for criminals and other matters. To exert stronger control over the sentences passed by the chief criminal court, he had the seal of the *nizamat* removed to Calcutta, and given into the custody of the *daroga* Sadr-ul-Haq Khan. The aim of this measure was to 'prevent unwarranted delay', and to 'give the Board an entire Controul over this department'.[166] The 'Controul' in reality passed to Hastings himself. In 1774, Hastings took personal charge of entirely revamping the *faujdari adalats* (criminal courts) in the districts of Bengal which he had come to regard as inefficient and corrupt. According to his plan, these courts should be staffed by Muslim law officers (*darogas, qazis* and *muftis*) and overseen by Company officials. It had been reported to him that many of the courts were not adequately staffed, and that their incumbents were sometimes absentees, ill-trained in Muslim law and prone to extort money from litigants in fines and fees. He was horrified to discover that a Hindu was acting as *daroga* in one *mofussil* court, disturbing his sense of proper forms of Mughal rule.[167] He wished to send out new men bound by official documents of appointment, 'a knowledge of the laws', an 'acquaintance with the Arabic tongue, and an unblemished reputation'.[168] Yet he declared himself incompetent to select qualified candidates in Islamic law, and insisted that the officers of the *sadr nizamat adalat* draw up lists of

[164] BRC, 31 August 1773, 'Board's reply to Governor Hastings', 29,079, fo. 21v.
[165] J. Fisch, *Cheap Lives and Dear Limbs. The British Transformation of the Bengal Criminal Law, 1769–1817* (Wiesbaden, 1983), p. 23.
[166] BRC, 23 November 1773, BL Add. MSS 29,079, fos. 22v–23r.
[167] Hastings to George Vansittart, Ft William, 18 May 1774, 20 May 1774, BL Add. MSS 29,125, fos. 301v–305r.
[168] Hastings to William Lambert, Ft William, 14 June 1774, ibid., fo. 319v.

suitable candidates to replace the existing officers of the district courts.[169]

If Hastings' interpretations of the Mughal constitution were often contested by *nawabi* elites, his attempted reforms of criminal justice reflected a certain overlap between the Company governor's sense of the proper ordering of justice, and notions of reform generated within late Mughal political culture. The idea that the institutions of the Mughal empire and of the Muslim law had become corrupted from within during the decline of Mughal power was commonplace among the Muslim intelligentsia of eastern India. The historian Ghulam Husain Khan Tabatabai, writing in the 1780s, complained that in the era of Mughal decline the honourable position of *qazi* was 'publicly put up for sale; so that people skilled in law, and in matters of distributive justice, entirely disappeared from the land'.[170] The office of the *qazi* was 'leased and under-leased' until the *qazis* became faithless bribe-takers.[171] Ghulam Husain specifically praised Hastings' efforts to root out corrupt practices in the office of *sadr ul sadr*, charged with 'watching over the capacities and morals of Cazies', which was previously being used to defraud holders of charity lands.[172]

Ghulam Husain was, however, much less impressed with Hastings' attempt to reconstitute the Mughal office of *faujdar* (literally, troop commander) as a kind of 'general Police for the Country'.[173] This was part of Hastings' broader campaign against the pervasive problem of *dakaiti*. He was frustrated that poor intelligence bedeviled his efforts to deal with rural violence and rebellion, because local landholders frequently colluded with the *dakaits*. Thus, in April 1774, Hastings appointed three *faujdars* in districts suffering from the worst disorders.[174] Yet Ghulam Husain regarded these new *faujdars* as faint shadows of the glorious Mughal past. He emphasized how *faujdars* under the Mughal empire were aristocratic figures, 'next in rank to the Nazems', appointed by the emperor himself to act as local troop commanders, and honoured by *mansabdari* rank and *jagirs* (revenue assignments). Ghulam Husain's own family had held the office in Bihar, commanding forces between 500 and 1,500 cavalry, sufficient to punish

---

[169] Hastings to Wm. Lambert, Ft William, 14 June 1774, ibid., fos. 319v–320r.
[170] Ghulam Husain, *Seir Mutaqherin*, vol. III, p. 160.
[171] Ibid., p. 165.   [172] Ibid., p. 168.
[173] Hastings to S. Middleton, Ft William, 16 April 1774, BL Add. MSS 29,125, fo. 283r. N. A. Siddiqi, 'The Faujdar and Faujdari Under the Mughals', in *Medieval India Quarterly*, 4 (1961), pp. 22–35
[174] Governor's Minute and Plan for the Establishment of Phoujdars, 19 April 1774, BL Add. MSS 29,079, fos. 26–30.

disobedient *zamindars* and chase banditti, so that the people 'enjoyed tranquility and comfort'.[175] The English, he suggested, hearing 'of the Fodjdary office, and how useful and salutary it was in former times, they have set up like offices everywhere in their dominions', in 'imitation of the ancient Princes'. Yet this was all 'to no benefit at all', for now this office was turned against 'the inhabitants of large towns and famous cities', and in trapping 'unwary people' to 'squeeze from them a few pence'.[176] They were mere thief catchers, rather than the great noble governors of old, doing jobs that were easily done in the time of Alivardi Khan by lowly officials like *kotwals* and *amils*.

Ghulam Husain's critique, like Reza Khan's critique of Hastings' judicial reforms, suggested again how British constructions of the ancient Mughal constitution adapted the lexicon of Mughal government to new uses. Ghulam Husain's critique pointed to an obvious problem in Hastings' attempt to revivify the Mughal office. The structures of patronage and military service which had sustained the Mughal nobility had been cut down; *faujdars* were no longer scions of Mughal armies, but subordinate officials dependent on the assistance of British sepoys. Hastings and the Company had cut off the head of the *nawab*'s government in Bengal, but they hoped against hope that the limbs would continue to function. Meanwhile, Hastings soon professed himself 'fatigued and plagued to death by the Fowjdarries and the Adawluts. I can confine neither to method nor the observance of orders, yet I must persevere till I have bought both into regular Channels'.[177] By the middle of 1775 only four *faujdars* were in office over the whole of Bengal, and Hastings asked to be relieved of the burdens of supervising them.[178]

Conclusion

The early years of Warren Hastings' governorship were often portrayed in old imperial histories as a moment of legislative brilliance, as a masterful imperial governor imposed his will to order on a degenerate Indian polity. By this means, Hastings was absorbed into the canon of imperial heroes, and the tyrannical excesses exposed in the later impeachment were redeemed by his far-seeing reformism and his benevolent stewardship of the natural rights of Indians to their own laws. Yet these accounts tended to erase the deep sense of pessimism and crisis

---

[175] Ghulam Husain, *Seir Mutaqherin*, Vol. III, pp. 175–9.
[176] Ibid., p. 182.
[177] Hastings to George Vansittart, 30 July 1774, BL Add. MSS 29125, fo. 339.
[178] Majumdar, *Justice and Police in Bengal*, p. 128.

that pervaded Hastings' own writings from this period, and the way that his reforms looked back to the imagined order of an earlier age of Mughal *imperium*.

After 1774, when parliamentary intervention substantially reduced Hastings' powers, and he was confronted by powerful opponents on the Bengal council, Hastings became a strident defender of his former administration. Before this, however, he was often a harsh critic of the systematic problems inherent in the Company's government. He regarded the growing powers of Company servants, young men bent on making their fortune, with alarm; the Company's commercial bureaucracy was a scant replacement for the old system of Mughal government. Company servants were ignorant of local languages and customs, but Indian complainants were powerless to resist their abuses and those of their associates; this he judged to be the 'root of all the evil which is diffused through every channel of the English government'.[179] Three years later, he was confronted by Persian treatises highly critical of the Company's administration, apparently written by partisans of Muhammad Reza Khan in Murshidabad. He admitted privately that 'one charge' came 'too near to the truth: I mean that which relates to the Exclusion of the old and experienced Muttaseddies [revenue officials] from Employment and Confidence, and the trust reposed in Servants of the English Gentlemen'.[180] Hastings' partial recognition of his Indian critics points to the anxiety at the core of his imperial project.

His centralizing initiatives in revenue and judicial administration were supposed to herald the reconstruction of a debased currency of sovereignty. Clawing back the state's prerogatives from overmighty subjects, Hastings can be compared to those British reformers who took the lead in the clearances of the Scottish highlands after the 1745 rebellion.[181] The Bengal *zamindars* with their vast domains, their law courts, their fines and market tolls, appeared to Hastings as unruly and divisive, like the Highland clan chiefs who were shorn of their distinctive hereditary jurisdictions in Hastings' teenage years. Hastings' strong sense of sovereignty carried the authentic traces of English Whiggism in the age of Blackstone. At the same time, in asserting the Company's sovereign rights, Hastings often invoked the idea of Mughal despotism to justify a reserved core of absolute power. In Hastings' view, Mughal legality, either with regard to land rights or Muslim law, was provisional

---

[179] Hastings to S. Middleton, 29 May 1774, BL Add. MSS 29,125, fo. 310r–v.

[180] Hastings to George Vansittart, 5 March 1777, BL Add. MSS 48,370, fo. 41v.

[181] For a good discussion of Whig reformers and the Highland chiefs, see Paul Langford, *A Polite and Commercial People: England, 1727–1783* (Oxford, 1989), pp. 217–18.

and subordinate to the reserved and absolute powers of sovereignty. This was an Asiatic twist on Blackstonian conceptions of unitary sovereignty which provided the essential ammunition for Hastings' later critics, notably Edmund Burke, and it would constitute one of the major themes of the later impeachment trial.

Meanwhile, the desire of the Company government to perform its constitutionality in elaborate rituals of recuperation, whether translations of indigenous legal treatises or 'questions to the natives', offered slim but significant openings for indigenous critics to insert their own alternative readings of Mughal custom into the fledgling colonial archive. Forcing the Company to confront dissonance within the official construction of the old constitution, 'native informers' provided valuable rhetorical ammunition for British critics of the Company, who would use these representations to assert the authenticity of their own views.

Between 1769 and 1774 an essential change had taken place in the politics of Bengal. After the experiment of the British supervisors in 1769, and the Company's 'standing forth' as *diwan*, the ills of Bengal could less easily simply be ascribed to the corrupt habits of degenerate Asiatic administrators. Shortfalls in the revenue collections, commercial difficulties and rural disorder were now the direct responsibility of the Company's governor and council in Calcutta and not the *naib diwans* of Murshidabad. With the assertion of sovereignty came the burdens of accountability. Hastings was keenly aware of his predicament as he faced the prospect of parliamentary legislation, and he watched with alarm the shortfalls in revenue collections under his farming scheme. He began collecting evidence about famine mortality in particular villages as a way to justify the revenue balances to the directors.[182] Yet he could not prevent the rising tide of opposition, or the redeployment of the Mughal constitution as the foundation of a substantive critique of the mercantile sovereignty of the Company.

---

[182] Hastings to Capt. Rennell, Ft William, 19 April 1774, BL Add. MSS 29,125, fo. 289v.

4 Philip Francis and the 'country government'

Around the year 1757, a Turkish man, born in Constantinople, educated in Paris, and a former servant of the French East India Company in south India, boarded an English ship in Bombay.[1] This Turk, variously known as Mustafa or Monsieur Raymond, quickly made friends with the English captain of the ship, a Mr Ranier. Mustafa described Ranier as possessing a 'general benevolence for mankind', and an 'uprightness', virtues that soon seemed to him to be 'characteristical in the English'. Captain Ranier and Mustafa became friends, partly because, in Mustafa's own words, 'I had learned his tongue with a rapidity that amazed us both';

with a mediocre dictionary and a bad grammar, I learned enough of English in the nineteen days from Bombay to Balassor, as to delight in Bolingbroke's philosophical works. The English itself is no ways Difficult, and to a man already master of some Latin and French it is a very easy acquisition.[2]

The story of a French-educated Turk, on an English ship in the Indian ocean, reading one of the pre-eminent political philosophers of eighteenth-century Britain is a vivid illustration of the dizzying transpositions involved in the expansion of British power in Asia. Mustafa stayed in Bengal, and made a fitful career out of service to high-ranking officers of the English East India Company as they laid the foundations of the British empire in India.[3] Haji Mustafa's somewhat unlikely story of his schooling in English raises the question of how British political ideas were exported to India, just as his self-presentation

---

[1] See the autobiographical account in a letter from Haji Mustafa to William McGuire, Orme Papers, OIOC, MSS Eur. OV/6, pp. 1–29.

[2] Ibid., pp. 3–4.

[3] In 1785–6, Mustafa translated the valuable contemporary history by a Mughal gentleman, Ghulam Husain Khan Tabatabai, *Seir Mutaqherin*. Apart from the above-mentioned letter in the Orme Papers, Mustafa's 'Translator's Preface', and a letter of dedication to Warren Hastings (15 February 1785), are the major sources for information about his life. Ghulam Husain Khan, *Seir Mutaqherin*, pp. 1–21.

points to the complex interactions between colonizers and colonized that constituted British Indian politics.

This chapter approaches the turbulent politics of Calcutta in the 1770s with both these issues in mind. It revisits one of the central political disputes of the British empire in India in its formative years, the extended conflict between Governor Warren Hastings and his greatest rival, Philip Francis (member of the Supreme Council of Bengal, 1774–80). The arguments between Hastings and Francis have loomed large in the historical record, because of their vituperative rhetoric, and also because of their intrinsic importance in the history of the East India Company. Philip Francis' attack on Warren Hastings raised fundamental questions about the nature of the Company government in Bengal, its relationship with the British state, and its effects on Indian society. It also laid the foundations for Hastings' later impeachment on charges of corruption in the British parliament.

Philip Francis' vigorous opposition to Warren Hastings was much studied in old imperial histories, often represented as a morality tale about the dangers of overwheening ambition and partisanship.[4] Francis was rescued from the imperialists by Ranajit Guha. His masterful study presented Francis as a sophisticated 'philosophe' eager to apply the latest theories of physiocratic political economy and agrarian improvement to the regeneration of Bengal.[5] Yet neither the old focus on personality nor Guha's high intellectualism have sufficiently accounted for the world of Haji Mustafa, oceanic politics, strange crossings and multiple identities. There is a need to situate the eruption of party disputes in Calcutta in the context of the interactive politics of colonial state-formation in Bengal, and also of broader shifts in the political culture of the British empire. This chapter argues that party disputes in Calcutta sprang from a confluence of forces pressing on the Company in Bengal. Ham-fisted efforts by the British state to discipline the overmighty Company coincided with Indian discontents, as diverse indigenous power holders tried to salvage their dignity from under the Company's fiscal and moral assaults.

These different elements were temporarily fused together through the artful rhetoric of Philip Francis, who drew on a powerful stream of British oppositionist ideology concerned with the erosion of public virtue and constitutional rights through executive abuses. In the 1760s

[4] See, for example, Ramsay Muir's attack on the 'malignity of Francis' in an introduction to the extended study by his pupil Sophia Weitzman, *Warren Hastings and Philip Francis* (Manchester, 1929), pp. xxviii–xxix.
[5] Guha, *A Rule of Property for Bengal*.

and 1770s, as the imperial state and its satellites pressed hard on metropolitan and colonial tax payers, militarizing states were generating ideological resistances throughout the British empire. Strategies of opposition that were pioneered by Haji Mustafa's long-dead English tutor, Henry St John Bolingbroke, and his 'country' party in the 1720s, were being dusted off all over the empire to express the discontents of the new era. Philip Francis drew an ideological line from these Atlantic discontents to Bengal, not least through redeploying the rhetoric of the ancient constitution in India. Francis' historical constitutionalism, long neglected by historians, represented a new milestone in the longer story of British appropriations of Mughal history for their own ends. By the 1780s, Francis' impassioned defence of the ancient rights of Indian princes and landlords was picked up by Edmund Burke and fed back into the new flowering of reformist Whiggism in London.

'To act generally for the nation'

Warren Hastings' reforms of the Bengal polity came too late to save the East India Company from parliamentary intervention. Public ferment against the Nabobs reached a new high point as Alexander Dow's and William Bolts' screeds hit the London coffee-houses. Sir George Colebrooke, the Company's chairman, was derided in the press as 'Shah Allum', a pun on the title of the Mughal emperor that alluded to Colebrooke's ill-fated speculation in alum, the white mineral salt used in dyeing.[6] In the House of Commons, committees were established to investigate the Company's affairs. One of these, General Burgoyne's select committee, became a forum for exposing the unscrupulous profiteering of Company servants, especially Lord Clive. Meanwhile, a government-appointed secret committee did the work of evaluating plausible avenues of reform for the chief minister Lord North.[7]

The resulting Regulating Act, introduced by Lord North in 1773 in the face of angry protests from the Company that its sacred chartered rights were being squandered, established a new and complicated framework for Company politics. The government acted aggressively to dampen down the heated electoral politics of East India house. The act provided for a more stable direction, and lessened the role of the turbulent court of proprietors; voting qualifications (in terms of stock holdings) were doubled, and directors were elected for longer four-year terms.

[6] C. A. Bayly (ed.), *The Raj: India and the British* (London, 1990), p. 122.
[7] Bowen, *Revenue and Reform*, pp. 133–50.

In parliament, North declared that the Company should be considered as 'farmers to the publick', for its Indian territories.[8] Yet his Regulating Act also suggested a relatively limited conception of British sovereign control over the Company government. There was no comprehensive attempt to extend the direct rule of the British crown to millions of new Indian subjects as Dow or Bolts had advocated. The act was designed to 'regulate' the East India Company rather than legislate for India. It granted a subordinate legislative authority to a newly created Supreme Council in Bengal, but this power was restricted to 'the said United Company's settlement at Fort William, and other factories and places subordinate or to be subordinate thereto'.[9] Inhabitants of the Company's settlements like Calcutta were construed as 'His Majesty's Subjects', but the rest of Bengal was presumed to be largely beyond the pale of British legislation.[10] The act simply confirmed that 'the ordering, management, and government, of all the territorial acquisitions and revenues in the said kingdoms of Bengal, Behar and Orissa' was vested in the 'Governor-general and Council', 'in like manner, to all intents and purposes whatsoever, as the same now are, or at any time heretofore might have been exercised by the President and Council or Select Committee in the said Kingdoms'.[11]

The thrust of the legislation was less therefore to provide a new constitution to Bengal, but rather to restrain the excesses of Company servants. To this end a new five-man Supreme Council was nominated in the Act of Parliament, and for the first time a Crown court, the Supreme Court of Judicature, presided over by British judges, would sit in Calcutta to have jurisdiction over 'His Majesty's Subjects in India'. To give greater cohesion to the Company's operations in India, the new Supreme Council was given supervisory powers over the Company's other Indian stations. And to bolster the separation between public and private interests in the Company government, the new councillors would be paid far more handsomely than ever before, the governor-general receiving £25,000 per annum and the other four councillors £10,000 each. This was supposed to discourage private profiteering, compensating these leading officials for regulations which forbade them to take gifts or to trade on their own account in India. After 1773 only the

---

[8] North's speech on 9 March 1773, cited in Bowen, 'A Question of Sovereignty', p. 171.
[9] Act 13 Geo.III, c. 63, *HCSP*, 24, p. 107.
[10] There was a significant exception here, which was the power granted to the new Supreme Court in Calcutta to hear complaints against Company servants or their employees in the interior; this measure is discussed more in chapter 5.
[11] Ibid., p. 94.

Lord Lieutenant of Ireland enjoyed a similarly generous salary to that of the governor-general of Bengal.[12]

The odd mixture of bold interventionism and deliberate conservatism that characterized the Regulating Act was nowhere more evident than in the choice of personnel for the Supreme Council. The existing governor, Warren Hastings, widely regarded within the Company as a sound administrator, was retained as governor-general, and another long-time Company servant, Richard Barwell was appointed councillor. The other three councillors, forming a majority, came from outside the Company service. General John Clavering (who was also appointed Commander-in-Chief of the Company's forces) and Colonel George Monson were well-connected soldiers and courtiers who had served in the West Indies and India, respectively. Philip Francis, a 33-year-old former clerk at the War Office became the most junior councillor after several others had turned down a perilous though well-paid trip to India.[13] These appointments represented a compromise between the interests of the Company (represented by Hastings and Barwell) and of the government (represented by the majority of Clavering, Monson and Francis.)[14] In fact, the new Supreme Council only succeeded in exporting to Bengal the bitter wrangling between the Company and the government which surrounded the Regulating Act at home. Hastings was furious to be associated in government 'with men strangers to the affairs of the Company and even to the Country of Bengal'.[15] The new men, meanwhile, had received from the recent inquiries of an angry parliament 'impressions very unfavourable to the existing system' in Bengal.[16] Philip Francis considered that the new men were bound to consider themselves 'the representatives of Government deputed to act generally for the nation; in contradistinction to Mr Hastings and Mr Barwell who may be supposed to act for the Company'.[17]

---

[12] Marshall, *East Indian Fortunes*, p. 185.

[13] Sutherland, *The East India Company in Eighteenth Century Politics*, p. 295.

[14] Ibid., p. 260. Sutherland described the 'characteristically elaborate compromise of the Act whereby the first holders of the offices were appointed in Parliament; the successor to the Governor-general (should he retire) was nominated; all replacements of the Council during the five years were to be made by the directors subject to the veto of the Crown; and the appointments thereafter by the directors without outside control'.

[15] Hastings to Richard Barwell, Fort William, 22 April 1774, BL, Add. MSS, 29,125, fo. 293v.

[16] Francis to A. Wedderburn, 3 April 1777, printed in Weitzman, *Warren Hastings and Philip Francis*, p. 217.

[17] P. Francis to C. Doyly, 1 March 1776, printed in ibid., p. 273.

As always in Company politics, there were further arcane elements constituting a background to tensions on the Supreme Council. Robert Clive, whose reputation and interests had been lambasted first by the rise of the Sulivanites in the directorate and then by Burgoyne's select committee, cultivated an alliance with the new councillors as a way of restoring his influence in Company affairs. Both Clavering and Francis spent time in Clive's household before leaving for Bengal.[18] Francis, meanwhile, resolved before he left for Bengal to 'adopt and unite all Lord Clive's friends to me'.[19] This would prove a sound method of attracting Clivite Company servants, overlooked by the Hastings/ Sulivan connection, into the camp of the majority. The alliance with Clive also indicated a plausible alternative line of policy which Francis and his fellow neophytes could adopt in Bengal. Warren Hastings had been busy since 1772 dismantling the system of shared power between the Company in Calcutta and *nawabi* officials in Murshidabad. Francis, in opposition, began to lament the destruction of the old system of 'double government', stating in a letter to Clive that 'experience proves the Wisdom of that System which was adopted by your Lordship in the year 1766'.[20]

Philip Francis began as the most junior of the three councillors, yet through his eloquence and longevity he had by far the greatest impact.[21] His relatively obscure career in England may not have suggested to Hastings a looming threat; but later historians have shown that Francis' early life may not in fact have comprised just the uneventful course of an ordinary 'man of business'. It now appears at least highly likely that Philip Francis was the mysterious figure concealed under the pen-name of the scandalous polemicist, Junius, who wrote a series of vituperative letters to the Public Advertiser in London between 21 November 1768

---

[18] For Francis, see Weitzman, *Warren Hastings and Philip Francis*, pp. 19–21. For Clavering, see letter of Arthur Fowke to his brother Francis, 29 March 1774, OIOC, Fowke Collection, MSS Eur. E3, No. 17.

[19] 'Hints for my own Conduct', cited by J. Parkes and H. Merivale, *Memoirs of Sir Philip Francis, K. C. B., with Correspondence and Journals*, 2 vols. (London, 1867), vol. II, p. 17.

[20] Francis to Lord Clive, Calcutta, 21 May 1775, printed in Weitzman, *Warren Hastings and Philip Francis*, pp. 239–41.

[21] Clavering was first in line to succeed as governor-general if Hastings succumbed to the majority's attacks; in the summer of 1777, Clavering thought he had succeeded when the news came through that Hastings' agent in London had submitted the latter's resignation. Hastings argued that this resignation was not valid, and retained his position; Clavering died soon after. See Keith Feiling, *Warren Hastings* (London, 1954), pp. 185–7. Monson died in September 1776, and Francis stayed on in Bengal until 1780.

and 21 January 1772.[22] Junius savagely attacked the government of Lord Grafton and his successor Lord North, and took up the cause of 'Wilkes and liberty'. John Wilkes, the metropolitan radical elected MP for Middlesex in 1768, was expelled from the House of Commons after convictions for libel.[23] The letters of Junius represented the persecution of Wilkes as a symptom of the wider erosion of constitutional rights by a corrupt executive and judiciary. Tax increases after the Seven Years War, the growth of the standing army and national debt, and unrest in America, all fed into the critique of ministerial tyranny, which found new voice in the burgeoning national press. The fame of Junius (and also the dangers of being identified as Junius) magnified dramatically after he wrote an open letter addressed to the king himself on 19 December 1769. This was regarded by ministers as treasonable and brought legal action down on the printers. Junius' letters were marked by what their modern editor has called 'an almost hysterical regard for the constitution' and a sense of urgency for its preservation.[24]

The Wilkes agitation was part of a wider resurgence of radicalism in British politics and of partisanship in parliament in the turbulent first decade of George III. In the House of Commons, factions clustered around disgruntled Whig magnates like the Earl of Chatham (Pitt the Elder) and the Marquis of Rockingham, who lost their grip on power under the new king. By the end of the 1760s, a more coherent party of opposition coalesced around the Yorkshire landowner, Rockingham, and its rhetoric echoed some of the long-standing themes of 'country' politics, pioneered by opponents of Walpole's hegemony in the 1720s and 1730s.[25] Like the old 'country' politicians, the Rockingham group

---

[22] The authorship of Junius has been the subject of long controversy ever since he wrote his famous letters to the Public Advertiser. The fullest account is given in John Cannon (ed.), *The Letters of Junius* (Oxford, 1978), Appendix 8. Cannon argued (p. 559) that Philip Francis was the most likely of the myriad candidates suggested in the long historiography of Junius, but he believed the evidence was still circumstantial rather than conclusive. T. H. Bowyer, 'Junius, Philip Francis and Parliamentary Reform', *Albion*, 27 (1995), pp. 397–418, argued that the proofs of Francis authorship were firmly established, especially after A. Ellegard, *Who was Junius?* (Stockholm, 1962). The latter study made a comprehensive stylo-linguistic comparison between all the major candidates and Junius, in which Francis came out a winner by a distance. Bowyer also showed the close similarities in Francis's moderate brand of parliamentary reformism to that of Junius.

[23] For a brief account, see Frank O'Gorman, *The Long Eighteenth Century. British Political and Social History* (London, 1997), pp. 223–4.

[24] Cannon (ed.), *The Letters of Junius*, pp. xxii–xxiii.

[25] For the origins of the 'country party', see Isaac Kramnick, *Bolingbroke and his Circle. The Politics of Nostalgia in the Age of Walpole* (Cambridge, MA, 1968).

emphasized the way that corrupt ministers were using the Crown's patronage power to unbalance the constitution, undermining the independence of parliament by a careful distribution of the resources of the treasury.[26] The opposition's chief rhetorician, Edmund Burke, railed against the evils of 'secret influence' in George III's court, traced back to the king's Scottish tutor the Earl of Bute. Not the least important feature of this Burkeian rhetoric was the refurbishing of the very notion of 'party'. Whereas ministers railed against party as a species of schismatic factionalism against the public interest, Burke defended the true principles of party, represented by the Rockingham Whigs, as essential to the proper policing of the ancient constitution.[27]

In the most comprehensive study of 'party ideology and popular politics' in this period, John Brewer showed how aristocratic Whig revivalism in parliament coexisted uneasily with a growing radicalism of politics 'out of doors'. Whereas the Rockingham group argued that the best remedy for present discontents was a change of ministers, restoring the great Whig magnates to their natural pre-eminence, radicals increasingly demanded more systemic changes, including expanding the electoral franchise to make a corrupt parliament more accountable to 'the people'.[28] Radical arguments were also inflected by the earlier 'country' critique of ministerial corruption, emphasizing (in a civic–humanist vein) the importance of restoring the constitution to first principles to guard against the corrosive effects of corruption. But early eighteenth-century 'country' ideology suggested that the remedy for corruption lay in the custodial virtue of the landed gentry, independent freeholders in the classical mould.[29] By the 1760s, however, radicals were arguing for broader reforms of parliamentary representation, not only more frequent elections and the removal of 'placemen', but also extending the franchise to accommodate new interests. Only these remedies, it was argued, could restore the ancient constitution to its proper balance, true to the legacy of freedom-loving Goths of old.[30]

Whether or not Philip Francis was indeed Junius, it is clear that he should be situated within this nexus of oppositionist ideology, falling somewhere between the lofty paternalism of the Rockingham group and the more aggressive demands of metropolitan radicals for

---

[26] Brewer, *Party Ideology and Popular Politics*, pp. 247–8.
[27] Ibid., pp. 17–18.   [28] Ibid., pp. 255–6.
[29] This theme was developed in J. G. A. Pocock, *Politics, Language, Time. Essays on Political Thought and History* (London, 1972).
[30] Brewer, *Party Ideology and Popular Politics*, pp. 260–1.

parliamentary reform.[31] As Guha showed, Francis was sympathetic to the commonwealth tradition in British politics; his heroes were pillars of republican virtue and independence like Brutus, Cato and, from British history, John Milton and Algernon Sydney.[32] After his sojourn in India, Francis became a noted proponent of moderate parliamentary reform, favouring shorter triennial parliaments, providing salaries for MPs, and broadening the franchise of the commons to rescue it from ministerial influence and restore civic-minded independence. There were strong echoes of 'country' and civic–humanist thought in Francis' work for the Society for the Friends of the People in the 1790s. He rejected more radical plans for universal manhood suffrage or annual parliaments, reasserting the connection between property, independence and virtue. His plan for extending the franchise to ratepayers sought to steer between the corruption of 'interest' and the 'license' of the mob.[33]

Francis' background in English oppositionist ideology in the crisis years of the late 1760s and early 1770s provides an important context for his elaboration of an opposition to Warren Hastings in Bengal. The fevered atmosphere of the age of Junius, marked by endemic fear of cabals, influence, executive tyranny and constitutional degeneration, helps to explain the virulence and urgency of opposition attacks on Warren Hastings after the new councillors arrived in Bengal in late 1774.[34] Furthermore, much of the language of oppositionist Whiggism exported easily to Bengal, where the military–fiscal juggernaut of the East India Company appeared to embody many of the worst features of the British imperial state, including high levels of taxation and debt, standing armies, private profiteering among government officials, bribery, corruption and secret influence. The irony, of course, was that these motifs would now be deployed in Bengal by the Crown's agents, appointed by the very minister, Lord North, who was accused by his opponents of analogous crimes against the English constitution.

This transposition of opposition Whiggism to Bengal involved rethinking the very nature of Indian politics. Britons usually characterized Mughal India, and Asiatic government in general, as a corrupt and

---

[31] Cannon, *Letters of Junius*, Appendix, p. 571; Bowyer, 'Junius, Philip Francis and Parliamentary Reform'.
[32] Guha, *A Rule of Property for Bengal*, pp. 69–70.
[33] Iain Hampsher-Monk, 'Civic Humanism & Parliamentary Reform: the case of the Society of the Friends of the People', *JBS*, 18 (1979), pp. 70–89. Bowyer, 'Junius, Philip Francis and Parliamentary Reform', pp. 406, 417.
[34] For Pocock's concept of a 'politics of paranoia', see Pocock, 'The Imperial Crisis', p. 254.

corrupting despotism, even though, as we have seen, the conquest of Bengal had provoked a partial rethinking of old stereotypes. Francis' achievement was to build on previous British discussions of Mughal history, as well as the representations of high-ranking Indians, to argue that there was a venerable ancient constitution in India, as well as a noble aristocracy of landowners. Both of these, in his view, together with the good name of the British nation, required to be rescued from the depredations of modern mercantile tyrants. In the critique of Company rule, Francis' political thought would take on a slightly dated 'country' tinge, echoing the old civic–humanist emphasis on landed property as the basis of political virtue. Even if there was no 'commonwealth' tradition in Bengal, and no House of Commons, Francis discovered in the figure of the *zamindar* a species of landed property that suggested a distinctive form of Asiatic political virtue. Fusing English 'country' rhetoric with physiocratic prescriptions about land as the basis of wealth, Philip Francis' attacks on the Hastings regime pitted the virtues of freehold property against the depredations of the monied interest.

Gathering materials

The arrival of the new 'majority' in Calcutta in October 1774 led, predictably enough, to a period of intense political conflict on the Calcutta council. Welcomed at the Calcutta docks by an official delegation from the governor, the new gentlemen were offended to be accorded only a 17 gun and not a 21 gun salute.[35] This set the tone for the ferocious battles for political supremacy in Bengal, in which all parties were swift to chide and just as swift to take offence. Within days, Governor Hastings' executive power was effectively overturned as the new men acted as a cohesive voting block to oppose the interests and views of Hastings and Barwell. Over the coming months the new majority, their views most often expressed by the daunting polemicist Philip Francis, set out to prove 'the total misgovernment of Bengal under Mr Hastings' Administration'.[36]

Official instructions from home empowered the new Supreme Council to investigate 'all Oppressions', all 'Abuses' and 'any Dissipation or Embezzlement of the Company's money'; and these

---

[35] Weitzman, *Warren Hastings and Philip Francis*, p. 23.

[36] Joint Address of Clavering, Monson and Francis to Ct. of D., 21 March 1776, printed in G. W. Forrest, *Selections from the letters, Dispatches and Other State Papers (preserved in the foreign department of the government of India), 1772–85*, 3 vols. (Calcutta, 1890), vol. II, p. 538.

orders begat a furious round of investigations and accusations.[37] The majority conducted accusatory inquiries on a number of fronts against the beleaguered governor. For example, they attacked his policy of hiring out the Company's troops to the *nawab* of Awadh to pursue a war of conquest in the territories of the Rohilla Afghans. One of the new councillors, George Monson, was told by an informant that the civil and military establishments of the Company in Bengal had grown so far beyond the resources of government that 'they are only to be supplied by making wars on the neighbouring states'. This policy he opposed as 'unnatural to the constitution of Bengal' and liable to unite Indian states against the Company. Rather he and the other councillors wished 'to turn our Minds to the Improvement of Cultivation and Manufactures' in Bengal.[38]

Yet, when the council majority looked to Bengal, they professed to see a scene of destruction wrought by the Company's voracious appetite for taxes and by the greed of individual Company servants. After inquiries by the majority, Hastings was forced to admit that he himself had received a gift of at least one and a half lakh rupees (about £15,000) from Munni Begum around the time of her elevation to guardian of the *nawab* in 1772, a payment justified as 'customary perquisites' or 'entertainment fees'.[39] The new men, fortified by large salaries, took a stern view of their public responsibilities that precluded entering into customary practices of gifting. They decided to refuse all 'Nazirs or presents', because even the relatively harmless receipt of small presents was 'very likely to be extended or abused'.[40] They became convinced, however, that the official records of the Company concealed a morass of double dealing and corrupt profiteering. Clavering reported to his brother, an MP, the comments of 'a black man', who told him 'within a month of my arrival, "I believe, Sir, you already find that this government is not what it appears to be on Paper"'.[41]

One of the central lines of inquiry undertaken by the majority concerned the activities of the committee of circuit (COC), headed by Governor Hastings, in 1772–3. The majority alleged that the COC had

[37] 'Instructions from the Court of directors to the Governor General and Council, approved by the General Court, 25 January 1774', OIOC, Francis papers, MSS Eur. E26, p. 14.
[38] Monson to Marquis of Rockingham, Calcutta, 28 November 1774, Wentworth-Woodhouse Muniments, WWM R1-1531a, Sheffield Archives.
[39] Marshall, *East Indian Fortunes*, p. 177.
[40] Secret Department, Majority minute and letter to the Ct. of D., Clavering papers, NRO 309, G.4, Box 1, No. 5, Northumberland CRO.
[41] Sir J. Clavering to Thomas Clavering, Calcutta, 17 November 1775, Clavering papers, NRO 309, G.4, Box 1, No. 2, Northumberland CRO.

corruptly lined its own pockets and those of its friends by letting lands to their Indian commercial agents or *banyans*, or by taking bribes from would-be farmers. Hastings' own *banyan*, Krishna Kanta Nandy, widely known to the British as 'Cantoo Baboo', was thought to stand 'foremost and distinguished by the enormous amount of his farms and contracts', over 13 lakh in farms and 16 lakh in contracts to provide the Company's investment.[42]

In August 1775, Clavering described how 'the descoverys we made of the indirect means by which the Governor and almost every man whether in the Company's service or not, had or were acquiring their fortunes, had spread a general alarm among them'.[43] In order to combat the fierce resistance to their inquiries into illegal profiteering and to promote their own agenda, the majority cultivated an eclectic set of alliances among both British and Indians in Calcutta. They exploited their patronage powers, as majority on the Supreme Council, to remove Hastings' friends from key positions and promote their own preferred candidates. In this way they would 'shew the people by some strong appearances that the power of conferring favours was in our hands'.[44] Among the majority's keenest allies were old associates of Clive who had not found favour under Hastings' rule. For example, Joseph Fowke, a former Company servant turned private trader, came down the river to meet the new men before they arrived in Calcutta and began producing information about 'the actual state of the Country'.[45] One of the majority's sources on abuses in the farming system was the former *banyan* to Lord Clive, a leading entrepreneur and revenue farmer in his own right, Maharaja Nabakrishna.[46]

Indeed, the evolution of the opposing factions in Calcutta after 1774 demonstrated the complex interrelations between Company politics and Indian society. Much of the fuel of the new opposition came from efforts of Indians to represent their complaints to the Company government. General Clavering described in one of his letters home how

the people had conceived that the new government was to redress all their grievances. They flocked round our palanqueens every time we went out, with numberless petitions. Those which were in English I constantly conveyed to the

---

[42] Minute of Clavering, Monson and Francis, 25 January 1776, Forrest, *Selections from the Letters, Dispatches and other State Papers*, vol. II, p. 477.

[43] Clavering to his brother, Sir Thomas Clavering MP, Calcutta, 5 August 1775, Clavering papers, NRO 309, G.4, Box 1, No. 5, Northumberland CRO.

[44] Clavering to Lord North, 7 January 1775, Clavering papers, NRO 309, G.4, Box 1, No. 1, Northumberland CRO.

[45] Clavering to his brother, Sir Thomas Clavering MP, Calcutta, 5 August 1775, Clavering papers, NRO 309, G.4, Box 1, No. 5, Northumberland CRO.

[46] Ray, *Change in Bengal Agrarian Society, c. 1760–1850*, pp. 42, 44.

council ... those which were in any of the Country languages, I had given to Mr Elliot who had offered himself to be my interpreter.[47]

According to Clavering, these petitions came from a wide range of sources. Once, his palanqueen was surrounded by 'a very numerous body of petitioners in a most outrageous manner'. It turned out that these petitioners were lowly salt-boilers from the 24 Pargana district, complaining against the local salt contractor. This contractor was the *banyan* of an Englishman, one Captain Weller, who was a member of Governor Hastings' household. According to Clavering's account, the salt-boilers complained that they were physically coerced into working for prices 'under what they received formerly'. When they had previously come to Calcutta to complain, they had been 'chained and sent down to the salt works again and compelled to work by Seapoys being put over them'.[48] Many of them had apparently 'escaped into the woods and were destroyed by Tygers'.[49]

More often, Indian petitions taken up by the majority were from status groups higher than the salt-boilers. Unsurprisingly, a common type of complaint came from *zamindars* deprived of their revenue collections under the farming system. The Rani of Burdwan, for example, lost little time in presenting herself to the new gentlemen, accusing the Company (as Clavering reported) of 'horrid acts of oppression towards her & her son, a minor'.[50] The *zamindari* of Burdwan had suffered an invasion of revenue farmers under Company rule, and Rani Bishnukumari was especially exercised by the growing power of the Burdwan *diwan* (chief revenue officer), Braja Kishor Roy, an ally of the Company who conspired to keep her out of the management of her minor son's estates.[51] The arrival of Francis and the new majority was the Rani's chance to fight back against Braja Kishor Roy and the Hastings regime. In this she had conspicuous success, coming to Calcutta early in 1775, providing the council majority with evidence of embezzlement of Braja and Company servants, and persuading them of her right to choose her own *zamindari* officers. In May 1776, after the expiry of the former revenue farms, the council majority restored the *zamindari* management to the Rani and her son.[52] Hastings, meanwhile, received intelligence that the ranis of

---

[47] General Clavering to his brother Thomas, 5 August 1775, Clavering papers, NRO 309, G.4, Box 1, No. 5, Northumberland CRO.
[48] Ibid.
[49] Clavering to Lord North, 7 January 1775, Clavering papers, NRO 309, G.4, Box 1, No. 1, Northumberland CRO.
[50] Ibid.   [51] McLane, *Land and Local Kingship*, pp. 229–30.
[52] Ibid., pp. 232–4, 245.

both Burdwan and Rajshahi were paying Francis and the majority for their help, though this appears at least highly unlikely given the great public and political stake the majority placed on its own whiter-than-white image.[53]

Zamindari petitions frequently appealed to the idea of ancient custom, often represented by the terms 'time immemorial' or 'antiquity' in the Company's official translations. For example, the petition from Rani Bishnukumari from December 1774 declared that 'the ancestors of my Husband Maharajah Tillook Chund have from time immemorial enjoyed the Zemindarry of the Burdwan District, which has been successively confirmed to them under every Government through which this country has passed'.[54] In fact, the Burdwan *zamindari*, like almost all the largest *zamindaris* was largely a creation of the late seventeenth and early eighteenth centuries. But basing rights on some concept of ancient custom was commonplace in eighteenth-century India, and this sort of self-representation fitted nicely with British respect for customary usages and ancient constitutions.[55] A similar idiom was deployed in the English translation of a petition from certain disgruntled property holders of the city of Dhaka. They complained that Company agents were surveying their charity lands which they had held rent free 'from the time of Akbar'. The government's predatory investigations, it was argued, violated 'the ancient usages and customs of the country'. 'From the first foundation of the city', they wrote, 'to this moment the above customs have been invariably retained, the inhabitants of every Royal City as of Moorshedabad, Rajahmahal, Poornea, and Patna who hold Lakherage [rent free] lands have never paid nor do they now pay a Revenue to government'.[56] Philip Francis, quick to spot any possible examples of the Company's oppression, used this petition to criticize Hastings, and especially Hastings' ally Richard Barwell, who was

---

[53] An anonymous note received by Hastings on 10 May 1775 included Philip Francis in a list of beneficiaries for a third share of Rs 200,000 in a gift from the Ranis. BL Add. MSS 29,198, pp. 325–8. In February 1775, George Vansittart reported that 'Nundcomar [the majority's chief Indian agent] I hear has received Rs 25,000 from the Ranny through Punjaub Roy.' Vansittart to F. Stuart, 23 February 1775, printed in Weitzman, *Warren Hastings and Philip Francis*, p. 249.

[54] 'Copy of a Petition of the Ranee of Burdwan to the Governor General and Council, 27 December, 1774', Francis Papers, OIOC, MSS Eur. E27, p. 171.

[55] Sumit Guha, drawing on materials from eighteenth-century western India, has suggested that 'antiquity' was 'perhaps the chief source' of right in early modern South Asia. Sumit Guha, 'Wrongs and Rights in the Maratha Country: Antiquity, Custom, and Power in Eighteenth Century India', in Michael R. Anderson and Sumit Guha (eds.), *Changing Concepts of Rights & Justice in South Asia* (New Delhi, 2000), pp. 14–29.

[56] BRC, 4 February 1775, OIOC, IOR P/49/50, pp. 451–4.

recently the Company's chief in Dacca. He queried 'whether it would be safe and prudent to shake and overturn so material and important an establishment of the Ancient Government of this Country'.[57]

If landholders formed one important group of complainants useful to the majority, then the displaced magnates of the *nawab*'s court in Murshidabad were another. 'Amongst the Black Men', wrote General Clavering to his brother, '. . . were two conspicuous for their fortunes, their abilities and their influence', Muhammad Reza Khan and his great rival Maharaja Nandakumar. He compared these to 'Chiefs of Partys' in England, and wrote that as in England these party chiefs 'hated one another and persecuted by turns when in place'.[58] Interestingly, Clavering thought that Hastings' eventual acquittal of Reza Khan after his 'impeachment' stemmed in part from Reza Khan's extensive network of friends in the Company service. Meanwhile, Nandakumar had become embittered with Governor Hastings after his own hopes of returning to power in Murshidabad were dashed and the governor's treatment of him was characterized by 'nothing more than the mere appearance of civility'.[59] After the majority's arrival, Nandakumar formed an alliance with Joseph Fowke, and worked actively to disgrace Hastings by digging up evidence of scandal.

Nandakumar's alliance with the majority made him intensely vulnerable to Governor Hastings' wrath; the latter was convinced that Fowke and Nandakumar were using coercive tactics to bring evidence forward. When the majority presented a letter from Nandakumar in council on 11 March 1775, alleging that Hastings had received over three and a half lakh of rupees in bribes from Nandakumar himself and Munni Begum in 1772, Hastings decided to press charges against Nandakumar and Joseph Fowke for conspiracy in the new Supreme Court.[60] Though a part of his allegations were subsequently proven, Nandakumar had overplayed his hand. In fact, before the conspiracy case against Nandakumar was heard, he was prosecuted for forgery on a separate case relating to apparently fraudulent claims made on the will of a Bengali banker, Bulaqi Das.[61] This case had been in litigation for several years in the *zamindar*'s court and the old Mayor's

---

[57] Francis' minute, BRC, 7 February 1775, ibid., p. 471.
[58] General Clavering to his brother Thomas, 5 August 1775, Clavering papers, NRO 309, G.4, Box 1, No. 5, Northumberland CRO.
[59] Ibid.
[60] B. N. Pandey, *The Introduction of English Law into India* (Calcutta, 1967), pp. 43–69.
[61] J. D. M. Derrett, 'Nandakumar's Forgery', *English Historical Review*, 245 (1960), pp. 223–39.

Court in Calcutta. Clavering believed that Hastings himself had deliberately 'kept the cause hanging over' Nandakumar before letting it loose in the Supreme Court, relying on clients of Muhammad Reza Khan as witnesses and his own friends in the board of trade as jurors.[62] Hastings' true role, if any, in this case was long unclear, but evidence from George Vansittart's diaries showed clearly that one of the governor's closest associates was instrumental in helping the executors of Bulaqi Das's will to prosecute their case as a criminal charge in the Supreme Court. Vansittart used his deep contacts in Calcutta society to marshal evidence, prepare witnesses, and to discover in advance of the trial the strategies of the defence.[63] Nandakumar was dramatically convicted and publicly hung, which was interpreted on both sides as a significant blow to the majority that would discourage further complainants against Hastings from coming forward.

The disputes among the British, and the resulting oscillations in Company policy, must have been confusing and alarming for many Indian observers. In March 1776, Hastings reported to Vansittart that 'all my Mussulman and Gentoo friends have been casting my nativity, consulting the stars, throwing Dice, and opening Corans at a venture, to know what will be the fate of the impending contests'.[64] Much was at stake for *banyans* and other Indian associates of the British in these conflicts, and the fate of Nandakumar dramatized just how dangerous the political environment had become. But the majority's arrival also represented an opportunity for some Indian power-holders to recover lost ground. In the feverish spring and summer of 1775, the other great party chief of Bengal politics, Muhammad Reza Khan, negotiated the morass of Company politics with some skill.

Reza Khan had lost a great deal under Hastings' reforms, and his possible resentment against the governor, as well as his role as the lynchpin of Clive's old system of double government, made him an obvious potential ally of the new men. The majority made their first approaches to Muhammad Reza Khan in a series of secret negotiations early in 1775.[65] Convinced that Hastings' administration was riddled with corruption, the majority regarded Reza Khan as 'the master Key to

---

[62] Letter of Sir John Clavering (no recipient given), 19 May 1775, Clavering papers, NRO 309, G.4, Box 1, No. 2, Northumberland CRO.

[63] L. Sutherland 'New Evidence on the Nandakuma Trial', *English Historical Review*, 72 (1957) pp. 438–65.

[64] Hastings to G. Vansittart, 30 March 1776, BL Add. MSS 48,370, fo. 20r-v.

[65] See 'Paper Brought by Mr Goring as a Message from Muhammad Reza Khan', OIOC, Francis Papers, MSS Eur. E28, pp. 341–2.

every secret Transaction that passed for many years'.[66] Even though the majority's friends offered various threats and inducements, Reza Khan refused to cooperate in the majority's search for allegations of personal corruption.[67] He thought it 'beneath his dignity' to inform against any one, but he was 'ready at all times to give the best advice in his power, for the future Management and Welfare of this Country'.[68] On 23 January, the new gentlemen gave notice in council that they had received a ceremonial visit from Reza Khan and that they would present a 'communication' resulting from this visit at an appropriate time.[69] In this visit, according to Clavering, Reza Khan, 'enter'd into a long discourse on the present state of this country', and the majority then 'desired he would commit the whole to writing'.[70]

Around this time, Hastings' friends began to hear reports 'that M.R.C. is gone over to the new folks ... Mr Hastings does not like such reports'.[71] Unlike Nandakumar, however, Reza Khan was careful not to burn his bridges with the Hastings camp. He kept open a line of communication with George Vansittart, and fed him information on the apparently coercive methods used by Nandakumar in plotting to bring down Hastings. Meanwhile, in March 1775, the majority introduced into the official minutes of the Supreme Council a treatise called 'Mohammed Reza Cawn's description of the former and present State of the Country, the Causes of its declension & the way there is of recovering & bringing it again into a flourishing condition'.[72] Clavering told Lord North that this treatise was simply a transcription

[66] Charles Goring to Lord Montague, Calcutta, 5 January 1775, printed in Weitzman, *Warren Hastings and Philip Francis*, p. 253. Goring was employed as a political agent by the majority.

[67] G. Vansittart to J. Graham, Calcutta, 25 March 1775, printed in Weitzman, *Warren Hastings and Philip Francis*, p. 249; see also letter from Aly Ibraheem Cawn. Recd 27 March 1775, printed in ibid., p. 252.

[68] 'Paper Brought by Mr Goring as a Message from M.R.C', OIOC, Francis papers, MSS Eur. E28, p. 341.

[69] Minute of the Majority, BSC, 23 January 1775, OIOC, IOR P/A/26, pp. 651–2.

[70] Clavering to Lord North, 26 February 1775, Clavering papers, NRO 309/G4, Box 1, No. 1, Northumberland CRO.

[71] G. Vansittart to F. Stuart, 23 February 1775, printed in Weitzman, *Warren Hastings and Philip Francis*, p. 148.

[72] This treatise was received by Francis in February 1775 and is recorded as 'Abstract of M.R.C.'s Account of the former and Present state of the Provinces', in OIOC, Francis Papers, MSS Eur. E28, pp. 345–57 (copy sent to Lord North). The majority also entered the treatise in the proceedings of the Supreme Council just as the corruption charges against Hastings were coming to a head. BSC, 13 March 1775, OIOC, IOR P/A/27, pp. 1435–51. There is another copy of this treatise, dated January 1775, in the Wellesley papers, BL Add. MSS 12,565, fos. 2–18.

of Reza Khan's views as expressed to the council.[73] On the other hand, George Vansittart thought, and perhaps was encouraged to think by Reza Khan, that much of this document was written 'as dictated by the new gentlemen'.[74] Vansittart also claimed that he had, as Hastings' agent, 'in a manner authorized him to write as he had done', in 'condemning the measures of the late administration'; he told Reza Khan 'that we should very well be able to defend ourselves against anything he might say in opposition to us'.[75] The Hastings camp, it appeared, were at this stage more worried about claims of personal corruption than general attacks on policy.

Despite Vansittart's claims, however, it seems unlikely that Muhammad Reza Khan's critique of Hastings' administration in this treatise was constructed solely to appease the majority. Removed from his position as *naib diwan*, and held under house arrest in Calcutta, Reza Khan had reason enough to be resentful of Governor Hastings. His treatise, while it needs to be treated with care, should not be written off as entirely fabricated by the new gentlemen.[76] Many of its sentiments accorded closely with Reza Khan's documented criticisms of Company policy going back to the late 1760s, and also with other contemporary Indo-Persian sources.[77] The start of the treatise, for example, emphasizes that 'every country has its different rules and Customs, by which it is Governed, and if they are not attended to, the Country must sink into Ruin.'[78] The idea that a ruler must attend to differences between localities in terms of climate, natural resources and social customs was also the starting point of another Persian commentary on the Company government, by the historian Ghulam Husain Khan Tabatabai.[79] Other general injunctions in Reza Khan's treatise, that the

---

[73] Clavering to Lord North, 26 February 1775, Clavering Papers, NRO 309, G.4, Box 1, No. 1, Northumberland CRO.

[74] 'Goring was almost daily with him for hours together instructing him what he should write, till his answers were brought into the form, in which you will see them on the Consults. of the 13 March'. G. Vansittart to J. Graham, Calcutta, 25 March 1775, printed in Weitzman, *Warren Hastings and Philip Francis*, pp. 249–50.

[75] Ibid., p. 250.

[76] Even Vansittart was not wholly firm on this point. He admitted, for example, that it was 'natural that M.R.C. should say the collections were better managed under him than since'. Vansittart picked out certain passages which he believed were inserted at the behest of the majority. These included: the sole emphasis on the farming system rather than the famine in explaining declining collections, as also the criticisms of the opium monopoly and the bank. Ibid.

[77] For a discussion which uses this treatise, perhaps too uncritically, as a straightforward statement of Reza Khan's views, see Khan, *Transition in Bengal*, pp. 13–16.

[78] Reza Khan's treatise, BL Add. MSS 12,565, fo. 2v.

[79] See Ghulam Husain Khan, *Seir Mutaqherin*, vol. III, pp. 157–8.

ruler should protect 'all Ranks of People' and make himself widely accessible 'immediately to hear all complaints' also reflected common motifs of Indo-Persian political ethics.[80]

Like other Persian treatises from this period, Reza Khan looked back to a former age of stable administration as his model of good government. But whereas the British often located this stability in a distant Mughal past, Reza Khan emphasized how the *nawabs* of Bengal, especially Alivardi Khan (1740–56), had themselves maintained good order. 'The Ruler ought to see', he wrote, 'that the established Rules and maxims be strictly observed ... as was the case from the Death of Aliverdy Cawn till the time Meer Jaffier was seated a second time on the Musnud after the trouble in 1763'. Robert Clive, according to Reza Khan, decided to 'reestablish the ancient form of Government, and give the People one man to look to for the transacting of publick Business'; he contrasted the vigour and dispatch of business under his management of the revenues with the cumbersome machinery of the new provincial councils.[81] This passage chimed with an important theme in Indo-Persian political norms, which emphasized the personal authority of the emperor and, by extension, his leading officials in the provinces.[82] In a similar vein, historian Ghulam Husain Khan later bemoaned the inefficiency and contention caused by the British preference for government by committee. A country, he wrote, 'having no apparent master, must in time cease to flourish'.[83]

Much of Reza Khan's treatise reads like a guide for beginners (as the new gentlemen were) to the systems of revenue administration in Bengal. He explained key terms, like *raiyat*, defined as 'an appellation not given alone to Husbandmen, but also to people of all ranks that compose the Empire'; and he detailed the cycle of seasonal harvests and how it intersected with the administrative calendar.[84] The largest section of the treatise was concerned, not surprisingly, with the land revenues and the failings of the present farming system. He described how the foundations of Mughal revenue administration were laid by the emperor Akbar, through the revenue assessment of Akbar's finance minister Todar Mal. Akbar established a pattern of just administration, with occasional moderate increases in the revenues which the people could afford. This was continued until the rule of Mir Qasim in the early

[80] Reza Khan's treatise, BL Add. MSS 12,505, fos. 2v–3r.
[81] Ibid., fos. 3–4.
[82] Chatterjee, 'History as Self-representation', p. 24.
[83] Ghulam Husain Khan, *Seir Mutaqherin*, vol. III, pp. 185–6.
[84] Reza Khan's treatise, BL Add. MSS 12,565, fos. 5v, 7v.

1760s, when 'the ancient system of government was set aside', and the revenues were increased 'without regard for the Welfare of the Country'. Now, he argued, 'the Gentleman, who are sent to the different Divisions, pursue the same plan, by which means the Zemindars, Talukdars, and Ryots are in great distress'.[85]

Criticisms of Hastings' revenue administration represented the meat of the majority's attack on the governor; again, however, we should not assume that Muhammad Reza Khan was merely parroting the majority's views. Indeed, his criticism of the revenue farming system echoed strong currents of opinion in Mughal politics that associated revenue farms (*ijara*) with oppression of the peasantry. Though the practice of *ijara* (leasing out revenue rights for an agreed price) was common at all levels of Mughal administration, and increased with the spread of the money economy in the seventeenth and eighteenth centuries, it was often regarded as morally suspect at the Mughal court because it was seen to encourage short-term rack renting of the peasantry.[86] Reza Khan argued that 'the Farmer, not having a Natural Interest in the place, has only his advantage in view'. He thought the farming system undermined the systems of official surveillance of local affairs that characterized best Mughal practice. 'The Rules now being laid aside, and others adopted, most of the Farmers do not pay the revenues monthly, and no enquiry is made in the Suddar [*sadr* – central government office] about them.'[87]

Some of Reza Khan's treatise echoed his earlier rearguard action, in 1770–2, to defend the independence of the *nawabi* by reference to earlier Mughal custom. For example, he stated that the ruler should not interfere with trade, and that merchants and bankers should be encouraged to trade freely.[88] As before, Reza Khan defended the hereditary rights of *zamindars*. 'The Zemindars and Talookdars are masters of their own Lands, they take care and improve them; as they are Hereditary, the Prince never deprives them of their Lands, but punishes them if they deserve it'. To emphasize the point that 'the Princes have no immediate property in the Lands', Reza Khan described how 'they even purchase Ground to build Mosques, and for burying places'.[89] In the light of Philip Francis' later defence of *zamindar* property, this part of Reza Khan's treatise may well have been of particular interest to the majority. Yet Reza Khan's views on the

---

[85] Ibid., fo. 9r.
[86] M. Athar Ali, *The Mughal Nobility under Aurangzeb* (2nd edn, New Delhi, 1997), pp. xxiii–xxiv; 83–4.
[87] Reza Khan's treatise, Wellesley papers, Add. MSS 12,565, fos. 10r, 12r.
[88] Ibid., fos. 13–14.   [89] Ibid., fos. 15v–16r.

hereditary rights of *zamindars* were consistent with his legal opinion on landed property given to the governor and council in 1773.

Even though George Vansittart feigned indifference to this attack on Governor Hastings, it is clear that the majority regarded the treatise of Reza Khan as a major prize. Not only did they enter it into the minutes of the Supreme Council, but General Clavering also referred to it in a letter to the Prime Minister Lord North, where he wrote that he was sending a copy to the court of directors.[90] One of the distinctive features of this period of British Indian politics was the prestige accorded to certain types of 'authentic' Indian informer, especially those who appeared to be strongly associated with the ancient constitution. Hastings could not afford to ignore the hostile opinions of Mughal notables. Indeed, in 1777, Hastings became deeply concerned at reports of 'mazhernamas' or petitions of grievances, allegedly produced in Murshidabad by supporters of Muhammad Reza Khan, and sent back to England. Hastings wrote to George Vansittart, who had now returned to England, wishing to pre-empt their publication: 'if you are certain that they have made their way to England, for God's sake publish them with proper Comments'.[91]

A high-ranking Indian ally like Muhammad Reza Khan could also provide much practical assistance to the majority. In order to carry out their plans of reforming the Bengal government, they needed to employ experienced administrators. To this end, in May 1775, the majority offered to restore Reza Khan to at least a large measure of his previous power. General Clavering thought 'that until European influence can be extinguished ... it will be impossible to collect a revenue equal to what the Country does yield', and he 'resolved to take the assistance of Mahomed Reza Cawn, on such terms as we should dictate to him'.[92] The majority could also frame their promotion of Reza Khan as a return to Clive's old system of delegated authority.[93] Not feeling justified, without orders from the directors, in recalling all the provincial councils and (in Clavering's words) 'putting all the inhabitants into the hands of Black agents', the majority proposed that Reza Khan should be appointed head of the *khalsa* (revenue) department in Calcutta, with

[90] Clavering to Lord North, 26 February 1775, Clavering papers, NRO 309, G.4, Box 1, No. 1, Northumberland CRO.
[91] Hastings to G. Vansittart, 28 March 1777, BL Add. MSS 48,370, fos. 41–4.
[92] Letter of Sir John Clavering (no recipient given), 19 May 1775, Clavering papers, NRO 309, G.4, Box 1, No. 2, Northumberland CRO.
[93] See Francis to Lord Clive, Calcutta, 21 May 1775, printed in Weitzman, *Warren Hastings and Philip Francis*, pp. 239–40.

a salary of Rs 2 lakh, and power to name the native *diwans* attached to the provincial councils.[94]

Once again, though, Reza Khan responded very cleverly to the apparent blandishments of his British patrons. Philip Francis was deputed to negotiate with him, and at the first interview he 'seemed willing to accept, but at the second, he refused absolutely'.[95] According to Francis, his 'objection went in general to the Inutility or Danger of any System that was to join Natives and Europeans in the Management of the Collections'.[96] According to Clavering, Reza Khan had decided that 'whilst the Provincial Councils subsisted his measures would be constantly thwarted and overset', and that he and his officers in Calcutta would be liable to legal proceedings in the new Supreme Court. Muhammad Reza Khan also appealed to his sense of honour, declaring that 'that he would serve the Company for nothing, but would not accept so small a salary as two lack'.[97] After his bruising experiences as *naib diwan*, with his rival Nandakumar languishing in a Calcutta jail, and with Governor Hastings making a determined fight back against the majority, Reza Khan decided to keep his own powder dry. This was sound policy, but also a fascinating reflection of the narrowing possibilities for elite Indian administrators under the new regime. The majority planned to revive Clive's system of delegated power, letting go of the details of territorial government. Yet the incident of Reza Khan's refusal also suggests how the British had rather quickly burned their bridges with some possible Indian allies. The rough treatment of Reza Khan in 1772 meant that he was unlikely to jump at the chance of once again entering the line of fire in the revenue administration.

Instead, he bided his time, and in October 1775 he did finally accept a more limited appointment from the majority, to return to the position of *naib subah*, with control over the *nawab's* household in Murshidabad, and jurisdiction over the network of *faujdari adalats* or criminal courts.[98] The salary was only Rs 240,000, close to the figure which he had regarded as derisory before; now he petitioned vigorously (and vainly)

[94] Letter of Sir John Clavering (no recipient given), 19 May 1775, NRO 309, G.4, Box 1, No. 2, Northumberland CRO.
[95] Francis to Lord Clive, Calcutta, 21 May 1775, printed in Weitzman, *Warren Hastings and Philip Francis*, pp. 239–40.
[96] Ibid.
[97] Letter of Sir John Clavering (no recipient given), 19 May 1775, NRO 309, G.4, Box 1, No. 2, Northumberland CRO.
[98] Proceedings of the Secret Committee, 18 October 1775, in Forrest (ed.), *Selections from the Letters' Dispatches and Other State Papers*, vol. II, pp. 431–6.

to increase it.[99] But this position had less of the other disadvantages which had led Reza Khan to refuse employment in the revenue line. He would be safely domiciled in Murshidabad, outside (as he hoped) the jurisdiction of English judges in the Calcutta Supreme Court. And he would be granted freedom to appoint law officers to administer the Muslim criminal law. The official policy of the Company continued to emphasize the distinction between civil (*diwani*) and criminal (*nizamat*) administration, and it is perhaps easy to see why the Company were content in the early stages of their power to leave to Indian officials the business of arresting, imprisoning and trying alleged criminals. For Reza Khan, the *nizamat* appeared to offer a relatively safe haven, sheltered from the Company's voracious appetite for tax revenues, where he could continue to nurture the traditions of Indo-Islamic empire. He would remain vulnerable to the slings and arrows of British factionalism, and was temporarily removed from his post in 1778 after the majority lost control of the Supreme Council, following the deaths of two of their members, Monson and Clavering. But he was restored again in 1779 on orders of the directors and continued to have formal control over the *nizamat* and the criminal courts until the reforms of Lord Cornwallis swept away these survivals from the age of the *nawabs* after 1790.

Competing visions

From the end of 1774, the majority and Hastings' camps quickly began to think of themselves as opposing parties, and they mobilized diverse resources to forward their respective goals.[100] Both sides put together complex coalitions of Company servants and Indian officials as they jockeyed for position in Bengal. During 1775 and 1776, the two parties also worked furiously to outline their contrasting visions for the future government of Bengal. As before, policy proposals were often grounded on some notion of an ancient constitution, and 'authentic' Indian sources were deployed to legitimize favoured policies. Ideas of Asiatic government were undergoing a subtle transformation as British officials responded to fiscal crisis in the aftermath of the famine, and as Philip Francis reinterpreted the ancient Mughal constitution through the lens of English Whiggism.

---

[99] N. Majumdar, *Justice and Police in Bengal, 1765–1793. A Study of the Nizamat in Decline* (Calcutta, 1960), p. 141.

[100] Clavering, in his early letters from India, already described 'two partys in the Council'. See Clavering to Lord North, 7 December, 1774, NRO 309, G.4, Box 1, No. 1, Northumberland CRO.

Warren Hastings and Richard Barwell produced a new set of revenue policies, recognizing the need both to explain the failures of the farming system and to devise a plausible alternative. Their 'Plan for the Future Settlement of the Revenues' of March 1775 was a calculated retreat from the previous farming scheme, which at the same time reminded its readers (in a preamble) the reasons why five-year farms had appeared appropriate in 1772: namely, the Company's disappointment with the old annual settlements for the *diwani* territories, the difficulty of ascertaining the proper value of the lands, and the hope that farmers granted security of five-year farms might be induced to improve the lands. 'We will not say', the Hastings/Barwell plan went on that 'the disir'd Improvement has in general taken place', an outcome which they blamed on 'the Farmers having engaged for a higher Revenue than the district could afford'.[101]

The new plan instead sought to stabilize rural property as a basis for taxation, by seeking to make tax settlements (based on the median of the previous three years of collections) with hereditary *zamindars*. *Zamindars* would hold rights to collect revenue over a fixed area for the duration of their lives, with the idea of strengthening 'Landed Property; for upon this we deem the whole success of the Plan to depend.'[102] Long term leases would thus render *zamindari* rights more valuable, and the government could make up arrears of revenue by forced sales of *zamindari* lands. The heirs of a *zamindar* would have an option to continue the lease, though the government would retain the right to raise the tax burden by a maximum of 10 per cent at the succession. The plan envisaged detailed surveys of lands by government, to make periodic reassessments and to monitor the tax burden on the peasantry. All new taxes imposed since the start of the Bengal year 1765 were abolished, and 'a Kind of Hustabood' (*hastobud* or tax survey) should be undertaken to achieve this goal.[103]

The plan recognized the superiority of hereditary *zamindars* as revenue intermediaries rather than temporary farmers. 'Whenever the Landed Property shall be put upon such a footing as to render it disirable and secure to Purchasers', the plan explained, 'we would wish that the Revenue of Every District should be settled with a Zemindar'.[104] Yet Hastings and Barwell implied that *zamindar* property was not yet sufficiently secure as to make sales of land a good security for the Company. Thus, the plan allowed flexibility to the government in leasing lands to revenue farmers where *zamindar* bids were deemed

[101] Plan for a future settlement, BL Add. MSS 12,565, fo. 23v.
[102] Ibid., fo. 29r.   [103] Ibid., fos. 24r, 34r-v.   [104] Ibid., fo. 33r.

insufficient or where *zamindars* were judged incapable. Lifetime leases to farmers 'in one respect would be more effectual; we mean by being granted to Substantial Men, who have money of their own to lay out in Improvments'.[105] Hastings and Barwell implied that *zamindars* were largely cash poor compared with revenue farming entrepreneurs. Government therefore retained the right to grant tax-collecting powers to other 'farmers'. While *zamindars* should always be allowed 10 percent of the collected revenues as hereditary perquisites (in accordance with the 'Ancient Constitution of the Empire'), they were 'for the most part Ignorant of or inattentive to business'. They had been corrupted by a despotic system which rendered them imperfect agents of agricultural improvement. 'It has been so long the Custom of Bengal to raise their rents to the full value of their Lands' that 'very few of them have any disire for their improvement'.[106]

The Hastings/Barwell plan was highly characteristic of Warren Hastings' approach to policy making. It was deliberately eclectic in its sources, referring sometimes to the 'constitution of the empire' (as in the provision to make *zamindars* and farmers answerable for murders or robberies committed in their territories) and sometimes deliberately subverting the old laws (as in the measure for replacing primogeniture with partible inheritance as a mode of succession for large *zamindaris* in order to bring them down to size).[107] Hastings and Barwell acknowledged that the Company had made mistakes in Bengal, driven by 'the Desire of acquiring a Reputation from a sudden Increase of the Collection'; but at the same time they tempered their enthusiasm for the Mughal empire, arguing that 'the Continual usurpations on the Rights of the People' were produced in part by 'the Remissness or the Rapacity of the Mogul Government'.[108] This was a pragmatic attempt, through trial and error, to remedy the defects of the five-year farms, offering extended leases on moderate terms to different classes of rural intermediaries.

It took the majority camp several months to produce a coherent alternative plan, although their minutes constantly brimmed with criticisms of Hastings' revenue policies. Their actions throughout 1775 tended to reinstate large *zamindars* who had been removed from their collections, and to restore the vigour of the 'country government', for example by reappointing Reza Khan to the position of *naib nazim*. Then, in January 1776, the majority's chief rhetorician Philip Francis produced one of the most famous policy documents in the early history

---

[105] Ibid., fo. 35r.   [106] Ibid., fos. 36r–38v.   [107] Ibid., fos. 38r, 42v.
[108] Ibid., fos. 41r–v.

of British rule in India, his 'Plan for a Settlement of the Revenues of Bengal, Bahar and Orissa.' This document has most usually been read as a precursor to Lord Cornwallis' 'permanent settlement' of the revenues in 1793, fixing the land-revenue assessment for all time on *zamindars*, regarded as proprietors of the soil. Situated in the cut and thrust of Bengal politics, what is perhaps most remarkable about this document is how many of its provisions – for reducing the tax burden on the peasantry and using *zamindar* property as security for revenues – were already anticipated in the Hastings/Barwell plan. At the same time, by introducing the notion of a 'permanent' freeze on the land tax, Francis' plan set itself as a direct and principled contradiction of all former policies pursued by the Company for managing the Bengal lands.

Not only Francis' insistence that taxes must be fixed for all time (and not just for one life as in Hastings' plan), but also the whole tone and tenor of his own minute differed markedly from the Hastings/Barwell plan. Whereas Hastings and Barwell had presented a set of pragmatic remedies for new circumstances, the Francis plan was a rousing declaration of constitutional principle, and a savage critique of the existing methods of the Company. Francis drew on the representations of Mughal officials and *zamindars*, and elaborated their 'ancient rights' in the manner of English Whigs defending their own 'ancient constitution' from executive tyranny. Francis' plan was an argument about constitutional history as much as political economy, which took the British re-evaluation of the Mughal empire to a new pitch.

From early on in his letters to England, Philip Francis had compared the *zamindars* of Bengal to the landed gentlemen of England. It was this analogy which made Hastings' farming system appear to him so shocking. In January 1775, he asked Lord North to consider 'the probable Consequences in England, if all the Lands were at once set up to sale by an Act of arbitrary power, without any Regard to the Rights of Freeholders, Copyholders and Lords of the Manors; in short, if the Monied Interest ... were at once to be put into possession of all the lands'.[109] Francis' language picked up on a conventional distinction in British political thought between the 'landed interest', which frequently symbolized stability, aristocracy and virtue, and the 'monied interest', which was seen to have swelled after financial innovations in the late seventeenth century (notably the founding of the Bank of England and the national debt). In 'country' rhetoric, the 'monied interest' was often

---

[109] Francis to Lord North, 13 January 1775, printed in Weitzman, *Warren Hastings and Philip Francis*, pp. 234–7.

associated with fears of excessive credit, speculation and corruption.[110] In the eyes of the majority, *ijaras* or revenue farms in Bengal also appeared by analogy to systems of revenue farming in France and continental Europe, connoting rack-renting and despotic government. General Clavering reminded Lord North 'with what horror the news was received in England of the French attempting to lett in farm the Revenues of Hanover', and how the farming scheme was repugnant to 'every idea that we entertain in England of property'.[111] The farming scheme was, Clavering thought (referring to the financial disaster of the 'South Sea bubble' of the 1720s) 'the most infamous project, the South Sea scheme not excepted, that was perhaps ever devised in any country'.[112]

Others had criticized the farming system by comparing it with tax farming in France; for example, in 1772 the noted Scots-born agronomist Henry Patullo had published an extensive comparison between Bengal and France calling for the British to make a new settlement of landed property in India.[113] Yet what was distinctive in Francis' plan of 1776 was his conviction that actual rights of landed property, in some sense analogous to those in Britain, existed within the constitution of the Mughal empire. His first sentence signalled that a radical revision of Mughal history, and the nature of Asiatic despotism, was being proposed in his revenue plan. 'The Company, I believe, had conceived an early, but erroneous, opinion that, by the constitution of the Mogul empire, the governing power was proprietor of the soil'. Therefore, rather than being content with 'a fixed tribute as government', they had sought 'to ingross the intire produce as landlord'.[114] In a physiocratic vein, he argued that this attempt to raise the rents to their greatest possible extent meant that 'the Government of this country has been living upon its capital; that is, they have annually taken a portion of its existing wealth, which ought to have been reserved for future production'.[115] This fallacy about the rights of government, therefore, lay behind the current decline of the land revenues.

---

[110] J. G. A. Pocock, *The Machiavellian Moment; Florentine Political Thought and the Atlantic Republican Tradition* (Princeton, 1975), pp. 446–7.

[111] Clavering to Lord North, 27 November 1775, Clavering papers, NRO 309, G.4, Box 1, No. 2. Northumberland CRO.

[112] Clavering to Thomas Harley, Calcutta, 15 January 1776, Clavering papers, NRO 309, G.4, Box 1, No. 3, Northumberland CRO.

[113] H. Patullo, *An Essay upon the Cultivation of the Lands, and Improvements of the Revenues of Bengal* (London 1772); see also the discussion of this in Guha, *Rule of Property for Bengal*, pp. 42–9.

[114] Francis, *Original Minutes*, p. 23.

[115] Ibid., pp. 24–5. For the physiocratic connection, see Guha, *A Rule of Property*, pp. 97–8.

Francis deliberately proposed to work against the grain of most conventional accounts of Asiatic government, in proving that Asiatic despotism was not incompatible with property. In this, he had some notable recent works to draw upon. For example, his idea that the 'form' of the Muslim governments in India was despotic, while not actually oppressive 'to the mass of the conquered people', was a clear echo of Alexander Dow's previous invocation of a benevolent Mughal despotism.[116] Yet Dow had still assumed that all land under the Mughals belonged to the king, and that a general sale of lands was consonant with this principle. Francis could also draw on the latest writings of Voltaire, which challenged the connection between despotism and imperial ownership of land inherited from Montesquieu and Bernier. Francis rehearsed Voltaire's distinction between the power to 'grant' and 'enjoy' the lands, arguing that imperial *sanads* which pretended that *zamindari* rights were dependent on the 'sovereign in capite', were really 'a kind of feudal fiction, of which the sovereign in fact never pretended to avail himself, as constituting a right to assume or transfer the possession'.[117]

Francis' reconstruction of the ancient constitution of the Mughal empire also drew on new sources of information from within the Company's archive in Bengal. In a general sense at least, his account of the virtuous Akbarian traditions of Mughal government echoed the treatise of Muhammad Reza Khan discussed earlier. Francis assumed that 'Bengal was in a much more flourishing state during the last century', and emphasized the importance of tracing 'the ancient policy of its government'.[118] He gave a summary history of the Mughal polity based on 'the records of the Khalsa, and from the information of some of the oldest servants in the revenue offices, supported by authentic documents'. Like Reza Khan, Francis traced the modern history of the Bengal land tax to Akbar's finance minister, Todar Mal. He thought that Akbar, the first Mughal conqueror of Bengal, had been concerned to 'conciliate the minds of the native Hindoos', and in particular to protect the rights of 'the Zemindars, the ancient proprietors of the soil'.[119]

---

[116] Francis, *Original Minutes*, p. 30. Alexander Dow had by now returned to Bengal and was patronized by the majority; General Clavering appointed him Commissary General of the Bengal army and spoke highly of him in his letters. See Clavering to Lord North, 26 February 1775, Clavering papers, NRO 309, G.4, Box 1, No. 1, Northumberland CRO.

[117] Francis, *Original Minutes*, p. 72. For Francis' use of Voltaire's *Essai Sur l'Histoire Generale* (1756), see Guha, *Rule of Property for Bengal*, pp. 99–101.

[118] Francis, *Original Minutes*, p. 31.   [119] Ibid., pp. 32–3.

Francis used a rough and ready comparison between the *jama* or total revenue demand given in the *Ain-i Akbari* (a great compendium of information about Mughal governance, described by Francis as 'the constitutions of the empire under Akbar') and the *jama* in 1728 (when *Nawab* Shuja Khan conducted a new revenue survey) to argue that the Mughal tribute from taxation had remained relatively stable over hundreds of years. By 1775, however, it had increased by almost ten million rupees. Francis argued that 'considerable infringements' began to appear on the 'ancient establishments' only in the reign of Alivardi Khan (1740–56), who killed the son and legitimate successor of Shuja Khan, marking a 'usurpation from the empire'.[120] *Abwabs* or permanent additions were made to the old *jama* which gradually undermined *zamindar* property. Echoing Reza Khan, Francis thought Mir Qasim's government between 1760 and 1763 was 'universally allowed by the natives' to be the period when 'the ancient establishments and the rights and property of the Zemindars were first shaken'.[121] Francis thought that Mir Qasim added new taxes by making *hastobuds* (surveys) of lands, overthrowing the traditional *jama* and 'totally excluding the Zemindars'. Francis' plan argued that this attempt to 'collect as great a surplus as possible' had continued under the Company, culminating with the attempt to enforce an 'increased and increasing revenue' under Hastings' five-year farms.[122]

Francis' blanket statement of the prior revenue policies of the Company gained in force for what it lacked in subtlety. There *were* indeed some radical reformers like J. Z. Holwell who had hoped to radically reduce the emoluments of *zamindars*, and these views were to some degree reflected in the 'Instructions to the Supervisors' of 1769. In general, however, Company officials at all levels had also paid lip service to the idea of preserving the hereditable rights of landholders. The conviction that Bengal since the famine had been over-assessed was widely shared in the Company service, not just by Francis' close allies, but even by Hastings himself. It remains true, however, that no Briton before Francis had talked with such conviction of the 'rights and property' of *zamindars*, or imagined that such property had been so fully secured under the apparently despotic regime of the Mughals. Hastings' plan of 1775 recognized a hereditary right in the

---

[120] Ibid., p. 36.
[121] Ibid., p. 38. Compare with the passage of Reza Khan's treatise which argued that 'Cossim Ally, when he was Nabob, increased the Bundbust, but he did it without regard to the Welfare of the Country.' BL, Add. MSS 12,565, fo. 9r.
[122] Francis, *Original Minutes*, pp. 41, 47.

zamindar only to a certain fixed share of the income from taxation. Moreover, Hastings continued to believe that property rights under the Mughals were constrained by the absolute rights of the emperor, and that landed property 'by the constitution is solely vested in the government'.[123]

Hastings and Francis further elaborated their differences late in 1776 over the issue of *hastobud* or revenue surveys. In September, one of the majority's members on the Supreme Council, Colonel Monson, died. This gave Hastings a casting vote on the council, and he used his powers to force through new reforms. Though the directors had not yet decided on how to proceed after the expiration of five-year leases in 1777, Hastings wished to move ahead with his plan for a general revenue survey. On 1 November 1776 he announced the appointment of a new 'temporary office' responsible for 'compiling and collating the accounts of past Collections', 'issuing orders for special accounts and other materials of information, and in deputing native officers on occasional Investigations'. The goal of this new body was to furnish government with information on 'the real value of the lands'.[124] Four Company servants, close associates of the governor-general, were appointed to the commission, know as the *amini* commission, to be assisted by Hastings' long-time ally from the *khalsa*, Ganga Gobinda Sinha.[125] This new revenue survey drew a furious response from Philip Francis, who regarded it as a 'union of confusion and impossibility', and as another attempt by the Company to engross the agricultural surplus of Bengal. He argued that it would empower corrupt *amins* to oppress local landlords.[126]

Hastings, on the other hand, vigorously denied that he aimed to increase the general revenue demand, arguing merely that he wanted to equalize the burden on different areas, relieve the peasantry of harsh exactions, and provide the ground work for a more lasting settlement.[127] The debates over the *amini* commission also revolved around different interpretations of Mughal history. Francis had argued in his general plan of February 1776 that general revenue surveys were an oppressive

---

[123] Hastings to L. Sulivan, Ft William, 10 March 1774, printed in Gleig, *Memoirs of Warren Hastings*, vol. I, p. 388.

[124] Minute of Governor General, 1 November 1776, Francis Papers, MSS Eur. E31, pp. 273–4.

[125] For a detailed account of the progress of the *amini* commission, see R. B. Ramsbotham, *Studies in the Land Revenue History of Bengal, 1769–1787* (Oxford, 1926), pp. 77–98.

[126] Francis' minute, 5 November 1776, in Francis, *Original Minutes*, p. 125.

[127] Hastings' minute, 12 November 1776, ibid., pp. 143–6.

innovation dating from the rule of *Nawab* Mir Qasim, and a violation of the ancient Mughal policy of stable taxes.[128] Hastings attacked Francis' ideas of the ancient Mughal constitution as 'points of mere speculation', arguing that the original assessment of Todar Mal was obsolete long before Mir Qasim's time, and noting that Todar Mal's assessment was itself an 'act without precedent', justified only by the 'absolute' will of Akbar. 'It is vain', he argued, 'to look for the constitution of a despotick Government in any other principle'.

As Hastings showed, Francis' idea that the revenue demand on Bengal had remained constant from Akbar's day into the late 1720s was contradicted by evidence of new surveys undertaken in the time of *Nawab* Murshid Quli Khan (1707–27).[129] Rather than violating an ancient constitution, Hastings argued that his plan would restore order after the catastrophic collapse of the old constitution. In this context he even implied a comparison between himself and Akbar, cherishing the rights of his subjects by extending the oversight of the central state: 'the same cause which induced King Akbar to establish an equal and permanent standard for the collection of the revenues in his time, equally requires that the same or other means as efficacious, be employed for the same ends in this'.[130]

Thus, by 1776, the British rulers of Bengal were competing over who best represented the virtuous traditions of Akbarian government. In response to Hastings' jibes, Francis once more invoked the 'justice, lenity and wisdom of the Mogul Government', 'whose name', Francis chided, the governor-general 'was ready enough to quote, whenever we wish to exercise the despotick Powers supposed to belong to it'.[131] He insisted that 'partial Hustaboods' may have predated Mir Qasim, but that a 'general Hustabood' was previously unheard of.[132]

While this debate was carried on by searching for precedents in Mughal history, Francis also invoked arguments drawn from the history of the English land tax. Again, his conviction that the Mughal empire had itself been a rule of property enabled him to draw analogies between the rights of property in England and India. Francis' attachment to ancient constitutions did not preclude an idea of universal reason; rather, local constitutions – in their best forms – were shown to reflect

---

[128] Francis' 'Plan for a Settlement', ibid., p. 38.
[129] Hastings' minute, 26 March 1777, Francis Papers, OIOC, MSS Eur. E32, pp. 126, 130, 133–4.
[130] Ibid., p. 133.
[131] Francis' minute, 28 March 1777, Francis Papers, OIOC, MSS Eur. E32, p. 188.
[132] Ibid., p. 191.

general principles. Francis saw no reason, for example, why principles 'unquestionably true in every other country, should not also be true for Bengal'.[133] Indeed, the history of the English land tax was uppermost in his mind as he criticized the *amini* commission. Based on quotas for counties, parishes and townships made in the 1690s, the rates of the English land tax rapidly fell behind real rental incomes in the eighteenth century, and the share of land tax in government revenue fell quite sharply from 35 percent in 1710 to only 17 percent in 1790.[134] Attempts to establish new rental surveys to revise anomalies in the land tax were strenuously resisted in parliament as an attack on private property. In opposing the *amini* commission, Francis cited the latest British authorities, James Steuart and Adam Smith, to argue that moderation and fixity in tax assessments were preferable to proportionate equality.[135] Inequality of assessment was 'not regarded in England' as an inconvenience, and should not be so in Bengal, despite Hastings' contention that the conditions in Bengal and the weight of the tax demand made inequality a more severe hazard.[136]

Thus, for all his trumpeting of Mughal precedent and 'authentic' records, Francis' version of the ancient Mughal constitution was heavily inflected by English Whiggism. This was because Francis regarded the historical forms of Mughal government and the principles of political theory rightly understood, as consonant rather than contradictory. Notably, Francis' account of Mughal history focused almost entirely on the figure of the *zamindar*.[137] Francis' plan gave little attention to the broader structures of Mughal bureaucracy or systems of surveillance, arguing that the *zamindars* themselves should be considered as 'instruments of government in almost every branch of the

---

[133] Francis' minute, 10 December 1776, Francis, *Original Minutes*, p. 120.

[134] Paul Langford, *Public Life and the Propertied Englishman* (Oxford, 1991) pp. 339–49; P. K. O'Brien, 'The Political Economy of British Taxation, 1660–1815', *Economic History Review*, 2nd series, 41 (1988), pp. 1–32. For a longer discussion of debates over tax rates in Bengal and Britain, see T. R. Travers, '"The Real Value of the Lands": the *Nawabs*, the British and the Land Tax in Bengal', *MAS*, 38 (2004), pp. 217–58.

[135] Francis' minute, 5 November 1776, *Original Minutes*, pp. 125–9.

[136] Francis, 'Plan for a Settlement', ibid., p. 55. For Hastings' counter arguments, in which he claims that the theoretical weight of assessment in England was only 1/5 of the rental value (4s in the £), whereas in Bengal it was 9/10, see Hastings' minute, ibid., p. 143.

[137] Francis wrote that 'it is reasonable to suppose, that the Subadar did, at particular times, and during convulsions of the government, extort more money from the Zemindars than their established quit rents', but he thought this involved a 'temporary act of violence, or occasional sums', by 'free-gift'. Francis, 'Plan of Settlement', ibid., p. 35.

civil administration'. 'By the ancient constitution of the empire', Francis claimed, 'the principal Zemindars were invested with fouzdarry jurisdiction and were answerable for the peace of their districts'.[138] Francis tended to regard other types of government officials, like *amils* or *amins*, with great distrust. He suggested, for example, that in the period between 1766 and 1769, when Muhammad Reza Khan himself was at the helm of the *diwani* territories, 'people of lower rank were employed as Aumils, or collectors, on the part of Government', multiplying oppressions and frauds in the revenues.[139]

Unsurprisingly, Reza Khan's account of the period between 1766 and 1769 was quite different. 'I sent one good and sufficient Man', he declared, 'to reside in each district'. Officials 'well-versed in business, were sent, who, in conjunction with the Zemindars, made proper Regulations'.[140] Nor had Reza Khan ever suggested, as Francis would, that the emperors after Akbar had left the original *jama* intact; rather, the revenues 'were increased by degrees by many pretences; but the people, being in good Circumstances, could well afford to pay the same'.[141] These significant details reflected quite different emphases in the two accounts. Whereas Francis' plan began and ended with private landed property, Reza Khan's treatise began and ended with the virtuous *hakim* (chief magistrate or ruler), attending to local custom, cherishing all ranks of people, hearing and deciding complaints, and sending out virtuous and experienced officials to enquire into local circumstances and punish rebels or wrongdoers. For example, whereas Francis regarded the institution of *hustabud* or revenue survey with suspicion, Reza Khan stated that in his administration the revenue rates were set 'after a proper examination what every Mehal [*mahal* or district] could afford'.[142] Reza Khan urged that the government must every month attend to changes in the revenues of different *mahals*, and if necessary send agents to investigate shortfalls.

A significant difference between the two views concerned the relationship between government and the peasantry. Philip Francis agreed with Reza Khan that peasants should be granted *pattas* or leases which specified and fixed their rental liability. But Francis also insisted that the *zamindar* was 'master of the land and to re-let it to whom

---

[138] Ibid., pp. 59–60.
[139] Ibid., p. 43. Francis did go on to somewhat exculpate Reza Khan himself, who was 'sensible of the decline of the country', and recommended 'that a more moderate rent should be fixed', ibid., p. 44.
[140] 'Mahomed Reza Khan's Description', BL. Add. MSS 12,565, fos. 4v, 10v.
[141] Ibid., fo. 8v.   [142] Ibid., fo. 10r.

he thinks proper'; in the past, he thought, the best security for tenants was 'the natural interest and relation, by which they and the Zemindars were mutually bound to each other'.[143] Reza Khan, by contrast, described an 'ancient maxim, which was, when the Ryots were thinning in a Mehal, or Village, a Man capable of the Charge was sent there as Supervisor, who, in conjunction with the Zemindars and Talukdars of the place, used to Comfort and Cherish them, lower their rents, and grant them new Pottahs from their Zemindars and Talookdars'.[144]

Reza Khan's emphasis on the fatherly rule of the emperor and his chief officers, constantly alert for oppression and seeking justice for their subjects, accorded well with other contemporary Indo-Persian treatises, and with long-standing currents of Mughal ethical literature. Indeed, Indo-Persian writers were much more likely to ascribe the decline of the empire to the rise and usurpations of rebellious *zamindars* rather than their supposed ruin by increased taxation under the late empire.[145] Indeed, while big *zamindars* were sometimes incorporated into the official ranks of the Mughal nobility, Mughal grandees tended to distain holding *zamindar* rights themselves. Instead they drew income from *jagirs*, or imperial assignments on the revenue, a prebendal form of right which was sharply cut back under Company rule, but which Francis tended to ignore.[146] Filtered through the world-view of English Whiggism, officials of central government appeared to Francis as lowly predators, whereas *zamindar* landlords were represented as vital links in the chain of 'subordination in society, through which the operations of the Government descend, by regular and easy gradations, from the summit to the base'. In much the same way, English aristocrats and gentry formed 'the real nobility in the ancient and rational sense of the English constitution'.[147] The idea of *zamindars* acting as *faujdars* seemed as natural to Francis as the gentlemen of England acting as JPs.

Francis' account of Indian history thus fused 'country' Whig emphasis on landed property, with a kind of ancient constitutionalism that had interesting parallels with conventional accounts of the ancient English constitution. Philip Francis imagined an ancient constitution for Bengal made up of the customary and legal rights of pre-Islamic Hindu property overlaid by the simple forms of Islamic empire. Just as some

---

[143] Francis, 'Plan for a Settlement', *Original Minutes*, p. 61.
[144] 'Mahomed Reza Khan's Description', BL Add. MSS 12,565, fo. 5r, v.
[145] For example, Ghulam Husain Khan, *Seir Mutaqherin*, vol. III, p. 181. See also McLane, *Land and Local Kingship*, pp. 11–12.
[146] Khan, *Transition in Bengal*, p. 12.
[147] Cited in Guha, *A Rule of Property*, p. 110.

English Whigs had learnt to deny the imposition of new feudal laws by the Norman conquerors, Francis argued that the natural wisdom of the Mughals led them to preserve entire the ancient customs of Bengal, represented in particular by the great landed estates of the ancient *zamindars* of Bengal. 'In general', he claimed, 'they [the Mughals] introduced no change, but in the army and the name of the sovereign'.[148] If this was a laudatory view of the Mughals, it was also built on a rather limited idea of the Mughal empire as a kind of distant military superstructure over a base of Hindu property.

Francis' idea of restoring the 'country government' of Bengal was also overdetermined by a crude distinction between Muslims as rulers and Hindus as subjects. According to 'the summary and simple principles of Asiatic policy', Francis thought, 'Moormen chiefly should be employed in the offices of government ... the cultivation of the soil should be left with the Gentoos, whose property it is, and the revenue fixed for ever.' The British should now, like the Mughals, 'stand paramount over the rest ... contented with a gross but moderate tribute ... and guarding the country from being ruined in detail by Europeans', so the natives can 'be left undisturbed in the full enjoyment of their own laws, customs, prejudices and religion'.[149]

Finally, then, it might have seemed that the ultimate beneficiaries of this Whiggish view were not the Mughals or the *nawabs*, rendered almost superfluous to the flourishing of Bengal, an ornamental residue from a former golden age, but the *zamindars* themselves. Yet, for them too, Francis' plan had stings in the tail. For the virtue of *zamindars* was regarded as residing in a more prosperous past and an improved future, not in a degraded present. Francis shared with Hastings the view that contemporary *zamindars* had been largely ruined by the oppressions of recent times. They had become 'rapacious and thrifty', and some would be 'incapable of managing their lands themselves'.[150] Thus, Francis' detailed plan for restoring *zamindar* property included provisions for guarding against the depredations of indolent *zamindars*. British supervisors would be appointed to oversee the initial period of the new settlement, and the Company would be empowered to appoint *diwans* to manage the lands of incompetents. Lands held by 'minors, idiots and females' would be committed to appointed relatives by a Court of Wards, and (as in the Hastings/Barwell scheme) inheritance laws would be adjusted so that the biggest estates would gradually

---

[148] Francis, 'Plan for Settlement', *Original Minutes*, p. 30.
[149] Ibid., pp. 29–30.   [150] Ibid., pp. 50, 58.

be broken down into smaller and more manageable units.[151] Readers of
the first half of this plan, with its reverence for ancient custom, might
have been startled by these radical prescriptions for engineering
a reformed *zamindari* system.

Not for the first or last time, ancient constitutionalism was being
harnessed to radical ends by arguments of necessity and novel circumstance. Perhaps the most portentous of all Francis' suggestions, as far as
the *zamindars* were concerned, was the notion that balances in the
revenues would be met through forced sale of lands.[152] As we have seen,
this was also the keystone of the Hastings/Barwell plan. Yet given
Francis' sense of the value of an ancient aristocratic class, and his
professed suspicion of the 'monied interest', this provision was the
source of a certain tension in his treatise. He admitted that in some cases
'a transfer of landed property to monied people, who are able to make
improvements, will be in some degree advantageous to Government and
to the country'. But he thought that this would be an occasional example
to *zamindars* rather than a sweeping or inexorable revolution in landed
property. For one thing, preference in any sales of land should always be
given to the next heir. For another, given the 'value set by the Zemindars
of Bengal on their inherited property', they would soon 'be roused from
their present supine and hopeless state, to exert every endeavour for the
preservation and improvement of their estates'.[153] In other words, the
operation of the market would eventually reinforce rather than undermine the hereditary aristocracy, and capitalism would work hand in
glove with gentility. Thus, Francis addressed the dialectic which John
Pocock has argued was at the heart of British political thought in the
eighteenth century, between land as a marketable commodity and land
as the bedrock of political stability and civic virtue.[154]

Francis conceived of the new land market as an alternative discipline
to 'the rigorous means hitherto in practise, and often ineffectually
applied; such as threats, imprisonment and stripes'.[155] But his idea of a
state-controlled land market was a far cry from the more flexible system
of lordship and surveillance described by Muhammad Reza Khan.
Reza Khan had stated that when *zamindars* did not punctually pay
their taxes or 'pleaded proverty, amils were sent into their Lands, who,

---

[151] Ibid., pp. 58–9.   [152] Ibid., p. 57.   [153] Ibid., p. 58.
[154] 'It seems to me that both classical and bourgeois conceptions of property and power
are to be found in the eighteenth century, and are to be found dialectically related'.
Pocock, 'Civic Humanism and Its Role in Anglo-American Thought', in *Politics,
Language and Time*, p. 91.
[155] Francis' 'Plan for a Settlement', in Francis, *Original Minutes*, p. 57.

in conjunction with them used to make proper Regulations, but they never removed the Zemindars and Talookdars'. The prince, he wrote, 'punishes them if they deserve it'.[156] From this perspective, forced sales for arrears appeared as a striking British innovation; and indeed, the large *zamindars* of Bengal, which had grown into sizeable little kingdoms under the *nawabs*, would shrink rapidly after 1793 when the British rule of sales for revenue arrears came into general force. According to modern analyses Francis was, however, to some extent right that land rights would continue to circulate eventually among established *zamindari* families and their associates rather than being swallowed up by a new 'monied' class of city based entrepreneurs.[157]

Based on the evidence of his revenue plan of 1776, Francis had often been called the father of the 'permanent settlement'. It is worth noting, however, that the eventual revenue settlement of 1793 was based on a rate assessment for Bengal higher than any government had ever collected in a single year, and this on the eve of a general slump in prices. Francis argued, by contrast, that the revenue demand of Bengal had been set too high by the Company and needed to be lowered. In the short term, the directors were reluctant to plunge into a new long-term settlement, or to decide between the rival plans of the contestants for power in Bengal. At the expiration of the five-year farms, they decided to delay plans for a new long-term assessment, and return to temporary, one-year settlements with preference to *zamindars*.[158] Francis could take some credit, however, that the gross *jama* of Bengal and Bihar was lowered for three years running between 1777 and 1779, and that Hastings' *amini commission* was condemned by the directors as a set of 'vexatious inquisitions'.[159]

Conclusion: the shifting ground of British Indian politics

The indecision of the directors over the revenue settlement reflected a wider unwillingness of the home authorities to address themselves to the fierce party conflicts in Bengal. After the passage of the Regulating Act,

---

[156] Reza Khan's treatise, BL Add. MSS 12,565, fos. 8r, 12r-v.
[157] S. Islam, *The Permanent Settlement in Bengal: A Study of its Operation, 1790–1819* (Dacca 1979), pp. 144–57. A few big *zamindars* regrouped their domains through a system of under-leases which shifted the risks on to under-tenants. McLane, *Land and Local Kingship*, pp. 267–70, and Marshall, *Bengal: the British Bridgehead*, p. 147.
[158] Ramsbotham, *Studies in the Land Revenue History of Bengal*, p. 86.
[159] McLane, *Land and Local Kingship*, p. 251. Letters from the Ct. of D. to the Governor and Council in Bengal, 4 July 1777, and 30 January 1778, reprinted in Francis, *Original Minutes*, pp. 203–5.

North's government was quickly overwhelmed by the crisis in North America. The wave on wave of disputatious letters, pamphlets and political agents sent home by the warring parties of Bengal were greeted with a certain embarrassment by ministers. The government was sympathetic to the majority, but was unwilling to provoke a major conflict with the Company. Hastings commanded a following among the Company shareholders, who were determined to maintain their sacred chartered rights of independence. The Company rebuffed a ministerial demand for Hastings' removal; then a bungled effort at securing his resignation, followed by the deaths of Clavering and Monson, meant that Francis was left fighting an increasingly shrill and desperate battle against Hastings' stubborn resolution to cling to power.[160] The outbreak of major conflict in 1778 between the Company and the Marathas in western India made it still more unlikely that the ministry would try to remove the experienced governor-general. Early in 1780, Hastings secured a temporary political deal with Francis, in which the latter promised public acquiescence in military and diplomatic policy in return for some valuable jobs for Francis' friends.[161]

Perhaps unsurprisingly, these inveterate enemies were not long reconciled. The party disputes in Bengal, fought on the emotive and highly personal ground of public virtue, had always been as much about honour and reputation as policy and intellect. An open conflict in council, in which Hastings believed the terms of the agreement had been betrayed, led to a duel on the streets of Calcutta in which Francis was hit a glancing blow to the shoulder.[162] When Francis returned soon after to England, Hastings wrote an exhausted victory note to his friend and patron, Laurence Sulivan:

what a victory! An exhausted treasury and an accumulating debt, a system charged with expensive establishments, and precluded from the multitude of dependencies and the curse of patronage from reformation, a government debilitated by the various habits of inveterate licentiousness, a country oppressed by private rapacity . . . and lastly a war either actual or depending in every quarter & with every power of Indostan.[163]

Hastings attributed these ills to parliament's actions in 1773, saddling him with obstructions on his council, and rendering him impotent to implement necessary reforms. Yet, ironically, his letter showed how

---

[160] Sutherland, *The East India Company in Eighteenth Century Politics*, pp. 301–17.
[161] This is described in Hastings to L. Sulivan, 30 January 1780, BL Add. MSS 29,128, fo. 232v.
[162] H. E. Busteed, *Echoes of Old Calcutta* (Calcutta, 1888), pp. 109–19.
[163] Hastings to L. Sulivan, 15 March 1780, BL Add. MSS 29,128, fos. 296r–v.

much the rhetoric of corruption and sense of political crisis was shared between the different parties in Bengal. In another sign of this ideological convergence, Hastings' close friend, George Vansittart, now back in England, went to East India House to read Francis' revenue plan and wrote to Hastings 'there are two or three points in it to which I should object but in general I approve it', and 'in many respects he has adopted your ideas'.[164] Underneath the 'contagion of party', there was an important sense in which leading British officials, in the aftermath of the controversial 'farming' system, were converging on an idea of saleable *zamindar* property as a basis for the revenue administration in Bengal.

Nonetheless, for all the blurred edges of party conflicts in Bengal, there was something clearly distinctive, and distinctively Whig, about Francis' sense of an ancient Mughal constitution teetering on the edge of collapse, and of landholder rights impugned by a rapacious mercantile despotism. One important legacy of Francis' Indian Whiggism was that it helped to redefine India as an issue in British party politics. When Francis left for India in 1773, the Rockingham Whigs were ranged on the side of Company shareholders against the ministerial invasion of chartered rights. After 1775, the Rockinghams, who had used Indian issues more for shortterm political advantage than as a plank of their political programme, began to shift their ground. The immediate catalyst was the dramatic imprisonment and death of the Rockingham ally, Lord Pigot, governor of Madras, by a cabal of Company servants – creditors of the *nawab* of Arcot. When both Hastings and North's government seemed either to favour this coup or not act decisively to root out corruption in Madras, the Rockinghamites, and particularly Edmund Burke, began to take a greater interest in Philip Francis' attempts to reach out to them with his jeremiads.[165] There was, moreover, a natural affiliation between Francis' ancient constitutional-ism and Burke's own political predilections. Burke would eventually take over Francis' sense of an ancient Indian constitution, and deploy it in his own theatrical attacks on Warren Hastings in the impeachment trial.

---

[164] G. Vansittart to Hastings, 17 December 1776, Add. MSS 29,138, fo. 17r.

[165] Sutherland, *The East India Company in Eighteenth Century Politics*, pp. 324–5. Letters in the Rockingham papers in Sheffield show that the majority were in active communication with the Marquis of Rockingham himself through Colonel Monson from the start of their Indian sojourn. Monson, who had served in south India in the 1760s, acted as an advisor to Rockingham on Indian affairs in 1767. See 'Letters of George Monson to 2nd Marquis of Rockingham', Wentworth Woodhouse MSS R1, 758, 761, 770, 1531a, 1537, 1561a, 1583a, 1638, Sheffield archives.

Meanwhile, despite Francis' patronage of Muhammad Reza Khan and the 'country government', the dynamics of colonial state-formation were working inexorably against the old nodes of Mughal and *nawabi* power in cities like Murshidabad, Dhaka and Patna. It was not just that the Mughal nobility, on whom Clive had once relied, were increasingly alienated from the Company's government by its parsimony and its brutal faction fighting. It was also that Whig interpretations of the Mughal constitution tended to abolish the moral core of older conceptions of empire in the structures of patronage, benevolence and lordship of the virtuous ruler. Meanwhile, Francis' idea of Mughal history further entrenched the notion of Muslims or 'Moors' as foreign invaders (by analogy with the Normans) and Hindus or 'Gentoos' as the ancient inhabitants of Bengal and the rightful owners of the soil. Meanwhile, Francis and the majority had popularized new stereotypes of corruption in the idea of an Asiatic 'monied interest' – the *banyans* who would later feel the lash of Burke's coruscating denunciations.

5 Sovereignty, custom and natural law: the Calcutta Supreme Court, 1774–1781

Party disputes on the Supreme Council were not the only destabilizing legacy of Lord North's Regulating Act of 1773. The act also created a new royal court of justice in Calcutta, 'the Supreme Court of Judicature at Fort William in Bengal', and the early history of the court was marked by bitter struggles between the judges and the Company government. Disputes over the jurisdiction of the court generated major debates about the scope of English law in India, the constitutional definition of the Company government, and the nature of Indian legal tradition and practice. In the process, the Company's claims to govern according to the ancient constitution of the country were subjected to new levels of scrutiny.

This chapter explores the impact of the Supreme Court on the colonial power's evolving view of itself. The court was designed to provide a beefed-up version of royal justice in Calcutta, replacing an old system in which judicial power was devolved to the Company and to British communities in India. Trying to extend domestic legal disciplines to an unruly frontier, the court soon clashed with entrenched conceptions of distinctive local privileges among the British in Bengal and also with the Company's claims to exclusive authority in the interior. Meanwhile, the Company's Indian subjects exploited new opportunities for legal redress, and the judges took an expansive view of their powers to hear cases involving Indian plaintiffs and defendants. The court's legal proceedings challenged the Company to justify the workings of its territorial government, especially its law courts (*adalats*), and rapidly exposed the gap between the rhetoric of regulated government, and the loosely coordinated network of power holders sheltering under the Company's sovereignty. The Company, meanwhile, was forced to validate its administrative practices by a strident defence of Asiatic customs, supposedly under attack from the alien invasions of the English judges.

A new court for Bengal

Law courts administering some version of English law had existed in the Company's settlements in India since the mid-seventeenth century. By a royal charter of 1726, Mayor's Courts were instituted in Bombay, Madras and Calcutta to administer civil laws to the British subjects, and the 'presidents' and councils of these settlements were empowered as Justices of the Peace (JPs) to hold criminal quarter sessions. The Mayor's Courts, consisting of a mayor and nine aldermen (seven of whom were to be 'natural born' British subjects) mediated in local trade, credit and inheritance disputes in the growing commercial settlements. In Calcutta, the Company's judicial powers were also assumed to derive in part from the Mughal grant of the *zamindari* of the three villages of Sutanuti, Govindpur and Calcutta after 1698; hence, the English courts coexisted with a '*zamindar*'s court' which determined civil and criminal cases involving Indians.[1] Cases involving Indian litigants were sometimes heard before the Mayor's Courts as well, with the consent of the parties, and the Calcutta Mayor's Court retained a Brahmin on its staff to advise on issues of Hindu law.[2] Indians not infrequently complained about encroachments by the Mayor's Courts on their laws and customs, but there is also evidence that Indian litigants used these courts in large numbers, to enforce debts or contracts and even to prove their wills.[3]

When parliament reviewed the Company's establishments in 1772–3, the existing system of corporations and JPs was coming to be seen as an inadequate vehicle for applying the law to a British and European population that was growing rapidly, and spreading out into the Bengal hinterland, beyond the juridical reach of the Calcutta courts. The secret committee of the House of Commons appointed by Lord North in 1772 to inquire into Indian affairs reported on the defects of the existing courts, in particular the general ignorance among the judges of the English law, the fact that their jurisdiction was limited to the Company's settlements, and that they were subordinate to the Company governor and councils who had the power to dismiss the mayor and aldermen.[4]

[1] B. B. Misra, *The Judicial Administration of the East India Company in Bengal, 1765–1782* (Delhi, 1961), pp. 123–45.
[2] Misra, *Judicial Administration*, p. 137.
[3] N. Brimnes, 'Beyond Colonial Law: Indigenous Litigation and the Contestation of Property in the Mayor's Court in Late Eighteenth Century Madras', *MAS*, 37 (2003), pp. 513–50. For disputes over the contentious issue of oathing, see Jain, *Outlines of Indian Legal History*, p. 53.
[4] '7th Report of the Committee of Secrecy', 6 May 1773, *RCHC*, 4, pp. 332–3.

Thus, when Lord North finally presented his Regulating Act to parliament in 1773, clause XIII provided for a new 'Supreme Court of Judicature' for Calcutta, to consist of four English judges (who were to be barristers of at least five years' standing) appointed by the Crown.[5] These judges were empowered with 'such Jurisdiction, and Authority, as our Justices of our Court of King's Bench have and may lawfully exercise'.[6] The seal of the court, replete with the royal arms, was to be lodged with the Chief Justice, who with the other judges would issue writs and summonses in the king's name. The new judges were styled as personal representatives of the Crown, and, along with the new councillors, they represented a new breed of the 'king's men' in India, with sources of fiat independent of the Company.

But the judges' role in Bengal was complicated by the uncertain legal status of the Company's dominions. Though North encouraged the idea that Bengal was a conquered territory under the ultimate sovereignty of the British Crown, that sovereignty had not been formally pronounced in the British courts or in parliament. In this circumstance of confused legal sovereignty, the letters patent outlining the court's jurisdiction were complex and vague. These regulations awarded the court a full civil and criminal jurisdiction for the town of Calcutta and subordinate British factories which were construed as British settlements.[7] It was stipulated, however, that cases of contract involving native inhabitants could only be heard where they had previously submitted to the jurisdiction in the contract, and that English criminal laws should only be applied 'as nearly as the Condition and Circumstance of the Place, and the Persons will admit of'.[8] Apart from this local jurisdiction, the court was also given a personal criminal jurisdiction over 'British Subjects' throughout Bengal, Bihar and Orissa, and power to hear any manner of suits against the Company, its servants 'or any other of our subjects residing there'. In a key clause of the charter of justice, the court was also empowered to hear suits against those 'directly or

---

[5] 13 Geo.III, c.63, *HCSP*, 24, pp. 72–5.

[6] 'Letters Patent, establishing a Supreme Court of Judicature at Fort William', 6 March 1774, printed in 'Report from the Committee on the Petitions of Mr Touchet and Mr Irving, Agents for the British Subjects residing in the Provinces of Bengal, Bahar and Orissa, & their several dependencies; & of Warren Hastings, Philip Francis, & Edward Wheler esquires; & of the East India Company Relative to the Administration of Justice, & c. in India' (henceforth 'Touchet Report'), *RCHC*, 5, p. 59.

[7] Ibid., p. 91. According to one of the judges, Calcutta was construed as a British settlement because of the military conquest (or reconquest) of the town by Clive and Admiral Watson in 1757. See entry for 11 November 1782, 'Notebooks of Justice John Hyde' (henceforth 'Hyde's Notebooks'), National Library, Calcutta.

[8] 'Letters Patent', Touchet Report, *RCHC*, 5, pp. 61, 63.

indirectly, in the service of the said United Company, or the said Mayor and Aldermen, or of any other of Our British Subjects'.[9] These expansive provisions ensured that the king's writ would run throughout Bengal, Bihar and Orissa, even without a declaration of legal sovereignty; and also that his writs would run against a vaguely defined group of indigenous inhabitants in 'the service' of the British. This opened up the potential for serious clashes between the Supreme Court's jurisdiction and the Company's agencies of government in the interior of Bengal.

The statutory constitution of the Supreme Court was in many respects a remarkable event, and a bold effort to impose legal controls on the operations of British governors, traders and settlers in eastern India. The institution of the court is only understandable in the context of the general clamour against corrupt Nabobs which fired up British politics in the early 1770s. After their arrival in Calcutta in 1774, the judges of the court, like the new councillors, used their powers to export these anti-corruption sentiments to Bengal. The judges were awarded high salaries, and at least two of the four were relatively high profile lawyers; Elijah Impey, the new Chief Justice, had been recorder of Basingstoke as well as counsel to the East India Company, while Robert Chambers had been Blackstone's successor as Vinerian Professor of Law at Oxford. They saw their court as a potential remedy for widespread lawlessness and corruption, and they were willing to employ innovative methods to do their duty. The judges' sense of mission is well indicated in a letter of Justice Robert Chambers to Lord North, describing the Regulating Act as 'an Effort of benevolent power endeavouring to rescue an oppressed and declining People from Insecurity and Unhappiness of Dominion exercised without Regularity or Knowledge', and himself as 'an Instrument of this glorious Purpose'.[10] Within a few years, however, the court was being accused both of invading the ancient customary rights of Indians and bringing the British empire in Asia to its knees.

The judges were caught up in the wider instability of legal doctrine associated with the expansion and transformation of empire. In landmark cases concerning Grenada and Minorca, Lord Mansfield, Lord Chief Justice of the King's Bench from 1756 to 1788, insisted that royal officials were subject to legal checks even in conquest

---

[9] Ibid., p. 61.
[10] Chambers to Lord North, 31 October, 1776, cited in Thomas M. Curley, *Sir Robert Chambers: Law, Literature, and Empire in the Age of Johnson* (Madison, WI, 1998), p. 186.

colonies.[11] Yet Mansfield advocated flexible accommodations of legal precedent to accommodate changing circumstances, for example, to allow non-Christians, formerly construed as 'infidels', to give evidence in English courts.[12] He also championed the preservation of indigenous laws in conquered territories, supporting the incorporation of French civil law into the new constitution of Quebec by the Quebec Act of 1774.[13] The judges in Bengal were eventually caught on the horns of a new legal dilemma: how to provide judicial review for colonial administration without being seen to encroach on indigenous custom and law.

The Supreme Court and British sovereign authority

While extensive records from a few high-profile cases are still extant, only fragmentary records survive from the bulk of the Supreme Court's business.[14] What does survive suggests that much Supreme Court business was a continuation of the role of the old Mayor's Court, administering civil justice to the complex commercial society of Calcutta. For example, the judges heard many suits regarding debts on the 'plea side' of the court, and they granted probate and administration of wills to 'British subjects', Christian or non-Christian, living in Calcutta. The Supreme Court retained Hindu and Muslim law officers (*pandits* and *maulvis*) to advise in cases involving Indian inhabitants.[15] It also held criminal 'quarter sessions' four times a year, involving jury trials which dealt with criminal cases arising in Calcutta, a role previously taken by the governor and council acting as JPs.

---

[11] Hussain, *The Jurisprudence of Emergency*, p. 24; see also F. Madden and D. K. Fieldhouse (eds.), *The Classical Period of the First British Empire, 1689–1783, Select Documents on the Constitutional History of the British Empire and Commonwealth*, 2 vols. (London, 1985), vol. II, pp. 320–3.

[12] Lieberman, *The Province of Legislation Determined*, pp. 89–92.

[13] P. J. Marshall, 'Britain and the World in the Eighteenth Century: iv, The Turning Outwards of Britain', *Transactions of the Royal Historical Society*, 11 (2001), p. 5.

[14] I was able to consult records of the early proceedings of the Supreme Court in the Calcutta High Court record room. I found unsorted and extremely fragmentary records from the late 1770s, but they do give some indication of the range of cases taken by the court. These can be supplemented by microfilm copies of the judicial notebooks of one of the judges, John Hyde, in the National Library in Calcutta. Some of these have been printed in W. K. Firminger, 'Selections from the Notebooks of Justice John Hyde', *Bengal Past and Present*, 3 (1909), pp. 27–64.

[15] Some of these law officers were highly esteemed scholars. 'Mudjum ul deen' was appointed a *maulvi* to the court in July 1782. Hyde wrote that he had previously belonged to the court of Shuja-ud-daula, the *nawab* of Awadh, and was now employed as the 'Head of a New College of Mahommedan students erected by Mr. Hastings.' This was the Calcutta *Madrassa*. Entry for 12 July 1782, 'Hyde's Notebooks'.

The Supreme Court was also used by the Company to sue its misbehaving servants, and for Company servants to sue Indian agents whom they accused of fraud.[16]

Yet the court quickly showed itself to be a new and potentially highly destabilizing force in Bengal politics. For one thing, the court appeared as a threat to the autonomy of the British community in Calcutta. Whereas the old Mayor's Court had been staffed by men of local influence, the judges of the Supreme Court were outsiders, not necessarily well disposed towards their compatriots in India. In 1781, the British inhabitants of Calcutta collectively petitioned parliament, loudly complaining of the expense, confusion and disruption caused by the Supreme Court, and demanding the right for trial by jury in civil cases. Indeed the period of the old Mayor's Court now seemed to some of them like a golden age of justice. Joseph Price, a free merchant, declared that the inhabitants of Calcutta, 'had very little law before the institution of the Court, but a great deal of justice'.[17] Among other things, British settlers in Calcutta complained that the court had penalized them for using corporal punishment on their Indian servants and workers.[18] The chief justice, Elijah Impey, complained to his friend that the committees formed to petition against the court were 'like your Bill of Rights men in England', and that 'they talk of their rights being indefeasible like Americans & in case of want of success to follow their example'.[19]

Apart from prickly British inhabitants, the judges also made enemies by their sometimes clumsy interventions in the party disputes which engulfed the Company's establishments in Bengal after 1774. It did not help that the Chief Justice Elijah Impey had been a friend of Governor Warren Hastings from their school days at Westminster.[20] Nor were the judges able to float free of the Company's elaborate nexus of patronage politics. Both Elijah Impey (who lost money in East India Company stock in the early 1770s) and Robert Chambers made various efforts to have themselves appointed to the Company's Supreme Council.[21] Whereas the three judges were paid salaries of £6,000 per annum (£8,000 for the Chief Justice), the councillors earned £10,000

---

[16] For example, William Richardson, the 'Pool-bundy' (or repairer of dams) in the 24 Parganas sued 'Gower Hurry Sing', a *sircar*, for fraud in the conduct of his duties. Entry for 17 March 1778, 'Hyde's Notebooks'.

[17] 'Touchet Report', *RCHC*, 5, p. 54.

[18] Pandey, *Introduction of English Law into India*, pp. 165–9.

[19] Impey to Kerby, 26 March 1779, BL Add. MSS 16,259, fos. 181–2.

[20] E. B. Impey, *Memoirs of Sir Elijah Impey* (London 1857), pp. 4–9.

[21] For Impey's financial struggles, see Impey to Dunning, nd. (probably 1777), BL Add. MSS 16, 259, fos. 79–81.

(£25,000 for the governor-general). The judges proved willing to compromise their supposed independence from the Company to swell their fortunes. Chambers, indeed, found it expedient to attach himself to the Clavering/Francis axis to forward his political ambition.[22]

Party politics also followed them into their court house. As party disputes hardened in the Supreme Council in 1775, the Hastings camp in particular chose to use the court to pursue its goals, as a way of circumventing their opponents' effective control, by majority voice, of the Calcutta council. The conviction and especially the hanging of Nandakumar (in August 1775) were especially controversial, given that Nandakumar was not only a political enemy of Governor Hastings, but also a Brahmin. The court was also divided over the legal propriety of this execution, at a moment when the use of capital punishment for crimes against property was becoming controversial in Britain. As concern spread about the impact of the Supreme Court, Chief Justice Impey carefully doctored the printed version of the trial which appeared in London in 1776 to suppress evidence of dissent among the judges.[23] British inhabitants of Calcutta later claimed that the hanging disturbed the 'Nation of Hindoos' because it 'shocked their Religious and Civil Prejudices as a People'.[24]

Yet the most dangerous aspect of the Supreme Court, from the point of view of the Company government, was its willingness to entertain suits against various kinds of government official for actions taken in their official business. The court's power to hear suits against Company servants and their Indian employees opened up a wide potential field for litigation, and appeared to undermine the authority of the Company's six provincial councils, acting as revenue tribunals and civil courts. For example, the Supreme Court issued writs of habeas corpus against the Calcutta provincial council on behalf of a revenue farmer imprisoned for arrears of rent.[25] The judges also sent a young clerk named Samuel Peat to Dhaka to act as 'Master-Extraordinary' on behalf of the court, helping suitors to seek legal redress against the Company without the trouble of coming to Calcutta. When Peat tried to arrest an officer of the Dhaka *faujdari adalat* (criminal court), he actually shot and seriously injured the brother-in-law of the Muslim *daroga* (superintendent).[26] Attempts by the Company to protect its Indian allies by invoking their

---

[22] Curley, *Sir Robert Chambers*, pp. 175, 262–75.
[23] Curley, *Sir Robert Chambers*, pp. 217–22.
[24] 'Touchet Report', *RCHC*, 5, pp. 44–6.
[25] Hussain, *Jurisprudence of Emergency*, p. 81
[26] 'Touchet Report', *RCHC*, 5, pp. 20–1.

immunity as servants of the *nawab* of Bengal, considered as a 'foreign prince', were quickly rebuffed by the judges. The court argued, by reference to the Company's records and to 'notorious fact', that the *nawab* no longer had any control over making war and peace nor over the treasuries of Bengal, so that his claims to sovereignty were defunct. Furthermore, Justice Robert Chambers argued that 'the East India Company can neither wage war, nor receive an ambassador, by any intrinsic authority of its own; it does both by the authority of the King of Great Britain, and under sanction of his sovereignty'.[27]

The actions of the court thus dramatized the continuing uncertainty over the legal definition of sovereignty in Bengal. In a bid to clarify the relationship between the Supreme Court and the Company government, the old school friends Warren Hastings and Elijah Impey together constructed 'A Plan for the Better Administration of Justice in the Provinces of Bengal' in early 1776.[28] Impey drew up the plan in the legal form of a parliamentary bill as 'less likely to be flung aside' when it was sent to England.[29] Impey's comment here illustrated both the frustration of British officials in Bengal at the fitful attention of ministers to their affairs, but also the changing orientation of Calcutta politics. Especially since the Regulating Act, British elites in Bengal needed actively to court not only the Company's directors but also ministers, lawyers and MPs. Indeed, Hastings' new judicial plan referred to the provisional nature of the Regulating Act, and the need for 'successive improvements, as necessity and experience might suggest them'.[30] In the case of the Hastings/Impey bill, the momentum for constitutional reform within the empire was emerging on the imperial periphery, but its focus was now of necessity on parliamentary statute.

The thrust of the plan was to join together the Supreme Court and the Company's own law courts in a single system of judicature to avoid future clashes between the two systems. Thus, the plan also sought to salvage and refurbish Hastings' previous 'Plan for the Administration of Justice of 1772.' The Company's *mofussil* civil courts would be retained, but they would be regulated and reviewed by a new high court, the 'Sudder Dewanny Adaulut', made up of the Supreme Councillors and

---

[27] T. B. Howell (ed.), *A Complete Collection of State Trials and Proceedings for High Treason and Other Crimes and Misdemeanors from the Earliest Period to the Present Time with Notes and Other Illustrations* (London, 1809–1826), vol. XX, p. 1130.

[28] The plan is discussed in Neil Sen, 'Warren Hastings and British Sovereign Authority in Bengal' in *JICH*, 25 (1997), pp. 59–81.

[29] Impey to Thurlow, 31 March 1776, BL Add. MSS 16,259, fo. 24r.

[30] G. W. Forrest (ed.), *Historical Documents of British India*, 2 vols. (New Delhi, 1985), vol. II, p. 300.

the Supreme Court judges sitting together. This 'high court' would regulate the lower courts, enact new legislation when required and act as a court of appeals. In a clear signal of the Company's main priorities, the plan took considerable pains to establish a regular legal framework for the prosecution of revenue defaulters in the district and provincial courts, and sought to limit the legal liability of the agents of these courts. Meanwhile, the criminal courts would revert to the system previously established by Warren Hastings, operating under a chief *daroga* and *qazi* in Calcutta. Again, however, the governor-general, his council and the judges would have powers to 'controul and govern' these Muslim courts.[31]

This plan was a remarkable effort to reconcile the competing claims of royal sovereignty and legal diversity in a unified administrative structure. It argued that 'the distinctions of Nizamut and Dewanny should be abolished, and the British sovereignty through whatever channels it may pass into these provinces should be all in all'. The plan warned of 'the uses, which may be made of these distinctions in securing the acts of Government from interruption by warrants and writs issued from the Supreme Court of Judicature will be found fallacious on examination, and may be perverted to the most dangerous of all abuses'.[32] Thus, Hastings and Impey sought a fuller measure of imperial sovereignty to strengthen the colonial establishments. At the same time, Philip Francis was also seeking clarification over the issue of sovereignty, arguing that 'the British government should declare His Majesty's Sovereignty over the kingdoms of Bengal, Bahar and Orissa'. Yet Francis saw this as a prelude to the re-establishment of the 'country government', suggesting that 'the Nabob may then hold by grant from the King, as he is now supposed to do from the Mogul'.[33]

Hastings and Impey, by contrast, argued that their proposed new high court was well adapted to guard 'the laws, usages and manners of the people'. To this end, it would be assisted in its deliberations by 'the Roy Royan, the Canongos and other chief officers of the Khalsa'. The provincial courts would be composed of the Company's provincial councils, assisted by *diwans*, *qanungos*, *maulvis* and *pandits*, and the district court would consist of 'the Naib Dewan and Canongos of each respective district'.[34] Meanwhile, the 1776 judicial plan, while building on Hastings' earlier plan of 1772, elaborated further on how best to construe the law in India. The 1772 model had stated that the 'Laws of

---

[31] Ibid., pp. 302, 304–5, 306.   [32] Ibid., p. 300.
[33] Cited in Guha, *Rule of Property For Bengal*, p. 145.
[34] Forrest, *Historical Documents*, pp. 301–3.

the Koran' for Muslims, or 'of the Shaster' for Hindus should be employed in cases of inheritance, marriage, caste and religious usages and institutions. Nothing was said to contradict the scriptural version of Indian laws in the plan of 1776. But the new plan also emphasized the importance of local usage and custom. The third paragraph of the plan stated that 'all the forms, usages and rules which have been generally practiced, or which have been constituted for the management and collection of the revenues, shall be valid and legal'. Indeed, Impey insisted that

the practise of the Court has been invariable guided by this maxim, and the Chief Justice on reading this article has declared that he considers the local laws and customs of the provinces, proved in the Court, as ruled by which he is to administer justice, in the same manner as the local laws and customs in England are understood to be part of the common law thereof.[35]

Here, then, was a powerful statement of a 'customary' approach to law in India, by analogy with the common law, which needed to be set against scriptural definitions of the Indian law. The view that local custom was the proper basis of law was a central tenet of the English common law tradition. Impey seems to have envisaged that the British courts would eventually discover an Indian common law based on 'the local laws and customs of the provinces, proved in the court'. The British usually thought that this law would involve the interpretation of principles derived from Hindu and Muslim scriptures and codes, especially in some critical areas of civil law. But, seen in the light of Impey's emphasis on customary law, the authority of scriptural laws derived from their supposed role in indigenous 'custom and usage'. Impey considered it his duty to investigate local custom by directing inquiries to knowledgeable local informers, not just *pandits* or *maulvis*, but also, for example, revenue officials in cases pertaining to administrative law. He wrote:

I do not pretend to intuition. I am arrived in a country where the Manners and Customs are dissonant widely from that which I have left. I endeavour to procure assistance from those whose offices, Learning and Experience ought to enable them to give information.

Impey noted that 'on Questions of the Hindoo Religion and Laws I have referred to the Pundits. On Questions of Mahomedan Law to the Molovies', but on issues of revenue he consulted officers of the khalsa or Company servants, making them answer specific questions under oath.[36]

---

[35] Ibid., p. 304.
[36] Impey to Lord North, Calcutta, 20 January 1776, BL Add. MSS 38,398, fo. 238r, v.

The Hastings/Impey plan thus sought to avoid costly clashes between the royal court and the Company *adalats* by uniting both into a system designed to discover an Indian common law. Yet the plan was destined, as Impey had feared, to be ignored by the home authorities. This was partly because of the determined opposition of the council majority, who portrayed the plan as a desperate grab for power on behalf of the judges, aiming 'to give the Supreme Court of Judicature a compleat and effectual controul over every part of the country'.[37] It was partly also because the plan made overly ambitious demands on ministers who were reluctant to grasp the thorny problem of sovereignty in Bengal, especially at a moment when troubles in America were consuming much of the government's attention.

The 'Patna cause': natural justice for India

Yet the conflicts between the Supreme Court and the Company government only intensified in the years to come. Impey declared in April 1777 that 'the Court is daily increasing in business. We are beginning to make the vultures of Bengal disgorge their prey.'[38] Individual Company servants or their Indian agents were frequently charged and found guilty of various civil charges arising out of their official activities. In such cases, the judges often criticized the Company government for failing to adhere to its own bureaucratic rules and regulations. For example, in the case of 'Binnodram Gose' versus 'Bunarrassy Gose' heard in February 1778, the court found that the plaintiff had been forced to pay charges to the officers of the *diwani adalat* in Dacca amounting to Rs 505. Referring back to Hastings' judicial regulations of 1772, Impey observed in court that 'I have heard and read that these Courts were to do justice without Fees.'[39]

Very often charges would be brought against Indian agents of Company servants rather than the Britons themselves. Impey felt that this was a natural consequence of the fears of Indian inhabitants of the power and influence of Europeans. Prosecuting the *banyans* or other underlings was thus the only means to achieve redress of grievances.[40] Yet Impey was not insensitive to the charge that his court was both undermining the authority of the Company government and encroaching into the realm of Indian law. In February 1778, for example,

[37] Minute of Majority, 21 March 1776, BL Add. MSS 16,265, fo. 102v.
[38] Impey to Lord Bathurst, 1 April, 1777, BL Add. MSS 16,259, fo. 52.
[39] Entry for 9 February 1778, 'Hyde's Notebooks'.
[40] Impey to E. Thurlow, 12 August 1778, BL Add. MSS 16,259, fo. 137r.

he expressed his reluctance to interfere with or overturn judgements made by the Company's *adalats*, because this would be 'in effect to abolish the jurisdictions'. Justice Hyde's view was that this consequence was a mere 'inconvenience' beside the greater evil of considering the judgements of the *adalats* as conclusive, 'because it is well known they are exceeding corrupt'.[41]

The issue of the Supreme Court's jurisdiction in relation to the Company *adalats* soon exploded over the judges in a case that perhaps more than any other came to define the early history of the Supreme Court. The so-called 'Patna cause', which was decided in February 1779, was one of the principal cases on which the Company founded its appeal to parliament against the jurisdiction of the Supreme Court.[42] The case was a vivid illustration of the contrasting claims of the Supreme Court judges and the Company as agents of justice in India. It showed how Elijah Impey was willing to use cases against Indian officials to discipline the Company government, and in the process to stretch the conventional remit of an English court by appeals to principles of natural law. At the same time, it suggested the pitfalls and contradictions involved in the Company's appeal to the customary norms of Indian law.

The 'Patna cause' originated in a dispute over inheritance, this time over the estate of Shabaz Beg Khan, a wealthy soldier and landowner from Afghanistan who had settled in Patna. As a cavalry officer he had served the British in the wars of the late 1750s and early 1760s, acting for a time as the agent of the high-ranking Company servant William Watts. Robert Clive had secured a noble title for the Khan from the Mughal Emperor Shah Alam, as well as *sanads* confirming him in his property in Patna. The Khan also acted as a revenue contractor for several regions of Bihar, paying revenues to the *naib diwan* of Patna, Shitab Rai and later to the Company's provincial council.[43] Shabaz Beg Khan was one of an elite class of intermediaries linking the

---

[41] Entry for 9 February 1778, 'Hyde's Notebooks'.

[42] For detailed secondary accounts of this case, see Pandey, *Introduction of English Law into India*, pp. 131–48; Curley, *Sir Robert Chambers*, pp. 278–87; and Lauren Benton, 'Colonial Law and Cultural Difference: Jurisdictional Politics and the Formation of the Colonial State', *Comparative Studies in Society and History*, 41, 3 July 1999, pp. 563–88, which examines 'the shift toward a hierarchical model of legal pluralism' (in which the state makes a 'monopoly claim to definitions of political identity') and how this shift occurred through the multiple contingencies of 'jurisdictional politics' (p. 564).

[43] For Shabaz Beg's career, from Kabul to Patna, I rely on George Bogle's report on the case, written in his capacity of Commissioner of Law Suits (responsible for coordinating the Company's dealings in the Supreme Court), BLC, 13 April 1779, OIOC, IOR P/166/82, pp. 2–3.

military—fiscal machine of the East India Company with the dynamic local economies of eastern India.

When Shabaz Beg Khan died in November 1776, he left a widow, Nauderah Begum, and a nephew, Behadar Beg, the son of the late Khan's brother who still resided at Kabul. After his death the Khan's complicated entourage appears to have split into opposing factions, one group forming around the widow and one around the Afghani nephew, squabbling over the spoils of his estate. After an initial period of dispute within the family circle, Behadar Beg took his claims to the inheritance to the Company's provincial council at Patna, alleging that he was the rightful heir to the estate by adoption. He claimed that the Begum had taken over her dead husband's house, retained his seals in her own hand and was despoiling his estate by carrying off the household goods.[44]

From this point events moved quickly in Behadar Beg's favour. The provincial council acting as the provincial *diwani adalat* referred his complaint to the *qazi* and *muftis* attached to the *adalat*, with orders that they should examine and take an inventory of the deceased's estate, and give an opinion on the proper rights of inheritance according to Muslim law. It took two or three days to make the inventory, and only after 'much difficulty' was Nauderah Begum persuaded to leave her apartments.[45] The *qazi* and *muftis* then decided on the right of inheritance. Their report to the Patna provincial council recommended that the proper division according to Muslim law would be three-fourths to the male heir (in other words, to Shabaz Beg's Kabuli brother, to be held on his behalf by Behadar Beg) and one-fourth to the widow for her maintenance.[46] The Begum, on the other hand, claiming full inheritance by virtue of a deed of gift (or *hebanama*), backed up by a record of the actual transfer of the property (an *ekrarnama*), refused to submit peaceably to the subsequent ruling by the provincial council. Instead she fled to a nearby Islamic religious compound (the 'Durgah of Shaw Arzaun in the environs of Patna') taking with her vital documents in the case, including her husband's seal, title deeds of his property, and slave women who should have formed part of the estate. While she was in the compound, a guard of sepoys was put over the Begum, and various 'harsh' measures were taken to force the Begum out of her sanctuary.[47]

The chief of the Patna provincial council, Ewan Law, suggested that the Begum took refuge in the 'durgah' to make herself appear 'more pitiable', and he professed concern that the seal of Shabaz Beg Khan

[44] Ibid., p. 3.   [45] Ibid., p. 9.   [46] Ibid., pp. 13–14.   [47] Ibid., pp. 17–18.

would be used to perpetrate more forged bonds on the deceased's estate. He argued that 'the Women of this Country, and particularly the Mussulman Women, are from their confined situation, bred up in too much ignorance and subjection to be capable of judging or acting for themselves'. The Begum was thus a tool in the hands of her male associates, who had likely forged the deed of gift in the first place. Law claimed that Behadar Beg had been 'publickly declared' by the Khan to be his heir, and that if the Khan had really wanted to leave a will he would have had it 'authenticated by the Cauzy'.[48] Law's account suggested how the details of this dispute were deeply bound up with the local authority of the *qazi*, and how Company servants were situating themselves as guardians of the imagined norms of Muslim patriarchy.

The Begum's actions in resisting the decrees of the Company may suggest that she was not so ignorant and abject as the chief at Patna imagined. Her next move was to go to Calcutta to issue a plaint to the Supreme Court against Behadar Beg, the *qazi* and the *muftis*, alleging assault, battery and false imprisonment.[49] The Company decided first of all to offer bail for all the defendants, and then to defend the suit on their behalf, claiming that the alleged crime was committed in the legal exercise of the Company's exclusive governmental authority. Hastings argued that the intervention of the Supreme Court, if left unchecked, 'threatened to break all the Bonds of Government'.[50] The trial was heard in November 1778, and on 3 February 1779, the Chief Justice issued a long and complex judgement in which he upheld the claims of the Patna widow, castigated the actions of the Company's provincial council and the Muslim law officers, and awarded damages against them of Rs 300,000 with Rs 9,208 costs.[51] Behadar Beg, the *qazi* and *muftis* were arrested and imprisoned, the *qazi* (a man of about 60) dying on route to Calcutta.[52] As so often, Indian officials bore the brunt of the blame for the perceived failings of Company rule.[53]

---

[48] Letter of the Chief at Patna, E. Law, to the President and Council at Fort William, BLC, 6 January 1778, OIOC, IOR P/166/79, pp. 135–44.
[49] Bogle's report, BLC, 13 April 1779, OIOC, IOR P/166/82, pp. 18–21.
[50] Governor-general's minute, BLC, 16 June 1778, OIOC, IOR P/166/79, pp. 346–7.
[51] Pandey estimated the total damages came to about £34,000. Pandey, *Introduction of English Law into India*, p. 137.
[52] The goods of the defendants were calculated at only Rs 47,574–10, so they were confined, until the Company paid off the balance due to Nauderah Begum (Rs 261,634), as ordered by parliament in the Bengal Judicature Act of 1781. Ibid., p. 138.
[53] Three members of the Patna council were subsequently sued by the Begum, lost the suit, and were charged Rs 15,000 in damages, but these were defrayed by the Company.

How then did the Supreme Court come to its judgement in the Patna Case, despite Impey's caution, expressed as we have seen in another case from 1778, about interfering in the Company's *adalats*? The real key to the legal proceedings in the 'Patna Cause' was the 'notice of justification' made on behalf of the defendants.[54] The defence rested not on a refutation of the proceedings alleged by the Begum to have occurred, but rather on the claim that the defendants had only acted under the legally constituted authority of the provincial *diwani adalat*. The defence, in effect, admitted the facts of the charges to be true, but denied that they amounted to a criminal offence. Thus, if the 'notice of justification' failed, then the defence would also fail.[55]

Before the trial, the Company's Supreme Council debated with their lawyers how the proceedings of the provincial *adalats* might be justified in English law. George Bogle, the 'Commissioner of Law Suits', noted that the attempt in a previous case to justify the proceedings of the Company government by the Mughal grant of the *diwani* tended to embroil the Company in inconclusive arguments about the historical role of this Mughal office; it would tend to produce a 'contrariety of evidence and opinions' and open up a 'wide untrodden field of argument'.[56] Thus, the ancient Mughal constitution, so often appealed to by Company policy makers, now seemed an imprecise basis for the legality of Company rule. Nor was 'usage and custom' a secure justification in this case, because the custom of the Company's *adalats* was 'too new, recent and vague'.[57] Thus, the safest ground of justification was the parliamentary Regulating Act which gave the right of the management of the Company's territorial acquisitions to the Supreme Council, confirming the powers previously exercised by the Company as *diwan*. Bogle noted that the parliamentary secret committee, in their seventh report of 1773, even took official notice of the new *adalats* established by Hastings' reforms of 1772.[58] Again, we can see here how the Regulating Act, for all its caution, was inexorably pulling the

---

[54] Before this notice was put forward, however, the first proceedings in the trial concerned Behadar Beg's 'plea to the jurisdiction'. The defence tried to argue that Behadar Beg was not 'in the service' of the Company; they argued that a revenue farmer, with a contractual obligation to deliver up a certain revenue, was different in this regard from an actual 'collector' of the revenues. The Court threw this claim out, and argued that Behadar Beg was 'in the service' of the Company through his obligations as an *ijaradar*. This was an interesting gloss on the question of which kinds of offices were regarded as 'real property' (like *zamindaris*) and which as mere administrative service. 'Touchet Report', *RCHC*, 5, pp. 237–9.
[55] Pandey, *Introduction of English Law into India*, pp. 136–7.
[56] Bogle's minute, BLC, 12 June 1778, OIOC, IOR, P/166/79, p. 311.
[57] Ibid., p. 313.   [58] Ibid., pp. 311–12.

Company government into the orbit of parliamentary sovereignty. Warren Hastings himself agreed with Bogle that the right of government, originally derived from the 'Dewanny', was 'now solely under the Act of Parliament'.[59]

In the event, it was this decision to argue that the authority of the *mofussil diwani adalats* derived from parliamentary statute that was the foundation of Elijah Impey's judgement against Behadar Beg and the Muslim law officers. The problem was that even the Supreme Council recognized the 'great irregularity of the proceedings of the Law Officers' by the standards of the judicial plan of 1772. According to these regulations, 'their business was solely to have declared the Laws', leaving the ascertaining of witnesses and judgement of the facts to Company servants on the provincial council.[60] Thus, Impey argued that if parliament had approved the powers of the British collectors, and latterly the provincial councils, to 'hear and determine' civil cases among Indians, then these provincial councils were then fully bound 'to hear and determine' such cases.[61] But in the case of Nauderah Begum, Impey argued, the provincial council had done no such thing. Instead they had referred both the investigation and the determination of the inheritance rights to their Muslim law officers. Impey's judgement, then, implicitly upheld the independent jurisdiction of the *adalat* properly constituted; what it denied was the power of the provincial council acting as an *adalat* to delegate their judicial authority to the Muslim law officers.

The Company, by justifying the actions of the *qazi* and *muftis* by reference to parliamentary statute, walked into a legal trap. Impey, following the prosecuting attorney, invoked the maxim of English law *Delegatus non potest delegare*[62] to make his point that the power 'to hear and determine' was a sacred trust attaching to judges, appointed by the sovereign power, that could not be delegated to others. And here his judgement made a crucial turn. Impey implicitly acknowledged the Company's arguments that such maxims of English law were invalid in the Indian context, by emphasizing that the maxim *Delegatus non potest delegare* was not merely derived from the positive rules of English law, but also from 'natural justice and common sense'.[63] This appeal to 'natural justice and common sense' is a fascinating and important

---

[59] Ibid., p. 314.
[60] Governor-general's minute, BLC, 16 June 1777, OIOC, IOR P/166/79, p. 148.
[61] 'Touchet Report', Appendix 16, *RCHC*, 5, pp. 246–8.
[62] Literally, 'the one to whom judicial power has been delegated, does not have the power to delegate it further'.
[63] 'Touchet Report', Appendix 16, *RCHC*, 5, p. 248.

feature of this opinion, because it refers us back to Impey's background as a practitioner of the common law.

As Lieberman in particular has shown, the idea of natural law not only underpinned conventional accounts of the nature of the English common law, but it was also used by legal reformers to expand or modify the common law to fit new exigencies. For Blackstone, for example, the legitimacy of the common law rested on a combination of historical and customary origins and congruence with natural law. The 'municipal law' of the English was thus a particular expression of the universal 'natural law', and no municipal law could stand if it was contrary to natural reason.[64] Following from this, English judges could appeal to natural law and reason to push the common law into new areas. 'Natural law and equity', for example, was the touchstone of many of Chief Justice Mansfield's critical opinions in the fast-developing sphere of commercial law.[65] Impey's appeal to natural law in the Patna cause was thus thoroughly consonant with the theory of the common law, but it was aimed rather differently than many of Mansfield's attempts at 'judicial determination'. Whereas Mansfield sometimes argued for modifications to common law precedent in the light of natural law principles, Impey was using natural law arguments to defend conventional rules of English law in a setting where they might be vulnerable to attack as inappropriate. Thus, Impey could use the idea that the English law was consonant with a broader 'natural justice' to justify the wisdom of parliament for extending that law into new territories, namely Patna.

This appeal to natural law and common sense was made still more explicit in the second half of Impey's judgement in the case. This addressed the defence's claims in mitigation of damages, which was that the defendants had acted, if not strictly according to legal powers, then at least in accordance with their own sense of duty *bono animo*. In adjudicating on the plea of justification, Impey stood on the comparatively solid ground of the English statute law, but now he was commenting on the procedures of investigation and judgement undertaken by Muslim law officers. Again, he made clear that his ability to comment on the behaviour of the *qazi* and *muftis* derived from his grasp of principles of natural justice. He declared that his comments on the justification were 'not narrow or confined to the Rules of any particular

---

[64] Lieberman, *The Province of Legislation Determined*, p. 38.
[65] See, for example, ibid., pp. 89–92, where Lieberman discusses Mansfield's judgement that 'the eternal rule of natural justice' insisted on allowing non-Christians to give witness under their own forms of oath in an English court.

system of Municipal Laws, but what would naturally arise to Men of common sense'. He declared he would regard the process of the Muslim law officers 'still more liberally', but it became quickly apparent that he found their behaviour, especially in turning a grieving widow out of her house, to be a violation of 'common humanity'.[66]

Again, in these novel circumstances, Impey relied on the notion of universal reason, natural law and common sense to see him through to an area of jurisdiction beyond the usual remit of English law. His training in the common law, he was implying, would not hinder his capacity to judge in the Indian context; rather it would assist him, by giving him sound ideas of 'natural justice' or 'common sense'. This section of the judgement bristled with horror at the ill-treatment of the Patna widow, and it was the fierce language of this attack on the *qazi* and *muftis* which left Impey open to the charge that he had overstepped the bounds of his competence in persecuting lawyers trained in a very different system of law than his own. The *qazi* and *mufti* were pilloried as 'wicked inhuman Oppressors', whose judgement for Behadar Beg was 'given merely on the Allegation of the Party', and whose examination of witnesses (which was in part performed through notes sent back and forward from the *qazi*) was 'too contemptible to deserve a single Observation to condemn it'.[67] Impey revealed himself to be prejudiced against the Indian officials of the *adalats* by previous complaints made to the court, and his opinion slipped into generalized racist condemnation of 'Black Officers'.[68]

Impey was not opposed to employing the Muslim law officers in cases of inheritance between Muslims. Indeed, he said 'it frequently does happen' that he himself referred such questions to the *maulvis* of the Supreme Court, who were salaried and 'sworn Officers of the Court'.[69] What he objected to were the powers informally awarded to *qazi* and *muftis* in Patna who did not even owe their appointments to the Company (they were still officially appointed by the *naib nazim* in Murshidabad) and who received scanty official reward.[70] He grandly declared, 'I shall always believe, till I am convinced to the contrary, that Principles of Justice are deeper rooted in the minds of my own Countrymen, than in the corrupt Natives of this Country, and especially

---

[66] 'Touchet Report', Appendix 16, *RCHC*, p. 248.
[67] Chief justice's opinion, 'Touchet Report', *RCHC*, 5, pp. 261–2.
[68] Ibid., p. 258.
[69] Chief Justice's opinion, 'Touchet Report', *RCHC*, 5, p. 247.
[70] Ibid., p. 261. The *qazi* was paid Rs 100 a month, the *muftis* even less. The clear imputation here was that they would inevitably seek remuneration from 'fees' or bribes.

than such Natives as are generally attendant as Officers on Courts of Justice.'[71] There may be a hint of irony here, especially in the first subordinate clause; the thrust of the judgement, after all, was a critique of Company servants who had not done their own duty as judges, but had palmed it off on others.

On the other hand, the venality of Indian lawyers had long been a commonplace notion in the Company's settlements. In Impey's judgement, the tension between the ubiquitous rhetoric of native depravity and the Company's efforts to incorporate indigenous power holders was being dramatically exposed. His ruling in the Patna cause was informed by a strong current of legal chauvinism, strengthened by his belief that the common law was consonant with universal or natural law. In fact, the implication of his opinion was that Muslims had respectable substantive laws, but that their judges knew (or at least acted on) no respectable form of judicial procedure. This view of Islamic law was in fact a commonplace of English legal theory; despotic states (of which Muslim states were the quintessential examples, from Turkey to India) were supposed to have very rudimentary and summary judiciaries, in contrast to the great complexity of English courts, which in Blackstone's famous invocation of the English as a 'polite and commercial people', acted as a bulwark of English liberties.[72]

A key element in Impey's judgement also depended on common stereotypes about Asiatic women, and especially Muslim women. These women were commonly imagined to be sheltered from the world from birth, and hence very vulnerable to the despotic authority of their male masters.[73] Thus, Impey positioned himself as a defender of the benighted Begum, emphasizing the horror to a woman of her stature of being rudely turned out of her house into the bazaar.[74] The Company government, taking a different tack, posed as defenders of the patriarchal norms of the Muslim law, which they argued typically frowned on a widow's claims to inherit more than a fourth of her husband's estate. Both of these positions shared in the notion that Indian women were relatively 'helpless', secluded and disempowered in Asiatic societies, while they drew different conclusions from this.

---

[71] Ibid., p. 247.
[72] See W. Blackstone, *Commentaries on the Laws of England*, Joseph Chitty (ed.), 4 vols. (London 1826), vol. III, pp. 325–6, and the discussion of this passage in Lieberman, *Province of Legislation Determined*, p. 48.
[73] For a contemporary discussion of a domestic despotism lying at the root of Islamic despotism, see Dow, *History of Hindostan*, vol. III, pp. xiv–xix.
[74] 'Touchet Report', *RCHC*, 5, p. 258.

For Impey, vulnerable Indian women needed to be protected from patriarchal tyrants; for the Company, violating Indian patriarchy disturbed the foundations of government and society. Neither of these views acknowledged the substantial evidence that Asiatic patriarchy was not so monolithic or totalizing as they imagined. Indeed, the role of women as head of some of the leading *zamindaris*, the role of matriarchs like Munni Begum in the *nawab*'s court in Murshidabad, and the determined legal strategy of Nauderah Begum herself, suggested that British stereotypes of oppressed Asiatic women substantially distorted, complex political realities.

From Patna to parliament: confusing outcomes

Impey's judgement in the Patna cause was consonant with his wider sense of his imperial purpose in Bengal. He believed that 'the Chiefs of the different subordinate factories have been used to exercise an uncontrouled despotic power in their several stations', and it was the duty of the Supreme Court to provide judicial remedies for their abuses.[75] He argued that he could provide such remedies while protecting the rights of Indian inhabitants to be judged by their own laws, partly by making enquiries of learned informers, and partly through the exercise of 'common sense'. His judgement in the Patna cause, however, suggested that his sympathy for Indian legal traditions was starkly limited, and that he was unwilling to explore the unfamiliar logic of Muslim legal practice with any rigour or sensitivity.

Meanwhile, the Supreme Court's dramatic interventions were now becoming intolerable for the Company. In its rough treatment of Behadar Beg, a revenue farmer, and the senior Muslim law officers of the important city of Patna, the Supreme Court was undermining the Company's alliances with vital Indian intermediaries. The Patna council was keen to emphasize how the attempted seizure of the old *qazi* struck 'general Terror into the Inhabitants of this City'.[76] A petition signed by 227 of the leading inhabitants of Bihar noted that 'when this country first became Subject to the Dominion of the Lords of Victorious Fortune, the English, great Fear and Apprehension prevailed in our minds. From the Diversity of our Faith and Religion, and from the Difference of Customs and usages, we doubted what Conduct those Gentlemen would observe towards us'; yet, thanks to the preservation of old laws and the authority granted to old officials, 'we were upon

---

[75] Impey to Lord Ufford, 9 January 1778, BL, Add. MSS 16,259, fo. 90r.
[76] BLC, 23 December 1777, OIOC, IOR P/166/79, p. 82.

the whole happy and satisfied'. Now, however, 'we consider Death to us as infinitely preferable to the dread we entertain' of the Supreme Court; some had fled the country to escape its jurisdiction, and 'Men of repute and honourable persons' had been ruined; they appealed to the English king that 'Justice shall be administered to us, according to the fixt Law of the Country, as it has even prevailed, according to our usage and customs.'[77]

After a prominent Hindu banker sued the raja of Kasijora (the largest *zamindar* of Midnapur district) for a debt in the Supreme Court, the Company sent a party of sepoys to put a stop to the attempt of the sheriff to arrest the *zamindar*.[78] The Supreme Court's interference in the Company's revenue system was especially alarming at a time when the Bengal treasuries were being stretched by wars on several fronts in central and southern India. Yet the Supreme Council took a great legal risk by stepping in so boldly to stop the process of the royal court of justice, and there followed a massive effort in parliament and in the press to justify the Company's actions. Urgent petitions from the Company were added to a petition from the British inhabitants of Bengal against the alleged abuses of the Supreme Court, and all this converged on the British parliament in 1781.

The Patna cause, along with the trial and hanging of Nandakumar, formed a major part of the subsequent inquiries of a House of Commons select committee into the impact of the Supreme Court in Bengal. On behalf of the Company, George Bogle, the Commissioner of Law Suits, prepared a detailed response to Impey's ruling in the Patna cause, which remains a fascinating explication of the legal and cultural dilemmas facing the British in Bengal.[79] Bogle defended the Muslim law officers as upstanding pillars of Patna society, unfairly condemned by the standards of an alien law. He painted the case as part of a conspiracy by the widow's corrupt agents to defraud Behadar Beg of his rightful inheritance by forged deeds. He strongly defended the *qazi* from charges of corruption, noting his venerable service to both the *nawabs* and Company, and insisting that 'it is one of the clearest points of Mussulman law, that her [the widow's] share is only a fourth; and that it is not in the husband's power, by any deed which takes effect after his death to give her more'.[80]

---

[77] 'Translation of Persian Petition from Native Inhabitants of Subah of Azeemabad [Patna] to the King', OIOC, MSS Eur. F218, fo. 30.
[78] For a detailed account of the Kasijora case, see Pandey, *Introduction of British Law into India*, pp. 176–95.
[79] 'Touchet Report', *RCHC*, 5, pp. 278–98.   [80] Ibid., p. 294.

Bogle was one of the few British observers who tried to consider more carefully the systemic rationality of the Muslim law. He saw that there appeared to be 'an informality, according to the English Law', in the way that the *qazi* first decided that the absent brother Allum Beg was the rightful heir, and then granted the property to Behadar Beg on his father's behalf. Yet, according to Bogle, 'Mussulman Lawyers' would insist it was a *qazi*'s duty to 'appoint a Guardian on behalf of the absent person'. Judged on 'liberal principles', this practice appeared to Bogle as analogous to the way that magistrates 'in more civilized nations' were empowered to appoint guardians and administrators.[81] Bogle's invocation of a hierarchy of civilization suggested that he too considered the Muslim law on a lesser plane than the English law. But he strongly denied the applicability of English legal doctrines, such as *delegatus non potest delegare*, in India. He argued that very few Company servants were well enough versed in Indian languages to administer justice themselves. Thus, it was necessary to delegate more power to Indian law officers, not only to discover the laws applicable, but also the facts of the case as well, because it 'requires a knowledge of the Law to try the Fact'.[82] Thus, in defending the *qazi* and *muftis*, Bogle was led into a remarkable admission of the incapacity of British officials to administer justice in Bengal.

The sheer volume of complaints against the Supreme Court, the general context not only of war in north India, but also of rebellion in North America, and the force of the Company's arguments about violations of 'native custom', all resulted in a swift defeat for Impey and the Supreme Court by the Bengal Judicature Bill of 1781. Parliament was inclined on this occasion to listen more to the voice of a hard-pressed colonial executive than a self-righteous judiciary. It passed a bill that supposedly clarified the provisions of the Regulating Act, but in fact secured new protections for the Company government from the jurisdiction of the Supreme Court.[83] Emphasizing the need for the Company's revenues to be 'collected with certainty', the court was disallowed from hearing cases concerning the revenues, except in cases of corruption or embezzlement by Company servants. Revenue farmers and *zamindars* were also exempted from the jurisdiction except in cases of 'Acts of Oppression' under the general authority of the governor-general and council.[84]

---

[81] 'Bogle's Report', BLC, 13 April 1779, OIOC, IOR P/166/82, pp. 147–8.
[82] Ibid., pp. 172–3; 'Touchet Report', *RCHC*, 5, pp. 296–7.
[83] The fullest account of the provisions of the bill is in Jain, *Outlines of Indian Legal History*, pp. 121–35.
[84] 21 Geo.III c.70, *HCSP*, 33, pp. 264, 266.

The bill also addressed the aftermath of the Patna cause, noting the need to protect the customary rights of fathers of families, and the inviolable spaces of Indian women's apartments. Provision was made for appointing 'Native counsellors' to advise the Supreme Court, as well as the Company courts. Meanwhile, Indian law officers were protected from complaints against their official actions, except in cases of manifest corruption; even in such cases, they would be given time to respond to written notice of any complaints. Meanwhile, Behadar Beg and the two surviving *muftis* were ordered to be released from confinement in the common jail of Calcutta and re-instated in their legal offices. Together with the family of the deceased *qazi*, they were belatedly granted financial compensation for their troubles.[85]

In passing the new statute, members of parliament spoke grandly of protecting the constitutional rights of the natives to their own laws. In the debate on the passing of the bill, one MP and former officer in the Company armies, General Smith, urged his colleagues to consider the wise example of ancient Rome, an empire that was 'satisfied to possess the revenues and the military power, leaving the inhabitants to conduct their internal police by their own native magistrates and laws', until Justinian committed the blunder (through the imperial law of conquest) of extending Roman law throughout the empire. In a different vein, Smith's speech also raised a different problem that was uppermost in the minds of many Britons in Calcutta: namely, 'the equalizing principle which this judicature tends to establish betwixt native and European'.[86] In a speech in committee, Edmund Burke pleaded with his compatriots to study 'the spirit, the temper, the constitution, the habits, and the manners of the people'. The people of Bengal were 'familiarized to a system of rule more despotic', and to force them to submit to the elaborate complexity of an alien law would be itself a form of 'tyranny'. Moreover, the English judges had violated the 'dearest rights' of Indians 'particularly in forcing the Ladies before their courts'.[87]

The conclusion to the early history of the Supreme Court was actually far more messy and contradictory than these parliamentary flourishes about the spirit of the laws would suggest. Before parliament passed its new Act, Warren Hastings had appointed Elijah Impey as judge of the

[85] Ibid., pp. 270–1, 279–81.

[86] W. Cobbett, *Parliamentary History of England from the Earliest Period to the Year 1803, from which last-mentioned Epoch it is continued downwards in the work entitled 'Cobbett's Parliamentary Debates'* (London, 1806–20), vol. XXI, pp. 1199–202.

[87] Cobbett, *Parliamentary History*, vol. XXII, pp. 554–5.

sadr diwani adalat in Calcutta, with powers to frame new regulations for the ordering of the inferior *adalats*.[88] For Hastings, this new alliance with Impey was not only a means of conciliating his damaged friend, but also of refurbishing the *adalats*, which had recently been shown to bear only a slight resemblance to their original institution according to the regulations of 1772. For Impey, the appointment came with a salary of Rs 5,000, as well as a chance to imprint some 'natural justice' on the 'despotic' agencies of the Company government. Impey's acceptance of this appointment, with the appearance of sacrificing his judicial independence, was later used by his enemies in an attempt to impeach the chief justice.[89] Yet, in his brief period as 'Judge' of the *sadr diwani adalat*, Impey composed new regulations for the Company courts which fulfilled his ambition, carried over from his earlier 1776 plan, of substantially reforming the Company's judiciary.

His code of regulations for the *diwani adalats*, enacted in July 1781, enshrined many of the concerns that Impey had raised in the Patna cause, and attempted to institute what he regarded as a more regular form of judicial process.[90] The aim of these 95 regulations was that 'a general uniformity may be obtained in the proceedings of the courts', overseen by a chief court of appeals. The *diwani adalats* were now given greater independence from the revenue branch; a Company servant acting as 'superintendent of the *diwani adalat*' was appointed to each of the six provincial stations of the Company government to work independently of the provincial councils of revenue. While these officials could not take cognizance of any case regarding revenues, they were now allowed to summon *zamindars* and *taluqdars* to hear complaints against them.[91]

Many of Impey's regulations reflected his deep-seated legal chauvinism and suspicion of Indian jurists. The Indian law officers (*qazis*, *muftis* and *pandits*) were to be disciplined through the strict administration of oaths, restrictions on fees and detailed provisions for record keeping. In a clear reference back to the Patna cause, the procedures by which the English judge should receive the legal opinions of the Indian law officers were elaborated in Regulation 38; *maulvis* and *pandits* were restricted to answering specific written questions about the Muslim

---

[88] Pandey, *Introduction of English Law into India*, p. 198.
[89] Ibid., pp. 199–214.
[90] Impey's Regulations are printed in J. E. Colebrooke, *A Digest of the Regulations and Laws, Enacted by the Governor-General in Council for the Civil Government of the Territories under the Presidency of Bengal, Arranged in Alphabetical Order* (Calcutta, 1807), pp. 37–87. They were also translated into Bengali and Persian.
[91] Misra, *Judicial Administration of the East India Company*, p. 270.

and Hindu laws delivered by the English judge.[92] The old provision for reference to Muslim and Hindu laws in specific civil cases was retained, with an extra proviso that, for civil cases not covered by Muslim and Hindu law, the British judges should act according to 'justice, equity and good conscience'.[93] As Derrett has argued, the technical meaning of this phrase was that the judges should look beyond 'municipal laws' and base their judgements on natural reason. In fact, this clause proved (especially in the nineteenth century) a way for certain maxims of English law to leak into the Indian courts, and with Impey's application of 'natural justice' in the Patna cause in mind, this should not surprise us.[94]

According to B. B. Misra, Impey was 'the first pioneer who elaborated the rules of process and evidence, materially altering the earlier principle of adjudication, which imported to the country courts the form and character of the British judicial system'.[95] Impey's code was later incorporated into the more famous Cornwallis codes after 1793, when British India settled into its familiar bureaucratic pattern, centred on British 'collectors' and 'magistrates' enforcing the imperial will in the countryside.[96] Thus, while parliament appeared to have beaten back the English law to Calcutta, an English judge's sense of proper judicial procedure was enshrined in the regulations of the Company courts. The Company's patronage of indigenous law officers turned out to be far more equivocal than their petitions to parliament might have suggested. George Bogle's view that more powers should be delegated to Indian jurists remained a minority view in the Company service, and Impey's regulations served to reinforce the idea that adequate judicial procedure must be imported through the superior legal intelligence of the British.[97]

Conclusion

In a general sense, the conflict between the Supreme Court and the Company had buttressed the idea of sharp constitutional difference

---

[92] Colebrooke, *Digest of Regulations and Laws*, pp. 64–5.

[93] Ibid., p. 74.

[94] J. D. M. Derrett, 'Justice, Equity and Good Conscience' in J. N. D. Anderson (ed.), *Changing Law in Developing Countries* (New York, 1963), p. 133.

[95] Misra, *Judicial Administration of the East India Company*, p. 274.

[96] J. H. Harington, *Elementary Analysis of the Laws Enacted by the Governor-General in Council at Fort William in Bengal* (Calcutta, 1818), pp. 30–1.

[97] Bogle continued to argue for greater powers for Indian jurists in the Company courts. See, for example, his letter to D. Anderson, Rangpur, Ft William, recd. 31 March 1780, BL Add. MSS 45,421, fos. 96v–97r.

between the Company's territories in India and the rest of the British empire. The Company's rule would in theory be built on indigenous law and custom, and its authoritarian structure of government was imagined to reflect the despotic nature of Asiatic government. At the same time, however, debates over the Supreme Court had rendered deeply problematic the Company's claim to govern Bengal in accordance with an ancient constitution.

The Company's decision to defend the exclusive jurisdiction of its law courts by reference to parliamentary statute rather than Mughal precedent suggested how the Company government was being drawn into the force field of parliamentary sovereignty, even though the formal definition of sovereignty remained uncertain. George Bogle's report on the Patna cause recognized the difficulty of justifying the details of the Company's government by reference to the 'Laws and Customs of this Country', when 'they are often repugnant to the principles of the Law of England', and they 'are not laid down in Books of Authority, but are founded on necessity, on practice, or on the opinions of the people'. Thus, if there was an ancient constitution underpinning the Company's administration, it was unwritten and unstable, and Bogle urged the 'necessity of establishing the Country Courts on some less questionable foundation'.[98] Impey's new code of regulations was a significant beginning in this direction, and provided the foundations for more expansive administrative legislation in the decades to come.

The debates around the Patna cause starkly revealed the failure of imagination which underpinned the emerging colonial attitude towards legality in India. Bogle apart, few British observers were willing or able to think through the intellectual and institutional workings of the Muslim law in Patna. Rather, they tended to comment on the 'irregularity' of their proceedings by reference to the Company's judicial regulations. The best that could be said, as in the Judicature Act of 1781, was that because of the 'long unsettled State of the Government' and 'Confusions attendant on the Revolutions there', 'it hath been difficult for the native Magistrates, and Men of the Law, to comport themselves to avoid Error in the Method of Proceeding'; it was therefore 'not fit that the most severe animadversion should be used'.[99] As it turned out, eighteenth-century Britons were better able to pay rhetorical lip service to the 'spirit of the laws' than to explore in any depth the different rationality of an alien law.

---

[98] 'Bogle's Report', BLC, 13 April 1779, OIOC, IOR P/166/82, pp. 184–8.
[99] *HCSP*, 33, p. 280.

6   Reconstituting empire, c. 1780–1793

Impey's regulations for the civil courts were a sign of the future. While parliamentary speeches extolled the beneficence of British rule in preserving the laws of India from alien invasion, the official language of the Company government of Bengal was gradually moving away from the idea of the ancient Mughal constitution. Debates over the Supreme Court appeared to reveal the fragility of 'custom and usage' and the irregular nature of a territorial administration buffeted by war, conquest and famine. Meanwhile, the gradual extension of parliamentary oversight offered a new source of legality independent of the Mughal constitution.

This chapter outlines how the idea of colonial state-building as constitutional restoration slowly dissolved in the new political climate of the 1780s and 1790s. Crucially, the empire of the Company was now more fully absorbed into the British imperial state. From the mid-1780s a more unified brand of British imperialism moved away from divisive disputes about the Mughal past, and announced itself more confidently as a decisive break from the history of Asiatic tyranny. As the East India Company service rebranded itself as a purified agency of imperial virtue, the entrenched critique of Asiatic manners finally overwhelmed the more fragile sense of Mughal imperium as a viable form of sovereignty.

In the 1770s, Warren Hastings and Philip Francis, armed with competing visions of the Mughal constitution, had fought to a stalemate. Hastings' absolutist interpretation of Mughal sovereignty, tempered by ancient legal traditions, provoked Francis' assertion of an ancient constitution of property. After Hastings' return to Britain in 1785, both these positions would be further refined and elaborated as Hastings faced impeachment in parliament on charges of 'high crimes and misdemeanours'. In Bengal, however, the new government of Lord Cornwallis (governor-general, 1786–93) increasingly abandoned the ground of the ancient constitution, even as it sought more rigorously to subordinate Indian officials beneath a purified British administration.

Armed with new legislative powers, Cornwallis generated an expansive code of administrative law, which announced itself as a new kind of constitution for Bengal.

The crisis of war and the Pittite resolution

As Philip Francis sailed from India in 1780, the Company was rapidly embroiling itself in a new and dangerous series of wars with a hostile alliance of Indian states. Ham-fisted attempts by both the Bengal and Bombay governments to intervene in the internal politics of the Maratha confederacy eventually drew not just the Marathas, but also the Nizam of Hyderabad and Hyder Ali of Mysore on to the field of battle. Military reverses, followed by desperate diplomatic manoeuvres, were a strong reminder that the Company remained only one among a number of powerful Indian states.[1] The wars of these years also had a major impact both on the Company's government in Bengal and on the wider politics of British imperialism. As in the 1760s, warfare in India led to fiscal crisis, and to a further attempt by British ministers to exert their authority over the tottering edifice of the Company.

In Bengal, the pressures of war galvanized Warren Hastings, now freed from Francis' opposition, to enact a series of administrative reforms. Although the main theatres of battle were in western and southern India, Bengal was charged with providing both troops and money to defend Bombay and Madras. In 1781, Hastings took the chance to centralize the administration of the Bengal revenues under a new committee of revenue made up of four experienced covenanted servants. The six provincial councils were thus abolished, in apparent fulfillment of Hastings' earlier plan (from 1772) to withdraw the British agents of the Company to Calcutta, and operate through Indian agency in the countryside. The new streamlined plan of administration was also designed to produce an immediate reduction in the costs of collection, from over five million rupees in 1779–80 to a projected fixed cost of just two million.[2] The Calcutta committee of revenue was empowered to set the revenue assessments and deal with refractory revenue payers, and it was assisted by the experienced *khalsa* official, Ganga Gobinda Sinha, as *diwan*. In the late 1770s, under pressure from Philip Francis, the revenue demand for Bengal had been revised down for several years

---

[1] This crucial period of warfare has not yet had a comprehensive modern treatment. For a brief account, see Marshall, *Making and Unmaking of Empires*, pp. 254–6.
[2] Misra, *Central Administration of the East India Company*, p. 124.

running. Now, under pressure of war, the Company raised the tax demand on Bengal and Bihar dramatically, by 9.4 per cent.[3] Balances were more strictly enforced, *zamindars* were removed from the management of collections and replaced by temporary collectors, and a new office was established in Calcutta to inquire into and reduce the amount of rent-free lands.[4]

As it turned out, the Company was often unable to collect the new higher tax demands; uncollected balances grew by five times between 1780 and 1783.[5] Sometimes the Calcutta council resorted to forced sales of *zamindar* lands to pay off balances, but these sales rarely in practice raised enough money to pay off old balances, and were regarded rather as a punitive measure.[6] One official recommended selling some *parganas* of the Nadia *zamindar* 'as a punishment for failing in his engagements' and 'a warning to others'.[7] The shortfalls in the Bengal revenues forced Hastings, as he had in 1773–4, to look to the treasuries of allied states to the north; but his attempt to squeeze more money out of the ruler Benares provoked a major revolt, the military annexation of Benares (1781), and further evidence of apparent oppression to energize Hastings' growing list of enemies in England.[8] The Company's debts also escalated alarmingly. By the end of the war, its capacity to service its growing debts both in India and in London was severely strained.[9]

Arguably, the Company's heavy debts were both its weakness and its strength in the coming years. As the *nawab* of Arcot had discovered in south India, heavy debts could promote ties of mutual dependence which a vulnerable state could fruitfully exploit. While the British government sought greater controls over the Company's operations, it was unlikely to want to take on the burden of the Indian debts itself; rather, because of the Company's pivotal role in the city of London, ministers would likely need to help the Company and pay off its creditors – an extensive network stretching from English banks and the British state itself, to the Company's own servants abroad, and Indian

---

[3] McLane, *Land and Local Kingship*, p. 252. See also minute of John Shore (who was the President of the Committee of Revenue in 1781), 18 June 1789, *Fifth Report*, vol. II, p. 64.

[4] Misra, *Central Administration of the East India Company*, p. 126.

[5] N. K. Sinha, *The Economic History of Bengal*, 3 vols. (Calcutta, 1956–70), vol. II, p. 105.

[6] For his sense of frustration at the low prices raised by sales of estates in this period, see John Shore, minute of 18 June 1789, *The Fifth Report*, vol. II, p. 25.

[7] Charles Croftes to David Anderson, 14 April 1782, Anderson Papers, BL Add. MSS 45,426, fo. 55r.

[8] Marshall, *Making and Unmaking of Empires*, pp. 254, 265.

[9] Ibid., p. 251; Furber, *John Company at Work*, pp. 236, 316–17.

bankers.[10] In India, meanwhile, debt financing, though often regarded as a problematic last resort, in fact offered a flexible means of funding expensive wars as well as forging important alliances within Indian financial networks.[11]

Hastings' tax hike of 1781 was reminiscent of the emergency wartime increases enacted by *Nawab* Alivardi Khan in the 1740s and by Mir Qasim in the 1760s. Yet the failure of both the *nawabs* and the Company to make these increases stick suggested that new expedients were needed to meet the growing costs of warfare. Territorial expansion, or guns for hire, was one method that Hastings and the Company were now familiar with. Debt financing, backed by a more stable and reformed tax system in Bengal, seemed to offer further possible solutions. As we shall see, by the 1790s the Company was trying to bolster the value of alienable *zamindar* rights as a potential security for the government revenue. This strategy would offer British governors the chance to act both as Whiggish upholders of ancient rights and responsible guardians of the Company's fisc.

In the meantime, however, British ministers exploited the Company's travails to impose more comprehensive political controls over Indian affairs. As the American war lurched to its disastrous conclusion, opponents of Lord North's declining authority viewed the troubles in India as a further example of his blundering maladministration. Preoccupied with America, North's government had postponed a comprehensive settlement of the relationship between state and Company, and ended up by supporting Warren Hastings and his friends among the directors.[12] Philip Francis found a ready audience for his attacks on Warren Hastings on two parliamentary committees established in 1781, a select committee dominated by Edmund Burke (a leading figure in the Rockinghamite opposition) and a secret committee led by Henry Dundas.[13] Edmund Burke, in particular, became the main channel for an impassioned critique of the Company's misrule of Indian territories, drawing heavily on Francis' arguments about Hastings' alleged tyranny in Bengal.[14]

---

[10] Lakshmi Subramanian, 'Banias and the British: the Role of Indigenous Credit in the Process of British Imperial Expansion in the Second Half of the Eighteenth Century', *MAS*, 21 (1987), pp. 473–510.

[11] J. R. Ward, 'The Industrial Revolution and British Imperialism, 1750–1850', *EHR*, 47 (1994), pp. 44–65.

[12] Sutherland, *East India Company in Eighteenth Century Politics*, pp. 351, 359–61.

[13] Ibid., pp. 361–3, 367.

[14] P. J. Marshall (ed.), *Writings and Speeches of Edmund Burke*. Vol. V, *India: Madras and Bengal, 1774–1785* (Oxford, 1981), intro., p. 19.

The reform of Indian abuses was widely acknowledged as a necessary component in the political reconstruction following North's resignation in March 1782 and the subsequent admission of defeat in America. Yet the Company remained a formidable entity, which continued to invoke the shibboleth of sacred chartered rights to fend off ministerial interference. Attempts to regulate Indian affairs also foundered on the fragility of successive ministries in an era of heated factionalism in parliament. The Fox–North coalition of 1783 succeeded in passing radical measures for reform of the Company in the House of Commons. Promising to address 'disorders of an alarming nature and magnitude' tending towards the 'utter ruin' of the British position in India, Fox aimed to place the management of the Company's affairs in the hands of commissioners, named in the bill and answerable to parliament.[15] Determined resistance from within the Company, widespread suspicion that the commissioners would entrench the power and influence of Fox's own party, and the desire of King George to rid himself of troublesome ministers, all eventually conspired to scupper Fox's bill in the Lords.[16]

However, as the commons vote for Fox's bill showed, parliamentary opinion was still firmly behind measures of Indian reform, and in 1784 the new Prime Minister, William Pitt the Younger, skilfully exploited the opportunity for decisive action. Forged in negotiation with the Company itself, Pitt's India Act was explicitly aimed at 'doing the most good to India, & to the Company, with the least injury to our constitution', not by introducing an 'absolutely new' system but by remodelling 'the old constitution of the Company'.[17] The directors retained control of commercial affairs and of the Company's patronage. The British government would enjoy the power to superintend and control the Company in issues relating to 'the civil or military government or revenues' of India. The act established a ministerial Board of Control to exercise these supervisory powers, while at the same time excluding the Company's shareholders from interfering in issues of Indian governance. Unlike North's bill of 1773, Pitt's Act would endure as a lasting framework for managing Indian affairs. Despite some early teething pains over the contentious issues of military appointments,

[15] Cobbett, *Parliamentary History*, vol. XXIV, p. 62; Marshall, *Problems of Empire*, pp. 40–1.

[16] John Cannon, *The Fox–North Coalition: Crisis of the Constitution, 1782–4* (Cambridge, 1973), pp. ix–xiii; Philip Harling, *The Waning of the Old Corruption*, p. 39.

[17] 'Pitt's Speech on the India Bill, House of Commons, 6 July 1784', printed in A. C. Bannerjee (ed.), *Indian Constitutional Documents, 1757–1947* (Calcutta, 1961), pp. 94, 99.

and how many royal troops the Company was supposed to support in India, relations between the Board of Control (led by Henry Dundas as President) and the Company's directors were remarkably harmonious.[18]

A major element in this new rapprochement was the reorganization of the Company's finances. Pitt and Dundas engineered a financial rescue package for the debt-ridden Company in the years after 1784. The cornerstone of this operation was the Commutation Act of 1784, by which customs duties on the Company's tea were cut from 119 to 12.5 per cent both to reduce the value of smuggled goods slipping through the government's net and increase the Company's own sales of tea. This last benefit was dramatically achieved, as the Company's yearly tea sales, purchased with silver sent from Europe and the profits of the sale of opium in Canton, rose from £6 million to £19 million.[19] The expanded tea trade offered an effective way for the Company to repatriate its 'surplus' revenues from Bengal. Meanwhile, new techniques of debt management were applied to the Company's growing 'home' and 'India' debts.[20] The most powerful symbol of the new financial management of the Company's affairs was the annual India budget presented by Henry Dundas to parliament. As P. J. Marshall has pointed out, whereas earlier British ministries dug for evidence of the Company's financial incompetence to justify statutory intervention, now one of Pitt's leading ministers made an annual defence of Indian finances for which he was in part responsible; the interests of state and Company appeared to be running in parallel once again, rather than at cross purposes.[21]

The great beneficiary of this new found stability was the new governor-general of India appointed by Pitt in 1786, Lord Cornwallis. Cornwallis personified the new sense of imperial responsibility prescribed in Pitt's Act. Vastly different in background and experience from previous governors, Cornwallis was a Whig aristocrat and military officer, who (despite his famous defeat at Yorktown) somehow avoided taking the blame for defeat in America and survived to embody a new species of imperial virtue in India.[22] Cornwallis' power base lay outside

---

[18] Marshall, *Problems of Empire*, pp. 43, 49–50, 98–9.

[19] Ibid., pp. 89–90; Bowen, *Business of Empire*, pp. 241–2.

[20] John Ehrman, *The Younger Pitt, vol. I: The Years of Acclaim* (London, 1969), p. 459.

[21] P. J. Marshall, 'The Moral Swing to the East: British Humanitarianism, India and the West Indies', in K. Ballhatchet and John Harrison (eds.), *East India Company Studies. Papers Presented to Professor Sir Cyril Philips* (Hong Kong, 1986), p. 79.

[22] C. A. Bayly and Katharine Prior, 'Cornwallis, Charles, First Marquess Cornwallis (1738–1805)', *Oxford Dictionary of National Biography* (Oxford, 2004) [http://www.oxforddnb.com/view/article/6338, accessed 21 June 2006].

the Company in the network of political and social connections that centred on Westminster and the royal court. He was untainted by the whiff of commercial priorities or private profiteering that clung to Clive and Hastings. Whereas these governors had contended with the shifting sands of a fluctuating directorate, and with sudden interventions followed by disinterest and indecision of previous ministries, now Cornwallis had the ear and trust of a powerful minister (Henry Dundas) with overriding control over Indian policy. Just as importantly, Cornwallis was awarded, at his own insistence, a concentration of powers in his own person which earlier governors could only dream of. Not only did he command the other presidencies of Madras and Bombay, but he also enjoyed substantial discretionary powers independent of the Supreme Council in Calcutta, as well as direct command of the Bengal armies.[23] Thus, if the politics of the Company calmed down after 1784, it was in part at least because the avenues of political dispute were deliberately closed off in a newly authoritarian structure of government.

Furthermore, extensive debates in Britain about Indian issues had created an approximate consensus around the previously thorny issue of revenue management and land rights in Bengal. Philip Francis and Warren Hastings' friends in London conducted a mini-pamphlet war in the early 1780s which aired their disputes over revenue policy. Fox's bill of 1783 substantially accepted Francis' view of *zamindar* property, ordering that all lands in Bengal should be considered 'the estate and inheritance of native land-holders and families . . . according to the custom of the country'.[24] Similarly, Pitt's Act of 1784 noted frequent complaints that 'divers Rajahs, Zemindars, Polygars, Talookdars and landholders' had been unjustly deprived of 'their lands, jurisdictions, rights and privileges'. The Company should inquire into their rights and then pursue measures for 'restoring' them that were 'agreeable to the Laws of the Country'.[25] Meanwhile, the directors of the Company were moving towards Francis' view that the land-tax demand in Bengal ought to be made fixed and unalterable.[26] After the ignominious beginnings of the Company's Asiatic empire, a permanent settlement of the land tax appeared to be exactly the kind of grand political gesture that could draw a firm line under the factious politics and confused policies of the Hastings era.

---

[23] Misra, *Central Administration of the East India Company*, pp. 33–4.
[24] Cobbett, *Parliamentary History*, vol. XXIV, p. 80.
[25] 24 Geo III, s. 2, c. 25, *HCSP*, 46, p. 76.
[26] Guha, *A Rule of Property for Bengal*, p. 161.

The Mughal constitution on trial

In the final years of his governorship, as the chorus of his critics swelled in size and volume, Warren Hastings had taken measures to counter Philip Francis' and Burke's view of him as a usurper of ancient rights, and oppressor of rajas and *zamindars*. Instead he portrayed himself as a great statesman, arbitrating the troubled affairs of north India, and offering British protection to the venerable institutions of the Mughal empire. For example, he continued to patronize textual scholarship in both Persian and Sanskrit. He sponsored the Company servant Charles Wilkins in his English translation of the Bhagavad Gita. Hastings also personally paid for the printing of the Company servant Francis Gladwin's translation of the *Ain-i Akbari*, or 'Institutes of Akbar', the massive compendium of administrative, geographical, religious and social knowledge compiled by the Emperor Akbar's chief minister, Abul Fazl.[27] This translation, more than any other, reflected the historicist idiom of Hastings' government. In Dow's *History of Hindostan*, Akbar had appeared as the model of enlightened toleration and benevolence.[28] Now Hastings recommended Akbar's 'institutes' to the Court of Directors as an authentic record of the 'original constitution of the Mogul empire', that would show them 'where the measures of their administration approach first principles, which perhaps will be found superior to any that have been built on their ruins'.[29] This statement may have been designed both to convey Hastings' solicitude towards the old Mughal constitution, and to insist that the Mughal constitution had in fact collapsed into ruins prior to the Company's conquests. Contrary to Francis' view, in other words, there was no ancient constitution still extant in Bengal to which British governors were answerable.

Hastings also came to believe that Persian sources offered encouragement to his own view of the Mughal emperor's absolute prerogative powers *vis-à-vis zamindars*. In an undated document entitled 'Explanation of the Term Zemindar', Hastings wrote that 'In no History or account of Hindoostan that I have read in the Persian Language, can I find a Definition of the Rights of Zemindars. Even the Ayeen Akberree is silent on this subject.' But he noted that the *Ain-i Akbari* prescribed severe punishments for a 'refractory Zemindar', and that 'instances of

---

[27] P. J. Marshall, 'Warren Hastings as Scholar and Patron' in Anne Whiteman, J. S. Bromley and P. G. M. Dickson (eds.), *Statesmen, Scholars and Merchants: Essays Presented to Dame Lucy Sutherland* (Oxford, 1973), pp. 247–9.

[28] Grewal, *Muslim Rule in India*, p. 18.

[29] Francis Gladwin, *Ayeen Akbery, or the Institutes of the Emperor Akber* (translated from the original Persian by F. Gladwin), 2 vols. (London, 1800), vol. II, p. xix.

the Expulsion of Zemindars are not infrequent in the History of Hindostaun'. He thought that *zamindars* were liable to be removed by the 'Emperors of Hindostaun according to their pleasure', and that they were 'liable to pay what Revenue the Sovereign thought proper to fix'.[30]

Apart from his continuing encouragement of British scholarship on the Mughal empire, Hastings extended his patronage to notable figures from the Mughal nobility and intelligentsia. From the early 1770s, Hastings was concerned to recruit well-educated Muslim officials to serve the Company government, especially in the *adalats*. The effect of the Supreme Court's harsh attacks on Muslim law officers very likely made this more difficult than before. In 1781, Hastings provided land on his own account as an endowment for a new college of Islamic scholarship in Calcutta, the Calcutta Madrassa. The costs of the new school, designed as a 'nursery for Muhammedan Law Officers and Judges' were later defrayed from assignments on the public revenues.[31] Meanwhile, he used the annexation of Benares to extend further the sway of what he regarded as the proper constitutional forms of the Mughal empire. The noted administrator and scholar, Ali Ibrahim Khan, a one-time prominent servant of *Nawab* Mir Qasim and a long acquaintance of Hastings, was appointed chief magistrate of Benares, acting alongside the new raja (a nephew of the deposed Cheyt Singh) and the British resident. Ali Ibrahim Khan corresponded directly with the governor-general and council, enjoying wide powers in both judicial and revenue affairs, and a large salary to reflect his high status.[32]

Ali Ibrahim Khan composed a series of contemporary histories in Persian, and maintained close communications with Warren Hastings even after the latter returned to England. In February 1786, he expressed his sadness at Hastings' parting from India: 'If you had remained', he wrote, 'a new town hall would have risen up, a Granary as a resource in time of Charity would have been built and a flourishing Gunge [market] in the name of the Company'.[33] One project from this imagined list of beneficence was in fact completed. In September 1786, Ali Ibrahim wrote that a *naubatkhana*, a kind of music chamber

---

[30] BL Add. MSS 29,233, fos. 56r–58v.

[31] A. C. Sanial, 'History of the Calcutta Madrassa', *Bengal Past and Present*, 8 (1914), pp. 83–112, 225–51.

[32] Ali Ibrahim Khan's monthly salary in 1781 was Rs 2,900 per mensem, which compares with the Rs 1,200 paid at this time to British collectors in Bengal. Shayesta Khan, *A Biography of Ali Ibrahim Khan (c. 1740–93): A Mughal Noble in the Service of the British East India Company* (Patna, 1992), p. 89.

[33] Ali Ibrahim Khan to Warren Hastings, 20 February 1786, BL Add. MSS 29,202, fo. 85v.

especially associated with rituals of rulership in north India, had now been completed and was inscribed in 'Persian, Hindoovee and English characters': 'By Orders of Mr Hastings, Ali Ibrahim Khan erected this building'. 'Drums and other instruments of Music are in the building and the Nobut sounds five times a day'.[34] This type of personal alliance with high-ranking Indian officials was an important feature of Hastings' governorship that would be less and less evident under his more determinedly 'British' successors.

Hastings' final act of self-conscious benevolence was the attempted restoration of the credit and authority of the Mughal *wazir*, the *nawab* of Awadh. The *nawab*'s position had been savagely undermined by the Company's fiscal demands since the 1760s and by the interference of successive British residents. In visiting Lucknow in 1784, Hastings declared his 'ambition to close my government with the redemption of a great government, family, and nation from ruin'.[35] His efforts to decrease the influence of the resident and resettle the finances of Awadh did little to allay the long-term erosion of the *nawab*'s power. Nonetheless, Hastings' ambition extended even to helping the son of the now captive emperor Shah Alam retain the Mughal throne in Delhi, recommending the scheme to the Calcutta Council as 'the generous side of the question' that would be 'applauded at home'.[36] Given the directors' constant emphasis on avoiding further military entanglements, this idea appears strangely optimistic, although it harked back to a longer-standing aim of governors in Calcutta since at least the 1760s to use the restoration of due Mughal imperial authority as a means of stabilizing north Indian politics.

Hastings' diplomacy was also designed to project his self-image as a cosmopolitan statesman on good terms with other scions of the Mughal empire, and he made increasing use of the medium of painting to publicize his efforts. Northern India, with its wealthy and status-conscious British and Indian patrons, became a notable centre of European art in the 1780s, and Hastings conducted his last tour of the great north Indian capitals with two well known artists, John Zoffany and William Hodges, in his entourage.[37] Zoffany painted Hastings sitting respectfully on the floor before the Mughal prince, Javan Bakht,

---

[34] Ali Ibrahim Khan to Warren Hastings, September 1786, ibid., fo. 86r.

[35] G. R. Gleig, *Memoirs of Warren Hastings*, vol. III, p. 153.

[36] Ibid., p. 191.

[37] For British artists in India in this period, see N. Eaton, 'Imaging Empire: Trafficking Art and Aesthetics in Colonial India c.1772–c.1795' (unpublished Ph.D. thesis, Warwick, 2000).

the son of the unfortunate Shah Alam II.[38] Meanwhile, Hodges' diary and paintings, later published in England, extolled the glories of Mughal architecture as well as the beneficent patronage of Hastings.[39]

Unsurprisingly, neither Hastings' efforts at self-publicity, nor the reforms of Pitt's India Act, were enough to divert Edmund Burke from his determination to bring the alleged crimes of the Company to account in Britain. Burke's campaign against Warren Hastings only grew in intensity in these years, culminating in the extraordinary political theatre of Hastings' impeachment trial (1786–94). Burke's lengthy and eloquent attacks on the person of Warren Hastings were closely related to a particular neo-Roman conception of politics. In this Tacitean tradition, the decline of republican virtue in ancient Rome dated from the growth of empire, as rogue generals on the imperial frontier turned their forces into a tool of faction, and subverted the balance and stability of Roman governance.[40] In Burke's passionate speech introducing Fox's India Bill in 1783, the danger that returning Nabobs would pollute the pure streams of British landed virtue was made vividly apparent. 'They marry into your families; they enter into your senate', he declared, and 'there is scarcely a house in this kingdom that does not feel some concern and interest that makes all reform of our eastern government appear officious and disgusting'.[41] The fear of the corrupting effects of imperial tyranny on the domestic constitution animated Burke throughout the trial and beyond. For him, the prosecution of Hastings' villainy was a necessary measure in preserving the national character and the checks and balances of the British constitution.

Viewed in the longer history of imperial politics, however, Edmund Burke's prosecution of Warren Hastings also appears as the culmination of a particular historicist and constitutionalist tradition. Like Philip Francis, with whom Burke and his fellow managers of the impeachment trial were closely associated, Burke met Hastings on the ground of Indian history, and in particular on the ground of the Mughal constitution. As we have seen, Hastings as governor took a stern view of the rights of government vis-à-vis landowners in Bengal, believing in the absolute, though properly reserved and beneficent, powers of Indian

---

[38] P. J. Marshall, 'Britain and the World in the Eighteenth Century: III, Britain and India', *TRHS*, 6th series, 10 (2000), pp. 9–10.

[39] William Hodges, *Travels in India, During the Years 1780, 1781, 1782, and 1783* (2nd edn, London, 1794); see also Natasha Eaton, 'Hodges' Visual Genealogy for Colonial India 1780–95', in Geoff Quilley and John Bonehill (eds.), *William Hodges, 1744–1797: The Art of Exploration* (London, 2004), pp. 35–42.

[40] Marshall, '*A Free Though Conquering People*', pp. 6–7.

[41] Speech on Fox's India Bill, 1783, in Burke, *On Empire, Liberty and Reform*, p. 311.

sovereignty. This was in accord, as he thought, with the extensive powers of Mughal government as ultimate owner of the soil. Hastings defended himself against the first charge of impeachment, in which he was accused of unfairly taxing and then dispossessing the raja of Benares in 1781, by reference to the inherited and absolute powers of Indian sovereignty, passing from the emperor, through the *nawab* of Awadh, and finally to the Company.[42] Yet, in his famously ill-received opening speech, Hastings pressed the language of absolutism to alarming extremes. In a phrase apparently written by his friend Nathaniel Brassey Halhed, he proclaimed that 'The whole history of Asia is nothing more than precedents to prove the invariable exercise of arbitrary power'.[43] Though Hastings subsequently tried to disown this statement, it may well initially have struck him as a thoroughly conventional description of the nature of Asiatic government.[44] Yet, it was a risky proposition for a British governor to appear so blatantly to associate himself with the traditions of Asiatic despotism, and Burke would exploit this passage in Hastings' speech to the full.

Drawing on the new knowledge of Mughal government, much of it generated within the East India Company, Burke leapt on Hastings' reference to despotic power and ridiculed him for his pretensions. Philip Francis had already tried to separate the notion of Mughal despotism from the taint of arbitrary power, arguing that private property had flourished under the benevolent and moderate rule of the Mughal emperors. Burke took this analysis still further. Though Burke had justified new limits on the scope of English law in 1781 by reference to the alleged despotic traditions of Indian government, he eventually insisted that the Mughal empire was not in fact a despotic regime, in the sense of a lawless tyranny. If there was indeed an ancient Mughal constitution, then this was sufficient proof of stability, fixity and legal government to render the notion of despotism redundant.[45]

For Burke, Warren Hastings' notion of the Mughal constitution was a farce. He ridiculed Hastings' claim to know 'the constitution of Asia only from its practices'. Hastings had simply made 'the corrupt practices of mankind' into 'the principles of Government', gathering them up to

---

[42] 'A Definition of the Nature of the Office of a Zamindar: sent for the use of Mr. Pitt, a day or two before the 13th June 1786, on which day he used it and voted for the Benares article (in Warren Hastings' hand-writing)', BL Add. MSS 29,202, fos. 32–7.
[43] Cited in Rosane Rocher, *Orientalism, Poetry and the Millennium: The Checkered Life of Nathaniel Brassey Halhed, 1751–1830* (Delhi, 1987), p. 134.
[44] Dirks, *Scandal of Empire*, pp. 107–8.
[45] For Burke's changing ideas about 'despotism', see Frederick G. Whelan, *Edmund Burke and India* (Pittsburg, PA, 1996), pp. 188–261.

'form the whole map of abuses into one code, and call it the duty of a British Governor'.[46] Elaborating on forms of Asiatic government, Burke described the Ottoman sultanate as a kind of limited monarchy, a 'Mahometan sovereign' who was 'bound by law'. Referring to the Institutes of Genghiz Khan, Burke declared, 'if there is arbitrary power, there can be no Institutes'; the 'Institutes of Tamerlane', from whom the Mughal emperors traced their ancestry, was further grist to this mill. Burke outlined the multifarious sources of law in Muslim polities: the Koran; *fatwas*, or 'written interpretations of the principles of jurisprudence'; *qanun*, which he thought 'equivalent to Acts of Parliament'; and the 'Rage ul Mulk, the Common Law or Custom of the Kingdom, equivalent to our Common Law'. 'They have', he concluded, 'laws from more sources than we have, exactly in the same order, grounded upon the same authority, fundamentally fixed to be administered to people upon these principles'.[47]

Burke thus pressed out the analogy between the ancient Indian constitution and its ancient English counterpart. This became still clearer in his discussion of Hindu or 'Gentoo' law, as a comprehensive and ancient body of written law, forming a system of 'natural equity modified by their institutions', or 'a whole body of equity, diversified by the manners and customs of the people'.[48] This was exactly the language which Britons conventionally used to describe their own common law. Burke further narrowed the conceptual distance between Europe and Asia in his description of the Mughal empire as a great confederation of princes analogous to the 'empire of Germany'.[49] Moreover, Burke (like Francis) argued that essential features of the ancient constitution of the Mughal empire had in effect survived the breakdown of central authority in the eighteenth century. Even in the 'troubled and vexatious era' of the independent *nawabs*, so Burke thought, the Hindu princes had maintained their honour and dignity, until they were 'given up finally to be destroyed by Mr. Hastings'.[50]

Burke's major arguments in the Hastings trial were not just about legal history, but about the role of sovereignty in history. What most fired Burke's rhetoric was that Hastings, a mere delegate of a commercial Company, should have been claiming a kind of despotic power. As a

[46] Burke's Speech on the Opening of the Impeachment, 16 February 1788, in P.J. Marshall (ed.), *The Writings and Speeches of Edmund Burke*. Vol. VI, *India: the Launching of the Hastings Impeachment, 1786–88* (Oxford, 1991), p. 350.
[47] Ibid., p. 364.   [48] Ibid., p. 365.
[49] Speech on Fox's India Bill, in Burke, *Empire, Liberty and Reform*, p. 296.
[50] Speech on the Opening of the Hastings Impeachment, 15 February 1788, in Marshall (ed.), *The Writings and Speeches of Edmund Burke*. Vol. VI, pp. 311–12.

delegate of the Company, Burke argued, Hastings acted under two main sources of power: first, the several royal charters authorized by parliament to be granted to the Company; and second, the 'grants and charters which it derived from the Emperor of the Moguls'. Whatever the nature of Mughal imperial sovereignty, Burke thought it absurd to imagine that the Mughals had delegated a despotic power to their subordinate governors. The power that Hastings 'supposed himself justified by, namely a delegated, subordinated, arbitrary power', was to Burke a nonsense. Meanwhile, it was evident that 'the East India Company have not arbitrary power to give him'.[51] Hastings, a mere delegate, had thus presumed to usurp the full powers of imperial sovereignty. Hastings appeared in Burke's rhetoric as a new kind of *nawab*, a usurper breaking the proper bounds of imperial subordination. Once again, we see how the rhetoric of usurpation, which the Company in the 1750s and 1760s had used so effectively against the *nawabs* themselves, could be turned back against a Company governor's own pretensions to sovereignty.

In contradistinction to Hastings' upstart pretensions, Burke was the prophet of a reconstructed imperial sovereignty. He saw the impeachment of Hastings as the dramatization of a new imperial dispensation, in which parliament was taking upon itself the virtual representation of millions of its subjects overseas. In a remarkable passage where Burke outlined the recent constitutional history of India, he envisaged a kind of mystical alliance between Mughal and British imperial sovereignties, designed to restrain the overweening powers of subordinate authority. By the treaty of 1765 with the Mughal emperor, by which the Company obtained the office of *Diwan* or 'Lord High Steward', the Company 'bound themselves, and bound inclusively all their servants to perform all the duties belonging to that new office' and 'to observe all the laws, rights, useages and customs of the Natives'. As the Mughal sovereignty was in effect 'annihilated or suspended' by the misfortune of the house of Timur, the responsibility of the East India Company to their earlier agreements was not itself abrogated; rather 'for the responsibility, they are thrown back upon that country for whence their original power' had emanated; namely, the king-in-parliament.

For when the Company acquired that office in India, an English corporation became an integral part of the Mogul Empire. When Great Britain assented to that grant virtually, and afterwards took advantage of it, Great Britain made a virtual act of union with that country, by which they bound themselves as to the

---

[51] Ibid., pp. 280–2.

securities of their subjects, to preserve the people in all their rights, laws and liberties, which their natural original Sovereign was bound to enforce, if he had been in a condition to enforce it.[52]

Thus, parliament itself now stood in for the Mughal emperor as the supreme sovereign and judge of the Company's fitness as Lord High Steward of the Mughal empire. The Mughal constitution, which had seemed to offer a template of rule to Company officials in India, was now in Burke's rhetoric partially absorbed into the orbit of the British constitution and of parliamentary sovereignty. This was because the law in India, like the law in Britain, was seen as a local or 'municipal' emanation of the one, universal, divine or 'natural law' to which all rulers were ultimately subject.[53]

Burke's arguments for imperial sovereignty chimed well with the new extension of central controls over the imperial provinces, but his wider analysis of Indian politics was much less influential. In the early days of the trial, cartoonists liked Gilray publicized allegations that Hastings may have bribed the king and his courtiers such as the Lord Chancellor Thurlow (a noted defender of Hastings) with Indian diamonds.[54] But the impeachment soon ran out of steam, as parliament was increasingly distracted by more the more urgent business of imminent war with the dramatic new threat of revolutionary France. Burke's break with his Whig colleagues over the French revolution split his political coalition, and left him an isolated and increasingly embittered figure. Meanwhile, the corruption of Nabobs appeared to have been tamed, as Pitt's India Act was generally seen to have worked well, and Lord Cornwallis was imagined to have thoroughly reformed the Company's Indian service. By the 1790s, Burke's venom against Hastings was increasingly viewed as ill-conceived and intemperate, and Hastings was acquitted on all charges in 1794.

While there were many factors in the eventual failure of the prosecution, one important cause was the scepticism which greeted Burke's elevated conception of the Mughal constitution among a British public long accustomed to thinking of Asia as a land of despotism. The 'rights, laws and *liberties*' (my italics) of the natives was a conceptual leap too far for a British audience now being schooled in the black arts of the Company's south Indian enemy, a new Siraj-ud-daula, Tipu Sultan of Mysore. Towards the end of the trial, news of Lord Cornwallis' victories

---

[52] Ibid., p. 282.   [53] Dirks, *Scandal of Empire*, pp. 288–90.
[54] M. D. George, *English Political Caricature. A Study of Opinion and Propaganda* (Oxford, 1959), pp. 192–3.

over Tipu were greeted with great shows of public enthusiasm in Britain.[55] Burke's elevated views of the obligations of sovereignty in India seemed to challenge not only the conventional stereotypes of Asiatic despotism, but even British conceptions of their own polity. After all, a certain form of despotism, in the sense of a supreme, final and uncontrolled power, could be said to exist in even the most free polities; Blackstone himself had famously described the British parliament as 'the place where that absolute despotic power which must in all governments reside somewhere, is entrusted by the constitution of these kingdoms'.[56]

It was notable that William Pitt the Younger, even while he voted for impeachment on the Benares charge in 1786, still did not accept the full burden of Burke's arguments about the constitutional restrictions on British authorities. The Benares charge turned on Hastings' demand of a special tribute which spurred the Raja of Benares to rebel. Pitt thought that every ruler, even in Britain, had a right to tax his subjects as much as necessary for the defence of the realm. 'It was impossible to suppose the existence of any state which had no provision made for extraordinary resources for extraordinary dangers'. [57] Pitt defended the ruler's right to absolute, discretionary powers in an emergency, especially in what he apparently regarded as a land of despotism. He decided, however, that in this particular case Hastings' treatment of the Raja of Benares broke through the bounds of acceptable or just behaviour. 'Though the constitution', Pitt declared, 'of our Eastern possessions were arbitrary and despotic, still it was the duty of every administration in that country to conduct itself by the rules of justice and liberty, as far as it was possible to reconcile them to the established government'.[58] This view, which clearly left greater flexibility for executive power, would have far more staying power than Burke's idealized model of the Mughal constitution.

Indeed, Burke's invocation of the ancient Mughal constitution proved to be a late flowering of the conception of the British empire in India as a form of constitutional inheritance – a political idiom which, by a considerable irony, Burke and Hastings in a broad sense shared. Eventually these two bitter enemies would take their places in the heroic

---

[55] P.J. Marshall, '"Cornwallis Triumphant": War in India and the British Public in the Late Eighteenth Century', in *Trade and Conquest: Studies on the Rise of British Dominance in India* (Aldershot, 1993).
[56] William Blackstone, *Commentaries on the Laws of England*, vol. I, p. 160.
[57] Pitt's speech, 13 June 1786, Cobbett, *Parliamentary History*, vol. XXVI, p. 103.
[58] Ibid., p. 110.

narrative of imperial history, Hastings as the governor who saved India, and Burke as the founder of a new tradition of imperial trusteeship. But their shared language of ancient constitutionalism would be largely forgotten, as the idiom of the ancient Mughal constitution fell into imperial disuse. Indeed the dramas of the trial may themselves have made the language of ancient constitutionalism less attractive for British officials in Bengal. Hastings' use of the Mughal constitution as a justification for a masterful executive steered too close to the winds of Asiatic despotism; whereas Burke's views of the historical constraints on Indian rulers appeared both to run against the grain of conventional European wisdom, and also to place unreasonable constraints on an empire of conquest.

One aspect of Hastings' defence chimed better with the currents of imperial politics. That was the idea that any Mughal constitution had so far broken down by the period of the Company's conquests as to be effectively in ruins. Hastings had developed this line of thought in his critique of Francis' view of the rights of Bengal landholders. It was further pursued in the trial.[59] This view of things suggested that British governors were not bound by Mughal precedent, though they might preserve elements from the old customs which were familiar to the people and not repugnant to the new rulers. An argument could be made, therefore, that what was needed was a new constitution for Bengal, blending British ideas of justice with traditional forms of Indian rule. This is what Lord Cornwallis would aim to provide.

The decline of the country government

The progress of the trial suggested how and why the old arguments about the Mughal constitution were running out of steam as strategies of legitimation for British politicians. Yet British invocations of the Mughal constitution had arisen not simply as a legitimizing device for a British audience, but also a way for British rulers to manage the alliances forged with different kinds of Indian official in Bengal. In the 1770s, both Warren Hastings and Philip Francis, as they had laid out policy positions for the future of Bengal, continued to imagine that British power in the region would be exercised largely through the agency of Indian officials. In Hastings' view, old offices of Mughal government like the *faujdars*, *darogas* or *amins* should be revived, and British collectors should be withdrawn from the districts. In Francis' plan of 1776, British district

---

[59] Marshall, *Writings and Speeches of Edmund Burke*, introduction, vol. VII, p. 22.

officers would only be necessary in the early days of the permanent settlement, but would afterwards withdraw to Calcutta, leaving the field for the 'country government' and the natural aristocracy of the *zamindars*. In both versions, the British would govern at some distance in their imperial capital, as if by analogy with the Mughal emperors themselves, and Bengal would be, if not self-governing, then at least self-regulating.

The idea of the ancient Mughal constitution was a vital element in the fantasy that the strange anomaly of the Company's empire could be redeemed by the internal mechanisms of India's own history. This fantasy was partially motivated by a persistent mistrust among directors and governors of the ambition and greed of the Company service, which was blamed for the disorders of the 1750s and 1760s. And yet the ideal of withdrawing British agents from the countryside invariably appeared as something to be aspired to in some future period of political order, rather than being considered actually practicable in the short term. Even when Hastings withdrew the six provincial councils in 1781, apparently fulfilling his plans to rely on 'native agency' in the districts, in fact he allowed the council chiefs and some other district collectors to remain at their stations (with European underlings) and to correspond with the committee of revenue.[60] In 1785, Hastings' temporary successor, John Macpherson, generalized the collector system, dividing Bengal into 33 districts under British collectors.[61]

Hastings sometimes blamed 'the curse of patronage' for what he regarded as a bloated Company service, and certainly the demands of Company servants for lucrative positions in the interior was one reason why ideas of native agency were compromised.[62] But this was part of a bigger problem; the idea that Bengal would become in effect self-regulating rested on unrealistic assumptions of the community of interests between the new British rulers and Bengal's administrative and landed elites, assumptions which threatened always to break down into mutual antipathy. Hastings' plans to revive Mughal offices, or Francis' desire to restore the 'country government', foundered on mutual misunderstandings and the persistent unwillingness of new British rulers to devolve too much power or too many profits to Indian subordinates. Meanwhile, Muhammad Reza Khan's sceptical response

---

[60] BRC, 9 February 1781, cited in 'Report on the Territorial Revenues of Bengal', Wellesley Papers, Add. MSS 12,566, fos. 45–6.
[61] Misra, *Central Administration of the East India Company*, pp. 127–33.
[62] Warren Hastings, *Memoirs Relative to the State of India* (London, 1786, repr. Calcutta, 1978), p. 68.

to Francis' overtures in the mid-1770s suggested an accurate appraisal of the limited scope for Indian high officials within the new colonial order.

Indeed, while Edmund Burke was expounding on the glories of the ancient Mughal constitution before the country gentlemen of England, a gentleman from Bihar, and a scion of the erstwhile Mughal empire, was composing a withering critique of the Company's efforts to appropriate the aura of Mughal legitimacy. Ghulam Husain Khan Tabatabai came from a Shia family with a long tradition of service to both the emperors and the *nawabs* of Bengal. Based in Patna, Ghulam Husain had made the hard transition from the Mughal lesser nobility to working as a *munshi* for the British.[63] He was probably encouraged to write his great Persian chronicle, *Seir Mutaqherin,* or 'history of his own times', by one of his patrons in the Company, Colonel Thomas Goddard. The history was completed in 1781 or 1782. Soon afterwards, Haji Mustafa, the French-speaking Turk who had settled in Murshidabad, published a translation of Ghulam Husain's work in Calcutta.[64] The translation testified to a continuing demand in Calcutta for the kind of knowledge available in Persian histories. Indeed, friends of Warren Hastings apparently conceived a plan to use Ghulam Husain's chronicle as supporting evidence for the defence in the impeachment trial.[65] Both Ghulam Husain and Haji Mustafa had known Hastings, and included words of praise for him in their texts.

Yet the dominant note of Ghulam Husain's chronicle was one of disillusionment with the innovations introduced by the British conquerors. As Haji Mustafa put it, there ran throughout Ghulam Husain's history 'a subterranean vein of national resentment, which emits vapours now and then, and which his occasional encomiums of the English can neither conceal nor even palliate'.[66] Inserted into the middle of the text was a treatise, similar in form to Muhammad Reza Khan's earlier tract, which detailed the ways in which the Company's rule violated the

---

[63] F. Lehmann, ' "The Eighteenth Century Transition in India', pp. 64–92. Ghulam Husain's paternal grandfather came from Persia to India to join the Mughal service and settled in Patna, the capital of Bihar. His mother was related to the *nawab* of Bengal, Alivardi Khan, and Ghulam Husain (born 1727–8) grew up in Alivardi's court, then moved to Delhi where he held administrative posts, before returning to Bihar where he was a tax farmer and revenue officer under Shitab Rai at Patna. Ibid., pp. 64–6.

[64] Ghulam Husain Khan Tabatabai, *A Translation of the Seir Mutaqherin, Or View of Modern Times,* Nota Manus [Haji Mustafa] (tr., ed.), 3 vols. (Calcutta, 1789, repr. Calcutta 1902–3).

[65] Grewal, *Muslim Rule in India,* p. 32.

[66] Ghulam Husain Khan, *Seir Mutaqherin,* vol. I, p. 6.

customs and ethics of the Mughal empire. This described how Mughal emperors had formerly lived among their people 'as kind and condescending parents among their children'. But for the last sixty years the old Mughal hierarchy, formerly governed with great vigilance by the emperors in Delhi, had broken down.[67] First it was replaced by independent provincial governors, who nonetheless had continued to follow the 'rules and maxims of government'. Already, however, evils had begun to creep into the system; offices were leased to the highest bidder rather than granted to virtuous officials, and 'a new sort of men, worse than the former' came to power.[68] Then came a revolution still more dramatic, in the 'introduction of European foreigners', new rulers who 'were quite alien to this country, both in customs and manners'.[69]

Ghulam Husain came from the broad category of the Mughal nobility and service gentry who had been rendered most vulnerable by the sudden decline of first the emperors and then the *nawabs*. Holders of *jagirs* (assignments on the revenues), pensions and offices under the old regime, they had been forced to rely on the uncertain patronage of the Company to maintain their wealth and status. In 1765 Ghulam Husain managed to secure the inheritance of his father's *jagir* in Bihar, but later he suffered large losses as a surety for a *zamindar* during the period of the five-year revenue farms (1774–5); after this, he entered Colonel Goddard's service with the Company army in Awadh.[70] The onset of Company rule had been profoundly dispiriting. He bemoaned the 'aversion which the English openly show for the company of the natives' and their ignorance of Indian languages.[71] Twice, Ghulam Husain travelled to Calcutta to settle personal business with the Company, but despite being favoured with an interview with Warren Hastings, he ended up alienated and disappointed.[72]

Ghulam Husain's treatise described the alarming loss of status suffered by elite Mughal warriors, scholars and administrators in the transition to Company rule. Yet, as Ghulam Husain presented it, this was not simply a function of the parsimony of the Company, and the siphoning off of political profits to Calcutta, but also of clashing systems of political norms and ethics. For example, the Company's preference for ruling through bureaucratic councils, behind closed doors, undermined the old principles of accessibility and good counsel

[67] Ibid., vol. III, p. 159.   [68] Ibid., pp. 160, 179.   [69] Ibid., pp. 161–2.
[70] C. A. Storey, *Persian Literature. A Bio-bibliographical Survey*, 3 vols. (London, 1927), vol. I, pp. 632–3.
[71] Ghulam Husain Khan, *Seir Mutaqherin*, vol. III, p. 163.
[72] Storey, *Bio-bibliographical Survey*, vol. I, pp. 633–4.

which animated Mughal rulers. Formerly, rulers used to establish fixed times for sitting in public and hearing complaints. Under the new system, however, it was never clear which council member should be approached by a petitioner, and access to council members was closely guarded by their Indian subordinates.[73]

The failure of the Company to take good counsel from the old nobility was a central concern of Ghulam Husain. In a fascinating passage, he recognized that the Company had tried to inform itself about the former customs of the Mughal empire, but argued that the project was a failure. He described how in England, the king could not give an order to the Company 'without the advice and consent of his Council', made up of 'Omrahs, or Great Lords of that land', as well as 'the principal inhabitants' of each city and town. Ghulam Husain approved of this system, calling it 'an admirable institution', 'extremely useful and beneficial'.[74] But, he went on:

Here in India, as well as in England, these people are guided by those institutions, and keep them among themselves; for as yet in what concerns the welfare of the people of these countries, and in all revenue matters, relative to these provinces, they trust to what rules and constitutions they have heard of here, and to whatever instructions they may have received from Mootsuddies,[75] and officers of their own appointing. These they have already committed to their books, and they have made of them so many rules to distinguish right from wrong; but the reason why such a custom has been instituted, and what might be its cause or ground, these are matters which they never discover themselves, nor ever ask of others, or if they comprehend anything in them, they willingly counterfeit ignorance, without anyone's being able to guess what they mean by counterfeiting that ignorance.[76]

Thus, British rulers, who in their own country consulted widely with great lords and 'principal inhabitants', were refusing to engage with the nobility in Bengal. Relying instead on the advice of lower-grade revenue officials, their understanding of the old 'rules and constitutions' was profoundly distorted.

Ghulam Husain argued, for example, that the Mughal office of *faujdars* had been misunderstood by the British; under the Mughals they had been great lords maintaining the honour and dignity of the empire in the districts, but the Company had made them into low-grade robber-catchers. Company rulers had also misunderstood the nature of *zamindars* under the Mughal empire. Ghulam Husain had discovered

---

[73] Ghulam Husain Khan, *Seir Mutaqherin*, vol. III, pp. 198–9.
[74] Ibid., pp. 153–4.   [75] *Mutasaddi* (a clerk or accountant).
[76] Ibid., pp. 154–5.

from 'intelligent persons' among the Company service that landlords in
Britain were very different from those in Bengal. In an apparent
reference to Philip Francis' ideas, he described how 'the English rulers
have thought proper to compare the Zemindars of this country to the
Zemindars of their own; men whose possession amount to no more than
a few thousand yards of ground'.[77] The Company had therefore been
excessively lenient to *zamindars* as a group, whom the emperors used to
discipline to protect the well-being of the cultivators. Ghulam Husain
was also well-informed, and deeply offended, about the proceedings of
the Supreme Court in Calcutta. 'A whole life is needful to attend their
long, very long proceedings', he wrote, and on the summons of the
court, 'a poor man' must 'directly forsake his wife and family' and trek
down to Calcutta 'where both air and water are bad'.[78] Ghulam Husain
was likely referring here to the *qazi* and *muftis* of Patna, whom he likely
would have known personally.

It is interesting to compare Ghulam Husain's idealized image of
former Mughal practice with Edmund Burke's encomiums on the
'ancient Mughal constitution'. Burke would no doubt have agreed with
one of Ghulam Husain's central premises, that 'the gradation of
climates' and 'the diversity of soil' produced 'a diversity in the genius of
inhabitants', which meant that rulers needed to attend carefully to local
customs.[79] Burke would likely also have recognized Ghulam Husain's
fears about the rise of commercial groups, and the buying and selling of
power, which had similarities with British critiques of East Indian
corruption and the 'monied interest'.

Yet Ghulam Husain's view of virtuous Mughal government had a
quite different emphasis from that of Burke, arising from their different
orientations to the Mughal empire, as well as to contrasting intellectual
traditions. Burke's was a rather academic, textual view of Mughal order,
which depended on translations of old legal texts and administrative
treatises. Ghulam Husain, on the other hand, portrayed himself and his
benighted class of Mughal state servants as the embodied representatives of the Mughal imperial tradition, pillars of virtue who were being
undermined by the ignorance and arrogance of the Company. Burke's
view of the ancient Indian constitution had a strongly aristocratic bent,
but (like Philip Francis) Burke focused much more on Hindu rajas and
zamindars than on Mughal noblemen like Ghulam Husain. For Burke,
the survival of *zamindar* property was a sign of the endurance of the
'ancient constitution'. By contrast, Ghulam Husain regarded the rise of

[77] Ibid., pp. 162, 205.   [78] Ibid., p. 210.   [79] Ibid., pp. 157–8.

the unruly *zamindars* as one of the symptoms and causes of the age of *inqilab* or revolution in India.

Ghulam Husain's treatise followed in a recognizable line of critiques of Company rule generated from within the *nawabi* milieu of Murshidabad and Patna. As others have argued, these critiques were also meant as increasingly desperate attempts to acculturate or absorb the British into the broad umbrella of Mughal sovereignty and Mughal custom. This book has shown how these attempts sometimes intersected with British efforts to legitimize their new empire by reference to constitutional forms apparently inherited from the Mughals, and to make alliances with pre-existing elites. Yet Ghulam Husain's history suggested that many of the old service gentry remained profoundly alienated from the new regime, even those like Ghulam Husain who found patrons among the British.

This was partly a matter of the brute exigencies of rule, and the Company's need to squeeze rupees out of old centres of wealth, power and patronage; and it was partly too a matter of contrasting values and mutually opaque intellectual and cultural traditions. Indeed, it is hard, analytically, to separate these strands out. For example, it may be, as Ghulam Husain argued and many other historians have agreed, that *zamindars* appeared closer to entrenched British ideas of what a land-holding aristocracy should look like, rather than Mughal *mansabdars* or *jagirdars* whose revenue assignments were dependent on service to the state. At the same time, however, British understandings of the Mughal constitution also focused so largely on the hereditary role of *zamindars* because these were gradually being revealed as indispensable intermediaries between the colonial state and agrarian society; whereas the Mughal nobility, deprived of old sources of protection and patronage, could be more easily suborned or sidelined. The vulnerability of the *nawabi* court and its direct dependents had been revealed as far back as 1769, when Muhammad Reza Khan was forced to withdraw his *amils* from the districts to be replaced by British supervisors. *Zamindars*, on the other hand, were less easily supplanted.

Ghulam Husain's history and Haji Mustafa's translation marked one of the end-points of the sense of Anglo-Mughal entente which animated figures like Hastings, Francis and Burke. Even between 1781 and 1782, when Ghulam Husain was writing his history, and 1789 when Haji Mustafa was producing his translation, Indian officials of different kinds had been more rigorously excluded from the deliberative heights of state power, as the Company looked for opportunities for bureaucratic retrenchments. In 1782, for example, the establishments allowed to the *nazim* for the administration of the criminal courts were cut by more than half.[80] Meanwhile, the office of *faujdar* was now abolished and replaced by British officers acting as supervisors of the Indian criminal courts. Indian revenue officials were also brought to book in this period for alleged frauds and oppressions. When Warren Hastings left Bengal in 1785, Ganga Gobinda Sinha, a key figure in the *khalsa* throughout the Hastings era, was elbowed aside during an investigation of alleged bribe taking and extortionate land purchases.[81]

Despite the rhetoric of ancient constitutionalism, Indian officials were always vulnerable under Company rule to being branded with the mark of Asiatic corruption. Even Burke's attacks on Hastings in the impeachment proceedings, while they were premised on a sympathetic view of pre-colonial Indian government, focused attention on Hastings' allegedly corrupt relationships with Indian revenue officials, who were supposed to have enacted his tyrannical policies. These attacks fed into a strengthening tide of attacks on native depravity in this period, which was further reinforced by the personal views of the new governor-general, Lord Cornwallis. Whereas Hastings had always professed a high opinion of Indian administrators, and made strategic alliances with them throughout his governorship, Cornwallis wrote that 'every native of Hindostan, I really believe, [is] corrupt'.[82] Under Cornwallis' watch, this kind of racial attack found further institutional expression in explicit restrictions on Indians and mixed-race Eurasians from serving in the higher offices of government. From 1793, Eurasians were officially excluded from the Company service for two generations. Meanwhile, no Indian could earn more than £500 per year in official emoluments (whereas British district collectors now earned more than £1,000 per year, and councillors could earn tens of thousands of pounds).[83] Oathing also became a potent institutional expression of racial distinctions. In Cornwallis' judicial regulations, British judges, like other officials, swore oaths to respect the Company's regulations when they took office. The Muslim jurists of the criminal courts, however, were required to repeat their oaths every six months, a provision that caused

---

[80] Misra, *Central Administration of the East India Company*, pp. 319–20.
[81] Marshall, 'Indian Officials Under the East India Company in Eighteenth-Century Bengal', pp. 115–16.
[82] Cornwallis to Henry Dundas, near Patna, 14 August 1787, in Charles Ross (ed.), *Correspondence of Charles, First Marquis Cornwallis*, 3 vols. (London, 1859), vol. I, p. 271.
[83] C. A. Bayly, *Imperial Meridian: The British Empire and the World, 1780–1830* (London, 1989), p. 149; K. Ballhatchet, *Race, Sex and Class Under the Raj: Imperial Attitudes and Policies and their Critics, 1793–1905* (London, 1980).

considerable resentment among Indian officials, for whom such public oaths were an offense to their status as respectable men.[84]

The language of native depravity was not new. The Company government had long rested on a racial division of labour; after all, Indians could not join the Company's covenanted service, and the higher ranks of military service were monopolized by Europeans. What was new in the late 1780s and 1790s was the growing respectability of the Company's covenanted servants themselves, who were being transformed in the new age of imperial unity from suspect mercantile frontiersmen into respectable pillars of empire. They paid a price for this hard won respectability, in Cornwallis' vigorous prosecution of illegal profiteering, especially in the Company's commercial departments.[85] At the same time, the salaries paid to British officials were substantially raised as compensation for lost opportunities of private trade. Cornwallis' effort to rationalize official salaries and cut back wasteful offices bore strong resemblance to the Pittite project of 'economical reform' of the domestic British state after the traumas of the loss of America.[86] In India, however, 'economical reform' had a strong tint of racial ideology, as the rhetoric of native depravity justified the high salaries paid to Europeans. 'Native corruption' now appeared to be a self-fulfilling prophecy, as the small salaries paid to Indian officials, for example the law officers, were regarded as one of the causes of their susceptibility to bribes. Thus, a major way that the new empire of 'British India' sought to distance itself from its troubled past was to redefine corruption as an Indian disease, and posit the reformed Company service, now differentiated into commercial, revenue and judicial lines, as the necessary agents of political virtue. A rising tide of evangelical Christianity would further reinforce this view.

Meanwhile, older arguments that had been previously used to limit the role of Company servants in the interior administration appeared now to be losing force. After two decades of training in the politics and administration of Bengal, a number of Company servants now appeared to have enough expertise in Indian languages that would enable them to

---

[84] Colebrooke, *A Digest of Regulations and Laws*, vol. II, p. 583. For the resentment of law officers about oathing, see R. Singha, 'Civil Authority and Due Process: Colonial Criminal Justice in the Banaras Zamindari, 1781–95', in Anderson and Guha (eds.), *Changing Conceptions of Rights and Justice*, p. 39.

[85] A. Aspinall, *Cornwallis in Bengal; the Administrative and Judicial Reforms of Lord Cornwallis in Bengal. Together with Accounts of the Commercial Expansion of the East India Company, 1786–93, and the foundation of Penang* (1st edn, 1937, repr. Delhi, 1987), pp. 13–16, 34.

[86] For this, see Harling, *Waning of the Old Corruption*.

navigate the thorny byways of revenue accounts. Whereas Hastings and Francis had relied on alliances with Indian informants to research and enact their policies, Cornwallis relied solely on recognized experts within the Company service; his main advisors were men like John Shore in the 'revenue line', Charles Grant in the 'commercial line' and Jonathan Duncan in the 'judicial branch'.[87] At the same time the Company's own bureaucratic records, rather than 'questions to the natives' or translations of Persian language treatises, were becoming the vital points of reference in disputes over law, property or taxation. As Ghulam Husain ominously noted, the British had already 'committed to their books' many disputes and precedents, and were now using them to make 'many rules to distinguish right from wrong'.

One old argument against European settlement in the interior was the lack of any effective legal checks. Now, however, a revamped Supreme Court apparently ensured that Company servants could be prosecuted for corruption, while after 1793, non-official Britons and Europeans were permitted to reside in the interior only on condition of being amenable to the Company's own law courts. The judges of the new courts were now British magistrates, so this regulation would not have the effects of placing Europeans under the 'corrupt' judgement of Indian lawyers. Furthermore, the old argument that British private trade would impinge on the rights of indigenous traders was now falling away before the notion that free trade would stimulate commercial growth in all directions. Now that the old system of *dastaks*, or commercial passes, had been abolished, British and Indian traders appeared to be on a level playing field.[88] Revenue officials were barred from private trade because of potential for conflicts of interest and local monopolies. It was thought that no British officer evading this rule could now escape scrutiny, given the checks of nearby commercial officials and (after 1790) British magistrates. Commercial agents on the other hand were allowed to trade, but within the customs regime established by the Company. Indeed, allowing the wealthy 'commercial residents' to trade was thought to be vital to the well-being of the rural economy.[89] The old sense, cultivated by Company directors and governors in the 1760s,

---

[87] Aspinall, *Cornwallis in Bengal*, p. 11, and Ainslie T. Embree, *Charles Grant and British Rule in India* (New York, 1962), pp. 97–8.

[88] Philip Francis was a notable exponent of this view; he argued in his revenue plan of 1776 that restrictions on private trade were understandable in the era when British traders made mischievous use of *dastaks* to achieve an unfair advantage on native rivals through customs exemptions, but they should now be lifted (except as they pertained to territorial administrators). Francis, *Original Minutes*, pp. 69–70.

[89] Embree, *Charles Grant and British Rule in India*, p. 100.

that the expansion of British private commerce meant robbing an Indian Peter to pay a British Paul was now waning.

The military and bureaucratic consolidation of Company power, and the concomitant withering of indigenous institutions, starved of influence and patronage, seemed to have reached a new stage of development by the mid-1780s. John Shore, who had worked as a Company servant in Bengal since 1772, wrote in 1785 that 'the general system of affairs in Bengal is wholly different from what it was ten years before; the scale of connections and interests is greatly extended, and English forms of policy and law are introduced; the natives no longer look to one of their own country and sect as the Supreme Head but to Europeans'.[90] Moreover, the ideological trajectory of British India and the material interests of the Company service were now more clearly intermeshed and mutually reinforcing. The very phrase 'British India', which gained a wider currency in this period, evoked a new imperial confidence. Earlier invocations of the 'ancient constitution' often entailed valorizing indigenous officials and institutions. Increasingly, however, a more unified and self-confident British elite now distanced itself from the Indian past, and argued that the advent of British rule was bringing untold improvements to formerly benighted Asiatics.

Towards a new constitution for Bengal

A full re-examination of the politics of Lord Cornwallis' governorship (1786–93) is beyond the scope of this book. But it is important to see how the old legitimizing language of the Mughal constitution lost its purchase in the new regime. In the Hastings era, the rhetoric of the ancient constitution became particularly associated with two major institutions of rule, the *adalats*, or civil or criminal courts, which were supposed in the 1772 Plan of Justice to represent a revival of a putative 'ancient constitution', and the *zamindars*, which Philip Francis had argued were the bedrock of the Mughal rule of property in Bengal. Yet in both these spheres of law and revenue, the idea of the ancient constitution, already compromised by bitter infighting, appeared to be less and less relevant to the Company's developing strategies of rule.

We can see this very starkly in the decline and eventual eclipse of the institutions of the *nizamat*. From the early 1770s, the Company had redefined the authority still allowed to the *nawabs* (as *nazims* of Bengal) as pertaining to the sphere of 'criminal law'. From the start,

---

[90] BRC, 18 May 1785, cited in N. Majumdar, *Justice and Police in Bengal, 1765–1793; A Study of the Nizamat in Decline* (Calcutta, 1960), p. 22, n.1.

British attitudes to the Muslim criminal law were conflicted, yet there was a consensus that English laws (especially in the criminal sphere relating to the sensitive issue of forms of punishment) should not generally be interposed in the native criminal courts. The continuing existence of the *nizamat* became highly politicized in the great party conflicts of the 1770s. On the one hand, Francis and his party deployed Muhammad Reza Khan, reappointed as *naib nazim*, as a symbol of their commitment to preserving the ancient forms of 'country government' from the depredations of the Company. On the other hand, the Company in general rallied round the *nizamat* and its officials as they came under attack or even prosecution in the Supreme Court.

As we have seen, the Company's defence of Muslim law officers was highly equivocal, and Elijah Impey's elaborate regulations for the civil courts had reinforced the view that there were no effective procedural laws within Muslim legal tradition. Meanwhile, Hastings appointed British magistrates to replace the *faujdars* in 1781, and during the war years he made extensive cuts in the expenses allowed to the *nizamat*. The consolidation of the territorial branch of the Company service, fanning out into the districts of Bengal as collectors and judges after 1781, accelerated the slow death of the *nizamat*. In 1789–90 Cornwallis collected the opinions of British magistrates in the interior of Bengal on the efficacy and performance of the Muslim criminal courts. These opinions recalled long-standing British criticisms of Islamic law and the apparent corruption of native officials. Henry Lodge's report from Bakarganj suggested how observations of the criminal courts were overdetermined by wider prejudices; 'I think there are hardly any among them qualified by principles for the office of Judge or Magistrate . . . Very few of the natives have a claim to integrity or character.' Added to these well-worn stereotypes, the small salaries awarded to the Muslim law officers were themselves described as an explanation of corruption. The Burdwan collector called these officials 'the dregs of the people'.[91] The reports complained of the unwillingness of Muslim law officers to execute convicted murderers, and of the 'slow, cruel and lingering death' that apparently followed from mutilations ordered by the courts.[92]

Cornwallis took little convincing that the Muslim courts were 'oppressive, unjust, and beyond measure corrupt'.[93] In a series of reforms between 1790 and 1793, the governor-general finally did away

---

[91] Cited by Aspinall, *Cornwallis in Bengal* (repr. New Delhi, 1987), p. 46.
[92] Misra, *Central Administration of the East India Company*, pp. 322–3.
[93] Cornwallis to H. Dundas, 8 March 1789, cited in Aspinall, *Cornwallis in Bengal*, p. 63, n. 1.

with the lingering institutions of the *nizamat* in Murshidabad, retiring the aged figure of Muhammad Reza Khan, and reconstituting the *sadr nizamat adalat* (chief criminal court) in Calcutta, made up of the governor-general himself and his council.[94] 'Courts of circuit' were instituted under British judges, who would meet up on their travels through Bengal with British district magistrates. Muslim law officers, the *qazis* and *muftis*, were reduced to expounding legal opinions in writing, after being presented with selected facts from the case by the British judges. These opinions were then reviewed and the decisions finally adjudicated by the judges. Cornwallis' new 'regulations' for the criminal courts made specific amendments to the existing pattern of Muslim criminal law, insisting on capital punishment for murder, replacing punishments of mutilations with transportation or long-term confinement, and abolishing the distinction made in the Muslim law of evidence between Muslims and non-Muslims.[95]

Interestingly, one member of the governing council, Peter Speke, dissented from the promulgation of the new judicial regulations of 3 December 1790, calling the new constitution of the *sadr nizamat adalat* 'an assumption, in fact, of the Sovereign Power in the fullest sense, not merely that of criminal jurisdiction, but of legislation'.[96] Cornwallis did not trouble himself too much about this dissent, yet when Cornwallis' regulations were reviewed by the Company's law officers in London, they agreed with Speke that his reforms of the criminal courts of Bengal had no adequate constitutional justification. Cornwallis claimed that he was acting under powers to regulate the judiciary exercised by previous Company governors in Bengal, and approved by parliament. Yet Cornwallis' extensive legislation was recognized by the Company's law officers as something qualitatively and quantitatively different from previous reforms. Previous parliamentary statutes, they showed, awarded only a limited legislative power to Company governors, to make by-laws for the English settlements and factories or (in the case of the 1781 Judicature Act) to make rules for the practice of the provincial courts. Nor could Cornwallis argue that he enjoyed the authority to remodel the *nizamat* within the constitution of the Mughal empire, because neither *diwan* nor *nawab* properly enjoyed that right.[97] In response to these opinions, and to shore up the legal

[94] Misra, *Central Administration of the East India Company*, p. 327.
[95] Ibid., pp. 323–5; Fisch, *Cheap Lives and Dear Limbs*, pp. 38–49.
[96] BRC, 3 December 1790, cited in Aspinall, *Cornwallis in Bengal*, p. 72.
[97] J. Anstruther's Opinion on Lord Cornwallis' Judicial Regulations of 1793, IOR, HM 414, fo. 66. See also the discussion in Misra, *Central Administration*, p. 38.

authority of the Bengal government, ministers hurried to provide a *post facto* authorization for Cornwallis' assumed legislative powers. A new act, passed on 20 July 1797, confirmed the existing legislation and authorized the governor-general to make a regular code affecting the persons, rights and property of the native inhabitants.[98] In the emerging imperial constitution, put together as it were on the hoof, the Company government in Bengal was emerging as a powerful proconsular regime, with substantial legislative authority delegated from the king-in-parliament.

This new legislative confidence inevitably undermined the old idea of a constitutional inheritance from the Mughals. By the 1790s, the administrative ruptures of British rule were rendering untenable a previous sense of political continuity. At the centre of the new Bengal code, or the 'Cornwallis code' as it was often known, was the idea of the 'permanent settlement' of 1793, by which the land-tax demand in Bengal was fixed for all time on the *zamindars*, now defined as proprietors of the Bengal lands. Yet by 1793, this settlement of property rights was no longer understood, as it was by Philip Francis, as a reversion to the pure forms of the Mughal constitution. Rather, Cornwallis and his henchmen tended to see the 'permanent settlement' as a break with the confusing, unstable history of property rights under the despotic rule of the Mughals, and a dramatic demonstration of the British desire to develop the colony of Bengal as a thriving concern for the long term. Landed property became a way of defining the new empire in opposition both to the old mercantile sovereignty of the pre-reformed Company, but also to the Asiatic despotism of the Mughals.

There was, in a limited sense, a direct line of political influence from Philip Francis' 1776 minute on the revenues to the eventual permanent settlement. Francis himself was quick to claim some credit for the measure when it was finally enacted.[99] But Francis' notion that property rights inhered in 'the laws and constitutions of India' was increasingly contentious. On the one hand, Francis' view seemed to have been reinforced by evidence that *zamindari* property could be sold and inherited under Mughal and *nawabi* rule. As Muhammad Reza Khan put it, 'the Revenue belongs to the King, but the Land to the Zemindar'. Yet the British often found such statements elusive and enigmatic; the question of where to draw the line between state and landlord, and how to adjudicate rights, often appeared to them ill-defined in the system of layered power-sharing that characterized Mughal government.

---

[98] 37 Geo. 3, c. 142, s. 8.   [99] Guha, *Rule of Property for Bengal*, p. 160.

The problem of the nature of the Mughal constitution was made more acute by a backlash against Philip Francis' views within the Company service in Bengal. In the mid-1780s, some Company servants produced a very different historical account of Bengal from that of Francis. They tended to see a powerful despotic state corroded from within by the systemic depravity and corruption of its native officials. In this view, the *zamindars* were mere tax officials, who had committed frauds on the peasants and their superiors in order to usurp a false claim to hereditary property in the land. The most strident advocate of this position was James Grant, a Company servant who was appointed 'chief sheristadar' of the *khalsa* in 1786, a new position created to ensure more detailed supervision of the central offices of revenue management and accounting. Grant qualified for this post after his extensive treatise on the revenues of the 'Northern Sircars', a coastal tract of land annexed by the Company to the south of Bengal, from which Grant argued that far greater revenues could legitimately be extracted.[100] He applied a similar analysis to the revenue record of Bengal, presenting to the governor-general and council his 'Historical and Comparative Analysis of the Finances of Bengal' on 27 April 1786.[101]

Grant's thesis, tangled up in tortured sentences and voluminous tables of accounts, was that the Company was being persistently swindled out of its rightful revenues by 'the indolence, ignorance and depravity of natives entrusted with uncontrouled executive management'.[102] From his own studies of Mughal revenue accounts, apparently acquired 'through a light and private purse',[103] he argued that a much larger revenue was collected from the Bengal peasantry but then concealed by the tricks of native accountants and *zamindars*. Grant's arguments depended on the shaky premises that Mughal assessments were actually collected in full, and that the Mughals typically sought to restrict *zamindari* incomes to a small proportion of the collections – an allowance in return for services rendered, rather than a form of hereditary property in the soil. Arguing from these premises he claimed that a full 10 crore of rupees, or £10 million, had been effectively stolen from the Company over a 20-year period since 1765, at the rate of

---

[100] *The Fifth Report*, vol. II, pp. xiii–xiv.
[101] Ibid., pp. 159–477. For an extended discussion of Grant's views, see F. D. Ascoli, *The Early Revenue History of Bengal and the Fifth Report* (Oxford, 1917), pp. 42–53.
[102] *The Fifth Report*, vol. II, p. 339.
[103] Ibid., p. 252; Ascoli suggested that Grant's Persian accounts, which purported to be copies of revenue assessments from 1722, were previously in the possession of Philip Francis – which, if true, would hint at the varied uses made by British officials of the same source materials. Ascoli, *The Early Revenue History of Bengal*, p. 46.

half a million pounds per year.[104] Grant's arguments thus harked back to the reformers of the 1760s such as J. Z. Holwell and John Johnstone, who had argued that the Bengal territories were capable of paying a much higher revenue once the real value of the lands was uncovered.[105]

Grant obtained sufficient influence over the board of revenue in Bengal that they publicly declared, on 30 March 1786, that a *zamindari* was a conditional office and that the sale of *zamindar* property would be restricted by the Company.[106] This suggested that Grant's views, while incongruous next to the pronouncements of Pitt's India Act, enjoyed some support in a Company service struggling to balance its books. Colonel James Murray, the commissary-general of Bengal and a supporter of Grant's views, collected a portfolio of 'authentic' information on revenue history, including a set of 'questions to the natives' and a Persian treatise which he commissioned from a 'native of rank' in 1785.[107] He argued that the revenues of Bihar could be almost doubled from their present rates if the collusions of Indian officials were punctured.[108] Yet such ambitious proposals, however tempting to a cash-hungry Company, also appeared grossly unrealistic given the persistent failure to collect substantially more rents from the Bengal countryside, most recently in Hastings' largely failed tax increases of 1781.

The tide of opinion in England, as well as the evidence of previous years' collections, suggested to the new governor-general, Lord Cornwallis, the need to make some kind of long-term settlement of revenues with *zamindars* on the approximate basis of previous collections. Nevertheless, Grant's and Murray's view about the constitutional position of the *zamindars* under the Mughals needed to be combated, especially because the court of directors professed that their aim was 'not to introduce any novel system, or to destroy those rules and

---

[104] Ibid., p. 45.

[105] Because Grant argued against Francis' view of *zamindars* it has often been assumed that his views were shared by Warren Hastings. A note in the Hastings papers, however, showed that Hastings thought Grant's strident proposals, especially for the resumption of rent-free lands, to be repellent and 'hurtful to humanity'. See the 'Criticisms by Warren Hastings of a Work by James Grant on the Sircars and Zemindarry Tenures in India'. B. L. Hastings papers, Add. MSS 29,233, fos. 66–74. This makes sense in the light of Hastings' persistent defence of the hereditary rights of *zamindars*, coexisting with the reserved and absolute powers of Mughal sovereignty.

[106] Ascoli, *The Early Revenue History of Bengal*, p. 42.

[107] See 'Mr Murray's Papers on the Revenues of Bengal', IOR, HM 68, pp. 705–56, and HM 387, pp. 419. The 'treatise on agriculture', the *Risala-i zira't*, has been published in translation with a useful introduction by Harbans Mukhia, *Perspectives in Medieval History* (Delhi, 1993), pp. 259–93.

[108] Col. James Murray to Thomas Morton Esq., Secretary to the Ct. of D., IOR, HM 387, p. 426.

maxims which prevailed in the well-regulated periods of the Native princes'.[109] James Grant's views were analysed and comprehensively rejected in a long minute by the new chairman of the board of revenue and member of Cornwallis' Supreme Council of Bengal, John Shore, on 2 April 1788.[110] Shore's minute, even while it refuted Grant's extreme hawkishness, showed how traditional notions of Asiatic despotism, associated with arbitrary whim and the curtailment of property, had survived the revisionist Whig versions of Mughal history. Unlike Burke, Shore did not deny the despotic nature of Mughal authority, nor the insecurity of property under the Mughals. Nor did he refute the idea that despotism had taken a corrupting toll on the manners and customs of the natives. Instead, Shore turned away from the unpromising ground of 'constitutional history' and emphasized the customary sphere of general 'usage' as a better guide to the issue of Indian property rights.

Shore first outlined Grant's main arguments: that *zamindari* was a conditional office and that the Mughal emperor (and hence by extension the Company) was the sole virtual proprietor of the lands by reference to the 'constitutional' forms of Mughal rule, especially the *sanads* or letters patent which confirmed the tenure of *zamindars* as conditional on fulfilling obligations to the emperor. In his response, Shore admitted that 'the constitution of the Moghul empire, despotic in its principle, arbitrary and irregular in its practice, renders it sometimes almost impossible to discriminate between power and principle'; it was necessary therefore to observe, not so much the unstable constitutional forms of the empire, but what 'has been left to the people', and to explore 'those usages which have subsisted for the greatest length of time'. Rights were in a strict sense incompatible with despotism; yet, even in a despotic government, rights could be discovered in 'what the subjects of the state claim for themselves', judged 'by the standard of reason, policy and natural justice'.[111]

In this vein of argument, the formal instruments of the Mughal constitution (such as *sanads* or even the *Ain-i Akbari*) became less significant material than the realm of actual practice and the customary usages actually subsisting in Bengal. Shore's account of Indian history

---

[109] Ct. of D. to Ft William, 12 April 1786, cited in R. H. Hollingbery, *The Zemindary Settlement of Bengal* (Calcutta, 1879), p. 42.

[110] 'Mr Shore's Minute on the Rights of Zemindars and Talookdars. Recorded on the Proceedings of Government in the Revenue Department', *The Fifth Report*, vol. II, pp. 737–52.

[111] Ibid., p. 737.

emphasized the evidence, partly from Halhed's *Code of Gentoo Laws* (1776), that 'property in land existed' under the 'ancient Hindoo government'. Shore was more circumspect with regards to Mughal history. Akbar, he thought, had intended to divide the produce of the lands into certain proportions (which were not exactly clear from the records) between 'the sovereign and the husbandman'. Shore thought that the long history of *hastabud* (revenues surveys) testified to this aspiration among the Mughals in general; he also referred to 'the common expression of the people, that "the land belongs to the zemindar, and the rent to the King", which from its universality is proverbial'.[112] Thus, the *zamindars* of Bengal, while they were left in possession of their lands after the Mughal conquest, were assigned only a specific portion of the rental value as their income, which does not 'destroy the right of property in the soil; although it greatly reduces the interest of the proprietors in it'.[113]

The workings of time, Shore argued, tended to increase the *zamindar*'s share in the soil, as they were able to conceal their growing incomes from central government; moreover, as the *zamindars* were employed by the Mughal conquerors as agents in the collection, they were able to use their administrative strength to increase their properties. *Zamindars*, in Shore's account, were seen 'in a double point of view, as hereditary possessors of the soil; and as the servants of the state'.[114]

Shore thus threaded a kind of middle position between Francis' sense that the Mughals preserved the pre-existing rights of Hindu property inviolate, and Grant's notion of direct imperial property in the soil. Shore referred to the 'institutes of TIMUR, the ordinations of Aurungzeb, and the Mahomedan Laws' to prove that Islamic governments were not enemies of property per se. But, in reviewing his materials, he claimed to discover

the sovereign's right to a proportion of the revenues of all lands not alienated by his sanction from the rental of government.

This principle 'will be found to reduce property to a mere name', by rendering it 'dependent on the equity and moderation of the governing power'. He argued, in line with the evolving official mind of the Company and the British government, 'we should endeavour to improve it by regulations, limiting the demands of Government to a precise amount'.[115] Thus, the Company's plans to fix the revenue demand on

---

[112] Ibid., pp. 738–9.   [113] Ibid., pp. 741, 746.   [114] Ibid., p. 746.
[115] Ibid., p. 751.

the *zamindars* was interpreted less as a return to the unstable terrain of Mughal finance, and more as a novel form of security in a previously despotic constitution.

Jon E. Wilson has recently argued that revenue officials of the Cornwallis era valorized the concept of 'custom', often referred to in the official archive as the 'custom of the country'; and that this notion, rather than a Mughal constitution, was increasingly used to explain the apparent existence of claims to right on behalf of *zamindars* and others, even under despotic regimes. Wilson has related this use of custom to naturalistic enlightenment narratives of conjectural history, which emphasized the workings of customary social practice independent of government.[116] Shore's argument from Indian custom or usage also contained a now familiar theme of ancient constitutionalism in India – his attribution a species of customary right to the ancient Hindus. Because almost all of the largest *zamindars* in Bengal were non-Muslim, it remained plausible for the British to imagine a continuous evolution of 'Hindu' property – even though most of the large *zamindars* of Bengal only built up their estates under Mughal and *nawabi* rule.[117] As in Francis' and Burke's admiring accounts of Mughal government, the continuity in Indian history was seen to rest on 'Hindu' property. Yet in Shore's view, the Mughal empire appeared more like the 'Norman Yoke', a conquest regime which threatened but never succeeded entirely in curtailing an earlier tradition of legal rights.

After Shore's skirmish with Grant, it is striking how quickly debates about property in Bengal moved away from the ground of historical constitutions on which they had rested since at least the 1760s. As Cornwallis and Shore debated the merits of declaring the decennial settlement of 1790 to be fixed in perpetuity, they argued not over the details of Mughal history, but over the practical consequences of the policy. For Shore, a truly 'permanent settlement' would fail to inspire the confidence of a landlord class habituated to the vagaries of despotism, but would prevent the British from making useful adjustments in demands on both landlords and peasants in the light of future experience.[118] For Cornwallis, fixity in perpetuity was necessary to

---

[116] Jon E. Wilson, 'Governing Property, Making Law. Land, Local Society and Agrarian Discourse in Colonial Bengal' (unpublished thesis, Oxford, 2000), ch. 2.

[117] Shore agreed with Francis in arguing that *zamindars* existed 'with some possible variation in their rights and privileges, before the Mahomedan conquests in Hindoostan', and that the Mughals 'employed the ancient possessors of the land as their agents in the collection of the taxes of the state'. Shore's minute, 2 April 1788, *The Fifth Report*, p. 744.

[118] Minute of John Shore, 8 December 1789, *The Fifth Report*, vol. II, pp. 518–27.

'stamp a value' on the Bengal lands, which meant in turn that the lands would serve as a more efficient security for the revenues. *Zamindars* would be encouraged to invest in and improve their resources to stay ahead of the government demand, avoiding the ignominy of forced sales for arrears of rent.[119] By this stage, neither party justified their proposals through reference to the Mughal constitution. Indeed both assumed that the idea of a permanent settlement was a radical innovation. Cornwallis hoped it would usher in a reformation in the manners of *zamindars*, as improvident and luxurious degenerates would be replaced by hard-working gentleman farmers. Moreover, by separating out the 'revenue' and 'judicial' lines of the Company service, and distinguishing revenue administration from the judiciary, the British would gradually train Indians out of their expectations of arbitrary government.

Contrasting with the rancorous disputes between Hastings and Francis, the gentlemanly debates between Cornwallis and Shore reflected a new era of British Indian civility, in which a necessary distance from the polluting effects of pre-colonial polities was becoming a given of imperial patriotism. Indeed, the policy, enacted in 1793, of declaring the revenue fixed for all time appeared to be a sudden reversal of the repeated efforts by both the *nawabs* and the Company to increase the income from land revenues. Some significant loopholes remained to be exploited by future governors, for example the power to resume rent-free lands and to raise internal customs duties.[120] Yet the dramatic finality of Cornwallis' gesture reflected the scale of the crisis of legitimacy that the Company had faced in Britain, and the need for a symbolic renunciation of its pretensions to uncontrolled power. In appearance at least, Cornwallis seemed to be bringing the Company government into line with the British state itself, in which the land tax was a moderate and falling burden on eighteenth-century landed estates. In fact, however, the tax demand on agriculture in Bengal remained out of all proportion to that in Britain; Edmund Burke, drawing from contemporary estimates, thought it nearer eight shillings in the pound compared with the British four.[121] Far from fixing the revenue demand at a moderate level, as Francis had argued, Cornwallis actually set the demand at a level higher than any single collection in previous years, arguing that the generosity of the state in renouncing its right to raise the assessment justified a premium on

[119] Minute of Governor-General, 3 February 1790, ibid., p. 538.
[120] Marshall, *Bengal: the British Bridgehead*, pp. 125–6.
[121] P. J. Marshall, *The Writings and Speeches of Edmund Burke*, vol. V, p. 467. I am grateful to Professor Marshall for pointing out this reference.

the initial demand.[122] In an era of low agricultural prices in the 1790s, huge balances accrued in the early years of the permanent settlement, and many *zamindars*, especially the largest estates, were dismantled under the law which ordered forced sales for non-payment of dues.[123]

Francis' 1776 plan had imagined the role of the *zamindars* under the Mughal constitution as 'instruments of government' in the localities. By 1793, however, the *zamindars* were hedged around by an expanding network of British officials. Distributed throughout Bengal, British district magistrates, judges and collectors administered a growing body of newly legislated administrative law.[124] The permanent settlement, as it eventually turned out, was a kind of quid pro quo, in which the British recognized the entrenched authority of rural land-controllers, but at the same time created a web of institutions to strengthen the security of the central state. By its provisions, *zamindars* were supposed to give up at least some of their traditional powers over tenants and local markets, and their rights to periodic remissions in years of bad harvests or inundations. As Sirajul Islam showed, the *zamindars* reacted bitterly to these measures and resisted them strenuously. In the face of this resistance, the colonial state eventually moved to reinforce *zamindari* powers to distrain the property of tenants to enforce rent collections.[125]

The elaborate legislative enactments of Lord Cornwallis were rapidly formed into the 'Bengal Code', an extensive set of regulations covering all areas of civil administration.[126] These regulations, regularly published in Calcutta, and gradually exported to the other north Indian territories conquered by the British after the 1790s, stood as the institutional bedrock of the emerging behemoth of British India, and they were declared to be in effect a 'new constitution for Bengal'.[127] This body of administrative law was a kind of mobile prefabricated constitution, which stifled the old project of historical constitutionalism and meant that it was unlikely to re-emerge in quite the same form, even as the Company later pushed up into the Mughal heartlands of north

---

[122] Siraj-ul Islam, *The Permanent Settlement in Bengal: a Study of its Operation, 1790–1819* (Dacca, 1979), p. 24.

[123] Marshall, *Bengal: the British Bridgehead*, pp. 144–9.

[124] McLane, *Land and Local Kingship in Eighteenth-Century Bengal*, pp. 269–71.

[125] Islam, *The Permanent Settlement in Bengal*.

[126] For a printed digest of the Bengal code, see J. E. Colebrooke, *A Digest of Regulations and Laws*.

[127] The idea that Cornwallis was providing 'a new constitution to so many millions of the Asiatic subjects of Great Britain' comes from a dispatch, drawn up under the Direction of Henry Dundas, President of the Board of Control for India, authorizing the enactment of the permanent settlement in 1793. It is cited in Marshall, *Problems of Empire*, pp. 68–7.

India. The Company state was emerging as a rule by administrative law created in a highly authoritarian structure of government. This government rested on an army and civil service organized by racial hierarchy, and a body of landlords empowered by the central government to bring down violent retribution on recalcitrant tenants. British power in India was built on a powerful connection between commercial monopoly and territorial tribute in India, and the global strength of the imperial state. Meanwhile in parliament, ministers were happy to proclaim 'year after year, that India is in a most flourishing state, and Bengal the best governed country in India'.[128] Not all MPs, however, were willing to accept such statements at face value. Philip Francis, for one, clung to the view that 'Bengal even under the best European government, must be, from the necessary effect of its political situation, a declining country'.[129]

The selective memory of colonial enlightenment

Even by the end of the eighteenth century, the British increasingly thought of their empire in India as a blessing for themselves and their subjects. It was becoming an empire of improvement and enlightenment rather than constitutional restoration. This view, while it inherited and reformulated certain features from the early language of ancient constitutions, also began to reconstitute India as an object of British knowledge. Rather than the Persian literature of Indo-Muslim governance, Sanskrit and the mysteries of ancient Hinduism attracted the brightest and most prestigious scholars of a new generation. Rather than the ancient Mughal constitution, the ancient civilization of the Hindus became the new holy grail of official orientalism. British India was constructing its own variant of what Pocock has termed the 'enlightenment historical narrative'.[130] In Europe, historians such as Edward Gibbon were creating a grand historical synthesis which posited a classical flowering of civilization, a long dark age of 'barbarism and religion', and a recent dawning of enlightenment working through the modern engines of reason and commerce. Similarly in India, Britons imagined a classical Hindu civilization, a dark age of 'barbarism and religion' under Muslim tyranny, and a modern era of colonial enlightenment.

---

[128] Major Scott's speech, 'Debate on the East India Budget', Cobbett, *Parliamentary History*, vol. XXIX, p. 1551.
[129] Francis' speech, ibid., p. 1547.
[130] J. G. A. Pocock, *Barbarism and Religion*. Vol. II. *Narratives of Civil Government* (Cambridge, 1999), introduction.

Two figures in particular were prominent in this latest ideological adjustment. First, and pre-eminently, Sir William Jones, judge of the Supreme Court from 1783 and founder of the Calcutta Asiatic Society (1784), worked to enunciate a novel understanding of the ancient Hindus.[131] If Elijah Impey had been pilloried as a violator of Indian law and custom, Jones would eventually be hailed as its chief interpreter. An earlier generation of scholars had begun to explore Hindu law, but they had largely worked through Persian translations. The Company servant Charles Wilkins studied Bengali and Sanskrit, working with the *pandits* of Benares. Now William Jones learned Sanskrit under the tutelage of the *pandits* of Nadia, a notable centre of philosophy and law. This was, in one sense, a broadening of British intellectual interests in India; but the inquiries pioneered by Jones also signalled a dramatic narrowing of British scholarship in India, which suddenly downgraded its former interest in Mughal political and constitutional history.

The tone was set by Jones' own annual discourses to the Asiatick Society of Bengal. His first address described his own voyage over the Indian ocean, which he envisaged as an amphitheatre, 'almost encircled by the vast regions of Asia', India, Persia and Arabia.[132] The classical image was well chosen, because the region he imagined as 'the nurse of sciences, the inventress of delightful and useful arts, the scene of glorious actions', was limited by period as much as geography, and tended to exclude the arrival of Islam and later the empire of the Mughals. For example, he would confine his famous discourse on India, one of 'the five principal nations' of Asia 'downwards to the Mahommedan conquests at the beginning of the eleventh century'.[133] The journal of the Asiatic Society, *Asiatick Researches*, despite boasting some fine Persian scholars (such as Francis Gladwin) as its members, was notable for its almost complete silence on Mughal history and antiquities, focusing instead either on more ancient languages and inscriptions or on natural history and geography.

Tellingly, Francis Gladwin's own declared aspiration to trace 'the most material changes that happened in the constitution of Hindustan' after the reign of Akbar in a new three-volume history was abandoned after the appearance of just one volume in 1788.[134] Gladwin would end his career as a relatively obscure scholar producing translations of Persian poetry. Jones meanwhile was widely celebrated for his work on

---

[131] For recent studies, see G. Cannon, *Oriental Jones; a Biography* (London, 1964); S. Mukherjee, *Sir William Jones* (Cambridge, 1968).
[132] *Asiatic Researches*, vol. I, p. x.   [133] Ibid., p. 477.
[134] Cited in Grewal, *Muslim Rule in India*, pp. 25–6.

the 'Digest of Hindu Laws', the 'Laws of Manu' and his famous discourses to the Asiatic Society. Here, he made the startling discovery of the linguistic affinities of Sanskrit with ancient Persian, Latin and Greek, arguing for a common source of world civilization in the ancient Iranian plateau. Jones' scholarship created a new point of affiliation between Britain and the remote peoples of its Asiatic empire, based on these linguistic traces, rather than the stewardship of an ancient constitution.[135]

William Jones actively participated in the hardening of attitudes towards the Mughal empire and its officials, claiming that 'if the natives know their own good, they cannot sigh for the harsh and imperious domination of the Moguls.'[136] Whereas earlier writers in the shadow of the 1769–70 famine yearned for the old prosperity of Mughal times, now India appeared to Jones as 'improveable beyond imagination'.[137] This was also the message of another pioneer of the enlightenment narrative of colonialism, the Company's own official historiographer, John Bruce. His *Historical View of Plans for the Government of British India* was a piece of propaganda designed to smooth the passing of the Company's new charter by parliament in 1793.[138] The idea of 'British India' in his title was itself a significant conceptual signal of the new imperial age. Bruce began his treatise by paying lip-service to the 'manners' and 'kinds of religion' of the subject peoples of British India;[139] yet the rest of his work moved very far from the thought-worlds of Bolts or Dow, Philip Francis or Edmund Burke.

Company rule in India was not a national embarrassment; rather, it was 'a new event in the history of mankind' and the 'wonder of foreigners'. The Company government was 'local, discrete and prompt'; and yet the British nation was 'engrafting by it, on Asiatic institutions, degrees of the mild maxims of British government and Laws'. After the loss of America, the nation now looked to the East Indies as 'the most important foreign dependency it possessed . . . to give splendor to its empire'. Confronting directly the critics of the Company, Bruce

---

[135] Kidd, *British Identities Before Nationalism*, pp. 54–5; Thomas Trautman, *Aryans and British India* (California, 1997); Tony Ballantyne, *Orientalism and Race. Aryanism in the British Empire* (Basingstoke and New York, 2002), pp. 26–30.

[136] G. Cannon (ed.), *The Letters of William Jones*, 2 vols. (Oxford, 1970) vol. II, p. 664.

[137] Ibid., p. 703.

[138] John Bruce, *Historical View of Plans for the Government of British India & Regulation of Trade to the East Indies, & Outlines of a Plan of Foreign Government, of Commercial Oeconomy & of Domestic Administration for the Asiatic Interests of Great Britain* (London, 1793).

[139] Ibid., p. 4.

ridiculed nostalgia for a 'golden age' in Mughal times. Rather, 'the provinces acquired by Great Britain have enjoyed a prosperity formerly unknown in Hindoostan', which could only 'be ascribed to the character of a free though conquering people'.[140] Asiatic empire had become for Bruce both a demonstration and a symptom of the glorious national character, rather than (as it was for Burke) a sign of its unravelling.

The ancient Hindu 'aborigines of the country', 'mild and super-stitious' in their manners, had enjoyed an 'improved state of the arts', but they were soon overwhelmed by their 'barbarous neighbours'. The Mughal empire was founded on 'the accidental talents and success of a few ambitious and able leaders'. It was a violent system of rule 'by arms, attended with the anxious propensity of promulgating a barbarous superstition with the relentless fury of persecution'. There was, however, a bright spot in this tale of woe, in the 'wise and mild institutions, which distinguished the reign of the virtuous Acbar'. Nonetheless, the Mughal government was 'absolute' and 'held in abhorrence by the Hindoos'. Mughal emperors were 'Sovereign Lords or Lords Proprietors of the Soil'. Though in many cases they suffered the 'ancient masters' of the land to remain, they also frequently exercised their 'absolute' powers to remove them; land tenures were thus 'feudal in spirit'. There were laws in the Mughal empire, but they were 'arbitrary in their spirit, and frequently partial and corrupt in their application'. Nonetheless, the 'simple and equitable maxims of the Hindoo Code of Laws' somehow survived this barbarous system alongside 'rigid Mahomedan jurispru-dence'. The Mughals taxed their subjects heavily, but they allowed *zamindars* to exercise some powers as 'a species of petty prince'.[141]

For Bruce, 'free government' was clearly incompatible with the spirit of native laws. Moreover, British officers abroad required 'full, prompt and discretionary powers'. Even Rome, 'the most free nation of antiquity', 'made its proconsuls absolute in the provinces, but responsible to the Senate and People'. Governor-general Cornwallis had used his ample powers to engraft 'the humane & equitable jurisprudence of Great Britain' on to the government of Bengal, distinguishing judicial functions from revenue collection, and rooting out an 'inherent evil in the Mogul system of government'.[142] Given the feudal spirit of Mughal land tenures, Cornwallis' award of property to *zamindars* 'has not proceeded from any positive title in the natives to their lands, but has been a concession from the British government',

---

[140] Ibid., pp. 6, 14, 38.
[141] Ibid., pp. 30–1, 335–6, 336–7, 341–2, 439, 468
[142] Ibid., pp. 345–6, 404, 422.

never before obtained even 'under the mildest of their native princes'; the 'permanent settlement' was thus an 'improvement on the system of Acbar'.[143] There were many ingredients here for future imperial ideologues to work with, not least the progressive narratives on which Bruce's historical view was founded: from feudal tenures to security of property; from barbarism to civility; from persecution to tolerance; from despotism to . . . well, to a different, more enlightened kind of despotism.

In justifying his new-found confidence, John Bruce could not escape the recent history of bitter struggles among the imperial elite. Given, he argued, that India was a 'novel and mysterious subject', then 'it is easy to account for the opposite opinions of the most intelligent servants of the Company'.[144] In his book, the warring tribes of British Nabobs were granted a kind of retrospective absolution and welcomed back into the fold of national character. Looking back to the turbulent 1770s, Bruce commented: 'Whoever was in the right, or in the wrong, in particular cases, is not now the question; but that the whole system of government was wrong.'[145] He meant by this that the system of power sharing between the Company and the national government had not yet been sufficiently stabilized in an efficient statutory framework. Pitt's Act, however, had clarified the position admirably. Those days of uncertainty and confusion were gone and best forgotten; divisions and weakness were replaced by unity and strength.

The labour pains of British India were rendered by John Bruce, as they were by many later historians, as a perfectly natural beginning to a difficult but necessary, and in its way admirable, enterprise. Gradually, right-minded Britons had worked out the logical outcomes of a reformed and benevolent empire. In this process of historical cleansing, different ideas about Britain's Asiatic empire had been swept away. The forgotten notion of an empire of ancient constitutions, drawing on the inherited wisdom of the Mughal empire and the expertise and know how of Indo-Persian elites, had always been a fragile and fractured construction. Yet the reconstruction of this view challenges the apparently ineluctable logic of later imperial histories. The idea of the ancient Mughal constitution had proved a necessary device for rethinking the nature of empire after the Indian conquests, and also necessary to discard when it proved an ideological handicap for the restless exigencies of empire.

---

[143] Ibid., p. 446.   [144] Ibid., pp. 115–16.   [145] Ibid., p. 360.

Meanwhile, though British reconstructions of the ancient Mughal constitution may briefly have disturbed crude stereotypes of Asiatic despotism, they also ended up reinforcing a divisive view of India's people as Muslim rulers and Hindu subjects, foreign invaders and ancient inhabitants. This was a view for which many later aspirants to power in south Asia have found a use; but it would be vigorously contested, as it was in the eighteenth century, by enduring strands of Indian patriotism which looked back to older empires as moral examples unheeded by the arrogance of the British.

7   Epilogue

This book implies that intellectual histories of European empires need to attend more closely, not just to the comparative analysis of European ideas of empire, but also to interactions of European ideas with conceptions of empire generated beyond Europe. In a landmark study, Anthony Pagden argued that European theories of civilizational and commercial progress were closely related to enlightenment critiques of earlier neo-Roman ideologies of universal lordship. Thus, enlightenment attacks on early modern European empires as cruel and rapacious tyrannies became the launching-off point for new theories of liberal imperialism in the nineteenth century.[1] This is a powerful and persuasive account, but it tends to leave out the complex story of European interactions with non-European imperial traditions like the Mughal empire, a story of confrontation and conquest, but also of selective appropriations.

Historians of South Asia will continue to debate the relative balance of continuity and change in the transition to colonialism and the long-term impact of colonial rule in the region. Proponents of a continuity thesis are accused of obscuring the profound rupture of colonial conquest. On the other hand, insisting on a radical or typological difference between pre-colonial and colonial regimes is a strategy that has long been used by defenders of empire as well as its critics. This book has argued that British views of the state in India were shaped by political presuppositions exported from British politics, as well as by the distinctive will to power of foreign rulers. Yet British presuppositions were also rethought through a process of encounter with indigenous political culture. Clearly, the contested history of the ancient Mughal constitution cannot be used to support a theory of continuity at the level of political discourse. It may, however, as it did for contemporaries, serve to blur the edges between the categories of 'British' and 'indigenous' politics in

[1] Anthony Pagden, *Lords of All the World. Ideologies of Empire in Spain, Britain and France c.1500–c.1800* (Yale, 1995), pp. 5–10.

the eighteenth century. While there was a clash of different political cultures in Bengal, these cultures were always dynamic and internally contested, and difference did not preclude the possibility of certain overlaps and intersections.

The promulgation of the Cornwallis code as a new constitutional settlement for Bengal marked a significant discursive break in the official rhetoric of British India. It was, however, not a total break, and the Cornwallis regime incorporated features inherited from the earlier discourse of ancient constitutions. The pattern of administering 'Hindu' and 'Muslim' law in Company courts was a significant legacy of the earlier era, which later evolved through the mechanisms of codification and precedent into the complex system of Hindu and Muslim personal laws. The idea of basing land administration on pre-existing forms of tenure remained in force, even if the custom of the country was increasingly divorced from the Mughal constitution.

This meant that records of pre-colonial tenures would long retain their legal pertinence in British India. In a remarkable confession, the young Bengal officer William Wilson Hunter admitted in 1868 that 'the rights of the governed are still ascertained. We are conscientiously striving to rule according to native usages and tenures; but no one can pronounce with certainty as to what these usages and tenures are.' This crisis of colonial knowledge sent Hunter back to the Company's eighteenth-century archive, arguing that 'the real land law of this country is to be found in those researches which were conducted by the rural officers during the first half-century of our rule'.[2]

Hunter's comments are a reminder that the long colonial engagement with the pre-colonial past, and with the moment of colonial transition, would pass through many further stages after 1793. Even if official narratives sought to distance the British Raj from earlier forms of Indian empire like the Mughals, the ghosts of imperial pasts could not so easily be killed off. Even Cornwallis knew that the British still relied on co-opting Mughal styles to bolster their fragile legitimacy in India. Thus, he resisted a request from no less a figure than the Prince of Wales to place a protégé in the office of Chief Magistrate at Benares. Cornwallis was reluctant to dismiss the learned Mughal official, Ali Ibrahim Khan, the current chief magistrate, because of the Khan's high prestige and the role of Benares as a sensitive point in north-Indian politics.[3]

---

[2] W. W. Hunter, *The Annals of Rural Bengal* (1st edn, 1868, repr. New Delhi, 1975), pp. 371–2.

[3] C. Ross (ed.), *Correspondence of Charles, First Marquis Cornwallis*, 2 vols. (London, 1859), pp. 27–8, 34–5. See the discussion of this incident in Bernard S. Cohn, *An Anthropologist Among the Historians and Other Essays* (Oxford, 1987), p. 432.

As British armies moved up the Ganges valley at the turn of the nineteenth century, the treatment of the still extant Mughal dynasty again became a live political issue. Writing to the Mughal emperor in 1803, Governor-General Richard Wellesley announced that the British conquests would be 'the happy instrument of your Majesty's restoration to a state of dignity and tranquility under the protection of the British power'.[4]

Meanwhile, Utilitarian philosophers like James Mill portrayed Muslim rule in India as an advance on the static degeneracy of the Hindus.[5] The British chose to retain the Mughal emperors in a confined and denuded sovereignty, until the rebellion of 1857 revealed the enduring appeal of the old empire among the north-Indian population. After that, the last Mughal emperor was exiled to Burma.[6]

Yet the British continued to try to associate their own rule with the aura of earlier empires in the reinvented medievalism of the great durbars or imperial assemblies.[7] The invention of an 'Indo-saracenic' style of architecture in the late nineteenth century also reflected the ongoing quest by a foreign empire to appropriate the ineluctable glamour of indigenous styles. Even Lord Curzon's white, neoclassical confection to the memory of Queen Victoria, the Victoria Memorial in Calcutta, could not evade unflattering comparison with the Taj Mahal.[8]

The language of ancient constitutions did not completely die out in colonial India after 1793. For example, it reappeared in a new context and in new form in South India. Here, where Islamicate state forms were newer creations, some British officials professed to discover and revive ancient Hindu constitutions from under the rubble of Muslim tyranny.[9] British officials in the south also used historicist arguments to resist the extension of the Bengal code and the landlord settlement, arguing instead for a 'ryotwari' policy of direct engagement with the peasantry. This view generated the idea of ancient village republics as self-sufficient nodes of Indian civilization, a notion that would have a long history

---

[4] Cited in Sen, *Distant Sovereignty*, p. xii.
[5] Grewal, *Muslim Rule in India*, pp. 85–7.
[6] Sugata Bose, *A Hundred Horizons. The Indian Ocean in the Age of Global Empire* (Cambridge, MA, 2006), pp. 41–2, 65–6.
[7] Bernard S. Cohn, 'Representing Authority in Victorian India', in Eric Hobsbawm and Terence Ranger (eds.), *The Invention of Tradition* (Cambridge, 1983), pp. 165–209.
[8] Thomas R. Metcalf, *An Imperial Vision. Indian Architecture and Britain's Raj* (Oxford, 1989), pp. 55–105, 203–10.
[9] See, for example, Mark Wilks, *Historical Sketches of South India. From the Earliest Times to the Last Muhammadan Dynasty* (1st edn, 1817, repr. New Delhi, 1980), and Bayly, *Indian Society*, p. 82.

in imperial and eventually nationalist thought.[10] Meanwhile, technologies of information gathering developed in eighteenth-century Bengal, such as the practice of putting written 'questions to the natives', reappeared in later debates about Indian tradition, for example, in the debates about Sati in the early nineteenth century.[11]

Between the lines of these archival moments of colonial encounter lurked an insistent question for India's foreign rulers, which would only grow louder with the passing of time: if British rule rested on Indian sources of information, why should the 'natives' not govern themselves? While the British project of reviving the ancient Mughal constitution proved to be short-lived, nostalgia for the lost empire of the Mughals remained an important element of Indian patriotism into the nineteenth century and beyond; and Indian scholars and politicians would continue to return to the pre-colonial past as a resource for a hoped-for post-colonial future.

[10] Clive Dewey, 'Images of the Village Community: A Study in Anglo-Indian Ideology', *MAS*, 6 (1972), pp. 291–328.
[11] Lata Mani, *Contentious Traditions. The Debate on Sati in Colonial India* (Berkeley, CA, 1998), pp. 32–41.

Bibliography

MANUSCRIPT SOURCES

BRITISH LIBRARY, ADDITIONAL MANUSCRIPTS (ADD. MSS)

David Anderson Papers
Egerton Papers
Warren Hastings Papers
Elijah Impey Papers
Liverpool Papers
Wellesley Papers
George Vansittart Papers

BRITISH LIBRARY, ORIENTAL AND INDIA OFFICE COLLECTIONS

India Office Records (IOR)
Bengal Law Consultations (BLC)
Bengal Public Consultations (BPC)
Bengal Revenue Consultations (BRC)
Bengal Secret Consultations (BSC)
Financial Department Proceedings
Home Miscellaneous (HM)
Murshidabad Factory Records (MP)

European Manuscripts (MSS Eur.)
Philip Francis Papers
Orme Papers
George Vansittart Papers

NORTHUMBERLAND COUNTY RECORD OFFICE, MELTON PARK, GOSFORTH

Clavering Papers, NRO 309, G.4

SHEFFIELD ARCHIVES, SHEFFIELD

Wentworth Woodhouse MSS R1, 758, 761, 770, 1531a, 1537, 1561a,
1583a, 163

GLOUCESTERSHIRE COUNTY RECORD OFFICE, GLOUCESTER

Papers of Gerard Ducarel, D2091, f7.

NATIONAL LIBRARY, CALCUTTA, INDIA

Notebooks of Justice John Hyde (microfilm)

BIBLIOGRAPHY

PUBLISHED SOURCES BEFORE *c. 1850*

Anon., *The Importance of British Dominion in India Compared to that in America*,
London, 1770.
*Narrative of the Proceedings of the Provincial Council at Patna in the suit of
Behader Beg against Nadara Begum; & of the Supreme Court of Judicature at
Calcutta, In the suit of Nadara Begum against Behader Beg & others. And in the
Criminal Prosecution instituted against Nadara Begum and her Accomplices for
Forgery – Forming together what is generally called in Bengal THE PATNA
CAUSE*, London, 1780.
Asiatick Researches, vol. I, Calcutta, 1788, repr. London, 1801.
Blackstone, W., *Commentaries on the Laws of England*, 4 vols., London, 1826.
Bolts, W., *Considerations on Indian Affairs Particularly Respecting the Present State
of Bengal and its Dependencies*, 3 vols., London, 1772–5.
Cobbett, W., *The Parliamentary History of England from the Earliest Period to the
year 1803, from which last-mentioned Epoch it is continued downwards in the
work entititled, 'Cobbett's Parliamentary Debates'*, 36 vols., London,
1806–20.
Colebrooke, J. E., *Digest of the Regulations and Laws, enacted by the Governor-
General in Council for the Civil Government of the Territories under the
Presidency of Bengal, arranged in alphabetical order*, Calcutta, 1807.
Dow, A., *The History of Hindostan, from the death of Akbar, to the complete
settlement of the empire under Aurungzebe*, 3 vols., London, 1768–72.
Francis, P., *Original Minutes of the Governor-General and Council of Fort William
on the settlement and collection of the Revenues of Bengal with a plan of settlement
recommended to the Court of Directors, January 1776*, London, 1782.
Ghulam Husain Khan Tabatabai, *A Translation of Seir Mutaqherin, Or View of
Modern Times*, Nota Manus Haji Mustafa (tr., ed.), 3 vols., Calcutta, 1789,
repr. Calcutta, 1902–3.
Gladwin, F. (trans.), *Ayeen Akbery, or the Institutes of the Emperor Akber, translated
from the original Persian by F. Gladwin*, 2 vols., London, 1800.

Gleig, G. R., *Memoirs of Warren Hastings*, 3 vols., London, 1841.

Halhed, N. B., *Code of the Gentoo Laws: or Ordinations of the Pundits*, London, 1776.

Hastings, W., in A. C. Banerjee (ed.), *Memoirs Relative to the State of India*, Calcutta, 1978.

Hodges, W., *Travels to India, During the Years 1780, 1781, 1782, and 1783*, 2nd edn, London, 1794.

Howell, T. B., *A Complete Collection of State Trials and Proceedings for High Treason and Other Crimes and Misdemeanors from the earliest period to the present time, with notes and other illustrations*, 33 vols., London, 1809−26.

Malcolm, J., *Life of Robert, Lord Clive*, 3 vols., London, 1836.

Mill, J. S., *Considerations on Representative Government*, London, 1856.

Montesquieu, C. de S. (1st English edn, 1750), in A. M. Cohler, B. C. Miller and H. S. Stone (eds.), *Spirit of the Laws*, Cambridge, 1989.

Patullo, H., *An Essay upon the Cultivation of the Lands, and Improvements of the Revenues of Bengal*, London, 1772.

Pownall, T., *The Right, Interest, and Duty of Government, As Concerned in the Affairs of the East Indies*, 1st edn, 1773, 2nd edn, London, 1781.

Scrafton, Luke, *Reflections on the Government of Indostan. With a Short Sketch of the History of Bengal, from the years 1739 to 1756, and an Account of the English Affairs to 1758*, 1st edn, Edinburgh, 1761, 2nd edn, London, 1763.

Smith, A., in A. S. Skinner (ed.), *The Wealth of Nations, Books IV−V*, London, 1999.

Steuart, J., *An Inquiry into the Principles of Political Oeconomy* (1st edn, 1767), A. S. Skinner (ed.), 2 vols., Edinburgh, 1966.

The Principles of Money Applied to the Present State of the Coin in Bengal, London, 1772.

Vansittart, H., *Narrative of Transactions in Bengal*, London, 1766, A. C. Bannerjee and B. K. Ghosh (eds.), repr. Calcutta, 1976.

Verelst, H., *View of the Rise, Progress and Present State of the English Government in Bengal*, London, 1772.

Watts, W., *Memoirs of the Revolution in Bengal*, London, 1760, repr. Calcutta, 1988.

PRINTED PRIMARY SOURCES

Bannerjee, A. C. (ed.), *Indian Constitutional Documents*, Calcutta, 1945−6.

Burke, E., in D. Bromwich (ed.), *On Empire, Liberty and Reform: Speeches and Letters*, New Haven, CT, 2000.

Calendar of Persian Correspondence, 11 vols., Calcutta, 1911−69.

Cannon, J. (ed.), *The Letters of Junius*, Oxford, 1978.

Eliot, H. M. and Dowson, J. (eds.), *History of India by its own Historians. The Muhammadan Period*, 8 vols., Calcutta, 1867−77.

Fieldhouse, D. K. and Madden, F. (eds.), *The Classical Period of the First British Empire, 1689−1783. Select Documents on the Constitutional History of the British Empire and Commonwealth*, 2 vols., London, 1985.

Firminger, W. K. (ed.), *Bengal District Records. Midnapur, 1768−70*, Calcutta, 1915.

(ed.), 'Historical Introduction to the Bengal Portion of the Fifth Report', *The Fifth Report from the Select Committee of the House of Commons on the Affairs of the East India Company, 28 July, 1812*, 3 vols., London, 1917–18.

(ed.), *Proceedings of the Controlling Council of Revenue at Murshidabad*, 12 vols., Calcutta, 1919–24.

Forrest, G.W., *Selections from the Letters, Dispatches and Other State Papers, Preserved in the Foreign Department of the Government of India, 1772–85*, 3 vols., Calcutta, 1890.

(ed.), *Historical Documents of British India, Warren Hastings*, 2 vols., New Delhi, 1985.

Fort William-India House Correspondence, and Other Contemporary Papers Relating Thereto, 21 vols., National Archives of India, Delhi, 1949–85.

Khan, Shayesta (ed.), *Bihar and Bengal in the Eighteenth Century: A Critical Edition and Translation of Muzaffarnama, a Contemporary History*, Patna, 1992.

Lambert, S., *House of Commons Sessional Papers of the Eighteenth Century*, 145 vols., Wilmington, DE, 1975.

Marshall, P.J. (ed.), in P. Langford (gen. ed.), *Writings and Speeches of Edmund Burke. Vol. V. India: Madras and Bengal, 1774–1785*, Oxford, 1981.

(gen. ed.), *Writings and Speeches of Edmund Burke. Vol. VI. India: the Launching of the Hastings Impeachment, 1786–8*, Oxford, 1991.

(gen. ed.), *Writings and Speeches of Edmund Burke. Vol. VII. India: The Hastings Trial, 1789–94*, Oxford, 2000.

Proceedings of the Committee of Circuit at Krishnanagar, Bengal Record Department, Calcutta, 1915.

Reports from Committees of the House of Commons, 1715—1801, 15 vols., London, 1803.

Sarkar, J. (ed. tr.), *Bengal Nawabs*, 1st edn, 1952, repr. Calcutta, 1985.

Sinha, N.K. (ed.), *Selections from District Records. Midnapur Salt Papers. Hijli and Tamluk, 1781–1807*, Calcutta, 1984.

SECONDARY SOURCES

Alam, M., *The Crisis of Empire in Mughal North India: Awadh and the Punjab, 1707–48*, Delhi, 1986.

The Languages of Political Islam: India, 1200–1800, Chicago, 2004.

Alam, M. and Alavi, S., *A European Experience of the Mughal Orient*, New Delhi, 2001.

Alam, M. and Subrahmanyam, S. (eds.), *The Mughal State, 1526–1750*, Delhi, 1998.

Alavi, S., 'The Company Army and Rural Society: The Invalid *thana*, 1780–1830', *Modern Asian Studies*, 27 (1993), pp. 147–78.

The Sepoys and the Company. Tradition and Transition in Northern India, 1770–1830, Delhi, 1995.

(ed.), *The Eighteenth Century in India*, Delhi, 2002.

Armitage, D., *The Ideological Origins of the British Empire*, Cambridge, 2000.

Armitage, D. and Michael, B. (eds.), *The British Atlantic World, 1500–1800*, Houndsmill, UK, 2002.

Ascoli, F. D., *The Early Revenue History of Bengal and the Fifth Report*, Oxford, 1917.

Aspinall, A., *Cornwallis in Bengal; the Administrative and Judicial Reforms of Lord Cornwallis in Bengal, Together with Accounts of the Commercial Expansion of the East India Company, 1786–1793, and the Foundation of Penang*, 1st edn, 1937, repr. Delhi, 1987.

Athar Ali, M., 'Recent Theories of Eighteenth Century India', *Indian Historical Review*, 13 (1986–7), pp. 102–10.

The Mughal Nobility under Aurangzeb, 2nd edn, New Delhi, 1997.

Bailyn, B., *The Ideological Origins of the American Revolution*, Cambridge, MA, 1967.

Ballhatchet, K., *Race, Sex, and Class under the Raj: Imperial Attitudes and Policies and their Critics, 1793–1905*, London, 1980.

Barber, W. J., *British Economic Thought and India, 1600–1858: A Study in the History of Development Economics*, Oxford, 1975.

Barnett, R., *North India Between Empires: Awadh, the Mughals, and the British, 1720–1801*, Berkeley, CA, 1980.

Barrow, I. J. and Haynes, D. E., 'The Colonial Transition: South Asia, 1780–1840', *Modern Asian Studies*, 38 (2004), pp. 469–78.

Bayly, C. A., *Rulers, Townsmen, and Bazaars: North Indian Society in the Age of British Expansion, 1770–1870*, Cambridge, 1983.

Indian Society and the Making of the British Empire. New Cambridge History of India, 2.1, Cambridge, 1988.

Imperial Meridian: the British Empire and the World, 1780–1830, London, 1989.

(ed.), *The Raj: India and the British, 1600–1990*, London, 1990.

Empire and Information: Intelligence Gathering and Social Communication in India, 1780–1870, Cambridge, 1997.

Origins of Nationality in South Asia: Patriotism and Ethical Government in the Making of Modern India, New Delhi, 1998.

'The First Age of Global Expansion', *Journal of Imperial and Commonwealth History*, 28 (1998), pp. 29–47.

The Birth of the Modern World, 1780–1914, Oxford, 2004.

Bearce, G. D., *British Attitudes to India 1784–1858*, Oxford, 1961.

Benton, L., 'Colonial Law and Cultural Difference: Jurisdictional Politics and the Formation of the Colonial State', *Comparative Studies in Society and History*, 41 (1999), pp. 563–88.

Bhattacharya, S., *The East India Company and the Economy of Bengal, 1704–1740*, London, 1954.

Blake, S., 'The Patrimonial–Bureaucratic Empire of the Mughals', *Journal of Asian Studies*, 39 (1979), pp. 77–94.

Bose, S., *Peasant Labour and Colonial Capital. Rural Bengal Since 1770*. New Cambridge History of India, 3.2, Cambridge, 1993.

Bose, S. and Jalal, A., *Modern South Asia: History, Culture, Political Economy*, London, 1998.

Bowen, H. V., 'A Question of Sovereignty? The Bengal Land Revenue Issue, 1765–7', *Journal of Imperial and Commonwealth History*, 16 (1988), pp. 155–76.

Revenue and Reform: The Indian Problem in British Politics, 1757–1773, Cambridge, 1991.

'British Conceptions of Global Empire, 1756–83', *Journal of Imperial and Commonwealth History*, 26 (1998), pp. 1–27.

The Business of Empire. The East India Company in Imperial Britain, 1756–1833, Cambridge, 2006.

'British India, 1765–1813: the Metropolitan Context', in P. J. Marshall (ed.), *The Eighteenth Century. Oxford History of the British Empire*, vol. 2, Oxford, 1998, pp. 530–51.

'Tea, Tribute and the East India Company, *c.* 1750–1775', in S. Taylor, R. Connors and C. Jones (eds.), *Hanoverian Britain and Empire. Essays in Memory of Philip Lawson*, Woodbridge, 1998, pp. 158–76.

Bowen, H. V., Lincoln, M. and Rigby, N. (eds.), *The Worlds of the East India Company*, Woodbridge, UK, 2002.

Bowyer, T. H., 'India and the Personal Finances of Philip Francis', *English Historical Review*, 110 (1995), pp. 122–31.

'Junius, Philip Francis, & Parliamentary Reform', *Albion*, 27 (1995), pp. 397–418.

Breckenridge, C. and Van der Veer, P. (eds.), *Orientalism and the Postcolonial Predicament: Perspectives on South Asia*, Philadelphia, 1993.

Brewer, J., *Party Ideology and Popular Politics at the Accession of George III*, Cambridge, 1976.

The Sinews of Power: War, Money, and the English State, 1688–1783, London, 1989.

Burgess, G., *The Politics of the Ancient Constitution. An Introduction to English Political Thought 1603–42*, London, 1992.

Busteed, H. E., *Echoes from Old Calcutta, Being Chiefly Reminiscences from the Days of Warren Hastings, Francis and Impey*, Calcutta, 1888.

Cain, P. J. and Hopkins, A. G., *British Imperialism: Innovation and Expansion, 1688–1914*, London, 1993.

Calkins, P., 'The Formation of a Regionally Orientated Ruling Group in Bengal', *Journal of Asian Studies*, 29 (1970), pp. 799–806.

Cannon, G. H., *Oriental Jones: a Biography of Sir William Jones, 1746–1794*, Bombay, 1964.

Chakrabarti, S., 'Intransigent Shroffs and the English East India Company's Currency Reforms, 1757–1800', *Indian Economic and Social History Review*, 34 (1997), pp. 69–94.

Chatterjee, I., *Gender, Slavery, and Law in Colonial India*, New Delhi, 1999.

Chatterjee, K., *Merchants, Politics, and Society in Early Modern India: Bihar, 1733–1820*, Leiden, 1996.

'History as Self-Representation. The Recasting of a Political Tradition in Bengal and Bihar', *Modern Asian Studies*, 32 (1998), pp. 913–48.

Chatterji, N., *Verelst's Rule in India*, Allahabad, 1939.

Chaudhuri, K. N., *The Trading World of Asia and the English East India Company, 1660–1760*, Cambridge, 1978.

Chaudhuri, S. (ed.), *Calcutta: The Living City*, 2 vols., Calcutta, 1990.
Chaudhury, S., *From Prosperity to Decline: Eighteenth-Century Bengal*, New Delhi, 1995.
The Prelude to Empire. Plassey Revolution of 1757, New Delhi, 2001.
Chowdhuri-Zilly, A. N., *The Vagrant Peasant: Agrarian Distress in Bengal, 1770–1830*, Wiesbaden, 1982.
Cohn, B. S., 'Political Systems in Eighteenth-Century India', *Journal of American Oriental Society*, 82 (1962), pp. 312–20.
An Anthropologist Among the Historians and Other Essays, Delhi, 1987.
Colonialism and its Forms of Knowledge: The British in India, Princeton, 1996.
Colley, L., *Britons: Forging the Nation, 1707–1837*, New Haven, CT, 1992.
Captives: Britain, Empire, and the World, 1600–1850, London, 2002.
Collingham, E. M., *Imperial Bodies: The Physical Experience of the Raj, c. 1800–1947*, Polity Press, Cambridge, 2001.
Curley, D. L., 'Maharaja Krisnacandra, Hinduism, and Kingship in the Contact Zone of Bengal', in R. B. Barnett (ed.), *Rethinking Early Modern India*, New Delhi, 2002, pp. 85–118.
Curley, T. M., *Sir Robert Chambers. Law, Literature, and Empire in the Age of Johnson*, Madison, WI, 1998.
Dalrymple, W., *White Mughals: Love and Betrayal in Eighteenth-Century India*, London, 2002.
Daniels, C. and Kennedy, M. V., *Negotiated Empires: Centers and Peripheries in the Americas, 1500–1820*, London, 2002.
Dasgupta, A. K., *The Faqir and Sannyasi Uprisings*, Calcutta, 1992.
Datta, R., *Society, Economy, and the Market: Commercialization in Rural Bengal, c. 1760–1800*, New Delhi, 2000.
Davies, C. C., *Warren Hastings and Oudh*, London, 1939.
Derrett, J. D. M., 'Nandakumar's Forgery', *English Historical Review*, 245 (1960), pp. 223–39.
Religion, Law and the State in India, London, 1968.
'Justice, Equity and Good Conscience', in J. N. D. Anderson (ed.), *Changing Law in Developing Countries*, London, 1963, pp. 114–53.
Dewey, C., *Anglo-Indian Attitudes: the Mind of the Indian Civil Service*, London, 1993.
Dickinson, H. T., *Liberty and Property: Political Ideology in Eighteenth-Century Britain*, London, 1979.
Dirks, N. B., *The Hollow Crown: Ethnohistory of an Indian Kingdom*, Cambridge, 1987.
Castes of Mind: Colonialism and the Making of Modern India, Princeton, 2001.
The Scandal of Empire. India and the Creation of Imperial Britain, Cambridge, MA, 2006.
Dodwell, H. H., *Dupleix and Clive: The Beginning of Empire*, London, 1920.
(ed.), 'The Development of Sovereignty in British India', *Cambridge History of India, vol. 5: British India, 1497–1858*, Cambridge, 1929, pp. 589–608.
Drayton, R., *Nature's Government: Science, Imperial Britain and the Improvement of the World*, Yale, 2000.

Eaton, R. M., *The Rise of Islam on the Bengal Frontier, 1204–1760*, Berkeley, CA, 1993.

Ehrman, J., *The Younger Pitt*, 3 vols., London, 1969–96.

Ellegard, A., *Who Was Junius?*, Stockholm, 1962.

Embree, A. T., *Charles Grant and British Rule in India*, New York, 1962.

Evans, E., *The Forging of the Modern State*, 3rd edn, London, 2003.

Feiling, K., *Warren Hastings*, London, 1954.

Firminger, W. K., 'Selections from the Note Books of Justice John Hyde', *Bengal Past and Present*, 3 (1909), pp. 27–64.

(ed.), 'Historical Introduction to the Bengal Portion of the Fifth Report', *The Fifth Report from the Select Committee of the House of Commons on the Affairs of the East India Company, 28 July, 1812*, 3 vols., London, 1917–18.

Fisch, J., *Cheap Lives and Dear Limbs: The British Transformation of the Bengal Criminal Law, 1769–1877*, Wiesbaden, 1983.

Fisher, M. H., *A Clash of Cultures. Awadh, the British and the Mughals*, Delhi, 1987.

The First Indian Author in English. Dean Mahomed (1759–1851) in India, Ireland and England, Delhi, 1996.

Counterflows to Colonialism: Indian Travellers and Settlers in Britain, 1600–1857, Delhi, 2004.

Fleischer, Cornell, H., *Bureaucrat and Intellectual in the Ottoman Empire. The Historian Mustafa Ali (1541–1600)*, Princeton, 1986.

Fletcher, F. T. H., *Montesquieu and English Politics (1750–1800)*, London, 1939.

Forrest, G. W., *The Administration of Warren Hastings, 1772–1785*, Calcutta, 1892.

Life of Lord Clive. 2 vols., London, 1918.

Foster, R. F., *Modern Ireland, 1600–1972*, New York, 1988.

Furber, H., *John Company at Work, a Study of European Expansion in India in the Late Eighteenth Century*, Cambridge, MA, 1948.

George, M. D., *English Political Caricature; A Study of Opinion and Propaganda*, Oxford, 1959.

Ghosh, D., *Family, Sex and Intimacy in British India*, Cambridge, 2006.

Gordon, S., *The Marathas 1600–1818*. The New Cambridge History of India, vol. 2.4, Cambridge, 1993.

Gould, E., *The Persistence of Empire: British Political Culture in the American Revolution*, Chapel Hill, NC, 2000.

Greene, J. P., *Peripheries and Center: Constitutional Development in the Extended Politics of the British Empire and the United States, 1607–1788*, Athens, GA, 1986.

'Empire and Identity from the Glorious Revolution to the American Revolution', in P. J. Marshall (ed.), *Oxford History of the British Empire, vol. 2. The Eighteenth Century*, Oxford, 1998, pp. 208–31.

Grewal, J. S., *Muslim Rule in India: The Assessment of British Historians*, Oxford, 1970.

Grover, B. R., 'Nature of Land Rights in Mughal India', *Indian Economic and Social History Review*, 1 (1963), pp. 2–15.

Guha, R., *A Rule of Property for Bengal: An Essay on the Idea of Permanent Settlement*, Paris, 1963.

   Dominance Without Hegemony. History and Power in Colonial India, Cambridge, MA, 1997.

Guha, S., 'Wrongs and Rights in the Maratha Country: Antiquity, Custom, and Power in Eighteenth Century India', in M. R. Anderson and S. Guha (eds.), *Changing Concepts of Rights & Justice in South Asia*, New Delhi, 2000, pp. 14–29.

Gupta, B. K., *Sirajudaullah and the East India Company, 1756–7: Background to the Foundation of British Power in India*, Leiden, 1966.

Habib, I., *The Agrarian System of Mughal India: 1556–1707*, 2nd revised edn, Delhi, 1999.

Hampsher-Monk, I., 'Civic Humanism & Parliamentary Reform; the Case of the Society of the Friends of the People', *Journal of British Studies*, 28 (1979), pp. 70–89.

Hardy, P., *Historians of Medieval India. Studies in Indo-Muslim Historical Writing*, London, 1960.

Harling, P., *The Waning of 'Old Corruption': The Politics of Economical Reform in Britain, 1779–1846*, Oxford, 1996.

   The Modern British State. An Historical Introduction, Polity Press, Cambridge, 2001.

Harlow, V. T., *The Founding of the Second British Empire, 1763–1793*, 2 vols., London, 1952–64.

Hasan, F., *State and Locality in Mughal India. Power Relations in Western India c. 1572–1730*, Cambridge, 2004.

Hollingbery, R. H., *The Zemindary Settlement of Bengal*, Calcutta, 1879.

Holzman, J. M., *The Nabobs in England: A Study of the Returned Anglo-Indian, 1760–1785*, New York, 1926.

Hunter, W. W., *Annals of Rural Bengal*, Calcutta, 1868.

Hussain, N., *The Jurisprudence of Emergency: Colonialism and the Rule of Law*, Ann Arbor, MI, 2003.

Impey, E. B., *Memoirs of Sir Elijah Impey*, London, 1857.

Irschick, E., *Dialogue and History: Constructing South India, 1795–1895*, Berkeley, CA, 1994.

Islam, S., *The Permanent Settlement in Bengal: A Study of its Local Operation, 1790–1819*, Dacca, 1979.

Jain, M. P., *Outlines of Indian Legal History*, 5th edn, Delhi, 1990.

Jasanoff, M., *Edge of Empire: Lives, Culture and Conquest in the East, 1750–1850*, New York, 2005.

Kent, S. K., *Gender and Power in Britain, 1640–1990*, London, 1999.

Khan, A. M., *The Transition in Bengal, 1756–75: A study of Muhammad Reza Khan*, Cambridge, 1969.

Khan, S., *A Biography of Ali Ibrahim Khan (c. 1740–93): A Mughal Noble in the Service of the British East India Company*, Patna, 1992.

Kidd, C., *British Identities Before Nationalism. Ethnicity and Nationhood in the Atlantic World*, Cambridge, 1999.

Koebner, R., 'Despot and Despotism; Vicissitudes of a Political Term', *Journal of the Warburg and Courtauld Institutes*, 14 (1951), pp. 275–302.

Kolff, D. H. A., 'End of the Ancien Regime: Colonial War in India, 1798–1818', in J. A. de Moor and H. L. Wesseling (eds.), *Imperialism and War*, Leiden, 1989, pp. 22–49.

Kopf, D., *British Orientalism and the Bengal Renaissance; the Dynamics of Indian modernization, 1773–1835*, Berkeley, CA, 1969.

Kramnick, I., *Bolingbroke and His Circle: The Politics of Nostalgia in the Age of Walpole*, Cambridge, MA, 1968.

Langford, P., *A Polite and Commercial People: England 1727–1783*, Oxford, 1989. *Public Life and the Propertied Englishman*, Oxford, 1991.

Lawson, P., 'Parliament and the First East India Inquiry, 1767', *Parliamentary History*, 1 (1982), pp. 99–114.

Lawson, P. and Lenman, B., 'Robert Clive, the "Black Jagir", and British Politics', *Historical Journal*, 26 (1983), pp. 801–29.

Lawson, P. and Philips, J., 'Our Execrable Banditti: Perceptions of Nabobs in Mid-Eighteenth-Century Britain', *Albion*, 16 (1984), pp. 225–41.

Lieberman, D., *The Province of Legislation Determined: Legal Theory in Eighteenth-Century Britain*, Cambridge, 1987.

Lobban, M., *The Common Law and English Jurisprudence, 1760–1850*, Oxford, 1991.

Losty, J. P., *Calcutta, City of Palaces. A Survey of the City in the Days of the East India Company, 1690–1858*, London, 1990.

McKracken, D., *Junius and Philip Francis*, Boston, MA, 1979.

McLane, J. R., *Land and Local Kingship in Eighteenth-Century Bengal*, Cambridge, 1993.

Maier, C. S., *Among Empires: American Ascendancy and its Predecessors*, Cambridge, MA, 2006.

Majumdar, N., *Justice and Police in Bengal, 1765–1793: A Study of the Nizamat in Decline*, Calcutta, 1960.

Marshall, P., 'British North America 1760–1815', in P. J. Marshall (ed.), *The Eighteenth Century. Oxford History of the British Empire*, vol. 2, Oxford 1998, pp. 372–93.

Marshall, P. J., 'Nobkissen versus Hastings', *Bulletin of the School of Oriental and African Studies*, 27 (1964), pp. 382–96.

The Impeachment of Warren Hastings, London, 1965.

'Indian Officials Under the East India Company in Eighteenth-Century Bengal', *Bengal Past and Present*, 84 (1965), pp. 99–102.

Problems of Empire: Britain and India, 1757–1813, London, 1968.

'British Expansion in India in the Eighteenth Century: A Historical Revision', *History*, 60 (1975), pp. 28–43.

East Indian Fortunes: The British in Bengal in the Eighteenth Century, Oxford, 1976.

A Free Though Conquering People: Britain and Asia in the Eighteenth Century, An inaugural lecture in the Rhodes Chair of Imperial History delivered at King's College, London, 1981.

Bengal: The British Bridgehead, Eastern India, 1740–1828. New Cambridge History of India, 2.2, Cambridge, 1987.

'Empire and Authority in the Later Eighteenth Century', *Journal of Imperial and Commonwealth History*, 15 (1987), pp. 105–23.

Marshall, P. J. (ed.), '"Cornwallis Triumphant": War in India and the British Public in the Late Eighteenth Century', *Trade and Conquest: Studies on the Rise of British Dominance in India*, Aldershot, UK, 1993.

'British Society and the East India Company', *Modern Asian Studies*, 31 (1997), pp. 89–108.

(ed.), 'The British in Asia: Trade to Dominion, 1700–1765', *The Eighteenth Century. Oxford History of the British Empire, Vol. 2*, Oxford, 1998, pp. 487–507.

'The Making of an Imperial Icon; the Case of Warren Hastings', *Journal of Imperial and Commonwealth History*, 27 (1999), pp. 1–16.

'The White Town of Calcutta Under the Rule of the East India Company', *Modern Asian Studies*, 34 (2000), pp. 307–31.

'Britain and the World in the Eighteenth Century, III: Britain and India', *Transactions of the Royal Historical Society*, 6th Series, 10 (2000), pp. 1–16.

'Britain and the World in the Eighteenth Century: IV. The Turning Outwards of Britain', *TRHS*, 6th Series, 11 (2001), pp. 1–15.

(ed.), *The Eighteenth Century in Indian History: Evolution or Revolution?*, Delhi, 2003.

'Warren Hastings as Scholar and Patron', in A. Whiteman, J. S. Bromley and P. G. M. Dickson (eds.), *Statesmen, Scholars, and Merchants: Essays Presented to Dame Lucy Sutherland*, Oxford, 1973, pp. 242–62.

'The Moral Swing to the East: British Humanitarianism, India and the West Indies', in K. Ballhatchet and John Harrison (eds.), *East India Company Studies. Papers Presented to Professor Sir Cyril Philips*, Hong Kong, 1986.

'Parliament and Property Rights in the Late Eighteenth Century British Empire', in J. Brewer and S. Staves (eds.), *Early Modern Conceptions of Property*, London, 1995, pp. 530–43.

Marshall, P. J. and Williams, G., *The Great Map of Mankind. British Perceptions of the World in the Age of Enlightenment*, London, 1982.

Mehta, U., *Liberalism and Empire. A Study in Nineteenth Century British Liberal Thought*, Chicago, 1999.

Metcalf, B. D., 'Too little, too much: reflections on Muslims in the History of India', *Journal of Asian Studies*, 54 (1995), pp. 951–67.

Metcalf, T. R., *Ideologies of the Raj*. New Cambridge History of India, 3.4, Cambridge, 1994.

Misra, B. B., *The Central Administration of the East India Company, 1773–1834*, Manchester, 1959.

The Judicial Administration of the East India Company in Bengal, 1765–1782, Delhi, 1961.

Monckton-Jones, M. E., *Warren Hastings in Bengal*, Oxford, 1918.

Moreland, W. H., *The Agrarian System of Moslem India*, Cambridge, 1929, repr. Delhi, 1994.

Mukhia, H., *Perspectives on Medieval History*, Delhi, 1993.

Muthu, S., *Enlightenment Against Empire*, Princeton, 2003, p. 10.

Nandy, S. C., *Life and Times of Cantoo Baboo: The Banian of Warren Hastings*, 2 vols., Calcutta, 1978.

'A Second Look at the Notes of Justice John Hyde', *Bengal Past and Present*, 97 (1978), pp. 24–34.

O'Brien, P. K., 'The Political Economy of British Taxation, 1660–1815', *Economic History Review*, 2nd series, 41 (1988), pp. 1–32.

'Inseparable Connections: Trade, Economy, Fiscal State, and the Expansion of Empire, 1688–1815', in P. J. Marshall (ed.), *The Eighteenth Century. Oxford History of the British Empire, vol. 2*, Oxford, 1998, pp. 53–77.

O'Gorman, F., *The Rise of Party in England. The Rockingham Whigs 1760–82*, London, 1975.

The Long Eighteenth Century. British Political and Social History 1688–1832, London, 1997.

O'Malley, L. S. S., *Bengal District Gazetteer: Midnapore*, Calcutta, 1911.

Pagden, A., *Spanish Imperialism and the Political Imagination. Studies in European and Spanish American Social and Political Theory, 1513–1830*, New Haven, CT, 1990.

Lords of All the World: Ideologies of Empire in Spain, Britain and France c. 1500–c. 1800, New Haven, CT, 1995.

Pandey, B. N., *The Introduction of English Law into India: The Career of Elijah Impey in Bengal, 1774–1783*, Bombay, 1967.

Parkes, J. and Merivale, H., *Memoirs of Sir Philip Francis, K. C. B., with Correspondence and Journals*, 2 vols., London, 1867.

Parthasarathi, P., 'Merchants and the Rise of Colonialism', in B. Stein and S. Subramanyam (eds.), *Institutions and Economic Change in South Asia*, Delhi, 1996, pp. 85–104.

Peers, D. M., *Between Mars and Mammon: Colonial Armies and the Garrison State in India, 1819–1835*, London, 1995.

Perlin, F., 'State Formation Reconsidered, part 2'. *Modern Asian Studies*, 19 (1985), pp. 415–80.

Pitts, J., *A Turn to Empire. The Rise of Imperial Liberalism in Britain and France*, Princeton, 2005.

Pocock, J. G. A., *The Ancient Constitution and the Feudal Law: A Study of English Historical Thought in the Seventeenth Century*, Cambridge, 1957, repr. 1987.

Politics, Language and Time: Essays on Political Thought and History, New York, 1971.

The Machiavellian Moment; Florentine Political Thought and the Atlantic Republican Tradition, Princeton, 1975.

Virtue, Commerce, and History: Essays on Political Thought and History, Chiefly in the Eighteenth Century, Cambridge, 1985.

(ed.), 'Political Thought in the English Speaking Atlantic, 1760–90; Part I, The Imperial Crisis', *The Varieties of English Political Thought 1500–1800*, Cambridge, 1993, pp. 246–82.

Barbarism and Religion. Vol. 2. Narratives of Civil Government, Cambridge, 1999.

Ramsbotham, R. B., *Studies in the Land Revenue History of Bengal, 1767–87*, Oxford, 1926.

Ray, Rajat, 'Colonial Penetration and the Initial Resistance', *Indian Historical Review*, 12 (1985), pp. 22–41.

The Felt Community: Commonality and Mentality Before the Emergence of Indian Nationalism, Oxford, 2003.

Ray, R., 'Indian Society and the Establishment of British Supremacy, 1765–1818,' in P. J. Marshall (ed.), *The Eighteenth Century. Oxford History of the British Empire*, vol. 2, Oxford, 1998, pp. 508–29.

Ray, Ratnalekha, *Change in Bengal Agrarian Society, c. 1760–1850*, Calcutta, 1974.

Raychaudhuri, T., *Bengal Under Akbar and Jahangir, an Introductory Study in Social History*, Calcutta, 1953.

Richards, J. F., *Document Forms for Official Orders of Appointment in the Mughal Empire*, Cambridge, 1986.

The Mughal Empire, New Cambridge History of India, 1.5, Cambridge, 1993.

'Norms of Comportment Among Mughal Officers', in B. D. Metcalf (ed.), *Moral Conduct and Authority: The Place of adab in South Asian Islam*, Berkeley, CA, 1984, pp. 255–89.

Rocher, R., *Orientalism, Poetry, and the Milennium: The Checkered Life of Nathaniel Brassey Halhed, 1751–1830*, Delhi, 1987.

Rothschild, E., 'Global Commerce and the Question of Sovereignty in the Eighteenth Century Provinces', *Modern Intellectual History*, 1 (2004), pp. 3–25.

Roy, B. K., *The Career and Achievements of Maharajah Nandakumar, Dewan of Bengal (1705–75)*, Calcutta, 1969.

Said, E., *Orientalism*, New York, 1978.

Sanial, S. C., 'The History of the Calcutta Madrassa (2 Parts)', *Bengal Past and Present*, 8 (1914), pp. 83–112, 225–51.

Schwartz, S. B. (ed.), *Implicit Understandings. Observing, Reporting and Reflecting on the Encounters Between Europeans and Other Peoples in the Early Modern Era*, Cambridge, 1994.

Sen, N., 'Warren Hastings and British Sovereign Authority in Bengal', *Journal of Imperial and Commonwealth History*, 25 (1997), pp. 59–81.

Sen, S., 'Colonial Frontiers of the Georgian State – East India Company Rule in India', *Journal of Historical Sociology*, 7 (1994), pp. 368–92.

Empire of Free Trade: The East India Company and the Making of the Colonial Marketplace, Philadelphia, 1998.

Distant Sovereignty: Nationalism, Imperialism, and the Origins of British India, New York, 2002.

Sengupta, J. C., *West Bengal District Gazetteers: West Dinajpur*, Calcutta, 1965.

Siddiqi, N. A., 'The Faujdar and Faujdari under the Mughals', *Medieval India Quarterly*, 4 (1961), pp. 22–35.

Land Revenue Administration Under the Mughals, 1700–1750, Delhi, 1970.

Singha, R., *A Despotism of Law: Crime and Justice in Early Colonial India*, Delhi, 1998.

'Civil Authority and Due Process: Colonial Criminal Justice in the Banaras Zamindari, 1781–95', in M. R. Anderson and S. Guha (eds.), *Changing Concepts of Rights and Justice in South Asia*, Delhi, 2000, pp. 30–81.

Sinha, N. K., *The Economic History of Bengal*, 3 vols., Calcutta, 1956–70.

Sinha, S., *Pandits in a Changing Environment: Centres of Sanskrit Learning in Nineteenth-Century Bengal*, Calcutta, 1993.

Smith, A., in A. S. Skinner (ed.), *The Wealth of Nations, Books IV–V*, London, 1999, first edition 1776.

Spear, T. G. P., *The Nabobs: A Study of the Social Life of the English in Eighteenth-Century India*, London, 1963.

Master of Bengal: Clive and his India, London, 1975.

Stein, B., 'State Formation and Economy Reconsidered', *Modern Asian Studies*, 19 (1985), pp. 387–413.

Thomas Munro: The Origins of the Colonial State and His Vision of Empire, Oxford, 1986.

Stokes, E., *The English Utilitarians in India*, 1st edn, 1959, repr. New Delhi, 1982.

Stone, L. (ed.), *An Imperial State at War: Britain from 1689 to 1815*, London, 1994.

Storey, C. A., *Persian Literature. A Bio-bibliographical Survey*, 3 vols., London, 1927.

Subramanyam, S., 'Frank Submissions: The Company and the Mughals Between Sir Thomas Roe and Sir William Norris', in Bowen, Lincoln and Rigby (eds.), *The Worlds of the East India Company*, Woodbridge, 2002, pp. 69–96.

Suleri, S., *The Rhetoric of British India*, Chicago, 1992.

Sutherland, L., *The East India Company in Eighteenth-Century Politics*, Oxford, 1952.

'New Evidence on the Nandakuma Trial', *English Historical Review*, 72 (1957), pp. 438–65.

Teltscher, K., *India Inscribed: European and British Writing on India, 1600–1800*, Oxford, 1995.

Tracy, J. D., 'Asian Despotism? Mughal Government as Seen from the Dutch East India Company Factory in Surat', *Journal of Early Modern History* 3, 3 (1999), pp. 256–80.

Travers, R., ' "The Real Value of the Lands." The British, the *Nawabs*, and the Land Tax in Bengal', *Modern Asian Studies*, 38 (2004), pp. 17–58.

'Ideology and Expansion in Bengal, 1757–1772', *Journal of Imperial and Commonwealth History*, 33 (2005), pp. 7–27.

Tribe, K., *Land, Labour and Economic Discourse*, London, 1978.

Washbrook, D. A., 'Progress and Problems. South Asian Economic and Social History *c*. 1750–1830', *Modern Asian Studies*, (1985), pp. 57–91.

'The Two Faces of Colonialism: India, 1818–1860', in A. Porter (ed.), *The Nineteenth Century. Oxford History of the British Empire, vol. 3*, Oxford, 1999, pp. 395–421.

Weitzman, S., *Warren Hastings and Philip Francis*, Manchester, 1929.

Whelan, F. G., *Edmund Burke and India: Political Morality and Empire*, Pittsburgh, PA, 1996.

Wilson, K., *The Sense of the People: Politics, Culture and Imperialism in England, 1715–85*, Cambridge, 1995.

The Island Race: Englishness, Empire, and Gender in the Eighteenth Century, London, 2003.

Wink, A., *Land and Sovereignty in India: Agrarian Society and Politics Under the Eighteenth-Century Maratha Svarajya*, Cambridge, 1986.

Wrightson, K., *Earthly Necessities. Economic Lives in Early Modern Britain, 1470–1750*, Yale, 2000.

Yang, A., *The Limited Raj: Agrarian Relations in Colonial India, Saran District 1793–1920*, Berkeley, CA, 1989.

UNPUBLISHED DOCTORAL DISSERTATIONS

Akhtar, S., 'The Role of the Zamindars in Bengal, 1707–72'. University of London, 1973.

Gordon-Parker, J., 'The Directors of the East India Company, 1754–1790', University of Edinburgh, 1977.

Gurney, J. D., 'The Debts of the Nawab of Arcot, 1763–1776', University of Oxford, 1968.

Lehmann, F. L., 'The Eighteenth-Century Transition in India: Responses of Some Bihar Intellectuals', University of Wisconsin, Madison, 1967.

Nichol, J. D., 'The British in India: 1740–63. A Study in Imperial Expansion into Bengal', University of Cambridge, 1976.

Stern, P., '"One body Corporate and Politick": the Growth of the East India Company-State in the Later Seventeenth Century', Columbia University, 2004.

Wilson, J. E., 'Governing Property, Making Law: Land, Local Society, and Colonial Discourse in Agrarian Bengal, c. 1785–1830', University of Oxford, 2001.

Index

Cambridge Studies in Indian History and Society

Other titles in the series